Evolving Halakhah

Evolving Halakhah

A Progressive Approach to Traditional Jewish Law

Rabbi Dr. Moshe Zemer

with a Foreword by
Justice Haim H. Cohn

Jewish Lights Publishing
Woodstock, Vermont

Library of Congress Cataloging-in-Publication Data
Zemer, Moshe, 1932–
[Halakhah shefuyah. English]
Evolving halakhah : a progressive approach to traditional Jewish law / by Moshe Zemer.
p.   cm.
Rev. translation of: Halakhah shefuyah.
Includes bibliographical references and index.
ISBN 1-58023-002-4
1. Jewish law—Reform Judaism. 2. Orthodox Judaism—Controversial literature. I. Title.
BM197.Z4613   1998
296.1'8—dc21   98–48902
                                                                      CIP

First Edition
10 9 8 7 6 5 4 3 2 1

Manufactured in the United States of America

Jacket Design: Bridgett Taylor
Text Design: Sans Serif Inc.

Jewish Lights Publishing
Sunset Farm Offices, Route 4
P.O. Box 237
Woodstock, Vermont 05091
Tel.: (802) 457-4000
Fax: (802) 457-4004

www.jewishlights.com

Dedicated to my Torah mentors in Israel:

JUSTICE HAIM H. COHN
May he be blessed with many more years of scholarship

PROF. YITZHAK D. GILAT ז״ל
When a wise man dies, how can he be replaced?

Contents

III. Conversion   121

Acknowledgements

I would like to express my gratitude to those who took part in the making of this volume:

Stuart M. Matlins of Jewish Lights Publishing, who put his faith in *Evolving Halakhah.*

Elisheva S. Urbas, the editor of this book, from whom I learned much.

Jennifer Goneau, the associate editor and Martha McKinney, editorial assistant, who worked faithfully on every aspect of its production.

Lenn Schramm for his dedication to the difficult task of turning ancient words and concepts into an accurate and readable English.

My loving wife, Ilana; our children, Hilla, Moriah, Barak, and Nahum; and our granddaughters, Nitzan, Dor and Ofek, who gave me the loving familial support that enables me to research and write.

Burton E. and Geraldyn R. Belzer, whose generosity helped make the translation possible.

Foreword

Justice Haim H. Cohn
Deputy President Emeritus of the
Israel Supreme Court

In this volume, Rabbi Zemer has collected his responsa and essays, including those previously published in newspapers and other periodicals—some of them rejoinders to halakhic rulings by Orthodox rabbis, others his answers to questions on topical matters raised by the general public. The hallmark of his writing is a strong reliance on the classic texts of Halakhah and an endeavor to solve problems of the modern age and polity in an enlightened and liberal spirit.

It is an ancient Jewish tradition that books, especially halakhic works, be prefaced by imprimaturs, approbations, and bans issued by the leading lights of the generation. The imprimatur is to avoid the allegation that the author may have presumed to teach Halakhah in front of his elders. The approbation is to keep readers from dismissing the author as an amateur who is not competent to write on such matters. Finally, the ban is to deter, intimidate, and even punish in advance any who might violate the author's copyright. There are many books to which great rabbis have prefaced the remark that the author does not need their stamp of approval because his praises and excellencies are well known and his name goes before him, while the importance of his book is obvious and needs no external proof. If nevertheless they added their approval, it was to encourage the author, support his efforts, and inspire others to follow in his footsteps.

When Moses Mendelssohn asked Rabbi Ezekiel Landau of Prague, the leading halakhic light of that generation, to give his approval to his German translation of the Pentateuch, the latter declined, and Mendelssohn regretted having asked. The custom,

Mendelssohn wrote later, was outdated: a good and useful book can speak for itself, whereas a bad and useless one cannot be salvaged even by the imprimatur of the greatest rabbi of the generation. It was not that Rabbi Landau did not esteem Mendelssohn, or that he objected to the translation of the Pentateuch into the vernacular (for it had long since been translated into Aramaic, Greek, and Latin); rather, in the manner of great rabbis, he was evidently leery of how the extremist fringe would react to his approval of someone who read and wrote profane books as well.

As for myself, I have no authority to issue approbations, certainly not when the author is the rabbi and I his disciple: it is he who gives the imprimatur and I who receive it. Nor do I need to recount his praises: he is well known in all the Progressive congregations in Israel and throughout the world. Nor does he need a ban, since we now have copyright laws on which all can rely. When he asked that I write a foreword to his book, however, I was glad to comply, if not in order to approve, then in order to do him honor.

Perhaps, though, what he asked me was to defend myself against his book, which might be taken as an indictment of my negligence and omissions, because as attorney general of Israel and later as a justice of the Supreme Court I held my peace and did nothing to promote progressive Halakhah. In my defense I can argue that some forty years ago I warned of the dangers threatening us from the attempts to stifle all innovators and reformers. As I wrote in an article, "Concern for Yesterday," that appeared in the journal *Sura* (1958):

> You cannot renew Jewish law and amend it to suit the needs of the time and place and make the people appreciate it without knowing it to the very last detail. But you *cannot* "know" it, because it is in the heavens, as it is written, "Who among us can go up to the heavens and get it for us" (Deut. 30:12). If you thought that the book is open and the table is set and the letters give forth light and wisdom, you were mistaken: it is an arcane lore that is given only to those who are suitable and pure; but the stranger who approaches it will be slain by the shafts of disdain and scorn of those who have mastered

the mysteries. Even if you have studied and not forgotten your learning, you are not fit to be numbered among those seated at the board of the oracle, as long as you have not received the seal of approval of the righteous rabbinic tribunal.

There are many sects of those who own the secrets, priests of the oracle: Rabbis who are not affiliated with the official rabbinate disdain all those who have not been properly ordained. The official rabbinate claims a monopoly on the knowledge of Torah law and its authoritative interpretation. The members of the Ultra-Orthodox Council of Torah Sages look upon the official rabbis as if they were sectarians and will not rely on their rulings in any matter. The religious court of the extremely Orthodox Neturei Karta deems the Council of Sages, and all the more so the official rabbinate, to be heretics. What is common to all is their assertion that the Torah was given exclusively to themselves, ministering angels as it were, and that there is no admission to its knowledge and study for *apikorsim*—heretics—or even for the progressive of the present day. . . . Small wonder that those few who have the ability and desire are slowly despairing.

In the forty years that have passed since I wrote those words, the situation has deteriorated further. The author of the present volume stands at the helm of Progressive rabbinical authorities; his rabbinical acumen and scholarship date from early youth. But everything he says and writes and demonstrates and quotes is, in the eye of non-Progressive rabbis, and of the Orthodox community in general, loathsome and untouchable. They will not so much as stoop to point out his errors for the simple reason that they will not defile their hands by opening his books. Such books, in their view, are even worse than leavened bread on Passover, which, although it may not be owned or seen and ought to be destroyed, can be sold to a non-Jew who will return it after the festival. Perhaps they deem it a positive commandment to burn them, like a Torah scroll written by an idolater. Were they to do so, they—like book-burners of every generation—would never discover the treasures hidden between its covers and what great rabbis and righteous men are quoted there.

There is no consolation in the fact that while they are united against the Progressives, with whom they have no common language, the Orthodox and their rabbis are split and divided among themselves, as they have always been. We witness the sorry spectacles of quarrels and controversies within their camp, where one delegitimizes another, who then retaliates even more impetuously. Those who are insulted and hold their peace are few and far between. The general impression given by the mutual recriminations and insults and the ostensibly halakhic sanction granted to this holy terror is that the Torah has become many Torahs, which are ranked according to their degree of zealotry and stubbornness, self-righteousness and arrogance; and all are the outcome of gross intolerance and an absence of love for fellow Jews and fellow human beings.

Let me preface this volume with words of encouragement and incentive to its author (and to all of us): Do not despair! There is no greater honor than the scorn, bans, and excommunications of those who over the generations have always disdained all reprovers and remonstrators.

Progress cannot be stopped; learning finds its way to remold the tradition; and may the verse be fulfilled in us: "Build up, build up a highway! Clear a road! Remove all obstacles from the road of My people!" (Isaiah 57:14).

Haim H. Cohn

Introduction

"One who makes a really truthful judgment" (BT Megillah 15b)—[by emphasizing really truthful, the Talmud refers to] one who judges according to the needs of the place and time in a way that will be truthful, . . . not that he always renders actual Torah law, because there are times when the judge must not rule in accordance with the strict letter of the law, in order to suit the time and circumstances. When he does not do this, even though it is a true judgment, it is not truthful.

RABBI JOSHUA FALK (1555–1614),
Derishah on *Turḥoshen Mishpat* 1

This book began as a response to my own perplexity. I had devoted years to studying the sources of Halakhah (Jewish law) at the Hebrew Union College and the Hebrew University and had found them to be evolutionary and ethical, as well as offering solutions to contemporary problems. But when I came on *aliyah* to Israel in the early 1960s to serve as the rabbi of a synagogue in the Sharon region, I was astounded at the apathetic and at times even hostile attitude toward the Jewish religion that I encountered in Israel.

When I lectured to the general public on religious matters, some of my listeners would object that Halakhah is inflexible and the antithesis of progress. They accused Halakhah of grave sins: it prevents young Jews from marrying, it disqualifies an entire community (the B'nai Israel of India), it mars innocent children with the stain of halakhic illegitimacy, it piles up obstacles for candidates for conversion, and it "chains" women whose husbands refuse to give them a divorce. In the opinion of those persons, Halakhah has no moral value in the modern age. Perhaps it served an important function in preserving the nature of our people in the past, but today it is antiquated and outmoded.

I tried to explain that Halakhah as it evolved was and remains a much more flexible and ethical system than is reflected by the rulings of the established Chief Rabbinate of this country. During my first decade in Israel, however, instead of publicizing my halakhic position I was compelled to wage public and legal battles in the media and courts in order to guarantee our synagogues' right to be allotted premises.

After several years a change occurred in my perception of the essence of the religious *kulturkampf* in Israel. I learned that victory will not come only from legal and public campaigns for equal rights. I realized that in addition, a difficult battle concerning the nature of Judaism and Halakhah must be waged on the ideological plane. My colleagues suggested that I write down my ideas about the humane and open approach of historical Halakhah, as contrasted with the inflexible rulings of the present-day official rabbinate. Consequently, more than twenty years ago, in response to the many immoral deeds that were being committed in the ostensible name of Halakhah, I began publishing articles based on halakhic sources. Later, when the Institute for Progressive Halakhah, associated with the World Union for Progressive Judaism, was founded, I was appointed its director. Over the years I have written about the approach of progressive Halakhah in several areas that are not usually considered to fall into the purview of religion, such as the Intifada and the exchange of terrorists for Israeli prisoners. These articles have been published in the daily press and scholarly journals in Israel and abroad, and finally led to the publication of a Hebrew collection of my writings in 1993, by Dvir Press, the oldest publisher in Israel. This book is an updated translation and revision of that volume, with several new chapters added.

In my writing I endeavor to present the rabbinic idea that Halakhah is ethical in its very essence. What is the import of the term *ethical?* For the Sages, discrimination against the destitute, widowed, and orphaned, or exploitation of the weak persons, constitutes injustice. It is intolerable when a group of rabbis declares that the pedigree of a particular group of children is defective. It is immoral when people are dying of hunger, even though food is available, or when an orphan girl is prevented from marrying and would carry the shame for the rest of her life.

The rabbis did not require philosophical or theoretical debates to realize this. They knew what an immoral action is and what is meant by sin: "Because they have sold for silver those whose cause was just, and the needy for a pair of sandals. You who trample the heads of the poor into the dust of the ground, and make the humble walk a twisted course! . . . They recline by every altar on garments taken in pledge . . ." (Amos 2:6–8). They also knew that it is a moral act to right wrongs: "Share your bread with the hungry, and . . . take the wretched poor into your home; when you see the naked, . . . clothe him, and [do] not . . . ignore your own kin" (Isa. 58:7). No further proof or reproof was required when the time came to take corrective moral action.

Nevertheless, our rabbis faced a grave dilemma, because some situations of injustice stemmed from the requirements of the codified Halakhah, based on a Torah precept or a regulation enacted by the Sages of antiquity. Is it possible to remain faithful to the prophetic imperative of justice while at the same time obeying the codified Halakhah that seems to discriminate against defenseless human beings? In this book I shall present many diverse approaches and methods that were developed by the rabbis in order to resolve this dilemma: acting in accordance with justice while preserving the framework of Halakhah. The principles and methods they employed were extremely sophisticated.

I shall attempt to clarify the ways in which, I believe, it is still possible today to act in the framework of Halakhah, safeguarding justice for individuals and society while not compromising our intellectual honesty. This book discusses the principles and criteria for halakhic decision-making and ruling of several rabbis of the twentieth century, erected as a bridge between our ancient heritage and the needs of the modern era.

This book is not limited to the academic or theoretical domain. It also considers the possibility of applying halakhic criteria and standards to extremely difficult problems of the lives of individual Jews and gentiles as well as of governments. Can these halakhic principles offer a remedy to the victims of Halakhah and thereby provide further evidence of the ethical evolution of Halakhah both in antiquity and today? These are only a few of the difficult issues that I shall endeavor to resolve in this book.

I

Foundations

Therefore Moses was given orally certain general principles, only briefly alluded to in the Torah, by means of which the Sages may work out the newly emerging particulars in every generation.

RABBI JOSEPH ALBO, Spain (fifteenth century)

1

Halakhah as an Evolving Ethical System

HARDLY A WEEK PASSES WITHOUT A REPORT IN THE ISRAELI media about some infringement of human rights against a halakhic background. If you browse through the newspapers you are likely to encounter incidents like the following:

A married woman was abandoned by her husband, who has refused to give her a divorce for more than thirteen years. She is "chained"—in Hebrew an *agunah*—even though a religious court ruled years ago that her husband must give her a *get* (a bill of divorce).

The Chief Rabbinate has published a halakhic ruling that a non-Jewish woman buried in a Jewish cemetery must be disinterred. (Later two Ultra-Orthodox yeshiva students exhumed the body and dumped it in a Muslim cemetery.)

A religious court has refused to convert a woman who was married to a Jew in a civil ceremony, because they are living together as man and wife.

The brother-in-law of a war widow is refusing to release her to marry another man unless she assigns him title to her home. The woman is unwilling to submit to this blackmail, and the rabbinate has denied her the right to remarry.

The rabbinate and the religious establishment have refused to allow a woman elected to a religious council to serve in this post because she is a woman.

Ultra-Orthodox Jews have stoned passing vehicles on the Sabbath "to preserve the sanctity of the Sabbath."

A young man has been proclaimed a *mamzer*—halakhically illegitimate—and cannot marry his fiancée, after his parents' twenty-year-old file in the rabbinate was examined and computerized blacklists were checked.

These are only a few of the many cases of discrimination and deprivation on a "halakhic" basis recorded in Israel every year. Frequently we hear the angry and disappointed responses of Israelis who conclude that Halakhah is cruel and outdated and totally unsuited to contemporary life.

Is this indeed the course of Halakhah as it was interpreted by the Sages of antiquity and over the generations? In this book I shall attempt to answer this question in the light of two fundamental postulates: first, that Halakhah is an evolving process; second, that Halakhah is intrinsically ethical.

Note that these are not external postulates, but principles inherent in Halakhah itself over the ages. In general, Halakhah has been an evolving process that deals with the changing reality of each generation. The elements of Halakhah rest on the ethics of the Torah and the prophets, and they manifest an extraordinary sensitivity to the weak and helpless.

In what follows, I shall attempt to prove the validity of these postulates by examining rabbinic texts that reflect the evolving and ethical nature of Halakhah. This demonstration is essential both to shed light on the nature of Halakhah in antiquity and in our own times and to ground the enlightened halakhic rulings presented in the rest of this book. It will become clear that such modifications of Halakhah are a necessary result of the perpetual struggle between the twin poles of Torah law and changing circumstances. This process, although difficult and painful, preserves the vitality of the Jewish tradition.

Did the Sages of past generations take account of changes in social and economic conditions? Did they act according to their conscience when confronted by injustice? Did they find ways to cope with altered circumstances? An examination of the history of Halakhah shows that the answer to all these questions is yes. Halakhic writings incorporate modifications rooted in certain halakhic principles. Below I shall analyze several texts that demonstrate that Halakhah is indeed evolutionary and ethical.

Afterwards I shall survey the history of the application of several principles that permit change in Halakhah, from talmudic times until the present. These principles pave the way to permission and leniency, despite a law that forbids. They provide examples that prove that Halakhah has always known how to preserve its vitality and flexibility. Our Sages set forth these rules and principles to make it possible to amend Halakhah without explicitly labeling the process as "change." These tools, intrinsic to Halakhah, enabled decisors to cope with changing circumstances and ethical problems.

THE "LANGUAGE OF THE COMMON FOLK" AND THE PURIFICATION OF *MAMZERIM*

A case study that clearly reflects how the talmudic Sages were guided by conscience may be found in their treatment of *mamzerim,* the offspring of an adulterous or incestuous relationship.

In the Talmud we read as follows:

> Hillel the Elder used to expound the language of the common folk, as it is taught: The men of Alexandria would betroth their wives; but [before] they entered the bridal canopy [for the marriage ceremony] other men would come and snatch them away. The Sages were going to rule that their children were *mamzerim.* Hillel the Elder said to them: Bring me your mother's marriage contract. They brought him their mother's *ketubah* and he found written there: "When you come under the canopy, be my wife." He ruled that their children were not *mamzerim* (BT Baba Metzia 104a).[1]

It was the custom in antiquity for the betrothal ceremony to precede the wedding by several months. According to Halakhah, a woman who has been formally betrothed, but has not yet celebrated the marriage ceremony under the bridal canopy (*ḥuppah*), is a married woman and must receive a *get* before she may remarry. Should she nevertheless live with another man without a prior *get*, the Sages view the new bond as an adulterous relationship and its offspring as *mamzerim*. When Hillel the Elder read over the marriage contracts (the *ketubot*, which are actually signed at the betrothal ceremony) of the mothers of those who had been declared *mamzerim*, he found that some of them included the phrase, "when you come under the canopy, be my wife," which is usually followed by the standard clause "and I shall honor and cherish you and provide for you as befits a Jewish husband."

Hillel took five Aramaic words out of the context of the Alexandrian marriage contract and interpreted them as if they constituted a legal condition formulated by the Sages, to the effect that "when you come under the bridal canopy with me, *[only then]* you will be my wife"—the implication being that should she not come under the *ḥuppah* with him, her betrothal would be retroactively null and void and consequently she would not require a *get*.

In other words, Hillel expounded the language of the common folk who wrote their own marriage contracts as if he were interpreting a carefully drafted legal document. According to Prof. Yitzhak Gilat, professor of Talmud at Bar-Ilan University:

> He gave the halakhic seal of approval to a custom of the common folk and based a judicial ruling on this custom, as if the formula had been coined by the Sages, and accordingly held that the children were not *mamzerim*.[2]

This is a classic example of the clash between the desire to safeguard the codified Halakhah, on one hand, and the harm done to children who are proclaimed *mamzerim* because of the sins of their parents, on the other. It was impossible to throw out the ancient law or conceal the fact that the mothers were *prima facie* already married women when they lived with the children's fathers in what were, consequently, adulterous relationships. Accordingly, Hillel the Elder opted to give a tendentious interpretation to the popular idiom incorporated into the women's *ketubot* as a way of saving their offspring from the stain of illegitimacy. There is no doubt that it was the dictates of his conscience that stirred him to take this audacious action.

LENIENCIES IN THE SABBATICAL YEAR

Both the Sages and the common people were meticulous in their observance of the precepts of the Sabbatical Year, that is, the septennial ban on plowing, sowing, and other labors in the field and vineyard. This strictness continued throughout the Second Temple period and for several generations thereafter—evidently until the Bar Kokhba Rebellion (132–135 C.E.). A halakhic midrash reports that Rabbi Judah bar Ilai, a disciple of Rabbi Akiba, ruled that in his day and age the Sabbatical Year precepts still had the status of Sinaitic commandments ordained by the Written Law: "What is the biblical basis for keeping the Sabbatical Year even though the Jubilee is not observed? Scripture teaches (Lev. 25:8), 'You will have seven sabbaths of years' " (*Sifra, Behar* 2:2). In other words, even though the Jubilee Year was no longer observed in his time, Rabbi Judah bar Ilai expounded the verse to prove that in his time the Sabbatical Year was to be observed because the Torah so ordained.

During the next generation, however, there was a sharp reversal in the attitude toward the Sabbatical Year. Prof. Gilat explains that after the destruction of the Temple, and even more so after the failure of the Bar Kokhba Rebellion, the Roman authorities raised their already heavy taxes. The Jewish farmers' increased poverty and tax burden made it extremely difficult for them to observe the Sabbatical Year regulations.[3] The economic condition of the Jewish community in the Land of Israel deteriorated, and the Roman authorities imposed heavy taxes every year, including the Sabbatical Year. As a result, the Sages began to deal leniently with those who violated the Sabbatical Year prohibitions by working their fields and vineyards. We read in a *baraita* (a statement by a *tanna*—a Sage of the period from about 10 C.E. until 200 C.E.—not included in the Mishnah when it was redacted by Rabbi Judah the Prince but recorded in the Tosefta, Gemara, or midrashim) that when a drought struck the country one Sabbatical Year, the entire community was urgently summoned for public prayer and fasting "on account of the livelihood of others" (Tosefta Ta'anit 2:8), or, in Rabbi Zeira's understanding of this phrase, "on account of the livelihood of those who were suspected [of violating the Sabbatical Year restrictions]" (JT Ta'anit 3:1).

In other words, the community's spiritual leaders recognized the need to fast and pray for rain, even in the Sabbatical Year, on behalf of those suspected of violating the Sabbatical Year prohibitions, so that there would be food for the people. In the words of Prof. Gilat, "the rabbis and Sages had to fast and decree a public fast so that the crops of the transgressors who sowed during Sabbatical Year would grow!"[4]

Rabbi Zeira's interpretation was based on the opinion of Rabbi Judah the Prince. We read of an indigent teacher, suspected of using produce grown in the Sabbatical Year, who was brought before that Sage for judgment. Rabbi Judah did not punish him. As he explained to the other Sages: "What should this unfortunate man do? He did it so he could live" (JT Ta'anit 3:1).

Rabbi Judah the Prince provided a halakhic basis for these and other leniencies by ruling that in his age the observance of Sabbatical Year stipulations was no longer directly mandated by the Written Law of the Torah but only by the Oral Law of the Sages. He held—in opposition to the view of Rabbi Judah bar Ilai—that in a period when the Jubilee Year is not observed, "the Sabbatical Year is observed on account of [the Sages'] rulings" (JT Shevi'it 10:3). This change of status created the basis for a more lenient application of the Sabbatical Year regulations.[5] To make it easier for the public to comply with a law whose observance was excessively onerous, Rabbi Judah the Prince reclassified the Sabbatical Year from a biblical *(mi-de-oraita)* commandment to a rabbinic *(mi-de-rabbanan)* commandment. This relaxed the restrictions on agricultural work during the seventh year and saved many from starvation.

There is no doubt that this example, and many others like it, buttress the thesis that Halakhah evolves and changes because of confrontation with altered circumstances. Alongside the natural development of Halakhah when it is confronted by changes in life and society, the conscience of the decisor also plays an important role. For example, Rabbi Judah the Prince evidently felt that the economic distress of the poor teacher was of greater moral weight than the Sabbatical Year precepts that the common people were transgressing.

AN EMERGENCY WEDDING ON THE SABBATH

Over the generations, rabbis have adduced various halakhic principles so that they could issue lenient and indulgent rulings. Maimonides did so with such vigor that we shall devote an entire chapter to his groundbreaking application of both established and original principles. Now, however, we shall examine two principles that figure in an important decision rendered some four hundred years ago. First, the Sages stipulated that in cases that could be defined as "emergency situations," a rabbinic prohibition could be interpreted leniently and even disregarded. For example, the Talmud relates that the Rav, the third-century Babylonian *amora* (one of the Sages of the Gemara, who flourished in the period 200–500 C.E.) permitted Hanukkah lamps to be carried on the Sabbath, in spite of the halakhic prohibition, so that they could be hidden from the ruling Zoroastrian priests, who considered such a use of fire to be sacrilegious (BT Shabbat 45a).

The second principle is that "great is human dignity, which takes precedence over a negative precept of the Torah" (BT Berakhot 19b)—specifically over the injunction "you must not deviate from the verdict that they announce to you" (Deut. 17:11), which is the basis for all rabbinic precepts.[6] Accordingly, "on account of human dignity, so that an individual not be disgraced in public, it is permitted to transgress rabbinic prohibitions."[7]

More than a thousand years after Rav, Rabbi Moses Isserles of Cracow (known as the Rama, 1525?–1572) employed these two talmudic principles to resolve a pressing problem. In one of his responsa he recounted the controversy over a dowry, which delayed the wedding of an orphan bride that was to have taken place on a Friday:

> When the shadows of evening began to fall and the Sabbath was approaching, her relatives who were to provide the dowry closed their fists and refused to give a sufficient amount. . . . Then the groom absolutely refused to marry her. He paid no attention to the pleas of the leaders of the city that he not humiliate a daughter of Israel on account of filthy lucre. . . . Then they finally agreed and the groom consented to go under the *huppah* and to shame a worthy daughter of Israel no longer. Thereupon I got up and conducted the marriage at that hour.[8]

"That hour," according to Isserles, was "in the dark of night on Friday evening, an hour and a half after night had fallen."

When some of the leading members of the Cracow community complained, Isserles found it necessary to justify conducting a marriage ceremony on the Sabbath. His apologia included the two talmudic principles just referred to.

One may permit a wedding after the start of the Sabbath when it is a "case of emergency," as it was in this incident, because "the maiden would have been put to shame if she had to wait for the wedding until the end of the Sabbath, after she had already immersed herself." In this difficult situation Isserles relied on the tosafist Rabbenu Jacob Tam (c. 1100–1171), who held that the Sages permitted betrothing a woman on the Sabbath in an emergency situation—although Rabbenu Tam had stated this as a matter of theory, not to be implemented in practice.[9] Isserles understood this to mean that "in a serious emergency we may permit such a marriage. There can be no greater emergency than this case, in which a grown orphan girl was being put to shame. It would be a lifelong disgrace to her, enough to set her apart from all other young women."

This led into his second rationale—the preservation of human dignity:

> Great indeed is human dignity, which takes precedence over a negative precept. . . . The prohibition [against marriage on the Sabbath] is only a rabbinic decree, to keep us from writing the marriage contract *(ketubah)* on the Sabbath, as is explained in the [Babylonian] Talmud; or because such a marriage might be deemed to be the acquisition of a possession on the Sabbath, as is explained in the Jerusalem Talmud. . . . In addition, we are concerned that the match might be broken off completely and there would be no marriage at all as a result of quarreling between the families, and "great is the value of peace between man and wife" (BT Ḥullin 141).

Rabbi Isserles demonstrated that these two principles provide the moral infrastructure for talmudic rulings on many questions. His concern for the unfortunate bride led him to officiate at her wedding in spite of halakhic prohibitions and the opposition of the leaders of the Cracow community. He acted and ruled on the basis of his conscience, as indicated by the conclusion of his responsum:

> The need of the hour leads us to be lenient in such matters which are only a rabbinic prohibition, because such rabbinic prohibitory decrees were not meant to apply in times of emergency. . . . To be sure, one must be strict in urging people to be energetic before the Sabbath, so that they will not have to face such an emergency. But when it has occurred, what can be done if the hour has moved along until darkness, and there is ground for concern that the match will be broken off or the maiden put to shame? Under such circumstances, he who relies on the above arguments to be lenient has done no harm. May he delight in peace and the joy of the Sabbath thereafter. The good deed that he has done will atone for him, if his intention was for the sake of Heaven and peace.[10]

The bottom line is that in an emergency it is permitted to take ad hoc action that does not serve as a precedent.

"Something That Was Unknown to Earlier Generations"

Beyond this, however, there are also situations that result from changing conditions and require a permanent reappraisal of a current custom or law. In another responsum, Rabbi Isserles cited several precedents that justify such innovation and change.

Until the abrogation of the Palestinian patriarchate in the fourth century, the Jewish calendar was not fixed in advance. Instead, the start of each month depended on the actual sighting of the new moon and a subsequent proclamation by the Sanhedrin (the Supreme Rabbinical Court in the Land of Israel during the late Second Temple until the fifth century C.E.).

Rabbi Isserles quoted the Mishnah that deals with the acceptance of witnesses to the appearance of the new moon:

> Originally [the Sanhedrin] accepted testimony about the new moon throughout the day. . . . [Later] it was ordained that testimony would be accepted only until the [time of the] afternoon offering. . . . After the Temple was destroyed Rabban Johanan ben Zakkai ordained that they might accept testimony about the new moon throughout the entire day (Mishnah Rosh Hashanah 4:4).

The start of each month was proclaimed by the Sanhedrin on the basis of the testimony of two witnesses who declared that they had seen the new moon. For technical reasons connected with the Temple ritual, at some point in the Second Temple period the Sages decided not to hear witnesses from midafternoon on; if the witnesses arrived then, the start of the new month was postponed to the next day. After the Temple was destroyed, the reason for this amendment no longer existed, and Rabban Johanan ben Zakkai repealed it. Rabbi Isserles challenged this action:

One must ask how Rabban Johanan went and enacted a rule that contravened the enactments and custom of the early authorities, if it is forbidden to modify the established custom in any matter?[11]

He raised a similar question about an even earlier precedent. According to Torah law, the Sabbatical Year cancels debts. With the development of commerce in the late Second Temple period, this ordinance had the unfortunate effect that people would not lend money late in each seven-year cycle, since they would not be repaid. To avert this situation, Hillel the Elder introduced the *prozbul,* a document whereby creditors transferred their accounts receivable to the religious courts, which, not being private individuals, did not have to cancel obligations owed them.

Hillel instituted the *prozbul* and the reason given there (BT Gittin 36a) is that he saw that the people were avoiding making loans, etc. But how was he empowered to institute a rule that contravened the established custom?

After a complex halakhic discussion, Rabbi Isserles answered his own questions:

Where something new has arisen that was unknown to earlier Sages, such as that there is reason to fear ruination or [the violation of] a prohibition, a fear that could not have existed in previous generations, it is certainly permissible to enact a rule, like all the enactments stated in the Talmud, because one can say that the earlier generations did not establish the prohibition with that situation in mind.

That is, the earlier generations did not institute a prohibition with regard to a problematic situation that has emerged only in our own time, because they could not have known the circumstances of the present day. In this way Rabbi Isserles grounded the authority for enacting new rules in every age, since when the earlier generations instituted their regulations they had no idea of such new situations. Here one can discern explicit consideration of the specific needs of every time and place.[12]

"Uprooting a Provision of the Torah"

The Talmud rules that the Sages have the authority to abolish a provision of the Torah. The Mishnah reports cases in which a man sent a *get* to his wife by means of a messenger.

> Originally a man used to set up a court [of three] elsewhere [without the knowledge of his wife and the emissary] and annul [the *get* before the emissary had conveyed it to the wife]; but Rabban Gamaliel the Elder ordained that they should not do so, as a precaution for the general good (Mishnah Gittin 4:2).

In other words, the original rule had been that a man could revoke the bill of divorce before it reached his wife. The president of the Sanhedrin, Rabban Gamaliel the Elder, amended the procedure to forbid this because of the possibility that neither the messenger nor the woman would know that the man had revoked the *get*. The woman, unaware that she was still married, might remarry and bear children who were halakhically illegitimate.

According to the Torah, a husband's annulment of the *get* before a religious court is indeed valid. However, in order to protect the woman against unwitting adultery and the consequent peril of bearing *mamzerim*, the rabbis enacted a regulation that in practice abrogated the Torah law. The *amoraim* of Eretz Yisrael approved of this approach: "It was well said by Rabban Simeon ben Gamaliel . . . [because] the rules [enacted by the Sages] abolish provisions of the Torah" (JT Gittin 4:2).[13]

RABBINIC REGULATIONS THAT PERMIT LENIENCY

In addition to the halakhic principles described above, the Sages invoked many other rationales for ruling leniently with regard to rabbinic and even toraitic prohibitions out of consideration for the needs of their people. Halakhah was not isolated from the lives of the community of Israel.

"Where There Would Be Suffering"

In certain cases, the Sages revoked or limited a prohibition in order to prevent loss or suffering to people, since their decrees were not meant to cause distress to their flock. For example,

> Where there would be suffering, the rabbis did not enact a prohibition. . . . Where there would be loss, our rabbis did not prohibit (BT Ketubot 60a).

"To Prevent Enmity"

Similarly, the Sages permitted certain forbidden actions "to prevent enmity," that is, if the prohibition was liable to lead to hostile relations with Jews or non-Jews. The question was raised whether one should care for the animal of a gentile in the same way one tends the animal of a Jew. The Sages ruled that if caring for animals is a toraitic law, one must surely care for the animal of a gentile. Even if it is only rabbinic in origin, one should still care for the animal "to prevent enmity" (BT Baba Metzia 32b).[14]

"For the Sake of Peace"

The rabbinic literature contains many regulations enacted by the Sages for the sake of peaceful relations among Jews and especially with non-Jews.[15] According to Rabbi Eliezer Berkovits, such regulations have a dual significance, since treating the indigent, ill, or suffering non-Jew with justice and mercy "can promote social harmony between non-Jew and Jew."[16] The Sages made wise use of this principle.

These three principles involve the loosening of rabbinic prohibitions. There are also precepts grounded in the Written Law that the Sages—including Hillel the Elder and Rabbi Judah the Prince—found ways to set aside.

"On Account of a 'Chained' Woman"

If a husband has vanished without a trace or refuses to divorce his wife, she becomes an *agunah* and may not remarry. In order to lessen the burden on Jewish women and release them from "living widowhood" if their husbands disappeared, the Sages amended the laws of evidence, even those stated explicitly in the Written Law.[17] Consider the ruling issued by the head of the Sanhedrin in the first century, after a bloody battle against the Romans:

> Many men were killed at Tel Arza, and Rabban Gamaliel the Elder permitted their wives to remarry on the testimony of a single witness. And the rule was established to allow a woman to marry again on the basis of hearsay testimony, testimony by a slave, testimony by a woman, or testimony by a slave-woman (Mishnah Yevamot 16:7).

According to the Torah, "a case can be valid only on the testimony of two witnesses or three witnesses" (Deut. 19:15). Nevertheless, in the problematic case where a woman's husband disappeared in battle and only one witness appeared to testify to his death, the Sages decided to permit her to remarry on the basis of this unsupported testimony. What is more, contrary to the law, they also permitted her to remarry on the basis of hearsay evidence or the testimony of women and slaves, which is generally not admissible.

Prof. Ze'ev Falk notes that

> This was not only an ad hoc decree. From that time on it was
> the rule for future generations, and we act accordingly to the
> present day. A woman may be released from the presumption of
> being married on the basis of testimony that would [in other
> cases] be invalid and on the testimony of a single witness only.[18]

These liberal rulings stemmed from the talmudic principle that
"on account of her chains the rabbis were lenient with the woman"
(BT Gittin 3a). The Sages drastically relaxed the rules of testimony
so that the woman could remarry.

ANNULLING A MARRIAGE

Again in order to keep Jewish women from being left as *agunot,* the
Sages took another bold step and found a way to allow a woman to
remarry even if she had not been divorced by her husband. They
instituted the rule that although marriage is grounded in the Written Law, nevertheless "everyone who consecrates a woman in marriage does so with the consent of the rabbis and therefore the
rabbis may annul the marriage" (BT Ketubot 3a and elsewhere).[19]

In the case of a marriage consecrated by means of money (or
any object of value, such as a ring) conveyed by the bridegroom to
the bride, the rabbis ruled that they could annul it by retroactively
expropriating the money involved. According to Rashi's commentary, the Sages retroactively deemed the ring to have been merely
an ordinary gift, relying on the principle that "whatever has been
expropriated by the court has been validly expropriated."[20] In
other words, the Sages declared that the ring was given to the
woman not for the purpose of sealing a marriage, but merely as a
gift; consequently, the couple had never been married.

There is a dispute as to whether the rule that a marriage may be
consecrated by money derives from the Written Law or only from
rabbinic law. All agree, however, that consecration of a marriage by

means of sexual intercourse derives from the Torah.[21] How could the Sages nullify a marriage consecrated in that way? According to the Gemara, "the rabbis deemed his intercourse with her to be fornication" (BT Yevamot 90b). The Sages ruled retroactively that the couple was not really married, because when he had intercourse with the woman the man's intention was fornication, not marriage.[22]

There is evidence that this annulment procedure was invoked by rabbis until at least the end of the fifteenth century. Rabbi Jacob Moses Toledano, successively chief rabbi of Cairo and Tel Aviv and Israel's minister of religious affairs (1958–1960), published

> an old manuscript responsum by a rabbi from Portugal dating to the year 1474, and I believe it is by Rabbi Joseph Hayoun, who was then the rabbi in Lisbon. . . . There he mentions a contemporary rabbi, named Rabbi Samuel ben Halat, who wanted to release several kinds of *agunot* by means of the aforementioned method of annulling the marriage consecration. Some of the rabbis of Portugal at the time followed his lead and acted in accordance with this ruling.[23]

The old manuscript cites the courageous remarks of Rabbi Samuel ben Halat, who begins with a question:

> Can religious courts annul the marriage consecration retroactively, when the courts see fit to do so, so that the woman will not be left an *agunah*, or not?

His firm answer is that they can, for several reasons. On the basis of a whole string of proofs, derived from the Gemara and other halakhic sources, he summarizes the case as follows:

> From this it follows that whether the [husband] made the consecration condition on the Sages' consent or not, the court can annul the marriage. . . . It follows that they can annul the marriage even against the husband's will.[24]

That is, it does not matter whether the husband explicitly accepted the rabbis' jurisdiction over the act of consecration; the rabbis have the power to annul it retroactively no matter what.

This opinion was too audacious for the aforementioned Rabbi Joseph Hayoun, who

> smote Rabbi Samuel on the skull and was very angry with him, and demonstrated fully that the Gemara never speaks of annulment of marriage consecration except when the consecration was improper from the outset or by means of a *get*, even though there are some doubts about it.[25]

Although there is no unambiguous decision in this halakhic dispute, we see that five hundred years ago there were rabbis who advocated the solution of annulling marriages.

CONDITIONAL MARRIAGE

In the twentieth century, too, rabbis have pondered ways to release *agunot*. In 1924, a group of rabbis in Turkey published a pamphlet entitled "Conditional Marriage Consecration." They proposed

> many conditions at the time of the marriage consecration, [for example] that should the husband later travel to a far place or quarrel with his wife for a long time and so on, the marriage would be annulled retroactively.[26]

The rabbis sent their pamphlet to contemporary scholars and requested their opinion, as has been the custom in recent generations. One of those who replied was Rabbi Toledano, who made his agreement to this procedure contingent on certain conditions, first and foremost the consent of all the leading rabbis of the day:

And I leave the matter conditional on the opinion of the greatest rabbis of our generation, who must discuss this proposal and decide whether to approve it or reject it.[27]

The tendency to make the implementation of a halakhic ruling depend on the consent of the leading rabbis of the generation became the norm for many recent decisors. In this they depart from their predecessors, who generally found the strength and confidence to decide on their own and accepted full personal responsibility for their rulings. The inability of individual rabbis to issue a ruling not backed by the consensus of their colleagues has paralyzed most attempts to enact new rules and find solutions to the *agunah* problem.

In the modern age, nevertheless, rabbis in four countries enacted provisions for annulling marriages. In 1804, Rabbi Abraham Eliezer Halevy of Trieste enacted an annulment procedure based on expropriation of the consecration money, with the approval of Rabbi Hayyim Joseph David Azulai and Rabbi Hayyim Yitzhak Moussafiyya.[28]

Shortly after the convening of the Sanhedrin in Paris (February 1807), the rabbis of France attempted to introduce a comprehensive provision for annulling marriages contracted in violation of civil law. The rabbis of Italy and Germany, who participated in the Sanhedrin, seem to have carried the day against this step, however.[29]

Rabbi Hayyim Palache (1788–1869), the leading rabbi of his generation in Izmir (Smyrna), Turkey, removed obstacles to the enactment of an annulment provision in Algeria. Some authorities maintained that because of the grave consequences of a woman's believing herself to be free when she in fact remained married in the eyes of Halakhah, only a court with extraordinary competence, like that of the Rabbi Ammi and Rabbi Assi (late third century), should be allowed to expropriate the consecration money. Rabbi Palache countered that such an eminent court was not required; any court in any place could expropriate the money, relying on the principle that "whatever has been expropriated by the court has been validly expropriated." He added that the right to abolish a

Torah regulation was all the more applicable when the generation is given to licentious behavior. Accordingly, in 1865 he ruled that his enactment could annul marriages contracted in violation of civil law.[30]

In 1874, Rabbi Elijah Hazzan (d. 1908), the chief rabbi of Alexandria, gave his consent to a similar enactment in the city of Constantine (Algeria), albeit with some reservations; this enactment received the approval of other leading rabbis of that time, including Rabbi Abraham Ashkenazi, the chief rabbi of Jerusalem.[31]

Finally, in 1901 the rabbis of Egypt instituted a provision for annulling marriages in their country. This too was based on the idea of expropriating the consecration money.[32]

In all these cases, Diaspora rabbis managed to overcome many obstacles and to institute rules that could save Jewish women from remaining *agunot*.

After enumerating numerous ways for annulling a marriage and tracing their history,[33] Rabbi Eliezer Berkovits concluded that "in my humble opinion I have demonstrated that in light of contemporary circumstances it is possible to enact rules and use them to annul marriages, in our own time as well."[34]

One can only regret that the Chief Rabbinate in a sovereign Jewish state, which has a monopoly over marriage and divorce, with the backing of the legislature, as well as ample means of enforcement at its disposal, has not found the courage to solve these problems with appropriate regulations.

As we have seen, enlightened decisors of past generations considered themselves bound by the codified Halakhah as presented in the Written and Oral Laws. At the same time, however, alert to the suffering of their people and the demands of their own conscience, they were willing to rectify injustices caused by the inevitable conflict between antique rules and the realities of their own age.

2

Maimonides and the "Lesser Evil"

AMONG THE MANY CASES IN WHICH THE ETHICAL AND evolving nature of Halakhah swayed major decisors, one of the most significant involved Maimonides (1135–1204). The elders of a twelfth-century Egyptian Jewish community asked him what action they should take regarding a young man of their community who had purchased a gentile female slave and was living with her in the same courtyard as his father's wife and her small daughters. The entire community was gossiping about the case. May he keep the woman with him, asked the elders, or must they compel him to send her away?[1]

Maimonides' reply should have been obvious, since he had already codified this issue in his comprehensive law code, the *Mishneh Torah:*

> If a man was suspected of having intercourse with a slave woman who was later emancipated, or with a gentile woman who afterward became a proselyte, he may not marry her; but if he has already taken her in marriage, they need not be parted (Laws of Divorce 10:14).[2]

But instead of applying his own halakhic ruling, Maimonides made an astonishing response:

After this evil tale [you have related], a *beit din* should force him either to send her away or to emancipate and marry her, even though [this latter action involves] something of a sin *(averah)*, because a man suspected of intercourse with a slave woman who was later emancipated may not marry her *ab initio.* Nevertheless in accordance with my ruling in a number of similar cases, he should manumit her and marry her. We have done this relying on three rabbinic dicta:

a. *Takkanat hashavim* (the "Provision for the Penitent");[3]
b. "It is better for him to eat the gravy and not the fat itself."[4]
c. "It is a time to act for God; they have violated Your Torah."[5]

Maimonides not only contradicted his own ruling in the *Mishneh Torah* but even admitted to his questioners that on more than one occasion he had abetted the commission of this sin. Then he mentioned, in passing, three talmudic *takkanot* (provisions or regulations), all of which may be seen as sanctioning the lesser of two evils and which he evidently considered to justify his self-contradictory action.

TAKKANAT HASHAVIM (THE PROVISION FOR THE PENITENT)

An early talmudic source recounts a controversy between Beit Shammai and Beit Hillel about a man who stole the main beam of a building and built it into his own mansion. Beit Shammai held that he must demolish the entire structure and return the beam to its rightful owner. Beit Hillel said that he need only pay its monetary value to the owner because of *takkanat hashavim*—the provision for the penitent.[6] Beit Shammai interpreted the biblical injunction "he shall return the stolen object, which he took by robbery"[7] in its literal sense; that is, the thief must restore the *original object* to its owner. He is obliged to return the stolen beam even if that means demolishing his own home.

Beit Hillel, on the other hand, understood that if a repentant thief is faced with the choice of destroying his dwelling or doing nothing, he may never make restitution. Therefore, this school allowed him to repent and right the wrong without undue damage to himself. Rashi explains that Beit Hillel's rationale is the "provision for the penitent": "For if you force him to destroy his dwelling and return the beam to its owner, he will avoid the act of repentance."[8] Beit Shammai ruled according to the literal meaning of the biblical law, whereas Beit Hillel opted for the lesser evil.

Maimonides incorporated Beit Hillel's decision into his code:

> A thief must return the stolen object itself, as it is written: "He shall return the stolen object which he took" (Leviticus 5:23). . . . Even if he stole a beam and built it into his mansion . . . the Torah states that he must destroy the entire structure and return the beam to its owner. The Sages ruled, however, on account of the provision for the penitents, that he may pay its value and not demolish the dwelling (Laws of Theft and Loss 1:5).

Here Halakhah preferred the rehabilitation of the miscreant to the imposition of strict Torah judgment. The Sages opted for the lesser evil—the payment of monetary compensation—rather than the literal enforcement of the biblical ruling.

Maimonides found a close parallel between Beit Hillel's decision and his own responsum. Beit Hillel allowed a thief to retain the stolen beam and his house, yet make restitution and become a *ba'al teshuvah* (a penitent). In the present case, Maimonides allowed the young man to retain his lover, but only after her status had been changed to that of a free woman and a Jew.

The emancipation of a slave is the equivalent of conversion. Actually, every gentile slave was a sort of pre-proselyte, who had already fulfilled the ritual requirements for conversion—circumcision, immersion, and acceptance of the yoke of the commandments—in order to serve a Jewish family.[9] When the master freed the slave, he or she was automatically a Jew, with all the rights and prohibitions that apply to a Jew.[10]

Thus, the slave woman in our case could marry a Jew after she was freed. More precisely, she could marry almost any Jew *except* her master, because he was suspected of cohabiting with her while she was a slave. According to Maimonides' ruling, however, if her former master married her despite the prohibition, the marriage would be valid *post factum,* and the community need not compel him to divorce her.

Maimonides understood that if the man were not allowed to free and marry the woman, he would undoubtedly keep her a slave and continue to live with her—a serious transgression, as we shall see—and would never repent. Maimonides considered the sin inherent in this condition, in which the man would be prevented from repenting, to be much graver than a violation of the rabbinic ban against marrying her. The young man needed to repent no less than a thief who stole a beam.

The great teacher considered that any obstacle to repentance must be removed. This is consistent with Maimonides' view of repentance, to which he attributes the highest religious value: "Great is repentance, which draws one close to the Divine Presence. . . . Yesterday this person was hated before God, defamed, cast away and abominable; today he is beloved, desirable, a favorite, and friend!"[11]

If violating the marriage prohibition was wrong, obstructing repentance would be a greater wrong. Maimonides, like Beit Hillel before him, chose the lesser evil.

"It is Better for Him to Eat the Gravy and Not the Fat Itself"

As further support for his ruling, Maimonides cited the aphorism, "it is better for him to eat the gravy and not the fat itself." This enigmatic adage is his own coinage, based on two talmudic sources:[12]

> If a pregnant woman smelled the [forbidden] flesh of a sacrifice, or of pork [for which she has a morbid craving], we put a reed into the gravy and place it in her mouth. If she then feels that

her craving has been satisfied, it is well; if not, she is fed the fat meat itself (BT Yoma 82a).

The gravy, too, is forbidden, but not to the same degree as the meat itself. The woman is fed this forbidden food, because she, or her fetus, or both might be in danger. It is a matter of *pikkuaḥ ne-fesh*—saving human life—and this takes precedence of almost all other commandments. Although the pork gravy is prohibited, licking less than an olive's bulk of the gravy is only a minor infraction, not as severe as eating the meat.

A second talmudic regulation supplies the first part of Maimonides' aphorism: "It is better for Israel to eat the flesh of animals that were about to die, but were ritually slaughtered, than the flesh of animals that have perished" (BT Kiddushin 21b–22a). Slaughtering a dying animal is a repulsive act, of course; but if we do not allow its owner to have the creature ritually slaughtered he is liable to consume the carcass after its natural death, thereby violating the much more serious transgression of the biblical commandment against eating carrion.[13]

"IT IS TIME TO ACT FOR THE LORD; THEY HAVE VIOLATED YOUR TORAH"

The third justification cited by Maimonides is this oft-quoted talmudic precept, which is based on the verse "it is a time to act for the Lord; they have violated Your Torah" (Ps. 119:126). Although the "plain meaning" of this verse would evidently take the first clause as the effect and the second as the cause—"it is a time to act for the Lord *because* they have violated Your Torah"—the Sages expounded it "back to front" (BT Berakhot 63a)[14] so that the first clause states the reason for the second: "violate Your teaching and infringe Torah law *because* it is a time to act for the Lord." As Rashi explains the passage, "when the time comes to do something for the sake of the Holy One, blessed be He, it is permissible to violate the Torah" (BT Yoma 69a, *s.v.* "a time to act").

A conspicuous example of the application of this principle involves Rabbi Johanan and his brother-in-law Rabbi Simeon ben Lakish (known as Resh Lakish), who lived in Eretz Yisrael in the third century. They were studying a book of *aggadah* (rabbinic legends) on the Sabbath, despite the then-current halakhic ban on committing the Oral Law to writing. The two justified their action by expounding the verse just cited: "'It is a time to act for the Lord; they have violated Your teaching'—they said it is better that [a specific precept of the] Torah be uprooted rather than that [the entire] Torah be forgotten by the Jews" (BT Temurah 14b). By the time of these two Sages, it had become almost impossible to commit the entire body of the Oral Law to memory.[15] To keep it from being forgotten, it was essential to disobey the injunction against writing down the Oral Law.

Another well-known Torah prohibition enjoins using the Divine Name in profane speech. Nahmanides expounds the verse from the Ten Commandments "you shall not swear falsely by the name of the Lord your God" (Exod. 20:7) as follows: "According to the plain meaning, it also bans uttering the Holy Name in vain." Today people avoid this prohibition by resorting to various substitutes for the Divine Name, such as *Elokeinu* and *Hashem.*

Despite this explicit ban, derived from the text of the Torah itself, the Mishnah reports a rabbinic ruling that permits uttering the Divine Name in daily speech:

> They instituted that a man should greet his fellow using the [Ineffable] Name; as it is written: "Boaz arrived from Bethlehem and greeted the reapers, 'Adonai (YHWH) be with you!' And they responded, 'May YHWH bless you!'"(Ruth 2:4) (Mishnah Berakhot 9:5).
>
> The Mishnah continues by stating the reason for this enactment: "'It is a time to act for the Lord; they have violated Your teaching.' Rabbi Nathan said: 'They have violated Your teaching because it is time to act for the Lord.'"

Rashi reconciles the contradiction between the Torah's ban on uttering the Divine Name in vain and this rabbinic enactment:

> Sometimes they overrule Torah laws to act for the Lord. A man who wishes to greet his friend and is thus expressing the Divine will, as it is written: "Seek [*or* greet] peace and pursue it" (Ps. 34:15), is permitted to violate the Torah and do something that appears to be forbidden (BT Berakhot 54a, s.v. "It says, 'It is a time'").

In other words, the Sages enacted this amendment as a way to increase peace among human beings. In the words of Rabbi Eliezer Berkovits:

> The concern for loyal and upright interpersonal relations is also part of Torah law, and everything that is done for this purpose is also done on behalf of Heaven. For this reason, if it is a time to act for the Lord, violate Your Torah.[16]

THE BEAUTIFUL CAPTIVE

Maimonides' responsum contains an additional justification for permitting the young man to marry his slave, although it is somewhat elusive. The questioners themselves, attempting to sound learned, had speculated that the woman might have the status of a *yefat to'ar*, a beautiful woman captured in war (see Deut. 21:10–14).

Maimonides replied that the situation of the female slave was not the same as that of a female captive. In the latter case, the Torah made a special provision that during wartime, a soldier could take the woman while she was still a gentile. In other circumstances this is forbidden; here, however, the Torah made allowance for human passions and permitted it. The situation is similar to that which prevails in the heat of battle, when the rabbis permitted the soldiers to eat forbidden foods, relying on the verse, "[the Lord will give you] houses full of good things, which you did not fill" (Deut. 6:10). The Sages ruled that these permitted "good things" might even include sides of bacon. When he codified this ruling in the *Mishneh Torah,* Maimonides stipulated that soldiers could eat pork and similar foods if they were hungry and could find only these forbidden foods, and could drink wine used for idolatrous libations.[17]

Why did Maimonides, who ignored most of the points raised by his questioners, nevertheless incorporate this reference to the laws of wine, women, and war into the responsum? On the face of it, special provisions for wartime are irrelevant to the case of the young man living with his slave woman. In fact, Maimonides' response begins with the demurrer that the subject of the responsum is not the captive woman, and concludes the section that deals with this law by admonishing his readers not to make any inference from that case.

But if the law of the female captive is irrelevant to the case of the female slave, why did Maimonides, who was such a stickler for brevity in responsa, devote a third of his reply to this subject? One answer may be that the question of the captive woman is in fact the key to the entire responsum. Maimonides quoted the talmudic rationale for this provision, namely, that "the Torah makes allowance for human passions" (BT Kiddushin 21b). The rabbis were aware of human weakness and how difficult it is for men and women to resist temptation and deny their bodily appetites. In his code, Maimonides cited this ground for leniency in cases where people cannot control their lust and cravings: "The Torah takes a person's impulses into consideration" (Laws of Kings 8:4). We have already cited the continuation of the statement in the Gemara, which is that "it is better for Israel to eat the flesh of animals that were about to die, yet were ritually slaughtered, than the flesh of animals that have perished." Both cases—the beautiful captive and the dying animal—deal with and make allowances for the weakness of those who are enslaved by their appetites.

Maimonides employed the law of the beautiful captive as an indirect but logical justification of his ruling that the young man could marry his slave. At first sight this precedent appears to be quite different from the three rabbinic regulations that are all variations on the theme of preferring the lesser evil, whereas the case of the captive woman is a biblical leniency that allows for the behavior of men in wartime.

In fact, the regulations concerning the beautiful captive, as codified by Maimonides and others,[18] really constitute another case of opting for the lesser evil. In his *Guide of the Perplexed,* Maimonides suggested that the permission to bring the captive gentile woman home actually places the returning soldier in a framework of restraint. The soldier may not be able to suppress his lust for her, but Halakhah requires him to "bring her inside his home" (Deut. 21:12). He is not allowed to take her forcibly while still in the field. He may not take more than one such woman. He may not have sexual relations with her a second time until she has finished the mourning process. He may not hinder her grieving and crying for her parents or prevent her from looking repulsive for the thirty days of her mourning period. Finally, even if he tires of her she may not be sold or treated like a slave.[19]

Thus, the codified Halakhah actually places limits on the soldier's ability to satisfy his desires. Had the Torah and the rabbis not regulated this matter, the soldier who lusted for a woman might have taken her without any restraints. He could have raped her whenever and wherever he wished, as often as he pleased, along with as many other foreign women as he could command. By permitting the soldier to take the captive woman as his wife, subject to strict limitations, the Torah and the rabbis were choosing the lesser evil.

THE VERDICT

Why did Maimonides go on at length about the beautiful captive and proceed to allege precisely these talmudic precedents, all of them based on choosing between two problematic alternatives?

What is the significance of resolving the conflict by opting for the more palatable option?

Maimonides cited these precedents to buttress his own decision. Allowing the young man to marry the slave woman after freeing her would not be an *actual* sin, but only "a sort of sin."[20] (This responsum was the only place in the halakhic literature where this category is mentioned![21]) But even if it is only "a sort of sin" and not a full-fledged transgression, the action is nevertheless a breach of Halakhah. It is self-evident that Maimonides took the halakhic process seriously.[22] He had himself codified the law that he now took into his own hands. Yet, he confessed to having been an accessory to this "sort of sin" several times in the past.

In fact, he was confronted by a conflict between two laws codified in his *Mishneh Torah*. According to the first, the young man who was suspected of having had intercourse with the slave woman was forbidden to marry her even after freeing her. The talmudic rationale for prohibiting the union was that their marriage might confirm the rumor that he had been sleeping with her while she was still a slave. The rabbinic prohibition is concerned with the public credibility of the original rumor.[23] Once freed, however, she became a full-fledged Jew, and their marriage, although forbidden before the fact, would be valid and they need not be divorced. Clearly, a statute that recognizes the forbidden marriage after it has taken place and is founded on the believability of gossip can hardly be considered a stringent law. Hence, transgressing it would only be a "sort of sin."

On the other hand, a man is forbidden to make a mistress of his slave.[24] Maimonides admonished his readers not to dismiss this iniquity *('avon)*[25] as inconsequential: "Do not think that this is a minor sin, because the Torah did not prescribe flogging for one who violates the prohibition; for this liaison also causes the son to turn away from the Lord,[26] in that a son born to a maidservant is a slave and not an Israelite. The result is that holy seed is profaned by becoming slaves."[27]

When Maimonides compared this grave consequence with the alternative of a valid and lasting marriage with the freed slave, now a full-fledged Jew, he knew that violating the prohibition was merely "a sort of sin." In comparison with the severe "iniquity" of living with her as a non-Jewish slave, the forbidden marriage appears to be the better of two bad alternatives and therefore permissible. He had no doubt which was the lesser evil, for he had previously so decided in other similar cases.

Such cases of men who wished to free a slave and marry her seem not to have been uncommon.[28] Many documents dealing with slave women have been found in the Cairo Geniza. Mordechai Akiba Friedman published twelve of them, which bear witness to the prevalence of this phenomenon. Most relevant here is the case of the daughter of the Nubian slave woman whom Eli ben Yefet had purchased in Ashkelon. He was ordered to appear before the rabbinical court of the exilarch, David ben Daniel, in the city of Fostat, Egypt, to clarify the status of his daughter, Malah (described as "the beauty of beauties"), who had just come of age. It was found that Eli had freed his Nubian slave and then married her. Their daughter was born after her mother had become fully Jewish. The document, dated 1093, states: "Her birth was in holiness and she is permitted to marry in the Congregation of the Lord."[29]

Maimonides concluded his responsum by instructing the rabbinical court of the young man's community to present him with the alternatives. He must choose whether to free her and marry her or send her away. The time for a decision had arrived and could not be postponed. Slave and owner had been cohabiting long enough. The procrastination must come to an end. Maimonides was permissive, but firm. He issued his verdict: the court should set a date by which the young man must marry her or send her away.[30]

Maimonides was not content with giving the couple his radically lenient responsum, which allowed them to be married. He related to the pair with tenderness, evincing a warm and human understanding of their predicament and hurt feelings. This is illustrated by the *obiter dictum* with which he ends the responsum: "Gently and with tenderness we help him marry her."

Maimonides responded to the ethical imperative of the couple's plight by ruling against his own code. This is an instance of case

law (responsa) overriding code law. Yet, Maimonides was not ruling for just the one couple but for an entire class of people.

Maimonides realized that his resolution of the issue was an
imperfect solution. Only God could repair our moral damage, as
He promised in the words of the prophet: "I shall remove all of
your dross" (Isaiah 1:25).

"THE LESSER EVIL" AS A HERMENEUTIC PRINCIPLE

"Choosing the lesser evil" is in fact an ancient rule of interpretation
that may be exemplified from the Bible, though not under this
name. Consider the following three cases:

1. Joseph, whom his brothers have not recognized, tells them
that Benjamin must stay behind in Egypt as his slave. Judah coun-
ters by offering himself instead: ". . . and let the lad go back with
his brothers. For how can I go back to my father if the lad is not
with me? I fear to see the evil that would come upon my father"
(Gen. 44:33–34). For all that slavery in Egypt is terrible, it would
not be as bad as causing the disaster that might befall Judah's aged
father. Here we certainly have a case of choosing the lesser evil.

2. The prophet Gad comes to King David to tell him that divine punishment has been decreed on the people, but the king may
choose whether it will be pestilence, famine, or exile. David, opting
for pestilence, replies: "I am in great distress; let us fall into the
hand of the Lord, for his mercy is great; but let me not fall into the
hand of man" (2 Sam. 24:14). Here too David chooses the lesser
evil.[31]

3. Another instance is found in the Book of Esther. At Mordecai's urging, Esther goes unbidden to King Ahasuerus, although entering the throne room without a royal summons is forbidden by
law and punishable by death. When she weighs this danger to herself against the cruel edict that mandates the annihilation of all of
the Jews in the Persian Empire, Esther chooses the lesser evil (Esther 4:8–16).

Similarly, Maimonides' responsum about the young man and his slave woman does not use the expression "choosing the lesser evil." Nor does it appear anywhere else in his work. Furthermore, although the principle was certainly applied, as we have seen, the phrase is not to be found in biblical or talmudic literature.[32] It is not included among the seven hermeneutic principles attributed to Hillel the Elder,[33] the thirteen of Rabbi Ishmael, or the thirty-two ascribed to Rabbi Eliezer son of Rabbi Jose the Galilean.[34]

What then, is the source of "choosing the lesser evil"? It appears to be a variation of *kal va-ḥomer,* an inference from the lighter or less important to the graver and more important. But unlike that inferential principle, which in the Western world goes by the Latin names *a minori ad maius* (from minor to major) and *a fortiori,* and which deals with matters of greater or lesser importance or stringency, "the lesser evil" compares and evaluates two phenomena or processes that are both bad and leads to a decision based on a judgment as to which is the worse and which the lesser evil.

Justice Haim Cohn[35] believes that this hermeneutic principle goes back to classical Greece and Rome. Plato has Socrates say that "when faced with the choice of two evils no one will choose the greater when he might choose the lesser."[36] Aristotle developed the idea further: "The lesser evil is reckoned a good in comparison with the greater evil, since the lesser evil is rather to be chosen than the greater."[37] Cicero used the expression *minima ex malis,* which is indeed literally the least of evils.[38]

Even though the Greeks and Romans knew this principle, gave it a name, and committed it to writing, and the Sages themselves applied it, it did not appear in the halakhic literature until about two hundred years after Maimonides. Rabbi Isaac ben Sheshet Perfet (known as the Ribash, 1326–1408) was chief rabbi of Algiers and head of its rabbinical court. Hundreds of his decisions were incorporated into the *Shulḥan Arukh.* One of his responsa contains the first known explicit reference to this hermeneutic rule, phrased as "I chose the least part of the evil."[39] The term cropped up again when Rabbi David ben Zimra (1479–1573) responded to a question about a conflict among members of a community.

He advised them that it would be preferable if they could pray together in harmony. But if they quarrelled most of the time, it would be better to worship separately, for this would be the lesser evil.[40] From the fifteenth and sixteenth centuries, the rule has been invoked frequently and under this name.[41]

Maimonides' reliance on this principle is further evidence that Halakhah is an evolutionary and ethical phenomenon. In all of these halakhic texts the rabbis enacted regulations in response to changes of time, place, and circumstance, or because their conscience demanded it.

3

The Essence of Evolving Halakhah

HALAKHAH AS IT DEVELOPED WAS AN EVOLVING ETHICAL SYS-
tem that found ways to cope with the particular conditions of each
generation. This statement leads to two difficult questions:

1. In antiquity, the Middle Ages, and even modern times, decisors issued lenient rulings and permitted the "transgression" of serious prohibitions concerning marriage and other ethically
problematic domains. Why, then, are the traditional rabbis of our
own day so severe, even when the codified Halakhah incorporates
ample precedents for ruling leniently? Are these decisors ignoring
the ethical dimension because they feel that the Halakhah as codified in the past has divine sanction and transcends merely human
ethical concerns?

2. Do the halakhic principles that enable progress, such as
those reviewed in chapters 1 and 2, make it possible to solve all halakhic problems in our age? Can a contemporary Jew who feels a
bond to the codified Halakhah live in accordance both with these
rules and with his conscience in our modern world, which is so different from that of the talmudic Sages?

Our answer to the first question is that despite the rigidity that
characterizes contemporary halakhic rulings and despite the widen-
ing gap between Halakhah and the conditions of daily life, it is still
possible to avail ourselves of the inherent flexibility of Halakhah
while showing our concern for weak and oppressed human beings.

I have already noted that a decisor must be endowed with certain character traits in order to rule humanely and against traditional stringencies. Many rabbis today, including some serving in the official rabbinate in Israel, are terrified that their Ultra-Orthodox colleagues will attack them for any lenient ruling. In recent years many decisors have demanded the concurrence of ten or more of the leading rabbis of the generation before any ruling they issued could be valid. Others have written long and closely reasoned responsa, to which they have appended the caveat that the ruling is given only as a matter of theory and must not be followed in practice.

There is such a great contrast between these rabbis and other decisors, of both the earlier and modern periods, who were not afraid to issue practical rulings even if they were controversial. The contemporary vogue of looking over one's shoulder at the extremists manifests a fear of flesh and blood, not necessarily of Heaven.

There *are* halakhic solutions to the painful situations of those who cannot marry freely and those who suffer for no fault of their own, as we shall see in the chapters that follow. In this book I shall attempt to show that the main responsibility for this obliviousness to human suffering does not stem from Halakhah itself but from certain contemporary decisors who do not understand—or perhaps do not want to understand—its humane and ethical foundations. I shall examine why these rabbis do not exploit the inherent flexibility of Halakhah to cope with changing conditions.

As we have seen, Halakhah is by nature and practice evolutionary, flexible, ethical, and progressive. It has roots in the distant past, but its methods allow it to deal with contemporary conditions. It can be applied to almost every human situation. Its determinations are a matter not only of ancient law but also of social justice and human rights. In other words, it deals not only with the dry letter of the law but also—and perhaps chiefly—with human beings as human beings and with Jews as Jews.

According to Ben-Yehuda's Hebrew dictionary, the original Hebrew term for a Reform Jew was "*metakken,* that is, one who repairs, in the sense of someone who wishes to make amendments and changes in life and religion."[1] The first Progressive Jews wanted to introduce amendments in the context of Halakhah, especially with regard to the liturgy and synagogue rituals. In 1818 a volume of responsa was published under the title *Nogah ha-tzedek*. Its authors—Rabbi Jacob Hai Recanati of Italy, Rabbi Aaron Chorin of Hungary, and others—cited precedents in the codified Halakhah to support various changes, such as the location of the lectern in the synagogue and the use of the Sephardi pronunciation in Ashkenazi synagogues. What these rabbis aspired to was, in fact, an improved or enlightened Halakhah.[2]

Their approach is in stark contrast to the Orthodox perspective that rejects all innovation and change in the Jewish religion. During his campaign against the reformers, the Hungarian rabbi Moses Sofer (or Schreiber, 1762–1839), generally known as the Ḥatam Sofer, gave currency to the slogan that "anything new is forbidden by the Torah in every place."[3] In one responsum he appended the observation that "the old and well-aged is better than the new,"[4] while in another he postulated that "anyone who makes changes has the weaker position."[5] The Ḥatam Sofer was systematically opposed to change, not only because of the inroads of religious reform but first and foremost in order to protect Orthodoxy against modernity. His philosophy had a strong influence on the character of Orthodoxy in subsequent generations.

Other rabbis, Orthodox and non-Orthodox, did not accept the Ḥatam Sofer's approach. They continued to issue innovative and creative rulings that relaxed the strict letter of the law and took human needs into account. In this book we shall have occasion to mention many such cases.

Although there were periods of relative fossilization or degeneration of Halakhah, nevertheless, as the result of contemporary circumstances and the frailty of a particular generation, Halakhah in its overall historical development remained balanced and self-amending.

It should be emphasized that this process of continuing rejuvenation was quite different from the familiar process of civil legislation, in which old laws are simply repealed and replaced by new statutes. Change in Halakhah is the result of deeper inquiry into and reinterpretation of older texts, employing the rules and principles—themselves enshrined in Halakhah—by which the Torah is expounded. Thus, there is no reason why decisors of the present generation may not rule leniently and permit what is at first sight questionable or forbidden, in accordance with the demands of ethics, their conscience, and evolving Halakhah.

But can all halakhic problems be solved by application of the halakhic methods for leniency? Down through the ages, rabbis wrestled with many difficult problems and found solutions to a large proportion of them—but certainly not all of them. They often found ways to erase the blot of halakhic illegitimacy,[6] once this had come to light, but rarely to permit a *kohen* to marry a convert to Judaism or a divorcée.[7] Even when they did find grounds for permitting such exceptions, frequently they were unwilling for their leniency to be cited as a precedent for similar cases that might arise in the future.

To clarify these questions further, we must now turn our attention to two fundamental issues: (1) the source of halakhic authority and (2) the criteria for halakhic rulings.

THE SOURCE OF HALAKHIC AUTHORITY

One obstacle to the attempts to rule flexibly and apply lenient postulates from the distant past derives from an attitude toward halakhic authority that is based on a fundamentalist conception of the essence and significance of divine revelation.

The view of halakhic authority held by Orthodox Judaism is quite different from that maintained by Progressive Jews. This latter term refers here to certain circles of rabbis and scholars affiliated with the Movement for Progressive Judaism (which goes by the names "Reform," "Liberal," or "Progressive"), with the Masorti (Conservative) Movement, and with the Reconstructionist Movement, and a number of Modern Orthodox rabbis. Milton Steinberg categorized the outlook of these circles as "modernist" (a term I shall use frequently below), as opposed to the "traditionalist" approach of Jews with a fundamentalist philosophy.[8] In fact, this difference is perhaps the major source of contention between Orthodox and non-Orthodox decisors. The Orthodox stance is summarized in a brief submitted by the Chief Rabbinate Council in response to a suit brought by the Israel Movement for Progressive Judaism, asking that its rabbis be granted the status of marriage registrars and the right to officiate at weddings in Israel.

The Rabbinate's brief advanced two main arguments: (1) The Torah given to Moses on Mount Sinai and the rulings of the Sages have absolute authority. (2) Nothing may be changed in Halakhah, whether in response to contemporary circumstances or to the urgings of individual conscience.

For the Chief Rabbinate, the postulate that the Torah given to Moses on Mount Sinai and the rulings of the Sages have absolute authority means that the opinions and practices of Jews who do not accept these basic tenets are religiously invalid, because such persons "do not see themselves bound [literally "chained"] by the Torah given to Moses on Sinai, and . . . by the rulings of the Sages over the generations and decisors throughout Jewish history."[9]

Although the Chief Rabbinate offered no textual support for its position that Halakhah is static and immutable because the Revelation on Mount Sinai was a one-time event valid for all generations, there are classical texts that may be interpreted as supporting this view. Citing the verse "these are the laws, rules, and instructions that the Lord established, through Moses on Mount Sinai, between Himself and the Israelite people" (Lev. 26:46), the Sages Ramarked that "this teaches that the Torah—its laws, details, and interpretations—was given through Moses on Sinai" (*Sifra, Beḥukotai* 8:12). In the Gemara, Rabbi Simeon ben Lakish holds that not only the Torah—that is, the Pentateuch—but also the Prophets and the Hagiographa, the Mishna and the Gemara, were all given at Mount Sinai (BT Berakhot 5a).

If everything was already revealed at Sinai, there is no room for innovation and change. Indeed, the conclusion inferred from the concept of a perfect revelation at Sinai is that "no prophet is permitted to innovate in any matter from this time on" (BT Shabbat 104a). If prophets are so restricted, how much the more are rabbis and scholars: "Even what a long-time student will one day expound before his teacher was already given to Moses at Sinai" (JT Pe'ah 2:4). It is this fundamentalist position that leads most Orthodox thinkers to reject the historical and scientific view of the evolving nature of the Bible and rabbinic literature held by modernist Jewish scholars.

On the other hand, there are also many passages in which the Sages recognized the fact that Judaism changes. Consider the well-known midrash that Moses visited the academy of Rabbi Akiba (early second century) but "did not understand their discourse [about the Torah he had received] and felt faint." Only when a student asked Rabbi Akiba for the source of his teaching, and the Sage replied that "it is a Halakhah given to Moses on Sinai," did Moses recover (BT Menaḥot 29b).

For the British Rabbi Louis Jacobs, this midrash could be interpreted as follows:

> The Torah that Akiba was teaching was so different from the Torah given to Moses because the social, economic, political, and religious conditions were so different in Akiba's day that, at first, Moses could not recognize his Torah in the Torah taught by Akiba. But he was reassured when he realized that Akiba's Torah was implicit in his Torah, was, indeed, an attempt to make his Torah relevant to the spiritual needs of Jews in the age of Akiba.[10]

Rabbi Jacobs' conclusion is buttressed by a statement of Rabbi Jose bar Ḥanina (a third-century Palestinian *amora*): "Matters that were not revealed to Moses were revealed to Rabbi Akiba and his colleagues" (Exodus Rabbah 5:9). This idea is at variance with the passage quoted above from the Jerusalem Talmud, which holds that anything that a Sage might ever expound had already been taught to Moses on Sinai.[11] But it reflects a recognition of a process that develops and supplements the Torah given at Sinai. The foundation of the authority to make innovations in the Torah, which troubled many generations, was expressed clearly by the fifteenth-century Spanish Jewish philosopher Rabbi Joseph Albo:

The Written Law cannot be understood except with the Oral Law; and the law of God cannot be perfect so as to be adequate for all times, because the ever-new circumstances of human relations, their judgments and their actions, are too numerous to be embraced in a book.

Therefore Moses was given orally certain general principles, only briefly alluded to in the Torah, by means of which the Sages may work out the newly emerging particulars in every generation.[12]

Albo understood that no written book, not even the divine Torah, could contain all the rules and laws required by future generations. The Torah is not perfect, in the sense that it does not embrace all future knowledge. The constant, dynamic changes in human society make it impossible to record the particulars of all customs and provide an account of all epochs to come. Hence, the Oral Law includes general principles that make it possible for the wise scholars of every generation to apply them and interpret the Written Law for their own age. One cannot help contrasting Albo's dynamic approach to the evolution of Halakhah with the position of those who believe that it all began and ended at Sinai.

By analyzing these and many other passages, liberal scholarship has reached the conclusion that "long before the rise of modern criticism some of the Jewish teachers had a conception of revelation which leaves room for the idea of human cooperation with the divine."[13]

How is the divine will revealed in Halakhah? According to Jacobs,

Revelation must be understood as a far more complicated and complex process of divine-human encounter and interaction and quite differently from the idea of direct divine communication of infallible laws and propositions, upon which the traditional theory of Halakhah depends. [14]

Evolving, modernist Halakhah, then, must be founded on such a reinterpretation of revelation. It relies on scholarly study of the classic texts of Judaism, which discovers variety, flexibility, and creativity in Halakhah and draws on new information derived from archaeological excavations and documents unknown to our ancestors.

This theological-halakhic position has implications for the authority of traditional Halakhah. For the non-Orthodox Jew:

> The ultimate authority for determining which observances are binding upon the faithful Jew is the historical experience of the people of Israel, since, historically perceived, this is ultimately the sanction of the Halakhah itself.[15]

Serious modernist Jews accept or reject the content of Jewish tradition not out of convenience or caprice but as a matter of principle, based on their liberal theological understanding of revelation, history, and Halakhah.

The Principles and Criteria of Progressive Halakhah

In chapters 1 and 2 we noted the progressive principles that are part of the codified Halakhah and that permit evolution, change, and grappling with customs and conventions. Despite the vast potential latent in these principles, however, we encounter many obstacles to dealing with the severe problems of our day. Some serious problems seem to have no solution in the framework of Halakhah, despite the sagacious principles incorporated into Halakhah itself that make it possible to rule leniently. Most Orthodox decisors of our day hold that there is nothing to be done about such cases because they lack the authority to rule permissively. The rabbis of earlier generations could boldly issue lenient rulings—they say—because their command of the Torah exceeded ours. If there is no way to keep some unfortunate persons from suffering at the hands of the codified Halakhah, that is, unfortunately, simply the way of the Torah.

Some Orthodox rabbis contend that these obstacles reflect the will of God, which is above human understanding. Hence, it is impossible to alleviate the suffering of those who cannot marry as they choose—the halakhically illegitimate and others—nor should one modify certain liturgical conventions, such as the prayer for the renewal of animal sacrifices in the Temple, or *Yekum Purkan,* an invocation in Aramaic recited every Sabbath on behalf of the welfare of the rabbis and scholars of the Land of Israel as well as their colleagues in Mesopotamia, who flourished more than a thousand years ago.

Modernist Jews have a different basic conception of the divine authority of Halakhah. The progressive view initiates and supports inquiry aimed at uncovering the latent principles of Halakhah and Jewish tradition and then applies them to reach halakhic decisions. Some of these principles may not fall into the category of codified Halakhah in the conventional sense of the term.

This theological position on the divine authority of Halakhah, together with a sensitivity to ethical concerns, inner spirituality, and social justice, is the crucial factor in the opinions issued by modernist halakhists. Some of the foremost thinkers of the twentieth century have set forth criteria for halakhic decision making and observance of the commandments by modern nonfundamentalist Jews. Most Orthodox decisors reject these criteria because the very process of choosing and selecting which traditional precepts should be observed is incompatible with the traditional view of the absolute authority of the divinely authored and sanctioned Halakhah.

The sections that follow review several principles and criteria for determining the halakhic attitude appropriate for modernist Jews. These principles have been gleaned from the writings of many thinkers affiliated with various streams of Judaism—Reform, Orthodox, Conservative. It is their approach to Halakhah, and not their movement affiliation, that warrants their inclusion here. Their concepts and criteria for rendering halakhic decisions are appropriate for a nonfundamentalist Halakhah. Although these criteria are not stated explicitly in the codified Halakhah, they are implicit in it and can be deduced from it.

Halakhah Is an Evolutionary Process

In the brief I submitted to the Supreme Court of Israel in the marriage-registrar case, I argued that Halakhah has continually developed and changed to confront changing reality in every generation. The history of Jewish law from the biblical period to this day is replete with changes, from substituting study and prayer for sacrifices, through upgrading the status of women (no marriage or divorce without the woman's consent), to allowing conversion for the sake of marriage (see chapter 9).[16]

These are only a few of the many developments within Halakhah, which, according to Rabbi Robert Gordis, who taught at the Jewish Theological Seminary, are the result of both outside influences and inner ethical insights. Gordis points out that these two factors have contributed to growth and change in Halakhah:

> The first was the necessity to respond to new external conditions—social, economic, political, or cultural—that posed a challenge or even a threat to accepted religious and ethical values. The second was the need to give recognition to new ethical insights and attitudes and to embody them in the life of the people . . .[17]

This concept of change and development may serve as a guide for modern Jews in assessing those *mitzvot* that evolved over time and are therefore relevant to our day. This criterion would set aside commandments such as *ḥalitzah* (release from the obligation of levirate marriage), which might have had some relevance in the distant past but have no spiritual meaning, even if reinterpreted, for Jews in the twentieth century.

Halakhah Is Pluralistic

A corollary of the evolutionary nature of Halakhah is its pluralistic character. Historical research proves that Jewish law was always diverse in nature and certainly far from monolithic. During the controversy between Beit Hillel and Beit Shammai about forbidden marriages, the two schools did not refrain from intermarrying, even though a particular union might be forbidden according to the halakhic ruling of one school but permitted by the other.[18]

Yitzhak Gilat, professor of Talmud at Bar-Ilan University, pointed out that in spite of the great differences between the two schools, they came to the recognition that "both [rulings] are the words of the living God" (BT Eruvin 13b) and that a person could act according to either view: "Whoever wishes to conduct himself according to Beit Shammai may do so, and according to Beit Hillel may do so" (ibid., 10b).

This freedom of halakhic ruling was accepted in practice during the time of the Second Temple. In the words of Prof. Gilat, "every Sage was permitted to render decisions in his town and home according to his own tradition and in consonance with his judgment, on the basis of the deliberations in the rabbinic sources."

The books that list the differences in the customs of the Jewish communities in Mesopotamia and the Land of Israel in the talmudic and post-talmudic age indicate great variation, ranging from whether poultry may be eaten with milk to whether the marriage of a childless widow to another man should be dissolved when her late husband's brother returns from abroad.[19]

Pluralism can be found in many codifications and rulings—for example, the hundreds of disagreements between Maimonides and his most prominent commentator-critic, Rabbi Abraham ibn Daoud (1120?–1198).[20]

Maimonides and the tosafists disagreed as to whether Christians should be considered to be idolaters. Maimonides, who spent all his life among Muslims, said they were. By contrast, Rabbenu Jacob Tam, the most prominent of the tosafists, who lived in Christian France in the twelfth and thirteenth centuries, ruled that Christians could be believed on oath because "they have the Creator of Heaven in mind."[21]

In the eighteenth-century imbroglio concerning a bill of divorce issued by the religious court of Rabbi Israel Lipschuetz of Cleves, in Germany, which was nullified by the *beit din* of Frankfurt-am-Main, Rabbi Jacob Emden was astonished that one court arrogated to itself the authority to overrule another independent *beit din:* "What power does a *beit din* have to rule for another country today, when we do not have a higher court as of old?"[22] The autonomy of each court to rule as it saw fit was not just an aspiration but a solid fact and reality.

In the twentieth century, too, pluralistic approaches have been applied to Halakhah. Rabbi A. I. Kook ruled that the agricultural lands of Eretz Yisrael could be worked during the Sabbatical Year, where there is extremely great urgency, by means of the fictitious sale of the land to a non-Jew.[23] Since the land then "belongs" to a gentile, Jews are allowed to carry out agricultural tasks they may not carry out in Jewish-owned fields. Rabbi Avraham Yeshayahu Karelitz (known as the Ḥazon Ish, 1878–1953), however, ruled that such a sale was invalid and consequently no Jew could work the land.[24] In the wake of the contradictory rulings by these two eminent scholars, different Orthodox communities still practice variant systems of Sabbatical Year agriculture in Israel.

Finally, we should refer to a dispute that has not yet been fully settled: the demand that the Jews of Ethiopia undergo full or token conversion (see chapter 10). Rabbi Yitzhak Isaac Herzog held that there were grounds to suspect halakhic illegitimacy among Ethiopian Jews, or even that, halakhically speaking, they were non-Jews. Accordingly he ruled that they should undergo full conversion.[25] Rabbi Ovadia Yosef and Rabbi Shlomo Goren both followed his lead, but later they changed their minds and ruled that the Jews of Ethiopia should be accepted as full-fledged Jews. The Chief Rabbinate Council, for its part, continues to demand token conversion. Rabbi David Shloush, the rabbi of Netanya and a member of the Chief Rabbinate Council, parted company with most members of the council and ruled that these Jews do not require any form of conversion whatsoever.[26]

Many more cases could be added to the list. But this brief survey provides ample demonstration that pluralism is an integral characteristic of Halakhah. Anyone who asserts a monopoly on Halakhah and alleges a monolithic approach that ostensibly exists in the history of Jewish law is both mistaken and misleading others.

Here, then, is another solidly grounded principle for issuing halakhic rulings: Since pluralism has always been an inherent part of Jewish religious life, one may legitimately choose the practices of any mainstream Jewish religious tradition, including those of non-Orthodoxy.

Halakhah and Ethics

Sometimes the codified Halakhah of past centuries may come into conflict with the insights and demands of modern ethics. Which should carry the day in such a case—Halakhah or ethics?

According to Orthodox Rabbi Eliezer Berkovits, this dichotomy is spurious: "The rabbis in the Talmud were guided by the insight: God forbid that there should be anything in the application of Torah to the actual life situation that is contrary to the principles of ethics."[27] If a ruling is halakhic, it must be ethical. If it is unethical, it cannot be halakhic.

What are the practical implications of this rule? Can the claims of individual conscience nullify or modify a Halakhah that is thousands of years old? Is it possible, as a matter of principle, to amend or modify halakhic regulations that contravene contemporary ethical and moral standards?

Professor Seymour Siegel, of the Jewish Theological Seminary, considered this question of the primacy of conscience with regard to selecting, revising, or abolishing particular laws:

> The ethical values of our tradition should have the power to judge the particulars of Jewish law. If any law in our tradition does not fulfill our ethical values, then the law should be abolished or revised. . . . Thus, if because of changing conditions, the specific laws no longer express the ethical values which Tradition teaches, . . . we have the responsibility to revise the laws, rather than allow them to fall into desuetude.[28]

Siegel applied this principle to matters involving halakhic illegitimacy, the marriage of a *kohen* to a divorcée or convert, a man's refusal to give a *get,* and similar cases.

I accept Prof. Siegel's view and believe that we should apply this ethical principle to issues of social justice in our respective countries. For example, there should be a modernist halakhic approach to the moral issues raised by the Intifada and the common practice of demolishing the homes of suspected terrorists.[29]

The Commandments Embody Holiness

Holiness may be defined as "supreme nobility, the summa of perfection and purity." The polar antithesis of the holy is the profane. What affinity can there be between holiness and flesh-and-blood human beings who must wrestle with the problem of observing the commandments on earth?

Julius Guttmann, who was a professor at the Hebrew University, dealt with the general rationale of the commandments as a whole rather than with the reasons for each individual precept. He maintained that holiness *(kedushah)* underlies what he called "the *mitzvah* character of Judaism." The Torah proclaims that the general purpose of the commandments is "so that you do not follow your heart and eyes. . . . But you shall observe all My commandments and be holy to your God" (Num. 15:39–40). "The origin of the commandments"—concluded Guttmann—"is in the idea of *kedushah*."[30]

The commandments are not an end in themselves but a means by which one may be sanctified and draw closer to God. The possibility of attaining *kedushah* is one of the criteria for observance of a commandment. Precepts such as prayer, Torah study, philanthropic deeds, and others should lead to sanctification. The litmus test of holiness should determine the value of every religious act in the daily life of Jews of our generation.

Internalizing the Commandments

Must we observe religious precepts only because the Torah and rabbinic codes mandate this? Is there any place for inner identification with the commandments, or must we be like disciplined soldiers who obey without question or hesitation?

How does a particular precept become part and parcel of one's inner being? Franz Rosenzweig suggested a progression from "Ich muss" to "Ich kann"—from "I am obliged" to observe because of an external injunction to "I am able" to fulfill the precept because of an inner call. What I am not yet able to accept may, in time, become acceptable, and therefore a commandment for me. The criterion for the observance of a commandment is whether I can internalize and observe it with full inner devotion and intent. This requires a constant effort of selecting commandments and trying them out. This is undoubtedly what Rosenzweig meant in his reported reply to the question "Do you put on phylacteries?": "Not yet." In Rosenzweig's own words, "The voice of commandment causes the spark to leap from 'I must' to 'I can.' The Law is built on such commandments and only on them."[31]

The Critical Approach to Halakhah

In recent years, there has been a change in how most Jews relate to the codified Halakhah of centuries past. Most Jews today believe that a Jewish woman is not her husband's property but a human being endowed with full rights in all spheres of life, including religious matters. Most Jews today are not interested in offering animal sacrifices and do not pray with full intent for the restoration of this ritual. The vast majority of our people attaches no spiritual significance to the impurity of a menstruating woman, the ritual uncleanliness of a dead body, or the defiling touch of vermin. In practice, the Jews in their daily life have determined that such regulations have lapsed.

To a large extent these conclusions have been reached not only as a natural popular reaction but also on the basis of the information available to contemporary Jews that was not at the disposal of our ancestors. The Sages were undoubtedly scholars of great intellectual power and moral giants, and sincerely devoted to the Torah, but they did not have the scientific tools that have given us access to archaeological discoveries, documents from other ancient cultures, and documents from our own past, such as those from the Cairo Geniza. Our ancestors did not and could not have the historical perspective that is the fruit of studying Jewish history as we are able to today.

The British Liberal Rabbi John Rayner has given clear statement to a principle of evolving Halakhah that is infrequently aired:

> There are whole vast areas of Halakhah . . . predicated on assumptions unacceptable to us, for instance, regarding the inferior status of women, the hereditary privileges of the priesthood, the desirability of sacrificial worship, the importance of ritual purity, the defiling effect of menstruation and the legitimacy in principle of capital and corporal punishment. . . . We cannot accord to the classical literary sources of the Halakhah more than a presumptive authority, and therefore what they legislate needs to be weighed against the individual conscience, the needs and consensus of the community, and still other considerations including historical and scientific knowledge as relevant.[32]

These are among the factors that a modernist Jew should weigh critically when deciding whether to observe a particular commandment.

The Major Thrust of the Tradition

The rules and principles set forth in this volume are a sort of viaticum for tradition and Halakhah. As with any guidebook, these principles will be useful only if we make the effort to delve deeply into our tradition and go beyond a superficial glance and incomplete understanding.

In the words of Rabbi Jakob Petuchowski of Hebrew Union College:

> In the process of examining the traditional material, one must not remain satisfied with first impressions. Rather should one pursue the meaning of a given observance in the Jewish past. Moreover, since, within a span of four thousand years, the meaning was not always uniformly understood and interpreted, it becomes particularly important to discover the main thrust within this tradition.[33]

If we examine closely the flux of Jewish tradition over the ages, we find that there was usually a balanced orientation that emphasized enlightened spirituality and generally stayed clear of extremism. We must find this mainstream in the tradition. It is not enough just to decide what is appropriate for our own generation. Tradition is what is passed on from generation to generation.

The Call of Individual Conscience

Conscience, as part of the divine image in which human beings were created, must be manifested not only in ethical conduct toward other people but also in observance of the commandments. Modernist Jews may meticulously observe a large proportion of the precepts of the Torah and Sages with a clear conscience, but there are many other precepts that they cannot accept. They are likely to discover that their consciences do not allow them to participate in the ritual of *halitzah* or the legal fiction of selling one's leavened products to a non-Jew for the duration of Passover. They may heed the voice of their conscience and do away with the entire concept of halakhic illegitimacy and the *halitzah* ceremony. They may store their leavened products in a separate and closed place throughout the seven days when they do not eat it.[34] The members of Kibbutz Yahel in the Arava, affiliated with the Israel Movement for Progressive Judaism, refused to sell their leavened products to a non-Jew, on the principled grounds that one should not have to rely on non-Jews in order to observe the precepts in the Land of Israel. Despite the rabbinate's threat that it would not be able to market its milk for the duration of the Passover holiday, the kibbutz held firmly to its principles. Ultimately a halakhic solution was found: the kibbutz's leavened products were declared to be ownerless for the week of Passover.

Responsibility to the Covenant Community

Most of the fundamental principles for evaluating the *mitzvot* and deciding which should be observed— like internalizing the commandments and heeding the voice of individual conscience—relate to the individual's struggle between his or her soul and heritage. Nevertheless, there comes a moment in the observance of the commandments when Jews are called upon to express their sense of responsibility to their people, to the Covenant Community—or *kelal Yisrael.* A Jew cannot live a full Jewish life alone. Many precepts can be performed only in public as part of a community: in a prayer quorum or *minyan;* in the synagogue; and at home. For citizens of Israel there is also the community of the Jewish state, which adds the responsibility of observing special precepts, such as defending our homeland and serving our people, as well as other civic obligations, which in Israel assume the character of *mitzvot.*

Beyond the individual, then, there is *kelal Yisrael,* which includes all Jews wherever they live. Each of us bears responsibility for the entire nation; we are all responsible for one another. We must observe certain precepts for the good of the collective even when we have personal reservations about them.

Accordingly, we must all ask ourselves not only whether a particular precept is compatible with our individual world view, but also whether observing it would harm or strengthen the Jewish people as a whole.

Rabbi Petuchowski has written that

> Everything . . . which contributes to the survival and to the unity of the Covenant Community of Israel must be regarded as a religious commandment. Everything, on the other hand, which hurts the Covenant must be avoided. Bearing this perspective in mind, the Reform Jew will observe many a *mitzvah* toward which he might feel no personal obligation, because it is not a matter of the individual only [but] also of the community as a whole.[35]

Following this principle, our halakhic decisions must take account of more than just ourselves and our synagogue, community, and movement. We must be aware of their ramifications for *kelal Yisrael.* When dealing with issues relating to marriage and personal status, to the physical and spiritual welfare of Jews who do not share our views, and to the relationship between Jews of the

Diaspora and Israel, we must be mindful that we are one people. In spite of diversity and severe conflict, we are all of us bound by that contractual covenant that our ancestors, and we ourselves, made with the God of Israel.

The Rationale for the Commandments

Finally, when we define the general principles by which we can find personal significance in the commandments we are in fact dealing with the age-old question of the rationale for the commandments. Over the generations, many scholars have delved into this topic, searching for the reason, background, and significance of each precept.

Even the Torah includes a few references to the rationale of commandments, such as, for example, the historical explanation for the *sukkah:* "In order that future generations may know that I made the Israelite people live in booths when I brought them out of the land of Egypt" (Lev. 23:43). Observance of the Sabbath is to remind the Jewish people that "a covenant for all time [was established] . . . between Me and the people of Israel" (Exod. 31:16–17).

In *The Kuzari,* Judah Halevi makes an analogy between the importance of prayer for the soul and of food for the body:

> Prayer is for [man's] soul what nourishment is for his body. The blessing of one prayer lasts till the time of the next, just as the strength derived from the morning meal lasts till supper. The further his soul is removed from the time of prayer, the more it is darkened by coming in contact with worldly matters. . . . During prayer he purges his soul from all that passed over it, and prepares it for the future.[36]

These and similar rationales can provide us with a deeper insight into the commandments, add a spiritual dimension that we might otherwise miss, and strengthen our bond to them. But there are also rationales that have just the opposite effect.

For example, the biblical commentator Don Isaac Abravanel (1437–1508) explained that the "reason and secret of *yibbum*" had to do with the reincarnation of the dead brother's soul in the child that his widow bears the surviving brother, who resembles the dead man. The precept is meant to prevent the reincarnation of the dead man's soul in a child born to his widow and fathered by a stranger who does not resemble the deceased:

> Jewish souls are moved or transferred from body to body. . . . And [Maimonides] means that the reborn soul should not take up residence in just any matter it happens to encounter, and that the Holy One, blessed be He, wanted to purify the soul of the Jewish dead when it returns to the earth [in] the body that most closely resembles the body and matter of the dead man, namely, the child born of his wife by [his brother], who is bone of his bone and flesh of his flesh, since [the dead man and his brother] were born of the same father. For this reason God commanded that the widow of the deceased not marry a stranger outside the family.[37]

If this is the reason why a childless widow may not marry the man of her choice, it is clear that this precept is quite devoid of value. The rationale for a commandment may sometimes constitute a negative proof that a particular precept has no spiritual significance for us and is not obligatory.

The nineteenth-century German Rabbi Zacharias Frankel reached two conclusions on the basis of his study of the rationale of the commandments and their significance:

1. We must respect all the excellent customs handed down to us by our ancestors, while rejecting those that give off a whiff of superstition.
2. We must continue organically the path of the Sages of the Middle Ages, whose regulations rejuvenated the face of Judaism.[38]

Thus studying the rationale of the commandments can lead to insights and revaluation or to a renewed appreciation of the observance of the commandments.

WHY WE NEED THESE PRINCIPLES

We should note that these progressive principles and criteria supplement the progressive rules of codified Halakhah and permit decisors of our age to continue in the path of the Sages, who dealt with the problems of their times and found appropriate solutions for them without having to rely on secular and extra-halakhic solutions. These criteria for observance of the commandments are derived from the worldview of modernist Jews and based on principles derived from the Jewish tradition. They permit modern Jews to blend what is essential from the past with the knowledge and needs of the present.

Contemporary Jews who are seeking a significant bond with their heritage need progressive principles and criteria to allow them to obey the voice of their conscience. These principles are especially necessary in the many cases of discrimination and injustice—for example, those whose marriage options are restricted, the halakhically illegitimate, and *agunot*—for which no solution has been found in the codified Halakhah. These are problems that usually cannot be solved by means of the aforementioned halakhic principles that permit progress. To solve them, contemporary scholars have developed criteria based on the fundamentals of historical Halakhah but adapted to the reality of our own day.[39]

In past generations, too, there were family tragedies that resulted from halakhic stringency, and the rabbis were powerless to help. Nevertheless, in some cases that seemed to be intractable, the Sages of those generations searched for and found solutions.

The Halakhah as codified in the past may not offer solutions to such cases. This is why contemporary decisors and thinkers have advanced their own principles, based on Halakhah and in the spirit of Halakhah, that make it possible to provide relief for today's version of those "oppressed by the Sanhedrin."

II

Marriage and Divorce

*[Matchmaking] is as difficult for the Holy One, blessed be He,
as the splitting of the Red Sea.*

GENESIS RABBAH 5:8.4

*One should certainly set aside for this couple, who are stand-
ing on the edge of such an abyss, the ban on marriage between
a convert and a* kohen.

RABBI JUDAH LEIB ZIRELSON OF KISHINEV
(nineteenth–twentieth centuries)

In the foregoing chapters, we have seen that in antiquity and the
Middle Ages the rabbis made an effort to find halakhic solutions to
extremely difficult ethical problems and to extend a hand to the
victims of Halakhah. Among the chief casualties were people prevented from marrying their chosen mates by the laws of personal
status.

We should investigate the paths followed by our ancestors
when they tried to cope with the moral contradiction between the
codified Halakhah and the unfortunate situation of those harmed
by some of its provisions. Cases like this are not found only in the
history books. Since the birth of the State of Israel and its religious
establishment, which enjoys exclusive control, granted it by the
secular legislature, in the sensitive areas of marriage and divorce, we
have been witnesses to a new dimension. In the past the Jews of a
town or district in the Diaspora almost always identified with the
ways of their rabbis, even when their rulings were harsh. Today the

vast majority of Jews in Israel are not Orthodox, and many do not accept the halakhic or moral authority of the official rabbinate in all domains. In particular, they have reservations about its approach to marriage and other matters of personal status.

Today, then, the question is whether it is possible to find a remedy for those whose personal status is affected by the inflexible approach to Halakhah. In this section I shall compare solutions proposed in the distant past with those of the present day, trying to find out whether evolving Halakhah can be of assistance here.

I shall investigate issues in the laws of personal status and their implications for the lives of Jews in a several areas: *yibbum* and *halitzah;* women who may not marry a *kohen* (including divorcées and converts); *mamzerut,* or halakhic illegitimacy; and other related matters. I shall inquire whether there is an alternative to the severe and inflexible path generally taken by the rabbinate in these areas today.

4

Yibbum and *Ḥalitzah*

ONE OF THE MOST DIFFICULT UNRESOLVED PROBLEMS IN the codified Halakhah is that of the *shomeret yibbum*—a childless widow who must either marry her late husband's brother (in levirate marriage, or *yibbum*) or, failing this, be released by him (*ḥalitzah*) so as to be free to marry another man. In many cases, however, a woman cannot obtain *ḥalitzah*. There have been cases of adult brothers-in-law who demanded a large cash payment in return for performing *ḥalitzah* or who adamantly refused to go through the ritual out of spite. In other cases, widows have had to wait years until a minor brother-in-law reached the age of thirteen and could release them. Unfortunately, such cases are not the province only of the distant past. Here I shall mention two of the many such real-life tragedies that have occurred in Israel in recent decades.

M.W. lost her husband in the Yom Kippur War. At first his oldest brother, Y.W., refused to release her by performing *ḥalitzah*. Later, after she signed a waiver of her rights to her apartment and any pension or benefits due her from the Ministry of Defense, he agreed. Her husband's five brothers told the rabbinical court that they had asked the widow to sign the waiver not for their own sake but solely in order to perpetuate the memory of the deceased brother.[1]

Another army widow who wished to remarry also faced the obstacle of *ḥalitzah*. Her late husband's brother absolutely refused to release her unless she paid him an astronomical sum. She did not understand how the rabbis could stand there watching her cry, begging not to be despoiled of her life savings. The Torah commands us not to oppress the stranger, orphan, and widow: Why, she demanded, did the rabbis emphasize *halitzah* instead of that humane precept? Why wouldn't they let her rebuild her life?[2]

These and many other press clippings collected over several decades reflect the fact that in Israel today a refusal to perform *halitzah* is a frequent and painful phenomenon. Many tragedies are caused by brothers-in-law and families, animated sometimes by greed, sometimes by a spirit of revenge.

In many cases the official rabbinate does everything in its power, within the limits of its understanding of Halakhah, to assist the poor widow. Its representatives try to persuade recalcitrant brothers-in-law; sometimes they require him to make large monthly support payments to her or even threaten him with imprisonment. But there is nothing they can do when the brother-in-law is outside Israel or is still a minor. Even if the rabbis and religious court judges ultimately succeed, many years may elapse before the widow can escape her chained status, rehabilitate herself, and remarry. The rabbinate has no way to compensate her for the waste of these potential years of marriage and parenthood.

Even when brother-in-law and widow agree to perform *halitzah* with the best of intentions, the strange ritual sometimes produces a painful emotional reaction. Both the widow who must spit and the brother-in-law who is being spat at feel humiliated. They cannot understand how this ceremony can have any religious or spiritual significance.

THE HALAKHIC BACKGROUND

Many volumes would be required to narrate the historical development of the laws of *yibbum* and *halitzah* and review the rabbinic discussions as to which of them is preferable.[3] We might think that the rationale for this precept is as stated by the plain meaning of the Torah, namely, to perpetuate the memory of the deceased brother—"that his name not be blotted out from Israel"

(Deut. 25:6). However, the Gemara states that the previous clause in the verse—"and the firstborn son whom she bears [to her brother-in-law] will be established after the name of his dead brother"—actually refers to the landed inheritance and movable property of the deceased. In other words, Halakhah does not rule that if the deceased brother's name was "Joseph, they call [the child] Joseph; Johanan, they call him Johanan" (BT Yevamot 24a).[4] Rather, "the brother's name" signifies the property he left behind.

There is no consensus about the historical and sociological reasons for the institution of *yibbum*.[5] Whatever they may be, it is clear that *ḥalitzah* was originally a humiliating rite intended to compel a surviving brother to marry his sister-in-law.

A halakhic midrash of the mishnaic era holds that there is no rational explanation for *yibbum* and *ḥalitzah;* rather, they are numbered among those precepts about which it was stated, "I, the Lord, enacted; you have no right to make any response to them" (*Sifra, Aḥarei Mot* 13:4, on Lev. 18:4). Maimonides, by contrast, does propose reasons for them. He asserts that the motive behind *yibbum* is quite clear and is made explicit in the story of Tamar and Judah (Gen. 38:8): "It was an ancient custom predating the giving of the Torah and the Torah left it in force." Why, then, did the Torah stipulate the practice of *ḥalitzah?*

> The actions of which it is composed [removing his shoe and spitting in his face] were considered shameful according to the customs of those times, and . . . on account of this the brother-in-law might perhaps wish to avoid this shame and consequently [perform *yibbum*] *(The Guide of the Perplexed* 3, 49)[6]

For most modern Jews, too, especially those who have had personal experience of this rite, "these actions" are still shameful. Yet, *ḥalitzah* today can serve no beneficial purpose—certainly not that of compelling the brother-in-law to marry the widow. In 1950, the Chief Rabbinate Council in Israel enacted a regulation for all Israeli Jews, "absolutely forbidding them to perform the precept of *yibbum;* they must perform *ḥalitzah.*"[7] Today *ḥalitzah* is merely the ceremony that accompanies the mandatory nonperformance of *yibbum.*

The major problem is the fate of a widow whose brother-in-law is unable or unwilling to be a party to the *halitzah* ceremony. Already in the talmudic age there were cases in which the Sages deceived the brother-in-law in order to get him to perform *halitzah.* We read in a *baraita* (a tannaitic tradition not included in the Mishnah):

> *Halitzah* induced by deception is valid. What is meant by *halitzah* induced by deception? . . . Whenever they say, perform *halitzah* for her and she will give you 200 zuz. Once a woman had a brother-in-law who was not fit for her. They told him, perform *halitzah* for her and she will give you 200 zuz. The case was brought before Rabbi Ḥiyya and he pronounced [the *halitzah*] valid (BT Yevamot 106a).[8]

According to Rashi's interpretation, this *halitzah* was valid, even though *halitzah* may not be conditional. When they deceived the brother-in-law into performing *halitzah,* the Sages decreed that the *halitzah* would be valid even if the condition was not fulfilled, that is, even if the sister-in-law did not give him the 200 zuz.

Why is it permissible to deceive a brother-in-law into performing *halitzah* if he has already rejected the impartial advice of the elders that he and his sister-in-law are not suited for each other? Rashi explains that if the woman does not want to enter into the levirate marriage and gives sensible reasons for her rejection of *yibbum,* and the rabbis endeavor to persuade the brother-in-law but he still insists on marrying her, we are permitted to deceive him by saying, "perform *halitzah* and she will give you 200 zuz. We deceive him; and if not, we compel him to perform *halitzah*" (Rashi on Yevamot 39b, s.v. *amar R. Kahana*).[9]

A question regarding a *shomeret yibbum* was addressed to the Spanish Sage Rabbi Solomon ben Abraham Adret (the Rashba, 1235–1310): "If the brother-in-law [gets wind of the deception and] wishes to leave her an *agunah,* are we required to compel him to perform *halitzah?*" He replied:

Whenever there is doubt concerning a *get* and she is forbidden
to [her brother-in-law], we are required to compel the brother-
in-law to perform *ḥalitzah* so that she will not be left an *agunah.* . . . [We do so] even if she is permitted to the
brother-in-law but he is recalcitrant and wishes to perform neither *ḥalitzah* nor *yibbum.*[10]

Here we have a clear and unequivocal halakhic ruling that *ḥalitzah* should be extracted by compulsion, if necessary, to prevent a
women from being left an *agunah* by a refractory brother-in-law.

An interesting case of deception and coercion of this nature
was brought before Rabbi Moses ben Mordecai Galante, a disciple
of Rabbi Joseph Caro, who was appointed rabbi of Safed in 1580.
Rabbi Galante describes the unusual case as follows:

In his time there was a case of a sister-in-law who [waited for]
yibbum for two years, and a fire raged among them every day on
account of the various claims and quarrels between the relatives
of the brother-in-law and the relatives of the sister-in-law; for
the brother-in-law said that he wanted to perform *yibbum.* . . .
One day the sister-in-law's relatives were advised to instruct her
to enter the synagogue, go over to the place where the brother-
in-law was sitting during the reading of the Torah, and spit at
him. So it was. She entered on Monday during the reading of
the Torah, stood in front of the brother-in-law, and spat at him
three times (each time the spittle was visible, as the law requires)
in the presence of the entire congregation. Each time she declared: "This is the brother-in-law who wishes to marry me. I do
not want you; I do not want you." Then she spat three more
times, as was attested by three members of the congregation who
stood nearby and constituted themselves a *beit din,* as they
wrote.

Following his summary of this astonishing case, the questioner
asked:

Now people ask, what is the legal status of this sister-in-law?
Is she forbidden to her brother-in-law and *ḥalitzah* must be

performed? Can this spitting make her forbidden to her brother-
in-law so that he must perform *ḥalitzah?*

The core of the question is whether spitting in her brother-in-
law's face in the presence of the entire congregation in the synagogue, including three men who constituted themselves an ad hoc
beit din, gave the sister-in-law the status of a woman who has been
partially released by *ḥalitzah,* so that the brother-in-law may not
marry her? In other words, was it a sort of *ḥalitzah*—against the
brother-in-law's will, and deficient with regard to the removal of
his shoe and an explicit statement on his part, but sufficient to
make her forbidden to him? The questioner continues: "And if you
rule that she should be released, we would like to know whether or
not a *beit din* can compel or coerce the brother-in-law to perform
ḥalitzah?"

Rabbi Galante replied with a long and closely argued responsum. After an exhaustive review of the sources, he concluded that
the action in the synagogue did not constitute a valid rite of *ḥalitzah.* Nevertheless, the incomplete and invalid *ḥalitzah* did render
yibbum impossible: "We learn that in our present case she is un-
suitable for *yibbum;* instead, she must be released." In this way
Rabbi Galante gave *post factum* sanction to the women's desperate
and dramatic act, which, by making it impossible for her brother-
in-law to marry her, forced him to perform *ḥalitzah* and release
her.

Another question remained, however. "Does a *beit din* have the
authority to coerce the brother-in-law?" It was clear that the
brother-in-law had an obligation to perform *ḥalitzah.* But could he
be forced to fulfill this obligation? Rabbi Galante concluded his responsum by ruling that "because [the woman] cannot be taken in
levirate marriage by her brother-in-law, we compel him to release
her."[11]

In his annotations to the *Shulḥan Arukh,* Rabbi Moses Isserles
cited the ruling by the Rashba, which can be seen as supporting the
ruling by Rabbi Galante:

Some say that if she spat at the brothers or did something similar and rendered *yibbum* forbidden, she is not considered to be recalcitrant because it is no longer possible to perform *yibbum*.[12]

There is no doubt that an ounce of prevention is worth many pounds of cure. Accordingly, Rabbi Isserles cited the ordinance introduced by Rabbi Israel of Brinn (1400–1480):

A man who marries a woman and has a brother who is an apostate may contract the marriage with the double condition that should she be left to the apostate to perform *yibbum,* she will retroactively be deemed never to have been married.[13]

This ordinance is the basis for many other regulations aimed at rescuing women who cannot receive *yibbum* or *ḥalitzah,* as well as other *agunot.*[14]

Courageous acts of this sort were not limited to a particular period. In various ages the rabbis took it upon themselves to stand in the breach, protect the defenseless, and enact new regulations to rectify injustice. Among these bold Sages was Rabbi Isaac Lampronti (1679–1756), the author of the halakhic encyclopedia *Paḥad Yitzḥak.* In Verona, he wrote, he added a condition to the marriage formula:

This is the language of the marriage formula that I arranged, with the consent of the rabbi, his excellency our teacher Rabbi Mordecai Bassano, of blessed memory: "If I leave behind viable offspring, who makes you exempt from *ḥalitzah* and *yibbum,* behold you are consecrated to me by this ring in accordance with the law of Moses and Israel. But if do I not leave behind viable offspring who makes you exempt from *ḥalitzah* and *yibbum,* then this ring is yours as an ordinary gift, and everything I have said is null and void and this marriage-consecration shall be like a pottery vessel that has no substance."[15]

This conditional marriage vow could obviate the distress of every woman who cannot receive *yibbum* or *ḥalitzah.* Should her husband die and leave her childless, then, according to the betrothal condition, the marriage is retroactively nullified. Since she was not married, she is not a widow; consequently, she is not liable to *yibbum* or *halitzah*. When Rabbi Lampronte tried to repeat it, however, he encountered opposition:

> But another time, when something like this happened in Verona, the aforementioned rabbi had his doubts in the matter and opted to act stringently, so she was married without the condition.

Although there were indeed rabbis who issued strict rulings, there was no lack of those who ruled leniently and did everything to make life more bearable for people. Rabbis from the talmudic period through the end of the Middle Ages found ways to rule that a childless widow could and should be released from entrapment by a recalcitrant brother-in-law.

THE SITUATION TODAY

The attitude of one prominent contemporary decisor stands in stark contrast to these and similar actions taken by rabbis who were sensitive to the suffering of these unfortunate women. A young widow asked Rabbi ayyim David Halevy (1923–1998), the Chief Rabbi of Tel Aviv, the following question:

> My husband passed away without children. My husband's brother is a minor. According to the religious court I must wait another five years until he can release me. . . . *halitzah* is a humiliating punishment for someone who does not want to perform *yibbum*. In any case, I do not understand why I have to wait so long until I am allowed to begin a new family. What is my sin?

Rabbi Halevy based the crux of his reply on "the Sages of the Zohar," and explained as follows:

When a man dies without children, his soul is troubled and can find no rest. The elementary rectification for this condition is *yibbum*. . . . But if there is no possibility or will to perform *yibbum*, there is a remedy of another type, which at least helps release the soul of the deceased from its link to this world. . . . The removal of the shoe has the power to restore a certain degree of repose to the soul of the deceased. . . . Even someone whose faith is not perfect would do well not to deprecate the precept of *halitzah*, so as to grant repose to the soul of the departed.[16]

What a gaping abyss there is between the widow's anguished cry and the rabbi's reassuring response!

The very fact of her question suggests that this response could not comfort the widow. We may assume that most women in her situation would not find it to be a satisfactory reply, intellectually or emotionally. Any non-Orthodox woman would certainly reject a mystical explanation of this sort, although those with a faith like Rabbi Halevy's might accept it. What counts, however, is the deed, not the explanation. In a case like this the rabbi has no practical solution to offer.

By contrast, a significant redress of this impotence accompanied the establishment of non-Orthodox streams in Judaism. As long ago as 1869, the convention of the Central Conference of American Rabbis (Reform), held in Philadelphia, resolved unanimously that "the precepts of *yibbum* and *halitzah* have lost all significance, importance, and obligatory force for us."[17]

A rabbinical conference held two years later in Augsburg, Germany, resolved that

The precept of *halitzah* has lost its importance because the circumstances that required *yibbum* and *halitzah* no longer exist. The idea underlying this law is alien to our religious and social outlook. The nonperformance of *halitzah* is no impediment to the widow's remarriage.[18]

These decisions, made more than a century ago after protracted discussions about *halitzah* and its implications, are generally accepted today by the Reform and Conservative movements throughout the world.

In the twentieth century, several Conservative rabbis in the United States wrestled with the problem of *halitzah*. Because *yibbum/halitzah* is a precept rooted in the Torah, Rabbi Isaac Klein (1905–1982) believed that the only way to release a widow from her chains would be the inclusion of conditions in the marriage contract whenever a woman might require *yibbum* or *halitzah*. The condition would retroactively annul the marriage should the husband die childless. Rabbi Klein did not deal with the many cases in which such a condition had not been stipulated in advance in the marriage contract.[19]

Rabbi Henry Fisher of the Jewish Theological Seminary conjectured that *halitzah* could be abolished. He reasoned that the requirement of *halitzah* depends on that of *yibbum* and arises only when the brother-in-law is unwilling or unable to perform *yibbum*. Because the rabbis have forbidden *yibbum*, there is no longer any real possibility of *halitzah* either, since its very existence depends on the possibility of performing *yibbum*. Fisher ruled that in the absence of obligatory *yibbum*, *halitzah*, too, is not obligatory, and a childless widow can remarry without any dependence on her brother-in-law, since he is forbidden to perform *yibbum* in any case.[20]

Rabbi Klein, however, rejected the idea that the impossibility of *yibbum* entails the abolition of *halitzah*, since even in Jewish communities where *yibbum* is no longer practiced, its prohibition is not *de jure* but only *de facto*.[21]

Rabbi Fisher held that the entire institution of *yibbum* is based on the principle that the woman is a chattel. When the husband dies without children, his relative and heir also inherits his wife or wives. In his eyes, there are three possibilities:

1. We may hold that this law has no validity in our day, because the notion that a wife is her husband's property is utterly incompatible with the moral foundations of our society. Consequently, we must reject this idea and cannot act in accordance with it.

2. We may ignore the Halakhah and allow it to die of neglect. He conjectured that most Conservative rabbis perform marriages without *halitzah* anyway, since they do not ask a widow whether she has children.
3. We can find a halakhic way to get around this Halakhah by means of a legal fiction, with our true intent being the abolition of *halitzah*.[22]

Rabbi Philip Sigal proposed that when a childless widow and her fiancé ask a rabbi to marry them, the rabbi may ignore the Halakhah of *halitzah* in favor of the dignity of human beings and the rabbinic authority to uproot a precept of the Torah. His recommendation was that rabbis act according to the talmudic principle of *shev ve-al ta'aseh*—sit still and do nothing: that is, they should take no initiative regarding *halitzah*. A rabbi should arrange a *halitzah* ceremony only when the brother-in-law and widow request it, and arrange a wedding for a woman who does not demand to be released. This would not be an abolition of the institution of *halitzah* per se, but only an application of rabbis' halakhic authority to waive the requirement of *halitzah* as a precondition for the widow's remarriage.[23]

Thus, in recent generations, rabbinic conferences and individual rabbis in the Diaspora have looked for ways to rescue these widows. Today this same resolution and openness are required in Israel. Although many halakhic problems are involved, we have adequate halakhic tools to solve them. For some reason the Chief Rabbinate, which has total control of all matters of marriage and divorce in Israel, is unwilling to use such tools to liberate these women from their humiliating state. The rabbinate could, if it wished, act in full compliance with Halakhah and include conditions in marriage contracts or arrange conditional divorces.

In the absence of compassionate boldness by the rabbinate, many Israeli women are forced to live out their lives alone, live with a man without a Jewish marriage, or have a civil ceremony abroad.

When the official rabbinate does not find reasonable solutions to this and other problems, the majority of the Jewish people are liable to seek solutions outside the framework of Halakhah—as we see happening today in so many areas.

This short survey of the Halakhah of *yibbum* and *halitzah* has shown that our Sages viewed the entrapment of a childless widow by a recalcitrant brother-in-law to be a serious ethical problem. Pricked by their consciences, they mobilized all their moral and halakhic powers to remove the impediments and obstacles. Many decisors have ruled, knowingly or otherwise, in accordance with the standard of Halakhah and morality (see above), and thus according to the principles of evolving Halakhah.

I must state unequivocally that the nonperformance of *halitzah* is not an obstacle to remarriage by a childless widow.

5

Marriages Forbidden to a *Kohen*

A *KOHEN* AND A DIVORCÉE

We should re-examine the ban on marriage between a *kohen* and a divorced woman in light of the thesis that Halakhah evolves. There is no doubt that the ban is stated explicitly in the Torah and reinforced by the Talmud and later decisors.[1]

Although antiquity attached great importance to the holiness of the priesthood, the rabbinic literature contains many references to *kohanim* who had forfeited their priestly privileges. This seems to indicate that there were *kohanim* who contracted forbidden marriages even during the period when the priesthood flourished.[2]

What is the rationale for the prohibition? The Torah ordains that members of the priestly caste "shall be holy to their God" (Lev. 21:6) because they serve in the Temple. This is immediately followed by the prohibition on their marrying three types of women: a *zonah* (literally "a prostitute," but interpreted by the rabbis as referring to any woman who has had sexual intercourse with a man forbidden to her), the offspring of a forbidden marriage by a *kohen* (as well as her descendants), and a divorcée. A woman who has been released from the obligation of levirate marriage is forbidden to a *kohen* by rabbinic regulation (BT Yevamot 61b; Maimonides, Laws of Forbidden Sexual Relations 17:7).

According to *Sefer Haḥinnukh* (thirteenth century), a *kohen* may not marry a divorced woman for the same reason he may not marry a *zonah*. About the former prohibition, the anonymous author wrote:

> Among the roots of the precept is that the priests were chosen to serve the Lord in perpetuity. Hence it is appropriate and obligatory for them to be holy and purer than the rest of the people in every matter, especially marriage, which is basic to men, so that a man always has some thoughts about his spouse. Consequently he was obligated not to marry a *zonah*, whose temperament is evil and bitter, lest she lead him astray and influence him from her vast experience to abandon his good ways and desirable intentions. She is also a shame and blemish to all who come near her, since everyone gossips about her impurity.[3]

The next section but one of *Sefer Haḥinnukh* discusses the ban on a *kohen*'s marrying a divorced woman: "Among the roots of the precept are what I wrote concerning the previous prohibition of a *zonah*."[4]

This view of the status of *kohanim* and divorced women raises a question that is relevant to the applicability of this prohibition in our own day: How do their respective positions today compare with their status in antiquity?

The Status of *Kohanim,* in Antiquity and Today

The most conspicuous difference between the status of *kohanim* in antiquity and today is this: Since the destruction of the Second Temple almost two thousand years ago, they no longer play the central role in the Temple ritual. The problems associated with the building of the Third Temple and consequent renewal of sacrifice are so complex that there is no great likelihood that it will be rebuilt speedily in our days or in the foreseeable future.[5] When the Temple was standing, it was essential that a *kohen* guard his status as a consecrated servitor, since the eyes of all Israel were on him. But the rituals in which *kohanim* participate today, such as the redemption of first-born sons and the priestly benediction of the

congregation, and their right to be called first to every public reading of the Torah (for the sake of civil harmony) are marginal as
compared with the centrality of serving in the Temple.[6]

What is more, for centuries leading decisors have questioned
the authenticity of their contemporary *kohanim*. In antiquity
there was documentary evidence of a *kohen's* lineage, and Israelite
women who married into priestly families, too, had verified genealogies. In contrast, according to Maimonides, "all *kohanim* in
this time are merely presumed to be such"[7] and cannot trace their
lineage "back to a *kohen* who served at the altar" (Laws of Forbidden Intercourse 20:1). Rabbi Isaac bar Sheshet (1326–1408)
issued a similar ruling and distinguished between his contemporary *kohanim* and those of antiquity. In his time, when *kohanim*
had no documentary evidence or other proof of their entitlement
to priestly status, their rights and obligations as *kohanim*
stemmed purely from the force of custom or presumption.[8] He
ruled as follows:

> Even with the *kohanim* of our generation, who have no docu-
> mented lineage but are only presumed to be so, the custom
> today is nevertheless to call one [to the Torah] first as a *kohen,*
> even if he is an ignoramus, before a great scholar of Israel.[9]

Similar rulings were issued by other decisors over the
generations.

In the sixteenth century, Rabbi Solomon Luria (1510?–1574)
wrote:

> Because of our transgressions and the protracted length of exile
> and decrees and expulsions, [the *kohanim*] have been commin-
> gled. Would that the holy seed had not been commingled with
> the profane! But the seed of priests and levites has almost cer-
> tainly been commingled, and if not in its entirety, then the ma-
> jority has been commingled.[10]

In the seventeenth century, Rabbi Abraham Gumbiner (c.
1637–1683) ruled: "One does not hold him to be a certain *kohen,*

since it is possible that one of his maternal ancestors was 'defiled'" (i.e., she was the descendant of a *kohen* who had contracted a forbidden marriage).[11]

In the eighteenth century, Rabbi Jacob Emden (1697–1776) issued a ruling about *kohanim* who kept the money given them in the ceremony of redemption of the first-born *(pidyon ha-ben):*

> It seems that they do not have the right to expropriate the money by virtue of their weak presumption [of priestly status], and I would almost say that as matter of law they must return [the money]. At the very least every *kohen* should himself feel the need to avoid committing what may be theft, since he may not be a *kohen.*[12]

We see clearly that the status of *kohanim* today is not the same as that of the descendants of Aaron in antiquity, and hardly need expand on this point. This has direct implications for the permissibility of a *kohen's* marrying a divorcée or one of the other women forbidden to him by Torah law.

The Status of Divorcées, in Antiquity and Today

The image of the divorcée presented by the Torah derives from the fact that the only pretext it knows for divorce is that her husband "found in her *ervat davar*"—an awkward Hebrew phrase that may be rendered literally as "an indecency of some matter" (Deut. 24:1), where this "indecency" is clearly related to sexual misconduct and perhaps even to incest or adultery. According to Beit Shammai, citing this verse and stressing the word *indecency,* "a man may not divorce his wife unless he has found unchastity in her" (Mishnah Gittin 9:10; BT Gittin 90a). In past generations, a divorcée was considered to be a woman of questionable morals, as reflected in the unfavorable description by the author of *Sefer Hahinnukh.* Otherwise, why would her first husband have divorced her? This seems to be the opinion of the School of Shammai.

The codified Halakhah, however, follows the opinion of the

School of Hillel, who cited the same verse but placed the emphasis on *some matter,* so that unchastity is not the only possible reason for divorcing one's wife: "Even if she spoiled a dish for him." Still, as Rashi explains, even "for Beit Hillel 'indecency of some matter' means either unchastity or something else distasteful."[13]

As Halakhah evolved, however, the accepted grounds for divorce continued to expand. Today they go far beyond the "indecency" of licentiousness or promiscuity. Over the generations a marked change also took place in the attitude toward divorce, and a woman was recognized as having the right to demand a *get*—a bill of divorce—for reasons connected with her husband's conduct, character, or even profession. The famous ordinance of Rabbenu Gershom (c. 960–1028), which bars a man from divorcing his wife against her will, further diminished the inequality between husband and wife with regard to divorce.[14]

In our own age, a divorcée is no longer considered to be morally inferior to any other woman or to the man she was formerly married to. Divorce was less common in antiquity than it is today, when an increasing percentage of Jewish marriages end in divorce.[15]

If we set the doubtful title of contemporary *kohanim* against the improved social status of divorcées today, we see that the disparity between them is no longer as great as that described in *Sefer Hahinnukh* and other writings.

On the other hand, there is an obligation that applies to every Jew: "It is a commandment for every man to marry a woman" (*Shulhan Arukh, E.H.* 1:2). The Sages emphasized the importance of selecting the right spouse and were aware of how difficult a task that is. Even for the Creator of the universe, Himself a matchmaker, pairing off couples "is as difficult . . . as the splitting of the Red Sea" (Genesis Rabbah 5:8, §4). If they have found each other—in response, they may believe, to a Heavenly voice that announced, "the daughter of this person for that person" (BT Sotah 2a; cf. BT Mo'ed Katan 18b)—and have decided to wed, can we be certain that theirs is *not* a match made in Heaven and that we have the right to rupture the bond between them?[16]

Note that if a *kohen* and a divorcée wed despite the ban, Halakhah makes two stipulations:

1. The marriage is valid *post factum*, with everything that this implies.
2. Their offspring may not serve as priests but can marry any other Jew, except that their daughters cannot marry *kohanim*.

Having taken into consideration everything presented above about the status of *kohanim* and divorcées today and the importance of compatibility in marriage, the Reform and Conservative movements have ruled that a *kohen* may marry a divorcée. These movements also permit marriage between a *kohen* and a woman who has been released from the obligation of levirate marriage, despite the rabbinic prohibition.

A *KOHEN* AND A CONVERT

According to Halakhah, a woman who was converted, even before the age of three, "is a *zonah* and forbidden to a *kohen*, because she is not a natural-born Jew" (Maimonides, Laws of Forbidden Sexual Intercourse, 18:3; based on BT Yevamot 60b). According to the Sages, a female convert, like a manumitted slave woman, falls into the category of the *zonah* mentioned in the Torah, and the ban on her marrying a *kohen* is stated explicitly in the Torah. The Tosefot explain that the rationale of the prohibition is that "she comes from among the idolaters, who are steeped in depravity."[17] Rabbi Yomtov ben Abraham Ishbili (the Ritba, 1250–1330) added that the fact that she was born a non-Jew labels her a *zonah* even if she has never had sexual intercourse.[18] According to this ruling, which can be traced back to the second century C.E., a female convert has the status of a *zonah* even if she is a virgin. This attitude towards converts is expressed in the Talmud by a statement attributed to Rabbi Isaac Nafa: "Evil after evil will come upon those who accept converts" (BT Yevamot 109b).

But the attitude toward converts is ambivalent. Another Sage, Rabbi Simeon ben Lakish, held that "the convert is more dear to the Holy One, blessed be He, than all the people who stood at Mount Sinai" (Midrash Tanuma, *Lekh Lekha* 6). If statistics have any significance here, one scholar has found that there are hundreds of biblical and rabbinic passages that praise righteous converts, but very few that denigrate them.[19]

In any case, the attitude toward converts has generally developed along the positive axis. Certainly there is no longer any emphasis on the suspicion of fornication by converts who derive from people "steeped in depravity."[20] As Maimonides wrote in his well-known responsum to Obadiah the Proselyte: "If we trace our ancestry to Abraham, Isaac, and Jacob, you trace yours to the One who spoke and the world came into being."[21] Such a lineage certainly cannot justify relegating a female convert to the biblical category of *zonah*.

Rabbi Ben-Zion Meir Hai Uziel (1880–1953, Sephardi chief rabbi of Israel from 1939) was once asked to rule in the matter of a non-Jewish woman who had married a Jew in a civil ceremony and now wished to convert. Rabbis have frequently rejected such prospective converts on the grounds that the conversion is deemed to be only for the sake of marriage. Rabbi Uziel, however, ruled that this woman,

> by entering henceforth the Covenant of Judaism, will draw closer and closer to the family of her husband and his Torah. . . . We are commanded to bring them [the woman and her children, who were to be converted along with her] closer and admit them into the covenant of the Torah of Israel.[22]

This is only one of the many halakhic rulings that permit conversion for the sake of marriage, despite the prohibition against accepting "a woman who converted for the sake of a man" (BT Yevamot 24b) and the requirement that the religious court thoroughly investigate her reasons for wishing to convert: "If she is a woman, they must investigate whether perhaps she has set her eyes on some Jewish lad" (Maimonides, Laws of Forbidden Sexual Relations 13:14).

As Rabbi Uziel's ruling shows, this is another issue where, in the light of changing circumstances, rabbis have had the courage to interpret the law in a lenient fashion in order to satisfy the command of conscience.

Rabbi David Zevi Hoffmann of Berlin (1843–1921) was asked about a non-Jewish woman who had been married to a *kohen* in a civil marriage and now wished to convert. Hoffmann ruled that the prohibition against a *kohen's* marrying a non-Jewish woman was more serious than that against "a *kohen* marrying a convert, which is at most only a negative prohibition. If so, in order to rescue a Jew from the more serious prohibition, it is certainly good to convert the non-Jewish woman."[23] In other words, the ban on marriage between a *kohen* and a convert is one of the negative commandments in the Torah, but it is much less grave than the ban on marriage between a *kohen* and a non-Jewish woman (the lesser evil). A marriage of the latter sort is invalid and the partners are forbidden to continue it, whereas that to a convert has *post factum* validity.

There remained the serious obstacle that a convert must accept the "yoke of the commandments," which includes the ban on a *kohen's* marrying a convert: "We can say that if she explicitly states that she does not wish to accept this precept, it is forbidden to accept her." Rabbi Hoffmann, however, offered a revolutionary solution to this problem:

> But in the present case she does not say so explicitly. Accordingly, even though we know that she will transgress this prohibition, in any case for the amendment of the *kohen's* conduct and the good of his offspring we can accept her. . . . Hence the religious court must not ask her about this, so that she will not say it explicitly.

The religious court must close its eyes to the fact that the new convert's acceptance of the commandments is almost certainly deficient, if this "blindness" makes it possible to rectify the *kohen*'s situation and avert the worse evil of his continuing to live with a non-Jewish woman, which is a clear transgression of a Torah prohibition.

Rabbi Hoffmann justified his bold step with the extraordinary rationale that

> We may also fear that it would be a profanation of the Divine Name *(ḥillul Hashem)*, Heaven forbid, if the woman had a nervous breakdown because she was not accepted, in that people would say that the Jews do not have mercy on a gentile woman and are not concerned that she might become ill and insane.

All the above notwithstanding, Rabbi Hoffmann was not willing to go so far as to allow her to marry the *kohen* in a religious ceremony after her conversion and preferred that they remain married only in civil law.

In his profound analysis, Prof. David Ellenson shows that the lenient halakhic rulings of Rabbi Hoffmann and other decisors constituted an almost total revolution in the attitude toward conversion for the sake of marriage, in contrast to the stringent rulings of the mid-nineteenth century.[24] Rabbi Hoffmann's humane approach and response to the needs of the time and demands of his conscience gave him the courage to find a way around the halakhic obstacles to the woman's conversion. The reason he offered was the possibility of a "profanation of the Divine Name," that is, the widespread publicity that would follow if the woman had a nervous breakdown as a result of the refusal to allow her to convert and continue to live with her chosen mate. Nevertheless, Rabbi Hoffmann could not carry his leniency to the point of allowing the two to wed in a Jewish ceremony.[25]

In the early twentieth century, Rabbi Judah Leib Zirelson of Kishinev (1860–1941) replied to a question submitted by a rabbi in Bulgaria concerning a young woman who had converted to Judaism out of sincere conviction and two years later had become engaged to a Jewish man.[26] After all the preparations for the wedding had been made, it was discovered that her fiancé was a *kohen*. The rabbi who submitted the question reported that her prominent family, who had consented to her conversion, was stupefied, while "the local Christians are stirring up the city over the great ignominy that the Jews consider the young woman to be a harlot." The groom was threatening to be baptized, along with his fiancée, if the rabbi refused to marry them in a Jewish ceremony. The Bulgarian rabbi asked for permission to marry them "in order to prevent profanation of the Divine Name and especially in this age, when antisemitism is so widespread."

In his response, Rabbi Zirelson considered the issue in the light of Halakhah and balanced the ban on marriage between a convert and a *kohen*, which applies to individuals, against the "collective precept" of saving the community from a possible pogrom. He also weighed it against the anticipated danger of the young man's abandoning Judaism, and ruled that

> one should certainly set aside for this couple, who are standing on the edge of such an abyss, the ban on marriage between a convert and a *kohen* . . . for the sake of preventing the perpetual betrayal of the entire Torah if the two abandon the Jewish religion in anger.[27]

Rabbi Zirelson also found grounds for leniency in the fact that the prohibition applies to female converts in general, whereas he did not know that she had had intercourse with a non-Jew, "so that her status as a *zonah* is only rabbinic in origin." Here he broke ranks with Maimonides, Joseph Caro, and other decisors, who held that the equation of convert and *zonah* is made by the Torah itself. Just as Rabbi Judah the Prince ruled that the laws of the Sabbatical Year were in force only as a matter of rabbinic regulation (see chapter 1), Rabbi Zirelson was able to issue a lenient ruling in this case by changing the status of the ban on marriage between a female convert and a *kohen* from toraitic to rabbinic. After the rabbi had thus opened the door of leniency, he took a bold step and walked through it:

Thus, the power to permit widens before us . . . so that one can indeed set aside the rabbinic prohibition of a female convert in order to avoid the general and perpetual transgression of positive and negative precepts that would follow the high-handed apostasy of two Jews.

Here we have a tangible danger, and "nothing stands in the way of saving lives."

Rabbi Zirelson ruled that the Bulgarian rabbi could conduct a Jewish wedding ceremony for the couple, as long as he made it widely known that his act should not be seen as a precedent and informed the groom that he and his offspring would forfeit their priestly status.

In these and other responsa, Rabbis Hoffmann and Zirelson demonstrated that they had the fortitude, vision, and scholarship required to issue unconventional halakhic rulings that prefer the lesser evil. A rabbi and decisor who would cope with the problems of his generation must satisfy stringent requirements of character. Rabbis Hoffmann and Zirelson, like Hillel the Elder, Judah the Prince, Maimonides, Rabbi Moses Isserles, Rabbi Moses Galante, and many others, had these traits and consequently were able to rule against the prevailing current.

The responsa of Rabbi Hoffmann and Rabbi Zirelson invoked the concept of "profanation of the Divine Name" to justify bold halakhic decisions permitting marriage between a *kohen* and a female convert. Can we apply this concept to our own day, when rabbis refuse to convert a woman who is married to a Jew, *kohen* or not, because she continues to live with him as a non-Jew? The concept of profanation of the Divine name is valid not only in response to a threat by the non-Jewish environment against a Jewish community. We can also discover profanation of the Divine Name in discrimination against Jews, ostensibly in the name of Halakhah, but against the dictates of conscience and ethics. It is no light matter to obstruct a match made in Heaven and wreak injustice on the couple and their children. When we examine the deeds of great rabbis of the past, we must ask whether in our day, too, the issue of saving lives militates against the refusal to convert a woman because her chosen spouse is a *kohen*. Is it not a profanation of the Divine Name to refuse to allow a Jewish man and a Jewish woman to marry because he is a *kohen* and she a divorcée or a convert? This is a classic example of a decree that the majority of the community cannot bear and must therefore, according to Halakhah itself, be repealed (Maimonides, Laws of Insubordination 2:5–7).

In light of the changes that have taken place over the generations in Halakhah's view of converts, conversion in order to marry, and the permissibility of a female convert's living with a *kohen* and even marrying him, and considering that Halakhah in any case deems such marriages to be valid *post factum*, the Council of Progressive Rabbis in Israel—like the Rabbinical Assembly of the Conservative Movement and the Central Conference of American Rabbis (Reform) in America—has ruled that a *kohen* may marry a convert.[28]

CONCUBINAGE

Various scholars and rabbis have suggested a way for a *kohen* to live with a divorcée or other woman who is forbidden to him, but without a formal consecrated marriage. What is the halakhic basis for this? Maimonides ruled that any *kohen* who marries, according to Jewish ritual and practice, a divorcée, *zonah* (including a convert), or the offspring of a forbidden marriage by a *kohen,* and has intercourse with her, is subject to flogging, like anyone who transgresses a negative commandment. If, however, their intercourse has not been religiously consecrated and is consequently to be deemed fornication, he is not liable to that punishment (Laws of Forbidden Intercourse 17:2, based on BT Kiddushin 78a). In other words, the Torah does not explicitly prohibit a *kohen* from living with a divorcée or *zonah* but only from consecrating a marriage with her. Some hypothesize that this might be the magical solution for such couples as well as for other couples who are halakhically barred from marrying.

Rabbi Jacob Moses Toledano thought that "the best regulation at present would be to restore the permission to take a concubine."[29] He cited a series of decisors to buttress his proposal. In academic circles, too, the idea has been raised of reviving the category of concubine for a woman who is forbidden to a *kohen*, as a way of giving a stamp of approval, both halakhic and civil, to the bond between the couple.[30]

Perhaps this idea seems reasonable to some decisors, as a desperate attempt to reconcile the contradiction between the codified Halakhah of antiquity and the feeling that preventing two unattached Jews from establishing a family is discriminatory and unjust. But there is no doubt that concubinage is unacceptable to a couple who want to consecrate their bond. Perhaps this is why the Israeli legislature and courts have not adopted the category of halakhic concubinage and recognize only common-law marriage as providing an "unwed" couple with a social and legal corporate identity.[31]

Enlightened Orthodoxy, too, would probably reject the possible restoration of this category. As one scholar put it, in no uncertain terms:

> The renewal of concubinage would be tantamount to abrogating the entire halakhic system of marriage and divorce . . . and open the way to a licentiousness that would eventually destroy our entire national existence. This is not the way.[32]

The reintroduction of concubinage would be another attempt to evade halakhic problems instead of confronting them; it is clear that the general public rejects this solution. Since there are ways to permit such couples to wed in accordance with the spirit of Halakhah, there is no need to revive the institution of concubinage.

6

Mamzerut (Halakhic Illegitimacy)

PERHAPS THE MOST TRAGIC RESULT OF THE RIGID APPROACH to laws of personal status is *mamzerut,* or halakhic illegitimacy. A *mamzer* (feminine *mamzeret*), the offspring of an adulterous or incestuous relationship, may marry only a convert or another *mamzeret/mamzer.* All descendants of such persons until the end of time are deemed to be *mamzerim* and are subject to the same marital restrictions.

This harsh condition appears not only in the tomes of decisors who lived five hundred years ago but also in contemporary Israel. Dr. Moshe Silberg, a justice of the Israeli Supreme Court for twenty years (1950–1970), summarized the most notorious case in modern Israeli history as follows:

> Two young people, a brother and sister [Hanokh and Miriam Langer] . . . came to the rabbinate and asked that a date be set for the brother's wedding. It was discovered that a small mark had been inscribed in the population register next to the names of the brother and sister, which those in the know understood to mean that they were *mamzerim.* It was also discovered that the annotation was added because the rabbis of Petah Tikva had ruled, in an earlier proceeding heard by them, that their mother had been married to another man, left him without a *get* [bill of divorce issued by a religious court], and married [their] father . . . ; that is, she was "a married woman" when she

married [their] father, and consequently he is a *mamzer*. . . . Because the brother is a *mamzer,* he is forbidden to join the community [i.e., marry a "kosher" Jew] and can marry only a woman who is herself a *mamzeret.* Because the brother's fiancée—his future wife—was not a *mamzeret* . . . the rabbinate refused to conduct their wedding.[1]

How did the Chief Rabbinate deal with this tragic case? Then–Chief Rabbi Isser Yehuda Unterman told a reporter who interviewed him that

he does not believe that this case [the Langers' *mamzerut*] should be seen as a tragedy of marriage. One cannot say that these people are barred from marrying. They can marry converts. And there are converts among us. There is even a selection to choose from.[2]

The rabbi's moral blindness to a case that embodied the bitter destiny of many citizens of Israel who have done nothing wrong is damning evidence of the inadequacy of the religious establishment and of its limitations when it must deal with contemporary problems.

To understand how evolving Halakhah relates to this phenomenon, we must investigate the history of halakhic rulings related to *mamzerut.*

THE *MAMZER* IN THE CLASSICAL SOURCES

The Hebrew word *mamzer* appears only twice in the Bible — once in the Torah and once in the Later Prophets. In Deuteronomy we read: "A *mamzer* shall not be admitted into the congregation of the Lord; his descendants, even in the tenth generation, shall not be admitted into the congregation of the Lord" (Deut. 23:3).

This verse leaves several questions unanswered: What is a *mamzer?* What is the meaning of "shall not be admitted into the congregation of the Lord"? What is the duration of the ban; that is, what is meant by "even in the tenth generation"?

What is a *Mamzer?*

What is the literal meaning of the word *mamzer?* The earliest source that "defines" the word is the Septuagint, the Greek translation of the Bible produced by and for the Jews of Alexandria, Egypt, during the third and second centuries B.C.E. The Septuagint renders *mamzer* by *ek pornês,* that is, "from a harlot." The ancient translators believed that a *mamzer* is the son of a harlot.

The word *mamzer* also appears in Zechariah 9:6: "And a *mamzer* shall settle in Ashdod. I will uproot the grandeur of Philistia." Here the Septuagint translators (evidently a different group working some decades later than the translators of the Pentateuch) rendered *mamzer* (as if it were short for *me-am zar*) by *allogeneis,* which means "of another race" or "of foreign origin." Here, then, a *mamzer* was understood to be a foreigner, an alien.[3]

In antiquity, then, at least two different primary significations were attached to the word *mamzer.* How did the medieval exegetes understand it?

Nahmanides (1194–1260), in his commentary on the passage in Deuteronomy, glossed *mamzer* as a designation for "a man who appears strange *(muzar)* to his brothers and friends, for it is not known whence he comes."[4] Rashi (1040–1105), by contrast, understood the phrase in Zechariah to mean "an alien people will dwell in Ashdod." Commenting on the passage in Zechariah, Abraham Ibn Ezra (1089–1164) noted that "Rabbi Judah ben Balaam said it was a term for a non-Jew; but in my opinion it means one born of a forbidden union." David Kimchi (known as the Radak, 1160–1235) summarized the various glosses on Zechariah as follows: "Some explain it as the name of a nation; others, as the offspring of a forbidden union among Israelites who lived by themselves in the Philistine cities and were separated from the congregation."

As we see, the translators and exegetes were not sure about the original meaning of the word *mamzer.* Is a *mamzer* a strange person? Is he a foreigner? Or is he the offspring of illicit sexual relations among Jews?

Whatever the "plain meaning," it is the halakhic understanding of the term that determines its application. The Mishnah delves behind the literal meaning and attempts to arrive at a precise definition of the term. This is understandable, since Halakhah deals with vital questions and must issue a ruling. According to the Mishnah:

> Who is accounted a *mamzer?* The offspring of any union that is forbidden by the Torah. Thus Rabbi Akiba. Simeon the Temanite says: [The offspring of any union whose partners] are liable to excision [i.e., death at the hands of Heaven]. The Halakhah is according to him. Rabbi Joshua says: The offspring of any union whose partners are liable to death at the hands of the court. Rabbi Simeon ben Azzai said: I found a family register in Jerusalem, in which was written, "such-a-one is a *mamzer* on account of [adultery with] a married woman"; this supports the words of Rabbi Joshua (Mishnah Yevamot 4:13).

Thus, this Mishnah offers three possible definitions of *mamzer:* those of Rabbi Akiba, of Simeon the Temanite, and of Rabbi Joshua.

1. Rabbi Akiba's definition is the most stringent. According to him, a *mamzer* is the offspring of a couple who engaged in forbidden sexual relations, including a *kohen* and a divorcée or a childless widow who remarries without first being released by her brother-in-law *(ḥalitzah).*[5] In the Babylonian Talmud we find a sharp response to Rabbi Akiba's extremism in this matter: "Rabbi Simai says: Rabbi Akiba makes a *mamzer* of everyone [born of an irregular union] except [the child] of a widow [married] to a High Priest" (BT Ketubot 29b). And Rabbi Yeshevav complains: "Come, let us cry out against Akiba son of Joseph, who used to say, 'in any case of illicit intercourse among Jews—the offspring is a *mamzer*'" (ibid.)

2. The definition advanced by Simeon the Temanite derives from the categories of forbidden incestuous relations enumerated in Leviticus chapter 18: intercourse with one's father or mother, sister, granddaughter, aunt, daughter-in-law, sister-in-law, and so on—that is, any illicit union that is punishable by death at the hands of Heaven.[6]

    We see that Rabbi Akiba's position was extremely harsh, since it attached the label *mamzer* even to the offspring of marriages that were perfectly valid (even if only *post factum*). But the codified Halakhah follows the opinion of Simeon the Temanite, not that of Rabbi Akiba.

3. Rabbi Joshua's opinion that a *mamzer* is the offspring of a union that makes its partners liable to capital punishment at the hands of an earthly court—such as adulterous relations involving a married woman—was adopted in Halakhah to supplement the definition of Simeon the Temanite. According to the authoritative ruling of the *Shulḥan Arukh,* "Who is a *mamzer?* Someone who is the offspring of any forbidden union between those liable [on account of it] to either capital punishment or death at the hands of Heaven (*Shuḥlan Arukh, E.H.* 4:13).

" . . . Shall Not be Admitted into the Congregation of the Lord"

Rashi explains that this means that "a *mamzer* may not marry a Jewish woman." The Mishnah (Yevamot 8:3) holds that the ban applies to both male and female offspring. Thus, a *mamzer* may not marry a Jewish woman, and a *mamzeret* may not marry a Jewish man.

The Duration of the Ban

The Sages interpreted the phrase "his descendants, even in the tenth generation, shall not be admitted into the congregation of the Lord" as implying a perpetual ban (*Sifre, Ki Tetze* 248). They based this reading on the verse that immediately follows the passage about the *mamzer:* "No Ammonite or Moabite shall be admitted into the congregation of the Lord; none of their descendants, even in the tenth generation, shall *ever* be admitted into the congregation of the Lord" (Deut. 23:4).

Summing up the halakhic discussion, Maimonides ruled as follows:

> Who is the *mamzer* mentioned in the Torah? One who is the offspring of forbidden sexual relations, except for the son of a menstruating woman, whose son is defective but is not a *mamzer.* But if a man has relations with any of the other women forbidden to him, whether by compulsion or willingly, whether highhandedly or by error, the child is a *mamzer.* This applies equally to males and females; they are forbidden perpetually, since it says "the tenth generation," which means forever (Laws of Forbidden Sexual Relations 15:1).

As we shall see below, the Sages found bold ways to mitigate the blow of *mamzerut,* limiting the inquiry into the families of those forbidden to marry and stipulating that "all families are presumed to be fit" (see chapter 7).

The halakhic literature is full of vacillation, doubts, and challenges to the absolute and inflexible Halakhah that leaves no room for human feelings or sympathy for the injured party. The Sages expounded the words of Ecclesiastes as referring to the pitiable state of *mamzerim:*

> I further observed all the oppression that goes on under the sun: the tears of the oppressed, with none to comfort them; their oppressors have power—but there is none to comfort them (Eccles. 4:1).

Comments the Midrash:

> Daniel Ḥayyata (the tailor) applied to *mamzerim* the verse "the tears of the oppressed." Their ancestors were transgressors—but what has it to do with these unfortunate people! This one's

father had illicit sexual relations—but how did he sin and what has it to do with him? "With none to comfort them," but "their oppressors have power"—[this refers to] the Great Sanhedrin of Israel, which assaults them through the power of Torah and rejects them in the name of "a *mamzer* shall not be admitted into the congregation of the Lord." "But there is none to comfort them"—the Holy One, blessed be He, said, "I must comfort them. For in this world they have a defect, but in the World to Come . . . he is all pure gold" (Leviticus Rabbah 32:8).

This passage reflects compassion and understanding of the plight of *mamzerim,* who are punished for a crime they did not commit. It constitutes a stinging rebuke of their tormentors, who are identified with a strict-constructionist Sanhedrin. But the Holy One, blessed be He, will Himself comfort them, and in the Messianic Age they will all be pure and without blemish.

MAMZERUT TODAY

Two aspects of the issue of *mamzerut* bear looking into: (1) What is the scope of the problem today? (2) How does the Israeli religious establishment deal with it?

The Scope of the Problem

From a strict Orthodox perspective, there must be tens of thousands of *mamzerim* in the world today. Only 11 percent of the six million Jews in the United States—the largest Jewish community in the world today—are affiliated with Orthodox congregations. Most Jewish marriages are conducted by a rabbi of one of the non-Orthodox movements. According to the best available estimates, one of every two or three couples in the United States gets divorced. Even if the Jewish divorce rate is lower than the national average, many Jewish marriages end in divorce. Perhaps only 10 to 15 percent of Jewish divorces involve a rabbinically sanctioned *get;* the vast majority of divorcing couples are satisfied with a civil divorce or a non-Orthodox *get.* A study conducted in Providence, Rhode Island, found that the percentage of Jewish divorcées who remarry is much higher than the corresponding figure among non-Jewish women. Of course, in the absence of a *get,* almost none of these second marriages are conducted by an Orthodox rabbi. Reform and Conservative rabbis, by contrast, require only a civil decree or a non-Orthodox *get* as a condition for remarriage. In the course of nature, many of the couples involved have children. What are the implications?

Because both spouses are Jewish, and the wife, who did not receive a rabbinically sanctioned *get* from her former husband, is still married to him according to Halakhah, hard-line decisors rule that their children are *mamzerim.* It is most likely that a large number of *mamzerim* have been born during the generations that Jews have been living in the United States; and all their descendants, too, are *mamzerim.*

Everything we know about how Jews lived in the Soviet Union (which had the third-largest Jewish community in the world) leads to the conclusion that a significant proportion of that community, too, may be *mamzerim.* Many decisors hold that the initial civil marriage to a Jew is halakhically valid, even in the absence of a religious ceremony. This validity derives from the sexual intercourse that took place between the partners and the halakhic tenet that "a person does not have sexual intercourse for the purpose of fornication."[7]

In the Soviet Union it was all but impossible to obtain a rabbinically sanctioned *get.* According to the stringent rabbinic opinion, any divorcée who remarried was in fact still married to her first husband; any children born to her are certain or doubtful *mamzerim* and barred from marrying other Jews.

This survey of the situation of two large Jewish communities indicates that hard-line rabbis must deal with the serious danger that our people are continually transgressing the severe Torah prohibition that "a *mamzer* shall not be admitted into the congregation of the Lord."

The Approach of the Religious Establishment in Israel

In chapter 1 we noted that one of the criteria to be invoked in halakhic rulings is the need to preserve the ethical character of Halakhah. The suffering of the innocent whose family tree has been blighted by the stigma of *mamzerut* should trouble every Jew and every sensitive person.

In the situation that exists in Israel today, a large gap yawns between the codified Halakhah and ethical imperatives. The prophet Jeremiah foresaw that "in those days, they shall no longer say, 'Parents have eaten sour grapes and children's teeth are blunted.' But everyone shall die for his own sins: whosoever eats sour grapes, his teeth shall be blunted" (Jer. 31:29–30). Nevertheless, today, in the State of Israel, children are being punished for the sins of their fathers and mothers. At a time when massive efforts are being invested to bring back those who were feared lost and compelled to abandon their Judaism all over the world, west and east, from places where our coreligionists face the danger of physical and spiritual annihilation, should we reject many of our brothers and sisters because of some supposed defect that is not their fault? Many remember the shameful episode of the B'nai Israel of India, an entire community whose members were deemed unfit to marry other Jews; the Ethiopian Jews in Israel have faced a similar situation (see chapter 10).

In the 1970s, the country was rocked by a series of cases concerning *mamzerim* and others forbidden to marry. In the years that have passed since, the issue has faded somewhat from the public consciousness. Is this because the religious establishment solved the problem of *mamzerut,* which so stirred up Israelis at the time of the Langer case? Was a solution found to the marriage blacklists, which wrecked the lives of many couples during recent decades (see chapter 7)? One might well assume that serious problems of this sort no longer occur, since we do not hear about them. And if it's not in the news, it doesn't exist; or, as the Sages put it: "Silence is tantamount to agreement" (BT Baba Metzia 37b). Such, at any rate, is the conclusion drawn by most people.

The truth, however, is that the rabbinate has not found a halakhic panacea for these unfortunates. On the contrary, their number has actually increased. The names of thousands of men and women whom other Jews may not marry are stored in the central computer of the Ministry of Religious Affairs, which can be accessed by every religious council in Israel.

Consider, for example, the case of one young man whom the rabbinate would not allow to marry his fiancée, on the grounds that he is a *mamzer*. This individual, whom we shall call Yitzhak, went to the offices of the religious council in Haifa to register for marriage, only to be told that he could not marry his fiancée because his name appeared on the marriage blacklist. His mother, a concentration camp survivor, had first married some forty years earlier. She and her husband were divorced before he emigrated from Romania. The woman stayed behind, because she could not obtain an exit visa. Some years later she remarried and gave birth to Yitzhak, her only son. Later the family received permission to emigrate to Israel; Yitzhak was three at the time. When the woman appeared before the district rabbinical court in Tel Aviv in 1963, the judges ruled that she had not been legally divorced from her first husband and had accordingly been a married woman, in the eyes of Halakhah, when she remarried and gave birth to Yitzhak. The ruling, relating to a boy of four, included the following paragraph:

> Please inquire as to the ID number of the child born to this woman and her present husband and tell the Ministry of Religious Affairs to add him to the list of those forbidden to marry.[8]

This ruling became known to Yitzhak only twenty-three years later, when the marriage division of the Haifa Rabbinate notified him that he could not receive a marriage license. Yitzhak and his fiancée began a long and woeful peregrination. First they were referred to the rabbinate in Tel Aviv, where the original verdict had been issued. The Tel Aviv court ruled that it had no authority to annul or amend the ruling handed down a quarter-century earlier. Yitzhak appealed to the Supreme Rabbinical Court in Jerusalem, but in vain. The couple threw up their hands and had a civil marriage ceremony in Cyprus.

Yitzhak and his wife later appealed to the *beit din* of the Council of Progressive Rabbis to free Yitzhak of the blemish of *mamzerut*, which would blight his future descendants as well, since *mamzerim* and their offspring remain unmarriageable in perpetuity. They also requested a Jewish wedding ceremony.

Does the rabbinate have any solutions to offer an individual adjudged to be a *mamzer?* They can suggest that he or she marry another *mamzer/mamzeret*[9] or a convert instead of his or her "kosher" intended. Sometimes rabbis advise a couple who cannot marry to live together without a religious ceremony (see chapter 5). Such proposals are of course rejected out of hand.

The "solutions" that the rabbinate proffers to *mamzerim* address, albeit inadequately, only the issue of their own marriage. Nothing is done to cleanse individual *mamzerim* or their descendants of the blot of *mamzerut*. The rabbinate's proposals fall under three headings:

1. Marrying another *mamzer:* "A *mamzer* may marry a *mamzeret* [if both are certain *mamzerim*]" (*Shulḥan Arukh, E.H.* 4:24).
2. Marrying a convert: "A male proselyte . . . may [marry] a *mamzeret* and every *mamzer* may [marry] a female proselyte . . . because the congregation of converts is not called a congregation" (ibid.).
3. Concubinage: If a *mamzer* has sexual intercourse without a marriage ceremony, he is not guilty of violating a negative commandment on account of *mamzerut* [but only on account of fornication]. He would not be liable to flogging for having sexual intercourse without marriage. The prohibition applies only in the case of a married *mamzer/mamzeret* (Maimonides, Laws of Forbidden Sexual Intercourse 15:2).

EARLY RABBINIC SOLUTIONS

This rigid approach seems to be a contemporary reaction. The tal-mudic Sages and medieval decisors proposed various enlightened ways to liberate Jews from the chains of their *mamzerut:*

Marrying a Female Slave to Cleanse One's Children

One solution dates back to the Mishnah. Rabbi Tarfon, a contem-porary of Rabbi Akiba, used to say:

> The offspring of *mamzerim* may be cleansed of the taint [of *mamzerut*]. If a *mamzer* marries a [non-Jewish] female slave, the offspring is a slave. If the father sets him free, the son becomes a free man [and the taint of *mamzerut* does not cling to him] (Mishnah Kiddushin 3:13).

Rabbi Eliezer, the Mishnah reports, rejected this solution as quite useless, since he held that the two categories of *mamzer* and slave were not mutually exclusive and "such a person is a *mamzer* slave" (ibid.). Nevertheless, the codified Halakhah is according to Rabbi Tarfon. In fact, Maimonides (Laws of Forbidden Sexual In-tercourse 15:4) and Rabbi Joseph Caro (*Shulḥan Arukh, E.H.* 4:20) ruled that this method is permitted even *ab initio*.

Rabbi Tarfon's method removes the stain from the *mamzer*'s descendants but not from the *mamzer* himself. Nor can it help a *mamzeret,* who cannot marry a non-Jewish male slave and in any case would convey her tainted status to her offspring.

Obviously in the modern era, when slavery no longer exists, this method is not practicable and is certainly not desirable.

The Fetus Spends Twelve Months in the Womb

In the Talmud we read of a decision rendered by Rabbah Tosfa'ah, a seventh-generation Babylonian *amora,* in the case of a woman whose husband went abroad. About a year after the husband's departure, his wife gave birth. The learned rabbi declared the child legitimate. According to Rashi, Rabbah Tosfa'ah was of the opinion that the mother could have carried the fetus for a full twelve months, so there was no cause to suspect that the woman had become pregnant after her husband had gone on his travels. The Gemara concludes that Rabbah Tosfa'ah acted in accordance with the majority opinion and that the Halakhah is according to him (BT Yevamot 80b). Maimonides, too, accepted this as the codified Halakhah, albeit with a cleverly veiled medical reservation: "A fetus does not remain in its mother's womb *more* than twelve months" (Laws of Forbidden Sexual Intercourse 15:19).[10] Hence if a woman gives birth within a year of her husband's departure or demise, we may attribute paternity of the child to him.

In his code, the *Arba'ah Turim* (generally referred to as the *Tur*), Rabbi Jacob ben Asher (1270?–1340) cited Maimonides and incorporated the ruling that if the husband remains abroad for less than a year, the child is not to be adjudged a *mamzer*. He also mentioned the opinion of *Sefer Halakhot Gedolot* (attributed to Rabbi Simeon Kaira of the ninth–tenth centuries) that even after a year a child is not held to be a *mamzer;* perhaps the husband returned secretly and had sexual relations with his wife.[11] Some commentators even conjecture that the husband may have made a secret flying visit to his wife by magical invocation of the Ineffable Name, which made it possible for him to travel back and forth in no time. The tosafists and Rabbenu Asher say that this idea is based on the story recounted in the Jerusalem Talmud about the father of the *amora* Samuel, who employed this special method to return from abroad and beget his son, the great scholar from Nehardea.[12]

According to another passage in the Jerusalem Talmud, an unidentified *mamzer* does not survive beyond the age of thirty days (JT Kiddushin 3:12). Hence, there is no danger of marrying such an individual.[13]

Did all these rabbis really believe that a fetus could remain *in utero* for a year or longer? It is unlikely that they accepted the notion that a man might pop back home from a distant country for a single night, unknown to his neighbors, in order to impregnate his wife. The idea that invocation of the Ineffable Name could make it possible to travel at near-light speed was indeed legendary. The connection between infant mortality and *mamzerut* was tendentious. The rabbis were so distressed by the ethical dilemma of *mamzerut* that they were willing to accept legal fictions of this type as the only way to resolve an otherwise insoluble problem.

Mamzerut and "Assimilation"

The Talmud states that "a family that has assimilated [into the community] may remain assimilated" (BT Kiddushin 71a). This has been understood to mean that a family of questionable lineage must not be cast out of the community and that no effort should be expended to investigate whether its ancestry is tainted. Various passages in the Gemara imply that the Sages did in fact know the identity of some *mamzerim*—for example, a family register from Jerusalem reported that "such-a-one is a *mamzer* from a married woman" (BT Yevamot 49a)—but made a conscious decision not to expose them. Perhaps the Sages were sensitive to their difficult status; perhaps they feared the baleful consequences of publicizing the matter.

From talmudic times on, this was the dominant policy with regard to investigating an individual's antecedents. In the sixteenth century it was codified by Rabbi Moses Isserles in his glosses on the *Shuḥlan Arukh:*

> With regard to a family with some blemish in its ancestry that is not known to the general public—once it has been assimilated a person who knows of the blemish is not permitted to reveal it. Instead he should leave it in its presumed fitness, since all families who have been assimilated into Israel will be fit in the Messianic Age (*Shuḥlan Arukh, E.H.* 2:5).

When the rabbis knew about cases of *mamzerut,* they preferred to keep silent about them. This may help explain why the halakhic literature contains so few actual cases of *mamzerim,* as opposed to academic discussion of the topic.[14]

MODERN RESPONSA ON THE PURIFICATION OF *MAMZERIM*

Human nature and sexual behavior seem to have changed little over the centuries, with the all-too-frequent consequence that innocent persons are condemned to suffer. Not only the Sages and medieval decisors had the moral courage to resolve the problem. Rabbinic authorities of the last two centuries searched the halakhic literature for practical solutions to their plight and found bold and innovative methods to release such Jews from the chains of *mamzerut*. A review of several cases from this period will exhibit ingenious halakhic methods for purifying *mamzerim*.

The Husband Who Didn't Die

In the late nineteenth century, a man abandoned his wife in Odessa and disappeared. Twelve years later his wife was notified by his family that he had died overseas. With the approval of the Odessa religious court, she went through the ceremony of *ḥalitzah* with her brother-in-law and later remarried. In due course she became pregnant by her second husband. Before the child was born, news arrived that her first husband was still alive; he had given his passport and papers to another man, and it was the latter who had died. The local rabbis felt they had no choice but to rule that she was an adulteress and the fetus she was carrying would be a *mamzer*.

The rabbi of Odessa consulted Rabbi Shalom Mordecai Schwadron (born in Galicia in 1835) about the woman and her child. Rabbi Schwadron replied that as a matter of Halakhah, she had to be divorced by both husbands and the child would be a *mamzer*. He thought he had a way around the latter problem, however. He suggested that the first husband divorce her by proxy and then revoke the *get* without informing the messenger or his wife. In accordance with the codified Halakhah, this procedure would cause her first marriage to be retroactively annulled. Thus, she would not have been a married woman when she stood under the *ḥuppah* for the second time, and the child would not be a *mamzer*.

Unfortunately, by the time the ruling was issued it was moot, because the first husband had already given the woman a valid divorce. Hence the recommended solution was theoretically valid but not applicable in practice. After weighing other halakhic options, Rabbi Schwadron reached the conclusion that there was no remedy for the child.[15] Nevertheless, he had developed a halakhic tool that could be used to purify *mamzerim* in similar cases in the future.

Four Generations of *Mamzerim* on the Island of Corfu

Israel, the son of Rachel Conegliano, was born on the Greek island of Zanthe in 1807. His mother had been separated, but not divorced, from her husband, Ḥayyim Gani. Rumor had it that a certain Raphael Hakohen of Corfu had fathered the child.

In 1830, when Israel Conegliano, now living on the island of Corfu, was about to marry, word of his problematic lineage reached the local rabbi, Shem-Tov Amarillo. He asked his colleague on Zanthe, Rabbi Joseph Ventura, to look into the case.

The latter questioned nine witnesses. Ḥayyim Gani, the estranged husband of the now-deceased Rachel, asserted that they had never had sexual relations after their separation. The *mohel* who had circumcised Israel testified that Rachel had confessed to him that Raphael Hakohen was the child's father. Some of the other witnesses supported these depositions, while others testified that Rachel had been visited by both Jewish and non-Jewish men. Two witnesses stated that she had become pregnant by a gentile.

Rabbi Ventura's conclusion was that the late Rachel Conegliano had indeed had an adulterous relationship with Raphael Hakohen, but he issued no ruling as to her son's status. It is not known whether Rabbi Amarillo on Corfu rendered an official halakhic verdict after receiving the report from his colleague. However, when he married Israel to Simha, the daughter of Shabbetai Judah and Ḥannah, in May 1830, he appended a codicil to their marriage contract (*ketubah*):

> I have announced to the tribes of Israel that their mother has committed adultery, their parent has acted shamefully. They are the children of fornication. It is not accidental that the starling follows the raven [i.e., bride and groom are as alike as birds of a feather]. "He will be called impure, impure" [Leviticus 13:45] and even the tenth generation may not enter the holy congregation.

Subsequent generations of rabbis on Corfu and in the eastern Mediterranean basin understood that Rabbi Amarillo had declared Israel to be an undoubted *mamzer*, and so too all his descendants. As a result, his children and grandchildren encountered difficulties when they attempted to marry. His daughter had to go to Constantinople, where she married her fiancé clandestinely. Back on Corfu, the birth of their son in 1852 led to a rabbinic pronouncement that he too was an undoubted *mamzer* who could not marry a Jewish woman of pure descent.

When this boy's younger sister became engaged in 1889, the incumbent rabbi of Corfu, Elisha Mapano, refused to allow the ceremony to take place on the island. Her father tried to compel the rabbi to back down by threatening to appeal to the civil courts. Rabbi Mapano thereupon enlisted the support of his colleagues around the Mediterranean and held his ground. The couple quietly decamped to Alexandria, where they were married by a local cantor.

Rabbi Elijah Ḥazzan, the chief rabbi of Alexandria, who had supported Rabbi Mapano, excommunicated the second couple, since they had been married in the city in contravention of his ruling, as well as the cleric who officiated at their wedding. He declared that the couple's offspring would be undoubted *mamzerim* in perpetuity and warned Jews in every community to beware of this family, which was impure from its founder Israel to his great-grandchildren throughout nine decades. Rabbi Ḥazzan circulated a series of responsa about the tainted family and enlisted the support of rabbis from other countries.[16] Not only were the names of the fourth-generation descendants of the family, the children of the banned couple, announced in every synagogue, the *mohel* was instructed to add a second name, "Kidor," to that of their son Pinhas, so as to label him a *mamzer*. This family could indeed be seen as suffering the punishment stipulated in the Second Commandment: "Visiting the iniquity of the fathers on the children to the third and fourth generation" (Exod. 20:4).

Meanwhile, Rabbi Jacob Saul Elyashar (1817–1906), the chief rabbi of Jerusalem, had begun an independent inquiry into the case at the request of members of the Corfu community. During the 1890s he, too, enlisted various rabbis and scholars to help research the halakhic and factual aspects of the affair. This led to a protracted and bitter halakhic dispute between the religious courts of Alexandria and Jerusalem.

Rabbi Elyashar and his colleagues reviewed the transcript of the testimony given on the island of Zanthe in 1830 about the circumstances of Israel's birth in 1807—some ninety years earlier—and reached the following conclusion (the actual ruling was authored by Rabbi Vidal Angel):

- Ḥayyim Gani, Rachel Conegliano's husband, was not to be believed when he claimed that he had not had sexual relations with his wife after their separation (the researchers wondered why he had not been questioned about the nature of the separation, when he and his wife were still living in the same city).
- Some witnesses had testified that Israel was fathered by a non-Jew. Had Rachel been alive in 1830, she might have confirmed this report. (Neither a husband who denies paternity nor a mother who confesses to adultery is believed, and the child is not a *mamzer* on the basis of their statements. But, according to Halakhah, a woman is believed if she avers that she was impregnated by a gentile or a slave, thus clearing the child of the taint of *mamzerut*.)
- The *mohel*'s testimony that Rachel had confessed her adultery to him was inadmissible hearsay evidence.

- The uncontradicted testimony of two valid witnesses is required to establish the existence of an adulterous relationship and consequent *mamzerut*. But this was not forthcoming in Zanthe in 1830, where some of the witnesses contradicted others.
- Early decisors, including Nahmanides, Solomon ben Abraham Adret, and Rabbenu Nissim Gerondi, concurred that if a rumor of illicit behavior was not investigated at the time when the misconduct was supposed to have occurred, but only much later, and the results of the inquiry were not clear, the rumor must be disregarded.

The conclusion of the Jerusalem rabbis was that Israel had been fathered by Rachel Conegliano's husband, Ḥayyim Gani! Alternatively, if she had been impregnated by another man, the presumption was that he was a non-Jew, because most of the residents of the city were gentiles.[17]

Thus Israel, the son of Rachel Conegliano, was declared to be a pure Jew and cleared of the taint of *mamzerut* in 1899, ninety-two years after his birth and eight years after his death! This had the domino effect of clearing all his descendants as well.[18] The Rabbinical court of Jerusalem promulgated and published the following decree:

A true judgment is rendered that this family is permitted to enter the Congregation of Israel and marry Jewish women. Their daughters may be taken as wives for anyone who chooses and no one may protest. A public declaration will be made that . . . their names shall be published, for there is nothing in all the testimonies, investigations, and clarifications that would ban them. They, their children, and all that is theirs are unblemished from the time that Mr. Israel Conegliano was born until this day. It is prohibited to treat them with contempt.[19]

The Child of the Eunuch's Wife[20]

Abraham Nahum was born in a village near Izmir (Smyrna), Turkey. When he grew up his skin was smooth and he had no trace of a beard. No objection was raised when he married a young Jewish girl in 1836, because he was still an adolescent and his appearance was not very different from that of his peers who had fathered children. Only later did suspicions arise that he was a congenital eunuch (the halakhic term is "sun eunuch" because he was already sterile when he first saw the light of day).

Two years after their marriage, his wife confessed to adultery with her husband's brother and other men, and the local religious court compelled Abraham to divorce her. Her son, Jacob, was proclaimed a *mamzer* because he was presumed to be the child of an adulterous and perhaps even incestuous relationship. When Jacob reached maturity, he moved to another community, where he married. When his identity became known, his two sons were declared to be *mamzerim*. Abraham Nahum remarried and died a few years later.

Rabbi Abraham Palache (1809–1899), the Chief Rabbi of Izmir, was asked to investigate. He convened a special *beit din* that included Rabbi Elyashar and Rabbi Shalom Moshe Hai Gagin, also of Jerusalem. At first Rabbi Palache believed that this was not a case in which one could invoke the halakhic principle that "most acts of sexual intercourse are attributed to the husband" (BT Sukkah 27a). Instead, he had to determine whether Abraham Nahum had indeed been a congenital eunuch and, if so, whether he had outgrown this condition. He resolved these questions as follows:

- A woman who had seen him naked at age four had described his genitalia to the people of the village; she said that the child's penis was the size of a *piñon* (pine-nut in Ladino). Since, however, Abraham had never been examined by a physician, it was impossible to state with certainty that he was a eunuch. This made his status as a eunuch doubtful.[21]
- According to the Mishnah, Rabbi Eliezer held that a congenital eunuch, unlike a castrated man, could be healed

(Mishnah Yevamot 8:4). This adds a second doubt: even had Abraham been a eunuch at four, he might have become potent by the time he was married. His second wife in fact testified that they had had normal sexual relations.

Given this double doubt concerning Abraham's diagnosis as a congenital eunuch, and the relevant halakhic precedents, Rabbi Palache's *beit din* ruled that the presumed eunuch was the father of Jacob. Even if this were not the case, the presumption was that the boy's mother had been impregnated by a gentile as a result of her promiscuous behavior while married. In either case, Jacob and his sons were fully cleared of the stigma of *mamzerut*.[22]

A *Mamzeret* in Egypt

In 1919, a *beit din* in Alexandria ruled that a married woman who had given birth to a daughter named Shoshana had been impregnated by a man other than her husband and that the girl was accordingly a *mamzeret*. In 1936, the case was brought before a religious court headed by the chief rabbi of Alexandria, Rabbi Jacob Moses Toledano (1880–1960), later Chief Rabbi of Tel Aviv and Minister of Religious Affairs in Israel. This court overturned the ruling of its predecessor and ruled that her mother's husband was indeed Shoshana's biological father, despite the testimony to the contrary presented to the original court. Here too, Rabbi Toledano presented the alternative hypothesis that the mother had had sexual relations with non-Jews, and, as stated, a child of mixed (Jewish and non-Jewish) parentage is not a *mamzer*. Rabbi Toledano permitted Shoshana to marry any Jew she wished.[23]

The Proxy Betrothal of a Yemenite Girl

A Jewish man from Yemen journeyed to Asmara in Eritrea, where he betrothed his minor daughter to a local Jew but failed to inform his family of the alliance. The daughter, who was still in Yemen, never discovered that she had been given the status of a betrothed woman and required a *get* before she could marry someone else.

When she reached maturity she married another Jew and bore him a son.

After the woman made *aliya* with her family, a stranger appeared and announced that he was her husband from Eritrea. The matter was brought to the *beit din* in Petah Tikva, which initially considered promulgating the standard verdict in such cases: requiring both husbands to divorce the woman and declaring the child a *mamzer*.

When Rabbi Reuven Katz consulted with Rabbi Yitzhak Isaac Herzog, then the Chief Rabbi, the latter proposed two avenues for resolving this problem:[24]

One option would be to question the validity of the betrothal in Asmara, because the groom's relatives were mixed in among the bystanders and the groom had not designated specific witnesses.[25] Unfortunately, this would actually make the boy's situation worse, since he would then be a doubtful *mamzer*, who can marry only a convert but not a *mamzeret*.

Instead, he suggested Rabbi Schwadron's idea of retroactively annulling the betrothal by having the first husband send a *get* by messenger and then cancel it without notice. Even though Schwadron had qualified this idea as "theoretical only," Herzog believed that this was a case in which it could be applied in practice.

Rabbi Katz, however, rejected this solution as impractical. Ultimately he discovered that one of the witnesses in Asmara was married to a non-Jewish woman, which disqualified him, invalidated the betrothal, and cleared the child of the stigma of *mamzerut*.

Civil Divorce without a *Get*

The rabbi of Lynn, Massachusetts, asked Rabbi Joseph Zussmanovich of Slobodka (a suburb of Kovno, Lithuania) about the status of woman who had been married to a Jew in a civil ceremony and subsequently been divorced by civil decree, without receiving a *get*. Rabbi Zussmanovich replied that "the question is serious with regard to the laws of a married woman [i.e., adultery] and the laws of a *mamzer* child," for decisors differ as to whether, following a civil marriage ceremony, the man is considered to have consecrated a marriage with his wife by the act of sexual intercourse, so that she requires a *get* before she may remarry.[26]

According to the Lithuanian rabbi, the case in question was not covered by the talmudic axiom that "a man does not have intercourse for the purpose of fornication" (BT Gittin 81b; Ketubot 73a; Yevamot 107a):

> Someone who goes to be married by the civil authorities does not think about [the halakhic possibility of consecrating a marriage through intercourse]. If so, it is clear that his marriage is not a halakhic marriage. . . . If so it is clear and true as a matter of Halakhah that any woman who was married only by the civil authorities, . . . even if she was divorced only by civil decree, is permitted to marry another man [without a *get*].

He sees this lenient ruling as "a great innovation in Halakhah and an important regulation to save thousands of cases in both Russia and America from the taint of *mamzerut*."[27]

Rabbi A. I. Kook issued a similar ruling in an almost identical case of a Jew

> who was married by the civil authorities and later . . . also divorced according to civil law. There could be better proof than this that he was totally uninterested in halakhic marriage, so why should we be concerned about it? . . . In a case of an *agunah* there is absolutely no reason to be concerned about this.[28]

Annulling the Conversion of the First Husband

Particularly well known is the 1972 ruling by Rabbi Shlomo Goren, which legitimized Hanokh and Miriam Langer and permitted them to marry, even though the two had been declared *mamzerim* by every level of the rabbinical court system in Israel. Rabbi Goren issued a carefully reasoned verdict and convened a special *beit din* that endorsed his ruling.[29]

Rabbi Goren's solution was to invalidate their mother's first marriage. From his inquiries he concluded that the first husband's conversion had been null and void, so that he was a non-Jew when he married their mother. Because marriage with a non-Jew has no halakhic status, the mother was not a married woman when she remarried, and her two children were therefore kosher.

Not long after he issued this ruling, Rabbi Goren was elected Ashkenazi Chief Rabbi of Israel. To the best of my knowledge, there has been no other case, during his tenure in that office or since, of children who were cleared of *mamzerut* by the rabbinic establishment in Israel.

The various responsa and cases cited above provide us with four ways to clear Jews of the stain of *mamzerut*. Two are based on a determination of paternity: ascribing paternity of the child to the mother's (first) husband or ascribing paternity of the child to a non-Jew. The other two are based on nullification of the mother's first marriage: retroactively annulling the mother's first marriage or determining that the first marriage had never been halakhically contracted.

Underlying all these solutions, advanced by eminent rabbis of the recent past and present, is an understanding of the injustice done to children who cannot raise Jewish families through no fault of their own. These rabbis found solid halakhic methods and, just as important, the courage to clear *mamzerim* and permit them not only to be "admitted to the congregation" but even to be fully cleansed of the stain of *mamzerut*. In these seemingly insoluble cases, bold and learned rabbis found ways to purify the children. We may infer that today, too, it may be possible to find halakhic solutions, in the spirit of these responsa, that can clear virtually every *mamzer*. Such halakhic means have in fact served Reform and Conservative rabbinical courts to remove the taint of *mamzerut*.

According to Rabbi Jose, "*mamzerim* . . . will be unsullied in the Messianic Age" (BT Kiddushin 72b).[30] We might say that the Sages of recent generations have shown that in practice, we need not wait until that time, and that *mamzerim* can be cleared even today, as was done by great Torah Sages in those days and in this time.[31]

With regard to the case of Yitzhak, mentioned earlier in this chapter, the *beit din* of the Israel Council of Progressive Rabbis, following the above halakhic precedents as well as the ethical criteria for rendering halakhic decisions, ruled that Yitzhak was free of all blemish and could marry his fiancée. Their offspring will be without halakhic flaw.[32]

7

Marriage Blacklists: "All Families Are Presumed to Be Fit"

THE RESPONSE OF A RABBINIC BODY OR A RELIGIOUS INSTI-
tution to the bitter suffering of young Jews who, through no fault
of their own, are prevented from establishing a family ought to be
a tenacious search for a way to remove the prohibition, for it is incumbent upon all of us to act compassionately and to emulate the
Lord in this particular: "Be like Him—just as He is merciful and
compassionate, so should you be merciful and compassionate" (BT
Shabbat 133b). In fact, the Israeli religious establishment takes
great pains to keep meticulous records of the names of those who
are halakhically barred from marrying other Jews[1] and to give them
and their children identity numbers that indicate this restriction to
those in the know. These blacklists, long kept secret, stirred up a
tempest when their existence became public knowledge.

Twenty-five years ago, the deputy director of the Rabbinate
Department of the Ministry of Religious Affairs and the Ministry
spokesman confirmed to journalist Daniel Dagan that the department maintained a central list with the names of hundreds of persons whose marriage options were limited by halakhic restrictions.[2]

Responding to a parliamentary question concerning this
"book of excommunicates," Dr. Zorah Warhaftig, then Minister
of Religious Affairs, acknowledged the existence of such lists and

of circulars sent to marriage registrars with the names of persons subject to various limitations on their right of marriage.

About a week later Dagan wrote:

> In the course of my investigation of the "book of excommunicates" I spoke with dozens of marriage registrars. All confirmed that they possess alphabetical lists of persons subject to various marriage restrictions. They added that the lists also include *[mamzerim]*, whose number they estimated at several dozen.[3]

As we see, the religious establishment's attitude on this question is vigorous and unyielding: Diligent inquiries must be performed to uncover the *mamzerim* hiding among us and prevent them from mixing with the Congregation of the Lord.

Although, for the most part, these blacklists have long since ceased to preoccupy the media and public opinion,[4] the religious establishment has not given up on the idea. Quite the contrary! Computerization has greatly facilitated the process of recording and storing the names of these "unmarriageables." Instead of a thin pamphlet distributed to marriage registrars throughout the country, as in the past, the Ministry of Religious Affairs now stores the data on these people and their children in its central computer. A clerk can input the details of someone who has come to register for marriage and receive an instant printout of his or her name—not much different from the computer of the border police, which checks whether a court order has been issued barring someone from leaving the country. Here, though, the query is whether an order has been issued that bars someone from marrying his or her chosen mate.

Both those who reject and those who favor such rosters start from the erroneous postulate that Halakhah requires keeping a blacklist; consequently, the Ministry of Religious Affairs is required to maintain and apply it, by both religious and civil law, because the Knesset has stipulated that "marriages and divorces of Jews in Israel will be conducted in accordance with the Torah" and has delegated exclusive jurisdiction in these matters to the rabbinical courts.

But Halakhah does not require maintaining such lists. On the contrary, they are totally contrary to Halakhah and to the spirit of Judaism.

To defend the existence of the blacklist, the rabbinical courts might allege the indisputable fact that in antiquity there were documented family registers and lists of those whose marriage options were restricted. The Mishnah reports that in the time of Ezra and Nehemiah the returnees from Babylonia were sorted into ten classes by ancestry, including *kohanim,* Levites, Israelites, "impaired" priests, proselytes, and *mamzerim* (Mishnah Kiddushin 4:1). Severe restrictions were imposed on intermarriage between those of inferior status and members of the first three classes.

Over the centuries these lists became more widespread. A remark by R. Simeon ben Azzai (early second century C.E.) reflects a situation quite similar to that prevailing today: "I found a family register in Jerusalem, in which was written, 'such-a-one is a *mamzer* on account of [adultery with] a married woman'" (Mishnah Yevamot 4:13).

The situation in Mishnaic times, when "unmarriageables" had commingled with the "kosher" population, led to an attempt to require thorough investigation of prospective brides. According to the Mishnah,

> If a man marries a woman of priestly stock, he must trace her family back through four generations—meaning eight maternal ancestors: her mother, mother's mother, and mother's father's mother, and the last-named's mother; also her father's mother and her mother, and her father's father's mother and the last-named's mother. For a Levite or Israelite woman, he must trace her descent back one mother more (Mishnah Kiddushin 4:4).

This seems to constitute a halakhic basis for investigating four or five generations of ancestors before allowing someone to marry. Clearly, such an inquiry is impossible in the absence of orderly records.

In fact, however, the Gemara does not accept this Mishnah: "Rabbi Judah said in the name of Rav: '[The requirement to check the fitness of the mothers] is according to Rabbi Meir. But the Sages said: All families are presumed to be fit'" (BT Kiddushin 76b). It is a general rule of halakhic decision making that when a single Sage (here Rabbi Meir) disagrees with his fellows, the codified Halakhah follows the majority opinion. Hence, there is no *prima facie* halakhic requirement to check pedigrees.

But a younger contemporary of Rabbi Judah reported that their common teacher, Rav, had added a caveat to the above. According to Rabbi Ḥama bar Giora, Rav said that "if a [family's ancestral fitness] is challenged, an investigation is required" (ibid.). What sort of challenge mandates an investigation? Rashi comments that "there is no need for an investigation unless two witnesses charge her with some taint of unfitness" (ad loc.). For Maimonides, "a family that has been challenged means that two persons testify that a *mamzer* or *ḥallal* [impaired priest] has intermarried with them or that they were slaves" (Laws of Forbidden Intercourse 19,18; the *Shulḥan Arukh* rules similarly).

From this we may draw two conclusions:

1. If there is no valid testimony alleging unfitness, there is no need to investigate the ancestry of prospective brides and grooms, since all families are presumed to be fit.
2. An inquiry is called for only if two qualified witnesses have told the religious court that there is reason to doubt a family's fitness. Anonymous tale-bearing is not enough. The rabbinate publishes lists of those who have registered to marry; if no one steps forward with a reason why the couple may not wed, they are presumed to be marriageable. The computer of the Religious Affairs Ministry cannot take the place of the two witnesses.

The Sages evinced sympathy for those of questionable lineage not only because they were loath to act unjustly and unethically, but also because they recognized the latent peril of such lists. There have been periods when the Jews of entire districts were deemed outcasts for the purpose of marriage, as stated by Rabbi Pappa Sava in the name of Rav: "The Jews of Babylonia are considered to be pure; the Jews of Mishon are all undoubted *mamzerim;* as for the Jews of Media and Elam, most are unmarriageable but some are fit" (BT Kiddushin 71b, according to Rashi's commentary). But the Sages, aware of the dire peril of dividing the people that would result from such wholesale disqualification, courageously accepted the grave responsibility of declaring that "all families are presumed to be fit."

The question remains, however: If I know with certainty that there is a halakhic defect in some person's ancestry, am I required to make this information available to the religious court?

Although the Sages could not alter the codified Halakhah on forbidden marriages, they found ways to get around it. Several talmudic and halakhic discussions reflect their approach. We are told that Rabbi Simlai asked Rabbi Johanan to teach him the "Book of Genealogies." The latter responded that that volume was not to be revealed to persons from the cities of Lod and Nehardea, and all the more so to a native of Lod who lived in Nehardea (like R. Simlai). This book, a midrash on the Books of Chronicles, evidently contained information about the questionable lineage of various families, especially from those cities. Eventually it was consigned to oblivion because of its potential for social damage (BT Pesaim 62b; see also the commentary of the Maharsha, ad loc.).

Another passage that attests the Sages' lack of interest in pursuing families of questionable lineage is found in the Tosefta: Despite the Sages' oft-reiterated distaste for the entire institution of the nazirite and their displeasure with those who subjected themselves to its rigorous strictures,[5] they decided that if a person took an oath to the effect that "I shall become a nazirite if I do not divulge [the identities of] families [with blemished ancestry]—let him be a nazirite and not divulge families" (Tosefta Nazir 1:3).

The rabbinic resolution that such information should not be divulged is expressed in Rabbi Isaac's dictum that "The Holy One, Blessed be He, acted righteously with Israel in that a family that has become 'assimilated' [i.e., knowledge of its tainted ancestry has vanished from public consciousness]—is assimilated [and fit to intermarry with other families]" (BT Kiddushin 71a). Rashi explains that one must not single out and expel such a family or try to find out "who has been assimilated and who has not; one should instead leave them be as doubtful; but in the Messianic Era they will be fit." Rabbi Moses Isserles, in his annotations to the *Shulan Arukh,* ruled:

> With regard to a family with some blemish in its ancestry that is not known to the general public—once it has been assimilated a person who knows of the blemish is not permitted to reveal it. Instead he should leave it in its presumed fitness, since all families who have been assimilated into Israel will be fit in the Messianic Age (*Shulḥan Arukh, E.H.* 2:5).

We have traced the historical development of the attitude toward naming "unmarriageables" from the lower seven of Ezra's ten classes (after the Return to Zion), then to the entire population of certain districts (third century C.E.), and on to the situation reflected in the responsa literature of the Middle Ages, when *mamzerut* was rare and one almost never heard about a second generation of *mamzerim.*

It seems unnecessary to belabor the point further. The inevitable conclusion of this survey is that if the Rabbinate and the Ministry of Religious Affairs were to adhere to the compassionate approach reflected in the rulings of the Gemara and later decisors, and evince sensitivity to the bitter suffering of the hundreds of their fellow Jews whose marriage rights have been unjustly restricted, they would certainly consign all such lists to oblivion, as the Book of Genealogies was in antiquity.[6] This discrimination can be eliminated by approaching Halakhah in a liberal spirit faithful to Jewish tradition, which ruled that "all families are presumed to be fit."

Summary

EVEN IN THE EXTREMELY SENSITIVE AREA OF LAWS OF PER-
sonal status, which can determine the future of individual human
beings for good or evil, evolving Halakhah finds bold ways to assist
those who have been mistreated by inflexible religious courts.
Lovers who had been declared ineligible to wed each other live together today with the blessing of intelligent and compassionate
rabbis who married them according to the law of Moses and Israel.
It has been demonstrated once again that the Torah is not divorced
from Jewish ethics; when the oppressed cry out for justice, rabbis
who know how to relax the rigidities of the law can find a way to
help them. The archaic institution of concubinage, whose revival
has been mooted by certain rabbis, is unnecessary. Today there are
methods, fully embedded in the framework of Halakhah, that permit such couples to establish a Jewish family.

In certain cases—such as those of divorcées or converts who
wish to marry a *kohen,* or childless widows whose brothers-in-law
cannot or will not release them—evolving Halakhah has found
ways to remove the obstacles. Basing its rulings on criteria other
than the rigidities of the Law—such as the necessary ethical underpinning of religious precepts and the pluralistic and evolutionary
nature of Halakhah through history—evolving Halakhah unites
couples who have been separated.

In the case of *mamzerut,* especially, evolving Halakhah has followed the lead of the great decisors of the past and found ways to
wash out this stain. If solutions that are compatible with our age
and our conscience have been found in this sensitive area, how
much the more may we expect them to be discovered in other domains of Halakhah as well.

III

Conversion

Nor let your lineage be ignoble in your eyes: If we trace our ancestry to Abraham, Isaac, and Jacob, you trace yours to He Who spoke and the world came into existence.

MAIMONIDES' RESPONSUM TO OBADIAH THE PROSELYTE
(twelfth century)

Although the problems associated with the laws of personal status—such as marriage and divorce—trouble the Israeli public more than any other matter under the control of the religious establishment, the question of conversion has become the most controversial halakhic issue of the last thirty years, both in Israel and in the Diaspora. The reasons for this lie in the realms of secular authority rather than the domain of religion.

The dispute goes back to the legal interpretation of the Law of Return, passed in 1950, and the Citizenship Law, enacted two years later, in order to permit every Jew to immigrate to Israel and acquire Israeli citizenship. In the first years after independence and passage of the laws, the meaning of the word *Jew* did not give rise to any serious problems. Evidently, Holocaust memories of Jews searching vainly for a refuge to save their lives had more influence than halakhic criteria or considerations.

In 1957, though, the director of the Population and Immigration Registry in the Interior Ministry, who was a member of the National Religious Party, instructed ministry clerks to take special care to verify the accuracy of the "religion" entry on the registration forms of new immigrants. The Interior Ministry was no longer willing to accept immigrants' self-affirmation of Jewishness at face value. In 1958, however, Haim Cohn, then the attorney general, and Israel Bar-Yehuda, the minister of the interior, issued new guidelines, according to which a new immigrant's good-faith declaration that he or she was Jewish would suffice. The leaders of the National Religious Party protested and soon resigned from the government.

The decades since that first crisis have seen many public storms, political crises, and fluctuations concerning the Law of Return. In the popular argot and the media, the matter is reduced to the question, Who is a Jew? Some argue that the real question is, What is halakhic conversion? Others assert, however, that the debate is connected chiefly with the determination of which rabbis and religious courts are qualified to accept converts. As noted, these problems did not bother the founders of the State of Israel during the first decade of independence, nor the leaders of the religious parties.

In the fury of political debate, the main point is often overlooked: the converts as human beings, as sensitive individuals. The impression given by the religious establishment when it repeatedly ignores the Torah precept "You shall not oppress a stranger, for you know the feelings of the stranger, having yourselves been strangers in the land of Egypt" (Exod. 23:9) is almost unbearable. Don Isaac Abravanel expanded on this notion in his commentary, explaining that this precept is

> a warning to the religious court . . . that when a convert comes before it for judgment they must not oppress him or coerce him and make him submit according to the strict letter of the law, even in those matters where it would be appropriate for a [born] Jew. They should treat him mildly and gently, because the convert's soul is suffering since he is in an alien land and he may think in his heart that you are pressuring him so hard because he is a stranger and alien. Consequently treat with him with kind and soft words—not that you should bend the law in his favor, but that you should treat him gently and not burden him.[1]

This moral attitude to the convert is characteristic of evolving Halakhah, which has the capacity to deal with problems of conversion and resolve the vast majority of them.

If the rabbinical courts and the rabbinate in Israel were to manifest the same consideration for the converts of our day, who in most cases have left their homelands, where they were members of the majority nationality and religion, to learn our language, customs, and laws, and encounter many problems, this situation would be inestimably better. Converts require sensitivity just as much as widows and orphans do. Abravanel interprets the approach of the Torah to mean that it does not *recommend* such conduct toward the convert, but *requires* it.

Indeed, over the years the debates and crises concerning the Law of Return have proliferated. There is no room here to relate all of them, given that many books have been written about the issue. Here I will concentrate on one case of conversion by way of investigating the meaning of the term *halakhic conversion*. In 1970, the Law of Return was amended to state that a Jew is a person born to a Jewish mother and who is not a member of another religion, or someone who has converted to Judaism, but the nature of the conversion was not defined by the law.[2]

8

Rabbi Goren's Reform Conversion

AFTER THE LATE DR. HELEN SEIDMAN WAS CONVERTED IN 1967 by the religious court of the Israel Council of Progressive Rabbis, the Israel Interior Ministry refused to record her as "Jewish" in the Population Registry.[1] Seidman petitioned the High Court of Justice to order the Minister of the Interior to register her as Jewish on the basis of her conversion. In 1970, the Attorney General informed the court that he found no legal basis to defend the minister's action. There was no doubt that the High Court was going to rule that the minister must register Helen Seidman as a Jew.

Minister Haim Moshe Shapira, the head of the Orthodox National Religious Party (NRP), and his party colleagues threatened a coalition crisis. Then, on June 15, 1970, Rabbi Shlomo Goren stepped into the breach and rescued the situation by convening an ad hoc religious court that took only three hours to convert Dr. Seidman anew.

As we shall see in this chapter, Rabbi Goren and his improvised *beit din* (religious court) in practice adopted the principles that Progressive Judaism applies to conversion. Nevertheless, the Regional Rabbinical Court and the Chief Rabbinate gave their full approval to Dr. Seidman's second conversion. My familiarity with the case stems from the fact that I guided and taught Dr. Seidman and, as head of the *beit din* of three Progressive rabbis, eventually converted her and her daughter Ruth.

All the signs indicate that the sole purpose of the Goren court's swift action was to enable the National Religious Party to remain in the coalition after it had threatened to bolt if Reform conversions were recognized for the purpose of Interior Ministry records. Because the Orthodox establishment contended that Reform conversion is *ipso facto* not according to Halakhah, Rabbi Goren's *beit din* had to convert her again in advance of her registration as a Jew. The express-lane proceeding averted a government crisis and allowed the NRP ministers to remain in the cabinet. The next day there was great rejoicing in the religious press; the main headline in the National Religious Party daily *Hazofeh* was "YOU ARE OUR SISTER!"

It is interesting to compare the approaches of Rabbi Goren's court and our Progressive court and see whether they meet the halakhic and moral criteria for conversion. We shall do so under five headings: (1) acceptance of the commandments, (2) marriage between a female convert and a *kohen*, (3) token circumcision, (4) conversion under duress, and (5) "express-lane" conversion. This will show what the two courts had in common and where they differed, thereby revealing the world views that underlie their actions.

ACCEPTANCE OF THE COMMANDMENTS

Halakhah requires that a convert undertake to accept the religious precepts of Judaism. The Gemara explicitly bans converting someone who rejects even one point of the Torah:

> One does not convert a non-Jew who comes to accept the Torah except for one point. Rabbi Jose son of Rabbi Judah says, even one refinement of a rabbinic precept (BT Bekhorot 30b).

On October 16, 1967, Dr. Seidman stood before the *beit din* of the Israel Movement for Progressive Judaism, to which she had applied for conversion because she was willing and able to accept the approach of Progressive Judaism to theology and observance of the commandments. Her intellectual honesty would not allow her to apply to an official rabbinical court, because she was unwilling to accept the commandments according to the Orthodox ideology. Her reasons had to do with her own worldview and the fact that she was a member of a secular kibbutz, Naḥal Oz, where Sabbath and *kashrut* (the dietary laws) are not observed and there is no ritual bath. (Incidentally, Dr. Seidman confirmed, the night before her reconversion by Rabbi Goren, that those were indeed her motives. She told me then that conversion by the Orthodox court would not prompt her to change her lifestyle and observe the commandments in accordance with the Orthodox interpretation. Dr. Seidman declared that she was already a Jew by virtue of her Progressive conversion. To undergo another conversion without believing in it would be hypocritical—but the pressure on her was intolerable.)

The Progressive *beit din* did not demand that she make commitments she would clearly be unable to keep. It relied on the sincerity of her desire to be affiliated with the Jewish people and to accept the Jewish religion and its commandments according to the views of Progressive Judaism. We examined her knowledge in several areas: religious precepts, both major and minor; the main tenets of Judaism; opinions and beliefs; laws and customs; history; the Bible; the Oral Law; the prayerbook, both the traditional and the Reform versions; blessings; and other matters. Dr. Seidman, who had studied for many months, had attained a mastery of these topics that satisfied Rabbi Goren's panel two and a half years later. She proved knowledgeable enough then for Rabbi Goren to convert her within three hours of his first meeting her, without demanding that she study further.

Of course, our *beit din* was not satisfied with quizzing her on the day of the conversion ceremony; we had insisted that she first go through a long process of studying and observing the commandments. We also required Dr. Seidman and her daughter Ruth to immerse themselves in a ritual bath. Then our court ruled that the two were righteous converts, and Dr. Seidman received the Hebrew name Rebecca daughter of Abraham. Not only did Rabbi Goren acquiesce in the Hebrew name given her by the Progressive *beit din;* he clearly accepted the fact that Dr. Seidman had accepted the commandments according to the views of Progressive Judaism, since she was going to continue living on her secular kibbutz and would not be observing the laws of family purity, Sabbath, and *kashrut* in the Orthodox manner.

Well-known Orthodox rabbis demurred at the manner of accepting the commandments in Rabbi Goren's rabbinical court. Rabbi Prof. David Bleich, the head of the Rabbi Yitzhak Elhanan Theological Seminary in New York, argued that

> All authorities agree that an application for conversion may justifiably be entertained only if the *beit din* is satisfied that upon conversion the candidate will become a God-fearing Jew and will scrupulously observe the commandments of the Torah. . . . All these authorities are in agreement that when it is evident that the candidate will be non-observant the conversion is null and void despite the candidate's oral declaration of acceptance of the yoke of *mitzvot.*[2]

Rabbi Bleich noted that even though Dr. Seidman's kibbutz was totally disregardful of the laws of *kashrut,* thereby casting some doubts on her intention to observe the commandments, Rabbi Goren had converted her on the basis of the fact that she was a vegetarian. According to Rabbi Bleich, this argument, though persuasive on the surface, is in fact deceptive. A vegetarian who lives on a secular kibbutz, where the kitchenware is presumed not to be kosher, cannot be considered to be observing *kashrut.*[3]

At a national conference on the Oral Law held several weeks after Dr. Seidman's second conversion, Rabbi Isser Yehuda Unterman, the chief rabbi, sharply criticized the whole affair. He clearly had Rabbi Goren and Dr. Seidman in mind, though he did not mention them by name:

> If a convert makes his home on a nonreligious kibbutz, it seems that even though he declares that he does not eat meat and will not work on the Sabbath we should say that he has not accepted the commandments. For if there is no observance of *kashrut*

where he lives it is forbidden to use their utensils; and even if he does not work on the Sabbath on a regular basis there will always be opportunities to desecrate the Holy Sabbath. It is hard to withstand these constant temptations.[4]

Rabbi Shlomo (Steven) Riskin, who was at the time rabbi of the Orthodox Lincoln Square Synagogue in Manhattan and a lecturer at Yeshiva University, challenged Rabbi Goren's action by juxtaposing it with a ruling issued by Rabbi Goren about a year after the Seidman conversion. In Rabbi Goren's well-known decision that removed the stigma of *mamzerut* from the Langer siblings, he nullified their mother's first marriage to a convert by holding that a convert who does not live in accordance with Halakhah and returns to his former lifestyle is no convert.[5] Rabbi Goren adduced rulings by Maimonides and Rabbi Joseph Caro and accepted the decision by Rabbi Meir Arik (1855–1926)[6] that when someone converts in order to marry a Jew, "if he conducts himself according to the Jewish religion the conversion is valid; otherwise, it is no conversion at all."[7]

We may indeed apply this ruling by Rabbi Goren to his own conversion of Dr. Seidman, who continued to observe the commandments in a manner not in accordance with the rules of the *Shulḥan Arukh*. In her case it was even clear in advance that there were some precepts she would not keep. If one adheres to the logic of his own Langer ruling, Rabbi Goren's conversion of Dr. Seidman was null and void.

If a conversion can be null and void because the convert does not observe the religious precepts, why didn't Rabbi Goren and his *beit din* devote more hours to teaching Seidman laws and customs? Why didn't they question her more meticulously until they were confident, with a reasonable degree of certainty,[8] that she would observe the commandments according to the Orthodox interpretation of Halakhah? His later ruling in the Langer case provided grounds for invalidating the conversion he performed at kibbutz Naal Oz. Rabbi Riskin, like others of his colleagues, was perplexed: "Unfortunately, [Rabbi Goren] has not yet penned a responsum explaining his action."[9]

This criticism is decisive, since without acceptance of the commandments in accordance with all precepts of Halakhah there is no conversion whatsoever, not even *post factum* (after the fact). One may, however, be more lenient with regard to other elements of the conversion procedure, such as circumcision and ritual immersion in the presence of the court. *Post factum*, we apply the principle that "he is a convert" (Maimonides, Laws of Forbidden Intercourse 13:18) to deficiencies in the various elements of the conversion process, "except for acceptance of the commandments, which is indispensable" for conversion and whose absence nullifies it (*Shulḥan Arukh, Y.D.* 268:3).[10] This means that if someone goes through the full rite of conversion before a *beit din* but does not accept the commandments, he or she is not a convert. But if a *beit din* recognizes someone as a convert, even though he was not properly circumcised or did not immerse himself before a religious court of three judges, but only in the presence of two ordinary Jews and at night (according to Halakhah, religious courts may sit only during daylight hours), he is nevertheless deemed to be a convert, *post factum.*

Perhaps Rabbi Goren took a leaf from the book of his future colleague in the Chief Rabbinate, Rabbi Ovadia Yosef, who had ruled leniently about converts accepted by the Karaites:

> There is no defect in their acceptance of the commandments, since the case does not resemble that of someone who does not accept one precept, rejecting it when, after having examined all the pros and cons, his feeble judgment decides against it. But this is not the case with these Karaites and those who join them, who do so because of their deficient knowledge.[11]

If a Karaite convert can be accepted by Rabbinite Jews even though the Karaites deny the validity of the Oral Law, Dr. Seidman's conversion by the Progressive *beit din* and by Rabbi Goren's religious court can be valid.[12]

Another possibility is that Rabbi Goren's court relied on a responsum by Rabbi David Zevi Hoffmann, the head of the Hildesheimer Yeshiva in Berlin, concerning the son of a Jewish father and non-Jewish mother, who, according to the questioner, "cannot be immersed to accept the commandments because he does not observe them." Rabbi Hoffmann replied that on one hand, converts are accepted *post factum* even if they were not informed of the rewards for observing the precepts and the punishment for violating them; on the other hand, acceptance of the commandments is a necessary step that if not done according to Halakhah, prevents conversion from taking effect. Nevertheless, Rabbi Hoffmann still had his doubts:

> In truth, for me the whole matter requires further consideration, for Maimonides wrote in Chapter 13 of the Laws of Forbidden Intercourse, *halakhah* 17: "It is obvious that informing him about the commandments is not indispensable. But how can he accept the commandments if he does not know them? It follows, then, *post factum,* that acceptance of the commandments is not indispensable either![13]

Rabbi Hoffmann recommended that the potential convert be taught the intellectual precepts that he was willing to accept in any case:

> The best course would be to teach him those precepts that he certainly wishes to accept, such as the bans on idolatry and illicit sexual relations and bloodshed, the precepts of charity and respect for one's parents and love for one's fellows, and the like. Then let him say simply that he accepts the precepts of the Jews. In any case none of this is indispensable.[14]

This is tantamount to saying that conversion is possible even if the candidate does not accept the commandments![15] Rabbi Hoffmann did indeed add that the matter "requires further deliberation but I do not have time to examine it now." Nevertheless he ruled as a practical matter, following the previous line of thought, that

> For the aforementioned reasons it seems to me that if he is immersed before three [judges] he is an undoubted convert, *post factum,* even if he did not accept the commandments.[16]

In a symposium held in the office of Rabbi Goren, then the chief rabbi of Tel Aviv, on January 27, 1972, I asked him about the halakhic problems associated with Dr. Seidman's conversion. He replied that he owed no one an explanation of the reasoning that led him to act as he had.[17]

Marriage of a Female Convert to a *Kohen*

In addition to the problems involved with Dr. Seidman's conversion per se, the Orthodox faced another serious obstacle. Her husband, Benjamin Seidman, is a *kohen,* and the Sages held that when the Torah states that a *kohen* may not marry a *zonah* (Lev. 21:7), the term also includes a female convert. Maimonides ruled that a female proselyte, "because she is not a natural-born Jew, is a *zonah* and forbidden to a *kohen*" (Maimonides, Laws of Forbidden Sexual Intercourse 18:3, based on BT Yevamot 60b). All subsequent decisors ruled similarly.

Rabbi Goren and his colleagues, like the Progressive *beit din,* converted Helen Seidman even though they knew that her husband was a *kohen* and she intended to continue living with him in contravention of the above ruling. Perhaps they relied on a resolution passed by a conference of Progressive rabbis in 1869, to the effect that a study of the sources leads to the conclusion that the ban on a marriage between a *kohen* and a female convert is no longer valid.[18] Or perhaps they were following another ruling by Rabbi David Zevi Hoffmann, who permitted the conversion of a non-Jewish woman who had married a *kohen* in a civil ceremony? One of the reasons Rabbi Hoffmann cited for his leniency was that "we may also fear that it would be a profanation of the Divine Name (*hillul Hashem*), Heaven forbid, if the woman had a nervous breakdown because she was not accepted, in that people would say that the Jews do not have mercy on a gentile woman."[19] Our own rabbis had studied these and other texts and ruled that, in the circumstances of the case, Helen Seidman should be allowed to convert.

The Progressive *beit din* not only converted Helen Seidman but immediately thereafter married her to her husband. In doing so we relied not only on the tenets of our own movement but also on a ruling by Rabbi Judah Leib Zirelson of Kishinev, who, when asked about a problematic case in Bulgaria, ruled that a *kohen* could marry a female convert. He held that it was a matter of saving lives and the couple must not be turned away. Rabbi Zirelson's innovation was that he defined the prohibition in question as rabbinic only, although a long line of codifiers, including Maimonides, Rabbi Joseph Caro, and others, had written that it was derived from the Torah. (There can be greater leniency with regard to waiving or bending rabbinic prohibitions.) Although Rabbi Zirelson hedged his ruling with strict limits to keep it from serving as a precedent, his responsum indicated that courage and scholarship can go a long way toward solving even such a difficult problem.[20]

It seems that here too Rabbi Goren accepted our outlook and halakhic position. His stance was clearly closer to ours than it was to the contemporary Orthodox consensus represented by Rabbi Bleich. The latter wrote that Helen Seidman's conversion in order to marry a *kohen* was *prima facie* evidence that she lacked a sincere intention to accept the commandments, since such a marriage is forbidden by Halakhah. He rejected the defense advanced by intimates of Rabbi Goren, namely, that many later decisors permit such marriages.[21] So far as Rabbi Bleich was concerned, Halakhah is crystal clear on this point: marriage between a *kohen* and a female convert is absolutely forbidden.[22]

TOKEN CIRCUMCISION

The media provided a detailed report of the conversion performed by Rabbi Goren, but omitted one small detail. His *beit din* did not insist that two-and-a-half-year-old Yehuda Seidman, born after his mother had been converted by Progressive rabbis, undergo a token circumcision (the removal of a drop of blood from the penis). If, as the religious establishment contends, that conversion was halakhically invalid, Rabbi Goren's *beit din* should have made him undergo token circumcision and then reconverted him (*Shulḥan Arukh, Y.D.* 208:3). If Rabbi Goren waived this step, one may presume that he accepted the validity of Dr. Seidman's conversion by our court, so that her son was born Jewish and there was no need for a token circumcision and conversion.

There may be another explanation. When a candidate for conversion has been circumcised in infancy in a *brit milah* ceremony—that is, the circumcision was carried out with the intention of fulfilling the religious rite of entering the Covenant of Abraham—the *beit din* of Progressive Judaism, relying on lenient rulings by eminent rabbis, tends to waive the requirement of token circumcision. Rabbi David Zevi Hoffmann was asked about the son of a non-Jewish woman who, according to his father, had been circumcised when he was eight days old; now the father wanted to have him immersed to be converted. Rabbi Hoffmann ruled that in this case there was no need for a token circumcision. If the circumciser knew that the infant was the son of a non-Jewish woman, he had undoubtedly circumcised him with conversion in mind. On the other hand,

> Even if you hold that the circumciser had no idea that the mother was not Jewish and thought that the infant was an undoubted Jew and did not circumcise him with conversion in mind, in any case and in every respect he circumcised him to fulfill the precept of circumcision.[23]

Obviously the precept of circumcision is the same for Jews and converts. According to Rabbi Hoffmann, the halakhic requirement that "a convert who is already circumcised must have a drop of blood drawn from him" applies only in the case of "an Arab who was circumcised or someone whose foreskin was removed for medical purposes and not with the precept in mind." In the case before him, the child was circumcised to fulfill the precept of circumcision. And in the case of circumcision "for the purpose of the precept of circumcision we have not heard that it is necessary to extract a drop of blood."[24]

The religious court of Progressive Judaism also relied on another halakhic precedent similar to the Seidman case. Rabbi Moshe Feinstein was asked about a woman who had undergone a Reform conversion. Some time later she bore a son

> who was deemed to be Jewish and circumcised as if he were Jewish. Now that they have become closer to God and His Torah, the woman agreed that her son should be immersed in the ritual bath, but did not want to have him undergo a token circumcision because the child is weak and will celebrate his bar mitzvah in a few days.[25]

In his responsum, Rabbi Feinstein stated that although, as a matter of principle, token circumcision was required, "in such a pressing case one may rely [on precedents and] not require a token circumcision, because he was circumcised for the sake of Judaism." The fact that the circumcision took place in a Reform community does not detract from it: "If three persons fit [to constitute a *beit din*] were present at the time of the circumcision, it is certainly valid; even if not, one can rely on the public knowledge that a circumcision was going to be performed."[26]

This responsum provides tacit recognition that *post factum,* a circumcision performed under Reform aegis can be recognized for the purpose of conversion. What is more, Rabbi Feinstein did not stipulate that the woman be converted again (this time by an Orthodox *beit din*) before her son could be converted, as religious courts in Israel demand of non-Jewish women before they will convert their children. Nevertheless, Rabbi Feinstein concluded his responsum with a recommendation that "the mother, too, because she is held to be a full convert, should be urged to immerse herself in accordance with the law."

These are the precedents and principles that guide the Progressive *beit din* in Israel. It is possible that Rabbi Goren, too, accepted them when he did not require that young Yehuda Seidman undergo token circumcision or immersion for the sake of conversion.

Yet, there seems to have been some other explanation for his leniency. A more likely reason was that Yehuda, unlike his mother
and sister, was already registered as a Jew by birth in the records of
the Interior Ministry. Because there was no threat that the High
Court of Justice would order that his registration be changed, converting him was irrelevant for saving the coalition.

With regard to each of the three elements of conversion analyzed
above, there was a grave contradiction between Rabbi Goren's declared intentions and his deeds. One one hand, he announced publicly that he was acting in order to repair the imperfection of the
conversion performed by our religious court, because in his eyes
the conversion was not according to Halakhah. On the other hand,
in practice he adopted our position with regard to acceptance of
the commandments, the conversion of a woman married to a
kohen, and token circumcision. But one cannot have it both ways.
If Progressive Judaism's approach to conversion is invalid because it
is not halakhic, then Rabbi Goren's reconversion of Helen Seidman
was equally invalid. If, however, the Progressive approach that was
appropriated by Rabbi Goren is correct and its conversions are
valid, there was no halakhic need for a second conversion. Rabbi
Goren could have offered one of two answers: (1) Conversion by
Progressive Judaism is invalid—but then so was his conversion,
since he adopted our approach. (2) The Progressive *beit din* converted Dr. Seidman in accordance with Halakhah—in which case
the second conversion was quite superfluous.[27]
     Despite the similarity in our procedures, I cannot omit men-
tion of at least two points where the Progressive rabbinate was
stricter than Rabbi Goren.

CONVERSION UNDER DURESS

No one ever doubted that Dr. Seidman agreed to the second
conversion because of the massive pressure exerted on her to save
the coalition. Government circles pressured the kibbutz association

to which her kibbutz belonged, and this in turn squeezed her own kibbutz, Naḥal Oz, to persuade her, using psychological pressure, to help save the coalition and convert a second time. Helen Seidman told me several times, including the night before the short-cut procedure, that she did not want to convert a second time. In her eyes, she and her children had been Jews since her conversion by the Progressive religious court three years earlier. If she could withstand the fierce pressure, she said, she would not convert again. Unfortunately, she could not withstand the pressure.

The Talmud refers to people who convert to Judaism under duress or out of fear as "lion" proselytes (BT Yevamot 24b). According to Rashi's commentary there, such converts are like the Samaritans, of whom we read in the Bible that "the Lord sent lions against them which killed some of them" (2 Kings 17:25), after which the survivors converted: "They worshipped the Lord" (v. 32).

The religious court of the Progressive Movement never accepts converts if it discovers that their application is involuntary and not in keeping with their conscience and belief and was submitted as a result of inadmissible outside pressures that have nothing to do with acceptance of the Jewish faith. On this matter we are punctilious and unshakable. We investigate and interrogate until we are convinced of the petitioner's sincere desire to join the Jewish people, in accordance with Maimonides' ruling that "when a potential convert comes to convert the proper way is to investigate whether . . . he has come to enter Judaism out of fear" (Laws of Forbidden Intercourse 13,14).

AN EXPRESS-LANE CONVERSION

Rabbi Goren's special religious court converted Helen Seidman in the space of three hours. Our *beit din* never performs a conversion within a few hours of its first meeting with the candidate. As noted above, we demand that candidates demonstrate a profound knowledge of Judaism, since we believe that it is important for them to be fully cognizant of the significance of the Jewish religion, its beliefs, and its precepts, both for themselves and for the Jewish people they are joining. Accordingly, conversions that we perform in Israel are predicated on candidates' spending an average of a year (depending on their prior knowledge, ability, and circumstances) to learn the material and become accustomed to the traditional ambiance of the Sabbath and festivals and the cycle of Jewish life, and then being circumcised and immersing in a ritual bath. We encourage candidates and welcome them cordially, as tradition demands, and promise them that if they sincerely comply with our requirements and master the material within a reasonable period of time they will be accepted into our faith, pursuant to Maimonides' principles for making them aware of the commandments:

> We inform him of the main tenets of the faith, namely, the Oneness of God and the prohibition of idolatry and go on about this at length. We inform him of some of the lesser precepts and some of the major precepts, but do not go on about this at length. . . . We inform him of the punishment for [transgressing] the precepts . . . but not of too many and not in excessive detail, lest this trouble him and divert him from the good path to a bad path. For initially one leads a person with kind and soft words only (Laws of Forbidden Intercourse 14:2).

There is no doubt that our religious court adhered to these requirements more meticulously than Rabbi Goren's *beit din* did.

Rabbi Goren seems to have considered it acceptable to ignore certain fundamental principles or dismiss them cavalierly, whereas Progressive Judaism is extremely strict about them, in accordance with the spirit of Halakhah. Nevertheless there are many points where our form of conversion is very similar to Rabbi Goren's, who adopted our approach in this case.

If we ignore his serious deviations from Halakhah and its intentions, as well as the substantive difference in our approaches and outlooks, in this particular case we Progressive rabbis could have saluted Rabbi Goren—just as *Hazofeh* greeted Helen Seidman—"You are our brother!"

The Lesser of Two Evils

In chapter 2 we examined a responsum by Maimonides in which he permitted a young man to free his slave woman and then marry her. Some contemporary scholars have mistakenly read the responsum as dealing with conversion.[28] Although this is clearly not what Maimonides had in mind, modern decisors have cited the responsum in lenient decisions about conversion.

Maimonides wrote the responsum sometime between his arrival in Egypt in 1165 and his death in 1204. As far as can be determined, it was never mentioned or quoted by any of his contemporaries or by rabbis of the ensuing centuries. The manuscript of the responsum dropped out of sight for four centuries.[29]

In 1765, about six hundred years after its composition, Rabbi Isaac ben Mordecai Tamah of Amsterdam translated the responsum from an old manuscript and published it in his collection of Maimonides' responsa, *Pe'er ha-dor*. Although the responsum was now accessible to rabbis and scholars, yet another century passed before it began to be cited as a precedent in halakhic literature. The first respondent to cite it as a precedent was Rabbi Abraham Palache (1809–1899), the chief rabbi of Izmir. He was asked about a gentile woman who had lived with a Jew and then converted to Judaism. Could the couple marry now? Rabbi Palache, after an extensive display of brilliant reasoning, permitted the marriage. He triumphantly quoted Maimonides' responsum about the young man and his slave woman.[30]

Palache's responsum was followed by a steady stream of responsa by Sephardi and Ashkenazi rabbis who quoted Maimonides' ruling about the slave woman as a precedent for conversion-related cases. Why did this halakhic ruling enjoy new popularity after more than six hundred years? How should we explain the resurrection of a responsum that had previously not been part of the process of the halakhic debate?

The initial silence of the rabbinic world, after the first publication of the responsum in 1765, may be accounted for by the fact that slavery among Jews was no longer prevalent, and questions about young masters and female slaves were quite rare. Since there were few, if any, questions on this subject, no responsa were written on the issue, and Maimonides' precedent was not needed.

However, with the onset of the Enlightenment and the Emancipation, Jewish communities began to face a new problem: intermarriage and conversion for the sake of marriage. Although Maimonides was not writing about conversion in the responsum, in the *Mishneh Torah* he set forth the close parallel between a slave woman who was freed and a gentile woman who converted.[31] It was thus only reasonable for learned decisors to transform Maimonides' six-century-old decision and apply it to their current halakhic needs.[32]

A brief quote from a responsum by Chief Rabbi Ben-Zion Meir Ḥai Uziel (1890–1953) may give us an idea of this transformation. Rabbi Uziel was asked whether it was permissible to convert a gentile woman who had married a Jew in a civil ceremony. Despite the many halakhic difficulties involved, he relied on Maimonides' ruling to overcome all obstacles:

> Our generation is experiencing a disaster with mixed marriages performed under civil auspices. Hence in many instances we must convert the man or the woman in order to save the Jewish woman or man from the sin of living with a gentile. We act in this way to save their children, too, who would otherwise be lost for Israel. We rely on the responsum of our rabbi and light, Maimonides of blessed memory.[33]

In this case, as in that of the Seidmans, we may hear the voice of Maimonides resounding through the centuries: "Gently and with tenderness we help him to marry her."

Afterword

ABOUT TWO YEARS AFTER I FIRST PUBLISHED MOST OF THE material incorporated in this chapter,[34] a pamphlet appeared opposing Rabbi Goren's candidacy for Chief Rabbi of Israel. The authors were prominent Ultra-Orthodox rabbis and yeshiva deans, including Rabbi Yehezkel Abramsky, the president of the Committee of Yeshivot; Rabbi Yaakov Yisrael Kanievsky; Rabbi Eliezer Menahem Shach, head of the Ponevezh Yeshiva; Rabbi Haim Shmuelevich, head of the Mir Yeshiva; Rabbi Moshe Hevroni, head of the Hevron Yeshiva; Rabbi Yosef Shalom Eliashiv, a member of the Supreme Rabbinical Court; and Rabbi Shlomo Zalman Auerbach, head of the Kol Torah Yeshiva. These rabbis referred, among other things, to my article about Rabbi Goren. They wrote:

> It is instructive that the express conversion conducted by Rabbi Goren for Helen Seidman gave new encouragement to the Reform in this country, to the point that "Rabbi" Moshe Zemer published an article in *Petahim* (Elul 5730 [September 1970]) in which he proclaims: "You are our brother," because "Rabbi Goren performs a Reform conversion." It is most interesting to quote from his article, in which he proves that in practice Rabbi Goren adopted the "principles of Reform conversion."[35]

The authors quoted almost my entire article in order to demonstrate the strong similarity, if not indeed identity, between Rabbi Goren's approach to Halakhah and mine. Did the Ultra-Orthodox rabbis responsible for this pamphlet understand that my criticism of Rabbi Goren far outweighed my praise for his acting in a way similar to our own *beit din?* Or did they see my essay as "acclamation," which in their eyes is really damnation, because it issued from the pen of a non-Orthodox rabbi?[36]

9

Ambivalence about Conversion

IN THE TWELFTH CENTURY, A RABBI IN THE LAND OF ISRAEL humiliated a proselyte by denigrating the allegedly idolatrous practices of his Muslim ancestors. The convert, Obadiah Ger-Tzedek ("the righteous proselyte"), complained to Maimonides, who reprimanded the rabbi and warned him that the Torah commands us to treat proselytes with tenderness and understanding.[1]

Eight hundred years have passed since then; yet, prospective converts are still being abused by rabbis all over the world. In some countries, candidates must traverse an arduous obstacle course before conversion. In others, rabbinical courts simply do not perform conversions at all.[2]

CONVERSION FOR AN ULTERIOR MOTIVE

One key to the ambivalent attitude toward converts is the principal requirement for conversion, *kabbalat 'ol hamitzvot* (accepting the yoke of the commandments), the sincere acceptance of the religion of Israel and its precepts. The oldest halakhic sources forbade conversion to Judaism for ulterior motives such as marriage.

The second-century sage Rabbi Nehemiah ruled that a person who converted for any extraneous reason—including a man who converted for the sake of a woman or a woman who converted for the sake of a man—is not a valid proselyte. Later, however, it was stipulated in the name of the third-century *amora* Rav that despite the ban on accepting proselytes with an ulterior motive their conversions, once performed, are valid.[3]

Over the centuries this *ab initio* prohibition was frequently circumvented. Not long before the expulsion from Spain, Rabbi Solomon b. Simeon Duran (the Rashbash, 1400–1467) of Algeria was asked about the return of *conversos* (marranos) and their descendants to Judaism. In his responsum, he quoted the codified Halakhah that it is forbidden to accept a person who wishes to convert to Judaism for any ulterior motive. He maintained, however, that this stricture applies only to gentiles without Jewish ancestors. By contrast, a candidate from among the *conversos* or their descendants is to be accepted in all cases. We are in fact obligated to draw them near and bring them under the wings of the *shekhinah* (the Divine Presence).[4]

The tosafists,[5] in their commentary on the talmudic debate between the positions of Rabbi Nehemiah and Rav, ask a pointed question: If conversion for an ulterior motive is not allowed, how could Hillel the Elder have accepted the gentile who came to him with the demand, "Convert me so that I may be High Priest"?[6] Their reply: Hillel was certain that this man's conversion would eventually prove to be for the sake of Heaven. A similar case involved the Roman courtesan who wished to convert to Judaism in order to marry a student in the yeshiva of the third-century *amora* Rabbi Ḥiyya; he accepted her because he was certain that ultimately she would become a sincere convert.[7]

How can one determine the intention *(kavvanah)* of a prospective convert and whether he or she will accept a fully Jewish way of life? How can we evaluate a candidate's sincerity, which is a "matter of the heart," part of his or her inner being, in the realm of thoughts and conscience that are not readily apparent? Rabbi Joseph Caro ruled that the *beit din,* the rabbinical court, possessed all the tools needed to determine whether a candidate would indeed be a sincere convert to Judaism. His conclusion was that "everything depends upon the discretion of the *beit din.*"[8]

THE NEGATIVE ATTITUDE TOWARD CONVERTS

In contrast to these affirmative attitudes, we also find a strand of antagonism toward the whole idea of conversion and converts. The third-century *amora* Rabbi Isaac, for example, said that "evil after evil comes upon those who receive proselytes. . . . [This can be deduced from a statement] of Rabbi Helbo, who said that proselytes are as troublesome to Israel as a skin disease" (BT Yevamot 109b).[9]

Why does evil come upon those who accept proselytes? Why are converts such a burden to Israel? The commentators offered several explanations.

Rabbi Isaac ben Samuel, a twelfth-century tosafist, explained that the warning against accepting converts referred to gentiles who were enticed to convert or were accepted at once, without fulfilling any of the requirements of conversion. Nonetheless, concluded the rabbi, we *must* receive gentiles who make a serious effort to convert.[10]

Elsewhere the tosafists offer an interesting explanation of why proselytes cause problems for born Jews. There are twenty-four (some say thirty-six) passages in Scripture that forbid us to mistreat converts. It is impossible for born Jews to fulfill all these commandments and not grieve converts![11]

Others say that converts are indirectly responsible for Israel's dispersion among the nations. This is deduced from one talmudic rationale for the Diaspora: "Why is Israel dispersed among all the nations more than are the gentiles? So that proselytes may join them" (BT Pesaḥim 87b).

Rashi maintained that the problem with converts is that they are not meticulous enough in their observance of the commandments. Born Jews who associate with them may be attracted to their ways and learn from their deeds (Rashi on Kiddushin 70b, s.v. *kashim*).

In Praise of Proselytes

Another tosafist, Rabbi Abraham the Proselyte, turned Rashi's reasoning upside down: Since converts have been taught to be experts in the commandments and are scrupulous to observe them, their piety stands in contrast to the backsliding Jews who do not act in accordance with God's will (Tosefot on Kiddushin 70b–71a, s.v. *kashim*).

Similarly, we find that tannaitic sources are almost unanimous in their praise of converts. The *Mekhilta,* a halakhic midrash traditionally dated to the second century C.E., declares that "proselytes are beloved" and proceeds to cite more than twenty Scriptural passages that enjoin us to deal generously with them.

Quoting the archetypal proof text for the appropriate behavior toward proselytes—"You shall not wrong a *ger* [literally 'stranger,' but also the standard Hebrew word for 'convert'], neither shall you oppress him, for you were *gerim* in the Land of Egypt" (Exod. 22:20)—the *Mekhilta* expounds: "'You shall not wrong him'— with words; 'neither shall you oppress him'—in money matters." The *Mekhilta* further admonishes us not to remind proselytes of their pagan past.[12]

The *Mitzvah* of Accepting Converts

Individual rabbis' view of converts as beneficial or harmful to Israel may be related to their opinion on a crucial issue. Is the admission of a non-Jew to Judaism a matter of the preferences of the local *beit din*? Or is it rather a positive precept to accept candidates for conversion and bring them into the Jewish fold? That is, are we commanded to convert gentiles to Judaism?

According to Maimonides, the verse "and you shall love the Lord your God . . ." (Deut. 5:5) "commands us to seek out and call upon all humankind to serve God and believe in Him. . . . When you truly love God . . . you undoubtedly search for unbelievers and the unlearned and bring them to knowledge of the truth that you have acquired."[13]

Maimonides goes on to quote the halakhic midrash *Sifre* on Deuteronomy:

> "And you shall love the Lord your God." . . . Make Him beloved by all His creatures, as did Abraham your father. . . . Just as Abraham loved God . . . and with his great understanding and faith sought out people [and led them] to the faith strengthened in His love, so shall you love God until you seek out and call mankind unto Him.[14]

Some commentators explain Maimonides' interpretation of this commandment as a call to receive converts and bring them into the fold: "This teaches that Abraham, our father, converted them and brought them under the wings of the Divine Presence."[15]

The eleventh-century scholar and poet Isaac ben Reuben of Barcelona listed the conversion of gentiles as a positive commandment, based on another verse: "You shall love the *ger*" (Deut. 10:19). As he phrased it in one of his liturgical poems,

> The proselyte who comes to be converted shall take refuge with you. When he says to you, "I shall take shelter with you," the [members of the *beit din*] will accept him and inform him of some of the light and some of the stringent commandments, lest he change his mind and say, "What have I done? I cannot go with these, for I am not used to them" (1 Sam. 17:39).[16]

Another Spanish sage, Rabbi Simeon ben Zemaḥ Duran (the Rashbatz, 1361–1444), was

> astonished that the acceptance of converts is not included in the list of [the 613] commandments. It is certainly a precept addressed to the *beit din* to accept converts and not to reject them, as we learn in the Talmud (BT Yevamot 47b): Once a prospective convert has accepted the yoke of the commandments, we circumcise him *immediately*, because "the performance of a mitzvah must not in any way be delayed."[17]

In the view of the Rashbatz, accepting proselytes is a positive commandment incumbent upon a *beit din*. Because it cannot be derived from any other precept, it should be counted independently, as a separate commandment in its own right, in the traditional number of the 613 Torah commandments.[18]

As we have seen, Jewish tradition incorporates contradictory and ambivalent attitudes toward conversion and proselytes, ranging from dire warnings of peril for rabbis who accept converts, and for the Jewish people as a whole, to the position that the Torah commands us to convert non-Jews. Which of these are merely the individual opinions of various Sages, and which inform the codified Halakhah that obligates later generations? How are they reflected in contemporary practice?

AN ETERNAL BAN ON CONVERSION

The negative approach to proselytes found its most radical expression in the total ban on conversion promulgated in Argentina in 1927 by Rabbi Saul David Setton (1851–1930), spiritual leader of the Syrian Jewish community of Buenos Aires.[19] The interdiction applied to all of Argentina "until the end of time" and is for the most part still observed by the Orthodox community in that country.[20]

Rabbi Setton's stated reason for forbidding conversions was that "life in [Buenos Aires] is exceedingly wanton, and everyone does as he pleases; there is no rabbi serving the Jewish community whose authority is respected by the government or any other party." One of the co-sponsors of the decree was Rabbi Aaron Goldman (1854–1932), who provided its halakhic and ideological foundation. Goldman, an outstanding talmudic scholar born in Russia, had in 1889 become the founder and spiritual leader of Moisesville, a Jewish colony about 375 miles north of Buenos Aires.

Goldman had no doubts as to why Jewish men in Argentina wanted to have their gentile wives converted:

"I was startled to hear and alarmed to see" (Isaiah 21:3) the news about the state of affairs in the land, namely, that there are men who have thrown off the yoke of Heaven. They have taken gentile wives and have fathered children from them. Then, to cover up their wantonness, they wish to have their alien wives and foreign children accepted as converts and included in the Congregation of Israel. . . . Who would be such a fool as to be taken in by their declaration that they sincerely wish to convert their alien wives and foreign children, since all their trickery and deceit are nothing but an attempt to whitewash their irresponsibility, in order to obtain religious sanction?[21]

Setton, who promulgated and implemented the "eternal" ban, had not always been opposed to conversion in his community. In 1915, acting on behalf of a *beit din* in Buenos Aires, he asked Goldman to assist in the conversion of a Syrian Arab who was living in their community. Setton warmly recommended this prospective convert, whose motivation was for the sake of Heaven. "Our hopes are great that you will promptly do everything and even more, . . . for it is known how great is the precept [of conversion] and its reward."[22]

In response, Goldman stated that it was impossible to accept proselytes in Argentina, because the rabbinic sources stipulate that the *beit din* must inform the prospective convert of some aspects of the punishment for violating the commandments, such as desecrating the Sabbath and eating forbidden foods.[23]

To my consternation, and that of every upright person, the scourge has spread here; many of our brethren have abandoned the Torah, and stringent precepts like the desecration of the Sabbath have become the lightest of the light. These violators so outnumber us that if one should find a Jew who keeps the Sabbath and the like, he would be considered on a par with a saint. There are so few that a child could make a list.

Now imagine that we warn the convert concerning all the above [precepts]. Afterwards, when he sees with his own eyes how many of our brothers trespass everything with contempt, he will surely ask: "What was all this that the rabbis of Israel

warned us? Is not the House of Israel just like all the gentiles?"
Are we not then responsible when, God forbid, he vilifies all the
disciplines of Judaism? . . . Therefore I'll have nothing to do
with this case.[24]

Goldman held an absolutist view. He insisted that converts could
be accepted only if they lived in a community where there was widespread observance of the commandments. Of course, such an environment was not to be found in the cities of Argentina at that time.

Absolutists frequently demand the fulfillment of conditions
and prerequisites that cannot be reasonably met. Rabbi Goldman
was not willing to accept even the finest candidate possible, because there was no sufficiently observant Jewish community where
he could live in Argentina. Conversion is indeed permitted by Halakhah; Goldman could not abrogate it by fiat. By raising insur-
mountable halakhic obstacles, however, he effectively eliminated
the possibility of conversion for those who accepted his authority.

This extremely stringent view led to the radical decree banning
conversion throughout Argentina for all time. The ban was ex-
ported to the United States as well, where it was adopted by the
Syrian Jewish community of Brooklyn in 1935, in the form that
"no future Rabbinic Council will have the right or authority to
convert non-Jews who seek to marry into our community." The
Buenos Aires ban on all conversions for all Jews everywhere in Argentina was later moderated into a prohibition against accepting
converts who wanted to marry into the Syrian and Sephardic Jewish communities of Brooklyn. The ban was reconfirmed and signed
by all the rabbis and lay leaders of the Syrian and Near Eastern
Jewish communities of the New York area, with added warnings
and proclamations, in 1946, 1972, and again in 1984.[25]

The Ambivalent Chief Rabbi

In the mid-1940s Rabbi Mordecai Jacob Breisch, the head of the
beit din in Zurich, proclaimed a ban on conversion for the sake of

marriage.[26] He wrote to the Chief Rabbi of Eretz Yisrael, Yitzhak Isaac Herzog, to request his support for the campaign by the Orthodox community of Switzerland against such conversions. Breisch published Herzog's 1947 responsum, which fully justified the total war against conversion waged by Breisch and his rabbinic colleagues:

> Although Halakhah has determined that those who convert for ulterior motives and not for the sake of Heaven are nevertheless proselytes *post factum,* I have a compelling reason to assert that this is not the law today. In the past, almost every Jew was constrained to observe the commandments; otherwise he would be rejected and held in contempt. This social situation strengthened the assumption that the gentile who had come to convert to Judaism was truly resolved to keep the Sabbath, etc. . . . But the situation is different today; it is possible to be a Jewish leader even though one desecrates the Sabbath and eats forbidden foods in public. Therefore, how can we make the assumption that the gentile has resolved, even if only at the time of conversion, to observe Judaism? This is especially so when the overwhelming majority of (and perhaps all) proselytes of this kind do not even begin to keep the fundamentals of our religion.[27]

Rabbi Herzog found grounds for revising the lenient talmudic ruling so as to justify the exclusion of prospective converts in this day and age. David Ellenson has analyzed his motives and the sociological background of this responsum:

> Herzog clearly viewed conversion in cases such as this as causing intermarriage rather than regarding them as a logical outcome of social conditions where Jews and gentiles socially interacted with one another. Hence he felt these conversions attenuated the strength of Judaism in the contemporary setting. . . . Herzog's responsum obviously stands as a stringent interpretation of, and perhaps even expansion on, Jewish law in this field. It reflects the embattled position Orthodox rabbinic authorities perceived themselves as occupying vis-à-vis the non-observant Jewish community and, as such, it represents the ever-increasing

polarity between Orthodox and non-Orthodox Jewries in the contemporary world.[28]

As Ellenson shows here and elsewhere, halakhic decisions cannot be understood in terms of rabbinic law alone but must be studied in the context of the sociological and organizational needs of the decisor and those whose position he supports.[29]

But when it came to a particular case, Rabbi Herzog had written a very different responsum on the same subject. He was asked about the validity of the conversion of a gentile woman who had married a Jew in a civil ceremony. Could this woman have a Jewish marriage with her spouse? In a closely reasoned responsum, written in 1941, the Chief Rabbi relied, as others have done, on the responsum by Maimonides that permitted a man to free his non-Jewish slave and then marry her, in clear contravention of talmudic law.[30] Rabbi Herzog held that "according to the situation, there are times one should waive such prohibitions so that a Jew will not be mired in sin." Furthermore, "a great deal depends on the judgment of the decisor and on his intention for the sake of Heaven."[31] Finally:

> If they were coming to ask whether to convert her or not, we would say, "convert her so that she may be married," for it is certain that they will not separate from one another and [then] the [Jewish] man would remain in a permanent state of sin, having marital relations with a non-Jewish woman. . . . Since the conversion was permitted even before the fact, it is obvious that they may have a Jewish wedding.[32]

Rabbi Herzog seems to be contradicting himself. How are we to explain the diametrically opposed approaches to conversion reflected in these two responsa, written only six years apart? Was Rabbi Herzog more lenient in this 1941 case because it related to a situation in the Land of Israel?

In the second section of this permissive responsum, however, Rabbi Herzog changed his tone and wrote in a manner that foreshadowed his reply to Rabbi Breisch:

Although the halakhah is in accordance with those who say that they are all converts (*post factum,* even if they converted for an extraneous purpose), nevertheless I have doubts about such conversions in our day; because in the days of the Sages and the Decisors, of blessed memory, there was almost no room within the Congregation of Israel for a nonobservant Jew. Therefore it was permissible to accept the promise of a convert to keep the mitzvot, even if there was a material motive for his conversion, because otherwise his existence would be precarious. However, to our great distress, the situation is so riotous today that Jews according to Halakhah are among the most unobservant of Israel, and many of them are leaders of communities, and even leaders of our nation. . . . Why should this gentile keep the commandments when so many Jews are not observant? . . . The [convert's] acceptance of the commandments is suspect when there is an ulterior motive for the conversion. . . . We must therefore deem these persons doubtful proselytes. The ruling must change when they come to us for conversion. We must reject them because . . . we would be allowing an admixture of the offspring of doubtful gentiles in Israel.[33]

Apparently, then, Rabbi Herzog was consistent in his basically negative position about conversion for the sake of marriage. Even while finding other halakhic precedents to justify permission for conversion and marriage in certain circumstances, he considered it necessary to qualify his leniency with the same caveat he later sent to the Swiss rabbis.

In December 1948, Rabbi Herzog wrote another lenient responsum in which he permitted the conversion of gentile women married to Jews "not for the sake of Heaven, but for the purpose of *aliya* to Eretz Yisrael."[34] After finding halakhic grounds for acceding to their request, he appended an almost identical admonition about the grave dangers of accepting proselytes.[35]

One key to Rabbi Herzog's ambivalent approach may be the identity of the questioner in each case. The Ultra-Orthodox rabbis of Switzerland were seeking his approval and support for their holy war against conversion. In this context he was more than willing to repeat his declaration of opposition to the acceptance of proselytes.

A decisor is not necessarily an impartial judge. Sometimes he is an advocate trying to help colleagues involved in halakhic polemics: responsa frequently involve advocacy.

In the specific cases mentioned above, where the women already had Jewish husbands, Rabbi Herzog issued lenient responsa. In these cases he also gave the answers that the women and his rabbinic questioners wished to hear. Even though he felt duty bound to repeat his reservations about the halakhic validity of conversion, he cited and ruled in accordance with halakhic decisions rendered by decisors in the nineteenth and twentieth centuries. In all these responsa the questioner received the reply, positive or negative, that was desired.

THE AFFIRMATIVE APPROACH TO CONVERSION

In his permissive decisions, Rabbi Herzog was in the excellent company of decisors like Rabbi Jehiel Jacob Weinberg (the last head of the Hildesheimer Rabbinical Seminary in Berlin) and others. These respondents stated that in the case of a gentile who was married to a Jew in a civil ceremony, the desire to convert should not be construed as impelled solely by the ulterior motive of marriage, since the couple were already living together and were legally married in the eyes of the civil authorities; they would not separate even if the conversion request were denied.[36]

Sephardi Chief Rabbi Ben-Zion Uziel actually expressed a sympathetic view of such a relationship:

> This woman is already married to a Jew. When she enters the Covenant of Judaism, she will draw closer and closer to the family of her husband and his Torah. Furthermore, her children and those who will be born to her in the future will be full-fledged Jews. This is like the actions of Hillel and Rabbi Ḥiyya, who were certain that in the end they would be proper proselytes. We are commanded to bring them closer and admit them into the covenant of the Torah of Israel.[37]

As we have seen, rabbis throughout the ages were disquieted by the insincere convert. What happens if a *beit din* errs when it accepts a candidate for conversion? Rabbi Elijah Guttmacher of Graditz (or Graetz, 1796–1874) maintained that rabbis should accept the convert even if they are not sure about the candidate's sincerity:

> If it is not certain that the candidate is acting from an ulterior motive, we must accept him, because we would be more liable if we rejected him than if we accepted him as a convert without halakhic justification. . . . If he misled us by saying that he is converting for the sake of Heaven, but he lied, and we accepted him on this basis, why the great commotion? We have found [in the Talmud and *Shulḥan Arukh* that there were similar cases not for the sake of heaven], and the *beit din* knew it and transgressed and accepted them as converts. Hence our candidate would be a full convert. All the more so, then, that if the *beit din* relied on his lie and thought he told the truth, there is no curse upon them.[38]

What is it that leads decisors to acceptance or rejection of converts? It may be the individual rabbi's attitude toward gentiles in general. It may stem from how a particular generation of Jews was treated by the surrounding gentile society. Often the decisive factor may be the respondent's general approach to halakhic ruling— open and accepting, as reflected in the decisions by Rabbis Guttmacher and Uziel, or hostile and excluding, as manifested by the rulings of Rabbis Goldman and Breisch. The negative attitude may be derived from a sincere belief that conversion is the *cause* of intermarriage rather than its result. Whatever the motivation and whatever the decision, there are ample precedents to support almost any ruling the decisor chooses to issue.

Perhaps the most appropriate resolution of this issue is found in Maimonides' responsum to Obadiah the Proselyte, where he gives his definition of a sincere convert as

> a person who has left his parents and native land and the sovereignty of his people, who are ruling; who by his understanding heart, has adhered to a people that is so abused and persecuted,

because he learned to . . . recognize that their religion represents truth and righteousness and recognized all this and followed after the Lord and entered beneath the wings of the Divine Presence . . . desiring His commandments and lifting up his heart to draw near to God in the light of the living. . . . God calls him the disciple of our father Abraham, who left his parents and birthplace and turned to the Lord.[39]

10

Disqualifying Jews from India to Ethiopia

MUST THE ETHIOPIAN IMMIGRANTS BE CONVERTED?

The conversion-related problems discussed in the previous chapters concern Jews all over the world. By contrast, the question of the conversion of the Ethiopian immigrants is unique.

Should the Ethiopian immigrants be made to undergo a token conversion as a condition for being accepted as full-fledged Jews? According to Halakhah as codified over the generations, are the newcomers from Ethiopia—the Beta Israel community—considered to be non-Jews or of doubtful lineage, so that only circumcision, immersion in a ritual bath, and acceptance of the commandments can bring them into the Covenant?

This does seem to be the conclusion of a document published in 1986 by the Chief Rabbinate, entitled "Guidelines for Marriage Registrars Concerning the Status of Ethiopian Jews." According to these guidelines, approved at a session of the Chief Rabbinate Council in late 1985:

> Because [the Ethiopians] have been cut off from the centers of Jewish life and Torah for generations, they have forgotten many of the basic tenets of Judaism. This protracted separation has

caused halakhic problems, chiefly with regard to their marriages, because many non-Jews have commingled with them over the generations, in a way that makes it impossible to clarify and prove their identity with certainty. Questions of lineage also arise because of the marriage and divorce procedures followed in their community. . . . Because of these doubts, acceptance of the commandments, circumcision, and immersion in a ritual bath (without a blessing) before three rabbis will be required of everyone who comes to register for marriage. . . . If it is proven that the applicant was circumcised according to Halakhah he will be required only to accept the commandments and immerse himself in a ritual bath.[1]

Is the Chief Rabbinate's attitude toward this community justified? Do the Beta Israel really have to convert to Judaism? To answer this question, we must briefly review the halakhic precedents relating to this community.

The rabbis' ambivalence about these dark-skinned Jews goes as far back as the first clear reference to them, in the writings of Rabbi David ben Zimra (the Radbaz), one of the leading rabbis of Egypt and the Land of Israel in the fifteenth and sixteenth centuries. He described them as

Israelites from the Tribe of Dan. Evidently they belong to the sect of Zadok and Boethus who are known as Karaites, because they do not know the Oral Law and do not light candles on Sabbath Eve.[2]

This classification of the Ethiopian Jews as Karaites would have made it extremely difficult for the Rabbanites to accept them. In another responsum, however, the Radbaz cleared them of this taint:

As for those who come from Ethiopia, . . . because there were no scholars among them who were learned in the Oral Tradition, they adopted the plain meaning of Scripture. If, however, someone had taught them they would not have spurned the words of our rabbis. Hence they are like an infant taken captive among the gentiles. Know that Zadok and Boethus lived in the time of the Second Temple, but the Tribe of Dan was exiled earlier [with the other northern tribes before the destruction of the First Temple].[3]

Nevertheless, he raised a serious problem, one that has continued to vex rabbis until the present:

> With regard to their lineage, however, I am apprehensive that although their marriages may be valid, their bills of divorce are not in accordance with the regulations of the Sages, because they know nothing of the form of bills of divorce and [the regulations of] marriage.[4]

In other words, marriages among Ethiopian Jews may be halakhically valid, but not their divorces. If a husband divorces his wife she remains married to him, in the eyes of Halakhah, because the form of the divorce is not as stipulated by Halakhah; thus, any children she might later have by another man would be deemed doubtful *mamzerim*.

THE LENIENT APPROACH: RABBIS HILDESHEIMER AND KOOK

The debate concerning the status of the Beta Israel peaked in the nineteenth century, when various Jewish leaders in Europe initiated a campaign to rescue the community. Rabbi Esriel Hildesheimer, one of the leading Torah lights in Hungary and Germany and the founder of the Berlin Rabbinical Seminary that later bore his name, published a manifesto calling on all European Jews to save Ethiopian Jewry from the danger of conversion by English Christian missionaries: "Woe concerning the state of faith among our Israelite brethren who live there! . . . For all of us have a single Torah and a single Father in Heaven and all Israel is responsible one for another."[5]

Rabbi Hildesheimer, who was extremely strict with regard to the laws of conversion, was not writing merely as a publicist promoting the rescue campaign. He explicitly raised the difficult question: "Are the Jews in Abyssinia truly the descendants of Abraham, Isaac, and Jacob?" By way of response, he mentioned the previously noted ruling by the Radbaz and other studies that "show clearly that the Israelites in Abyssinia, who are known as Falashas, truly came from an Israelite origin. . . . They believe in the Mosaic Creed and at every time and season conduct themselves as full-fledged Jews."[6]

In the twentieth century, Rabbi Abraham Isaac Kook followed Rabbi Hildesheimer's lead. In a manifesto entitled "To All Our Jewish Brethren in Every Place," which he published in 1922, he described the situation of the Jews of Ethiopia:

> Far from the center of Jewish life, tens of thousands of Jews have been living there for more than 2,000 years and, despite all the travails and afflictions they have experienced, they remain faithful to their religion and their people."[7]

The clear inference to be drawn from this manifesto and other of his writings is that Rabbi Kook had no doubt about the Jewishness of the Beta Israel.

THE STRINGENT APPROACH: RABBIS HERZOG, NISSIM, AND GOREN

Rabbi Kook's successor as Ashkenazi Chief Rabbi, Rabbi Yitzhak Isaac Herzog, initiated a halakhic revision concerning the Jews of Ethiopia:

> The main question is whether they are the descendants of converts or come from Israelite origins. All the more so, if they are the descendants of converts it makes matters easier. The fear is that they contracted halakhically forbidden [adulterous or

incestuous] marriages which their [halakhic] distortions permit, or that, if divorce is practiced among them, they certainly do not follow Torah Law. For these reasons there is a suspicion of *mamzerut*.[8]

Hence, Rabbi Herzog preferred to see the Beta Israel as the descendants of non-Jews who had converted; this solution would resolve the problem of *mamzerut*, since this category does not apply to non-Jews. Rabbi Herzog alleged anthropological support for his approach: "It is my impression that scientists are absolutely certain that the Falashas come from non-Jewish stock that converted at some time in the past."[9] The bottom line in his ruling was that "as far as I know they are doubtful Jews" and "there is a suspicion of *mamzerut* among them."[10]

Ultimately, in accordance with the views of Rabbi Herzog and his colleague the Sephardi Chief Rabbi Yitzhak Nissim, it was decided that Ethiopian Jews should be converted by immersion and token circumcision. A writ issued by a Jerusalem religious court in 1955, signed by three religious court judges and a circumciser, states that "with the consent of the Chief Rabbis it was decided to convert the Falashas." This is followed by a list of eight Ethiopian immigrants who were converted.

We do not know what halakhic answers Rabbi Herzog found for his questions about the status of the Ethiopians; the court record states only that "the Chief Rabbis' grounds for this decision were recorded and are to be found in the offices of the Chief Rabbis."[11] The Chief Rabbinate, however, is not in the habit of publishing the reasons for its rulings in controversial matters such as this one, which makes it extremely difficult for the general public to understand how it reached its conclusions.

Chief rabbis since Rabbi Herzog have tended to view the Beta Israel as Jews, and even as "full Jews" (Rabbi Ovadia Yosef). Nevertheless, they have continued to demand full conversion. In July 1974, Chief Rabbi Shlomo Goren ruled that

If we determine that they are Jews in every respect, this raises a problem of their marriage, as was raised by the Radbaz in his responsa [concerning the suspicion of *mamzerut*]. This does not happen if they are not declared to be unquestioned Jews and by being converted are made fit to intermarry with other Jews.[12]

DOES CONVERSION REMOVE THE TAINT OF *MAMZERUT?*

Here Rabbi Goren exposed the real reason for the demand that the Ethiopian Jews convert. Because the establishment rabbis have not laid to rest the apprehension that the Beta Israel may be tainted by the stigma of *mamzerut,* in that their marriages were valid but not their divorces, they would rather view them as doubtful Jews with gentile antecedents and require that they undergo a token conversion. Because there is no such thing as *mamzerut* among non-Jews, the Ethiopians would then be eligible to marry other Jews.

In conclusion, Rabbi Goren ruled that "in order to find a Jewish halakhic solution to the problem of the Falashas and to avoid all grave doubts concerning their identity, if it is desired to bring them to Israel they should undergo token conversion in accordance with Halakhah."[13] The whole purpose of this conversion, then, is to remove the Ethiopians from the status of doubtful Jews.

But it is the rabbinate that assigned them this status of maybe–Jews/maybe–non-Jews in the first place, despite all the rulings we have reviewed that deem them "full Jews," merely to make it possible to require them to undergo token conversion and eliminate any suspicion of *mamzerut.* This halakhic approach, which was never explained to the Ethiopians, perplexes and pains not only them but all Jews to whom both these immigrants and Halakhah are dear.

Almost all the Ethiopian immigrants reject the demand that they convert, a step they consider to be unnecessary and humiliating. Clearly, no one bothered to explain to them that the whole procedure is only a legal fiction intended to indirectly remove any possible stain of *mamzerut.* The community's vigorous opposition seems to have won the day; at some point the Chief Rabbinate re-treated and no longer demands full conversion, including circum-cision, but only immersion and acceptance of the commandments.

Why did the rabbinate concede its demand that Ethiopian men undergo circumcision (that is, the token circumcision of shedding a drop of blood from the penis), even though Rabbis Herzog and Goren demanded full conversion? The Chief Rab-binate Council explained its decision as follows: "It became clear to the present Chief Rabbinate Council that most of them circumcise their sons in accordance with Halakhah. Accordingly it was de-cided that anyone who was circumcised according to Halakhah will not be required to undergo token circumcision."[14]

This lenient response by the rabbinate is astonishing in view of its concomitant demand that the Ethiopian Jews undergo token conversion. This demand, as we have seen, stems from the notion that the Beta Israel are doubtful Jews and only conversion can re-move the doubt. But a doubtful Jew is also a doubtful non-Jew. How, then, can the rabbinate argue that the circumcision per-formed in Ethiopia was halakhic? In the sixteenth century, Rabbi Joseph Caro held that in the case of a Jew who was circumcised by a non-Jew, "it is necessary to extract a drop of blood from him, since he is no better than a baby born without a foreskin."[15]

According to the rabbinate, the Ethiopians are only doubtful non-Jews. Circumcision is a Torah precept, and the operative prin-ciple is that we rule stringently in cases of doubt concerning a Torah precept (BT Beitzah 3b). This should require the rabbinate to rule stringently in this matter and require token circumcision. Evidently, the anxiety that this demand would spark a rebellion by the Beta Israel against the whole idea of token conversion deterred the rabbinate from doing so.

Conversion under Duress Is Not Halakhic Conversion

The rabbinate and the religious establishment adopted all sorts of stratagems and even resorted to threats to force the Ethiopian immigrants to immerse themselves for the purpose of conversion, even if in the sea instead of a ritual bath. It is questionable whether such an immersion would fulfill the halakhic requirements for conversion, since the Ethiopians would not be doing so with the sincere intention of conversion. The rabbinate's attempt to compel the Beta Israel to convert is contrary to Halakhah, which bans coercion in this matter—including external pressure and overt or tacit threats related to marriage or some other problem—and insists that conversion be free and voluntary. The halakhic term for those who convert under compulsion is "lion converts" (BT Yevamot 24b: see 2 Kings 17:24ff.); Maimonides disqualifies candidates for conversion who are motivated by fear (Laws of Forbidden Intercourse 13:14). The fact that the rabbinate retreated from its demands step by step speaks volumes about the weakness of its position.

A Solution Is Found

Into this dark situation, Rabbi David Ḥayyim Shloush, the Sephardi Chief Rabbi of Netanya and a member of the Chief Rabbinate Council, beamed a ray of light. He found a solution to the problem of doubtful lineage from the time of the Radbaz until the present. He maintained that

> The Radbaz did not ban [the Ethiopian Jews], writing only "I am apprehensive." Because they were exiled during the time of the First Temple and do not know the form of bills of divorce and marriage vows, it seems to follow that they do not celebrate marriages in accordance with the regulations of the Sages and consequently there is no *mamzerut*.[16]

In his book and in a learned halakhic ruling that he published, Rabbi Shloush presented various persuasive halakhic rationales that demonstrate the complete Jewishness of the Ethiopians and their fitness to intermarry with other Jews, without conversion or any other ceremony.

Rabbi Shloush also mobilized history to his cause and offered the precedents of the rabbis who had given their sanction to "the far-flung communities of Bokhara, Dagestan, the Caucasus, and their provinces, who were devoid of all [knowledge of rabbinic law]," and certainly did not know the form of bills of divorce and marriage vows.

Unfortunately, the faithful Beta Israel have been made to suffer by the political game played by the Chief Rabbinate, despite lenient decisors such as Rabbi Shloush. For the most part, the members of the community have had the courage to persevere in their refusal to undergo token conversion.

Their stubborn persistence and refusal to accept the rabbinate's dictates won out for the community. In response to a petition submitted to the High Court of Justice against the Chief Rabbinate, Rabbi Mordechai Eliyahu, then the Sephardi Chief Rabbi, proposed to designate Rabbi Shloush as the countrywide marriage registrar for the community, charged with "handling all the problems of registering the marriages of Ethiopian Jews. Wherever they live in the country they should apply to him in this matter."[17] In September 1988, the Chief Rabbinate appointed Rabbi Shloush as the nationwide marriage registrar for Ethiopian Jews, thereby putting this practical remedy into force.

This provided a solution to the problem of token conversion, since Rabbi Shloush was on record as holding that the Ethiopians are full-fledged Jews and need not undergo any form of conversion. Even though the Chief Rabbinate's demand has not been retracted in theory, it has been neutralized in practice, because Rabbi Shloush is willing to marry members of the community without having them undergo immersion for the purpose of conversion.

As we see, there has been a gradual erosion in the Chief Rabbinate's position on the conversion of the Ethiopian Jews. In 1954–1955, Chief Rabbis Herzog and Nissim ruled that they must undergo full conversion, including circumcision, immersion, and acceptance of the commandments. In 1974, Chief Rabbi Goren seconded their demand. In 1985, the Chief Rabbinate Council, led by Chief Rabbis Avraham Shapira and Eliyahu, waived the demand for token circumcision and said that immersion was enough. At the end of 1988, the Chief Rabbinate set up the arrangement with Rabbi Shloush, whose practical implication is total abandonment of the demand that the Ethiopians convert, even though the resolution of the Chief Rabbinate requiring token conversion remains technically in force.

Thus, the struggle of Beta Israel has been partially successful, with the help of a bold rabbi who has consistently ruled about the Ethiopian Jews:

> They are as fit as all other Jews. Because their ignorance is the result of compulsion, the Falashas should be brought closer and educated. Especially in our days, the time of the ingathering of the exiles, we should be bringing our brethren from every place closer and making them into a single unit, and the children will return to their country.[18]

THE B'NAI ISRAEL OF INDIA

In retrospect, it was to be expected that the Ethiopian Jews' tenacious struggle to be recognized as full-fledged Jews, both as a community and as individuals, would be crowned with success.[19] Not only were their own history and halakhic background on their side, there was also the parallel with the successful struggle three decades ago by the B'nai Israel community of Bombay, India, which ended in the utter rout of the Chief Rabbinate.

Despite the great differences between the Beta Israel and the B'nai Israel, the communities have a similar background. Both trace their roots to the distant past: the Ethiopians, to the time of the First Temple; the B'nai Israel, to the Hasmonean period. Both groups were isolated and cut off from other Jewish communities.

As a result, each developed its own approach to Jewish Law, including elements not found in the rabbinic tradition, and were ignorant of rabbinic precepts. Both communities were loyal to the God of Israel and the Torah in accordance with their beliefs and understanding, suffered martyrdom, and remained faithful to the Jewish People and the Land of Israel. Their mere survival, in the face of persecution and attempts to assimilate them, is a miracle.

The first contact between the B'nai Israel and the outside Jewish world seems to have been in the mid-eighteenth century. Rabbis of the nineteenth century ruled that the B'nai Israel were Torah-observant Jews. In 1859, Rabbi Samuel Abed of Safed ruled that they "observed all the precepts of the Written Law and the Oral Law and all their actions are in accordance with the practices of Jewish people."[20] Their case suffered a setback in 1914, however, when a religious court in Baghdad declared that "those B'nai Israel found in the cities of India have the status of Karaites and it is forbidden to intermarry with them."[21]

About the same time, a religious court in Jerusalem ruled categorically that "it is forbidden to intermarry with the B'nai Israel. They are banned forever, until and after the coming of the Messiah."[22] Accordingly, ruled this court, "if someone takes a wife from among them, his children are *mamzerim*."

The doubts and suspicion of *mamzerut* dogged the B'nai Israel for decades, just as it did the Beta Israel. Some rabbis accepted both communities as full-fledged Jews, whereas others deemed them doubtful *mamzerim* or even non-Jews and ruled accordingly.

THE SUCCESSFUL STRUGGLE BY THE B'NAI ISRAEL

Despite the halakhic rulings of the early twentieth century that rendered them outcasts, the destiny of the B'nai Israel changed course after thousands of them immigrated to Israel, where the rabbinate's attitude toward them was ambivalent. Chief Rabbi Uziel ruled that "the Jews known as B'nai Israel are from the holy stock of Judaism,"[23] whereas Rabbi Herzog vacillated: "It is questionable whether these B'nai Israel are the descendants of converts or of Jewish descent."[24] Nevertheless, he ruled that "marriage is not forbidden with a member of that sect who adheres to Judaism fully and behaves as a kosher Jew in everything related to the laws and sacred matters of Israel."[25]

In 1962, the Chief Rabbinate Council published a halakhic ruling affirming that there were no doubts about the Jewishness of the B'nai Israel. At the same time, it noted that "halakhic questions have arisen concerning the regulations and laws of marriage and divorce practiced by them." Accordingly, the council ruled that "there is no basis for banning marriages with the B'nai Israel, and it is permitted to intermarry with them." But there was a fly in the ointment, for the ruling continued: "Marriage registrars must conduct appropriate inquiries in every case, in compliance with the guidelines of the Chief Rabbinate."[26]

These guidelines mandated, in part, an inquiry and investigation whenever "a request was submitted to register the marriage of a member of the B'nai Israel community with someone who was not a member of that community."[27] Both the community and the general public saw this instruction as rank discrimination against the B'nai Israel and a nullification of the recognition of their Judaism. A fierce public debate ensued in the Israeli and world Jewish media as well as in the Knesset. For two years the B'nai Israel and others staged stormy demonstrations and sit-down strikes outside the Jewish Agency building in Jerusalem.

Then the matter was settled, not by the Chief Rabbinate but by the government of Israel. On August 17, 1964, Prime Minister Levi Eshkol told a special session of the Knesset that the government had reached a decision in the matter of the B'nai Israel:

> The Government of Israel again declares that it views the B'nai Israel Community of India as Jews in every respect, with no reservation or difference, equal in rights to all other Jews in every matter, including matters of personal status. . . . The Government avers that it is essential that the rabbinate take account of public opinion and find a way to eliminate the reasons for their

sense of discrimination and remove all motives therefor.[28]

This situation is quite unlike what happened to the Beta Israel, on whose behalf the government of Israel begged the rabbinate to deign to find a solution to their problem. The Eshkol government made it plain that the rabbinate must rectify the situation at once, or the government would step in and issue its own ruling!

11

You Shall Not Oppress the Stranger

SOME YEARS AGO WE WERE TREATED TO A NEW SOLUTION for the problem of registering converts. When the then minister of the interior, Rabbi Yitzhak Peretz, was informed that the law did not permit him to persist in his refusal to register non-Orthodox converts as Jews, he came up with a magical formula: the nationality line on the identity card of every person converted outside of Israel would read "Jew (converted)."

What are the halakhic and moral implications of this solution? The Sages understood the verse "you shall not oppress the *ger* [stranger]"[1] (Exod. 22:20) to mean "do not oppress him in words": it is forbidden to oppress or wound a convert by means of language (*Mekhilta of Rabbi Ishmael,* Mishpatim 12).

What constitutes "verbal oppression" in our days? Rabbi Peretz declared himself astonished by the public storm that blew up in the wake of his instruction to add this identifying and discriminatory mark to the files of the immigrant converts, disingenuously asserting that the idea was meant to make things easier for them, not more difficult. He also maintained that such an annotation would be "a badge of honor for the convert."

About this and similar ruses, the mishnaic commentator Rabbi Obadiah of Bertinoro (fifteenth–sixteenth centuries) wrote:

171

"Do not oppress one another, but fear your God" (Lev. 25:17)—
this refers to oppression in words, since whether they are good or
evil can be known only by the heart of the speaker, who alone
knows whether he intended them for evil or for good.[2]

Rabbi Peretz certainly knew whether he meant for his new regulation to help converts or make their lives miserable. His track
record suggests that the former was not his intention. In any case,
he explicitly told the media that the true objective of this annotation was to alert marriage registrars that they should "investigate
whether these converts were converted according to Halakhah."

There is no doubt that this falls into the category of verbal oppression and constitutes a grave insult to the community of converts. The Gemara holds that causing pain to human beings by
means of harsh and deceitful words is worse than damaging their
property: "Fraudulent words are worse than financial fraud" (BT
Baba Metzia 58b).

The Sages, relying on the verse that provides the title for this
chapter (Exod. 22:20), which concludes, "for you were strangers in
the land of Egypt," ruled that it is forbidden to mention a convert's
past. "Hence Rabbi Nathan used to say: do not reproach your fellow with your own blemish" (*Mekhilta* on that verse). All of us, all
the Israelites of antiquity, were strangers in Egypt, and we must not
speak lightly of converts—strangers among us in our day—and
treat them according to different standards.

Maimonides emphasizes the full equality of converts in his responsum to Obadiah the Proselyte:

Because you have come under the wings of the Divine Presence
and joined us, there is no difference between us and you. . . . We
read in Isaiah: "Let not the foreigner, who has attached himself
to the Lord, say 'the Lord will keep me apart from His people'"
(Isa. 56:3). There is no difference at all between us and you in
any matter. . . . Nor let your lineage be ignoble in your eyes: if
we trace our ancestry to Abraham, Isaac, and Jacob, you trace
yours to He Who spoke and the world came into existence.[3]

Maimonides buttresses his argument by citing the Torah: "There shall be one law for you and for the resident stranger; it shall be a law for all time throughout the ages. You and the stranger shall be alike before the Lord" (Num. 15:15).

Rabbi Peretz was prepared to offend all Jewish converts for extraneous reasons. Such behavior toward converts has an instructive parallel in another responsum of Maimonides. A certain rabbi in the Land of Israel had humiliated Obadiah the Convert and reminded him that his ancestors had been idolaters:

> Your rabbi answered you improperly, distressing and shaming you. . . . He committed a grave sin . . . and ought to ask your forgiveness. . . . The Torah admonishes us about the convert in 36 places . . . [and one of them is:] "you shall not oppress the stranger," which refers to oppression in words.[4]

This was not the first time that the religious establishment affronted all converts in pursuit of political gain. In 1974 a proposal was floated to institute a one-year moratorium on filling in the nationality line on the identity cards of all immigrant converts. Vigorous public opposition led to the withdrawal of this idea. What the two ideas have in common is the willingness of the religious establishment to cast aspersions on all converts in order to prevent the registration of non-Orthodox converts as Jews, in the context of their efforts to amend the Law of Return through extra-legislative means.

Rabbi Peretz argued that his proposal was based on the rulings of Maimonides. Someone should have drawn his attention to what that great decisor said about the status of sincere converts:

> Know that the obligation laid upon us by the Torah concerning converts is very great. We have been commanded to honor and fear our father and mother, and to hearken to the prophets to listen to them. . . . But concerning converts He ordained heartfelt love—"you shall love the stranger"—just as He commanded us to love His Name—"you shall love the Lord your God."

Maimonides further emphasizes that a convert is

a person who has left his parents and native land and the sovereignty of his people, who are ruling; who by his understanding heart, has adhered to a people that is so abused and persecuted, because he learned to . . . recognize that their religion represents truth and righteousness and recognized all this and followed after the Lord and entered beneath the wings of the Divine Presence . . . desiring His commandments and lifting up his heart to draw near to God in the light of the living. . . . God calls him the disciple of our father Abraham, who left his parents and birthplace and turned to the Lord.[5]

Every person in Israel, and certainly every rabbi, must heed these words—not only in theory, but also in practice.

Afterthought on Conversions

ANOTHER ASPECT OF EVOLVING HALAKHAH HAS BEEN EVIdent in our discussion of conversion: the dynamic interplay between Torah Law and the demands of life.

Rabbi Goren's motives for converting Helen Seidman were in part political (rescuing the religious parties and government coalition) and in part theological ("repairing" the conversion performed by Progressive rabbis by reconverting her "halakhically" and in conformity with Orthodox practice). As we have seen, though, the basic principles that underlay his conversion of Dr. Seidman were similar to if not identical with those followed by the religious court of the Council of Progressive Rabbis in Israel. Rabbi Goren deviated from our procedure in some particulars, chiefly because he was lenient about the prohibition against conversion under duress and performed an express conversion in a matter of hours—something that our *beit din* would never do.

The crux of the matter is that Rabbi Goren's procedure was almost identical with ours. This reaffirms that the dynamics of life frequently compel rabbis to act in accordance with evolving Halakhah, even against their will.

The Chief Rabbinate's handling of the conversion of the Beta Israel, too, ultimately coincided with the principles of evolving Halakhah, despite the chief rabbis' strong reservations. The rabbinate was forced to retreat stage after stage and to accommodate the community. At first it ruled that its members were Jews, but demanded that they undergo full conversion; then it was willing to make do with token conversion and waive symbolic circumcision; finally it agreed to allow them to marry without conversion. Even though the rabbinate found halakhic rationales—which were really "legal fictions"—for every relaxation of its requirements, the true reason for its ultimate leniency seems to have been the Ethiopian immigrants' stubborn refusal to knuckle under to the demand that they "convert," in which they were supported by vigorous public pressure.

Instead of adopting a bold and moral stance, as is the way of evolving Halakhah, the rabbinate was forced to withdraw step by step until its rulings about Beta Israel were devoid of practical content. The rabbinate never made an effort to find a solution based on a halakhic and ethical perspective that takes account of changing reality. Having opted for token conversion, it was forced to liberalize against its will. Had it acted from the outset in accordance with the progressive, ethical principles of Halakhah, it could have steered the affair in the direction it took in any case, but controlled the process rather than been dragged along after events.

Still another aspect of the progressive approach to Jewish law has been evident in this section: the pluralism that is manifested in every one of the issues discussed here. In almost every case, great rabbis disagreed with other great rabbis and invalidated conversions performed by their colleagues. Today, as in antiquity, Halakhah is essentially pluralistic.

IV

The State of Israel and Gentiles

Who is the greatest hero of all? . . . One who turns his enemy into his friend.

AVOT DE-RABBI NATHAN

When you go out as a troop against your enemies, be on your guard against anything evil.

DEUTERONOMY 23:10

The verse cautions against a time when sin is widespread. It is well known among the customs of troops that go out to war that . . . the most upright person in his nature becomes cruel and wrathful when the troop goes out against the enemy. Accordingly, Scripture warns him, "be on your guard against anything evil."

NAHMANIDES (thirteenth century)

One of the most difficult problems that confronts the State of Israel is how it relates to non-Jews—both our neighbors in Arab countries and in the territories (Judea, Samaria, and Gaza) and those who are residents and citizens of the state.

If the attitude that Jewish tradition evinces toward converts is not univocal, its attitude toward non-Jews is all the more ambivalent. Empathy for the non-Jew who is created in the image of God coexists with fierce condemnation.

On one hand, the Sages set down many utterances in praise of non-Jews: "The righteous among the nations have a share in the World to Come" (Maimonides, Laws of Repentance 3:5, based on Tosefta Sanhedrin 13:2). The Sages also ruled that "we support poor non-Jews along with poor Jews" and visit their ill and bury their dead (BT Gittin 61a). There are even passages that establish full parity between Jews and non-Jews: "I call to witness the heavens and the earth, that for both non-Jew and Jew . . . everything is according to their deeds, and thus the Holy Spirit descends upon him."[1]

On the other hand, there are also many harsh and derogatory expressions about non-Jews: "You [the Jews] are called 'human'; but non-Jews are not called 'human'" (BT Yevamot 61a). "Non-Jews feel comfortable with licentiousness" (BT Ketubot 11a). "Why are idolaters filthy?" asks the Gemara, and replies, "because they eat unclean animals" (BT Shabbat 145b).

The many statements on both sides of the ledger constitute yet another demonstration of the pluralistic nature of our tradition. But does Jewish tradition nevertheless have a normative position vis-à-vis the gentile? Scholars have found that the attitude toward non-Jews depended on the period, the place, the nations among whom the Jews were living, and the worldview of a particular decisor.

In countries where the gentiles and their rulers were relatively tolerant, the rabbis evinced a moderate to sympathetic attitude. But in places where the non-Jews and their rulers were hostile, persecuted our people, and expelled or even murdered them, the rabbis composed harsh diatribes against them.

What position should we adopt toward the non-Jewish minority now that we are the sovereign majority in the State of Israel? Does Halakhah teach us to respect the rights of the minority over whom we rule? Or shall we treat them as our ancestors were treated in the Diaspora?

Judah Halevi dealt with this problem in *The Kuzari*. His rabbi-protagonist argued that the Jews were closer to God in their current state of subjugation to the gentiles, in that they had no power in this world. The king of the Khazars offered a quick rejoinder: "This might be so, if your humility were voluntary; but it is involuntary, and if you had power you would slay [your enemies]."[2]

In the entire book, this is one of only two points that the king makes against the Jews that the rabbi cannot refute. He quietly acknowledges that "thou has touched our weak spot, O King of the Khazars."[3]

The chapters that follow were written shortly after the beginning of the Intifada, when Israel had been occupying Judea, Samaria, and the Gaza District and ruling over the Palestinians there for more than twenty years. Today, entering its sixth decade, the State of Israel is strong, despite its many security, economic, and social problems. The Jewish state has proved itself on the battlefield in six wars. Can a strong Israel also demonstrate its moral stature when it rules over an Arab minority that demands political freedom and human rights? We are duty bound to inquire whether evolving Halakhah offers answers that can guide us in finding ethical and realistic solutions and help us escape the terrible maze in which we are lost.

What can we answer when we hear an echo of the Khazar king's prophecy: "If you had power you would slay [your enemies]"? Would that we not be compelled to reply, as Judah Halevi did, "Thou has touched our weak spot, O King of the Khazars."

In this section we shall consider several ethical and religious problems associated with various aspects of the conduct of the independent Jewish State and how it deals with the problems of its citizens.

We shall deal with our relations to the non-Jewish minority over whom we rule, on the levels of both principle and practice. We shall consider difficult problems between us and our neighbors and among ourselves. This is not an academic discourse without practical implications, but one that is topical and relevant, since our future and that of the entire Middle East depend on our actions. We shall see that in the view of evolving Halakhah, the ethical path is ultimately the practical one.

12

The Sabra and Shatilla Massacre

ON FRIDAY AND SATURDAY, SEPTEMBER 17–18, 1982, hundreds of Muslim residents of the Sabra and Shatilla Palestinian refugee camps in western Beirut—unarmed men, women, and children—were murdered by Christian Phalange militiamen. The media all over the world described the atrocities: shattered and swollen corpses piled high in the late summer heat.

Although the Israel Defense Forces, then occupying Beirut, were not involved in the massacre, the Israeli commanders on the scene had allowed the Phalangists to enter the refugee camps, despite the Christians' known hatred for the Muslim refugees and the long annals of revenge and blood feuds between the communities. Any intelligent person might have reasonably feared that the Christians would attempt to avenge the death of their leader, Bashir Jemayel, the president-elect of Lebanon, who had been assassinated several days earlier. There were reports that Defense Minister, Ariel Sharon, had himself given the army the green light to let militiamen into the refugee camps. Questions were asked about the direct responsibility of senior army officers and government ministers.

A fierce storm erupted in Israel, accompanied by public demands for an official inquiry into why the Defense Minister and senior commanders had allowed the Phalange militia to enter the camps, even though they had been alerted to the potential for catastrophe.

An estimated 200,000 persons participated in a rally in Tel

Aviv a week after the massacre. Speakers called on the government to appoint a state commission of inquiry to determine who, if anyone, bore direct or ministerial responsibility. The government was slow to comply; finally, on September 28, 1982, it appointed such a commission, known as the Kahan Commission after its chairman, the then president of the Supreme Court, Justice Yitzhak Kahan.

Much has been written about this massacre from the military, political, and moral perspectives. As Jews we must cope with this tragedy by adducing the applicable principles of the Torah and Halakhah and following the guidance of specifically Jewish morality.

Here I shall concentrate on three issues associated with the tragedy in the refugee camps: our relations with non-Jews, our leaders' responsibility for such tragedies, and their obligation to investigate.

OUR RELATIONS WITH NON-JEWS

Is the murder of Muslim children, women, and old people a Jewish matter? Or is it only a case—as was reportedly said at a meeting of the Israeli Government—of "*goyim* killing *goyim*" and has nothing to do with us as Jews?

According to the Torah, the tragedy did indeed concern us, because the victims were our fellow human beings, created like us in the image of God. The talmudic Sage Ben Azzai held that the verse "this is the record of Adam's line. . . . When God created man, He made him in the likeness of God" (Gen. 5:1) is *the* cardinal tenet of the Torah (JT Nedarim 9:4). One commentator explains that this is the cardinal tenet of the Torah because it teaches us that "all human beings come from the same ancestor."[1] The other principal commentary on the Jerusalem Talmud holds that the importance of the verse is implicit in the words "He made him in the likeness of God"; consequently, "when a person considers this he will be extremely chary of his fellows' dignity."[2]

Thus, the Torah teaches us that all mankind is descended from a single pair of human beings who were created in the Divine Image. It follows that we must relate to all persons, both Jews and non-Jews, as equal before the Lord God.

Jewish tradition recognizes the unique value of all human life. According to Halakhah, the witnesses in capital cases are to be admonished as follows:

> Consequently Adam was created alone, to teach you that anyone who causes a single soul to perish has as it were destroyed an entire world; but anyone who preserves it has as it were preserved an entire world (Mishnah Sanhedrin 4:5).[3]

To sum up, Jewish tradition requires us to see non-Jews as our brothers and sisters, because we are the children of the same Creator. Thus, we cannot evade the fact that this loathsome massacre constitutes a moral and religious problem for us as Jews.

OUR LEADERS' RESPONSIBILITY FOR THE TRAGEDY

In spite of the differences, an instructive parallel to the practical question of ministerial responsibility for the Sabra and Shatilla massacre can be found in Halakhah. This is the biblical and talmudic law of *eglah arufah* (the "heifer whose neck is ritually broken"), the ritual performed when the body of a murder victim is discovered in the open country between Israelite cities. The elders and judges, the leaders of the people, must deal personally with this matter; the rite includes the following declaration by the elders of the town closest to the site where the corpse was found: "Our hands did not shed this blood, nor did our eyes see it done" (Deut. 21:7).

Why should the elders have to utter this denial of guilt, when no one suspects that these dignitaries committed the crime? The Mishnah raises this very question—"could we imagine that the elders of the court were shedders of blood?"—and then proceeds to answer it: "[the dead person] did not come to us only to be sent away without food, nor did we see him [leaving the town] and let him go without an escort." (Mishnah Sotah 9:6). The nineteenth-century compendist Rabbi Baruch Epstein made plain the tragic connection between the stranger's death and such acts of omission: "If they did not feed the visitor or accompany him when he set out; as a result he may not have had the strength to withstand his assailants. Similarly, if they let him travel alone on the highway they put him in danger."[4]

The town fathers must scrutinize their own actions and declare that they did not cause the death of this unfortunate stranger, even indirectly or unwittingly. Maimonides, in his commentary on the Mishnah, explains that this is an all-embracing, comprehensive responsibility borne by the leaders, who must proclaim that "we did not sin or transgress in the matter of the deceased, which would be tantamount to having caused his death."

The leaders must declare publicly that they did not create the conditions that made the murder possible. Thus, we see that our leaders bear overarching responsibility for everything associated with the conditions that help create an attitude toward the stranger that facilitates his murder, even though they are not directly implicated in the crime.

Our Leaders' Obligation to Investigate

The nation's leaders cannot simply repeat a verbal formula and consider themselves quit of the affair. They must also make a diligent inquiry into the entire matter.

The writ of appointment of the "commissions of inquiry" of antiquity declared that they must first of all investigate the conditions that made the tragedy possible. This is how Maimonides phrased it in *The Guide of the Perplexed:*

> The elders of that city shall call upon God to bear witness that they were not remiss in repairing and watching over the roads

and protecting all the wayfarers. [They must declare that his death] in spite of this [was] not due to [their] having neglected the general interest.[5]

But an investigation of the environmental and social conditions is not enough. We must look into the heart of the matter: Who is guilty of the murder?

Don Isaac Abravanel assigned the blame to the nation's leaders if they refused to conduct a vigorous investigation:

> But the true answer, as I see it, is that the people's sin and transgression should be imputed to their leaders. . . . The guilt, too, pertains to their leaders, because they did not find out who the killer was and eradicate him, as is incumbent upon the judges and elders of the city (commentary on Deut. 21:7).

How can this guilt be purged?

> When the [leaders] do what is upright in the eyes of the Lord and are meticulous in leading and judging the people . . . [it is forbidden] that they not also speedily investigate to find out who killed that corpse. On the contrary, He commanded that they investigate further to eradicate the blood and identify the murderer. . . . In this way they will be doing what is upright in the eyes of the Lord (ibid., 21:9).

Both Maimonides and Nahmanides hold that the public nature of the investigation is beneficial in and of itself, because then "many people will speak about it" (Nahmanides ad loc.). That is, involving the general public in the inquiry will heighten interest in the case: "Thus, because of the matter being universally known, the killer could perhaps be recognized" (Maimonides, *The Guide of the Perplexed*, 3, 40).

This is the procedure laid down in Halakhah. We must hope that the leaders of modern Israel know how to steer their course and adopt the principles of Halakhah and ethics found in our heritage.

When the investigation was completed, the priests could

sincerely and unhesitatingly ask the Lord to "absolve . . . Your people Israel whom You redeemed, and do not let guilt for the blood of the innocent remain among Your people Israel" (Deut. 21:8). Only then could God be expected to be appeased and forgive the people (BT Sotah 46a).

We, too, stood in need of atonement and forgiveness when, only a few days after the massacre, we intoned the Yom Kippur liturgy, confessing from the depths of our hearts "the transgression that we transgressed before You, wittingly and unwittingly," and beseeching the Lord to pardon all our transgressions. Many worked to amend our defect, praying that we would merit fulfillment of the Lord's promise to Moses: "I pardon, as you have asked" (Num. 14:20).

The report of the Kahan Commission, submitted on February 9, 1983, recommended that strong disciplinary action be taken against several senior officers, including their possible discharge from the Israel Defense Forces. It concluded that Defense Minister Sharon bore responsibility for the tragedy "in that he paid no attention to the danger of acts of revenge and bloodshed against the population of the refugee camps." Consequently, "the Defense Minister ought to draw the appropriate personal conclusions" and resign, or be dismissed by the Prime Minister. A few days later Sharon did in fact grudgingly resign as defense minister.

In the final analysis, this case reaffirmed the ancient principle that the leaders are responsible for what happens among the people.

13

Demolishing Houses in the Territories: A Halakhic Perspective

FOR AN ENTIRE YEAR, FROM APRIL 1984 TO APRIL 1985, the Israeli military authorities refrained from sealing or blowing up Arab-owned houses in Judea, Samaria, and the Gaza Strip. Members of the Knesset and Jewish settlers in the territories called for renewing this form of punishment for terrorists and stone-throwers; in mid-1985, the policy of demolishing the homes of suspected terrorists was reinstituted. Why was this form of punishment suspended for a year and then reinstated? What are the halakhic and moral dimensions of the punitive policy, which Israel inherited from the British Mandatory government that preceded the establishment of the state?

In 1984, the authorities sealed the home of the father of suspected terrorists in the Jerusalem neighborhood of Abu Tor. In reaction, a member of a Progressive congregation sent the following query to the Israel Council of Progressive Rabbis: "Does this practice of the military authorities—punishing the innocent with the guilty . . . and applying a different law to Arabs than to Jews suspected or accused of similar crimes—conform to Halakhah?"

I relayed her question to Rabbi Solomon B. Freehof, the leading American Reform decisor and a world-renowned halakhic authority, who sent us the following response:

Actually, as far as I know, there is no legal decision in the post-talmudic codes or responsa on this theoretical question. But there is, indeed, an interesting discussion of it in the Talmud. It is found in Avodah Zarah 4a, at the bottom of the page. There the Talmud takes up Abraham's argument with God about destroying the city of Sodom, an act which might very well destroy the righteous inhabitants together with the evil ones. The Talmud bases its discussion on the verse in Ezekiel 9:6, where God's agent is told to put a sign of punishment[1] on various people. The text in Ezekiel actually says: "Begin [the mark of guilt] at the sanctuary." But the Talmud modifies the word *sanctuary* to mean "my holy ones." And then, of course, it deals with the question: Why should the righteous people be marked for punishment? It then gives the following rather remarkable answer: "If a man is wholly righteous (the Talmud uses the unusual expression, 'if he has obeyed the commandments from *Alef* to *Tav*' [the Hebrew equivalent of *from A to Z*]), even so he will deserve punishment if he has failed to use his influence to dissuade or restrain the wicked people."

We may, therefore, well say that this is a talmudic justification for the action of the Israeli authorities. If these other Arabs, themselves innocent of this particular crime, could have made an effort to dissuade or restrain the criminals, but actually made no such effort, then, according to the Talmud, they share the guilt even if otherwise they are innocent.[2]

This creative responsum by an eminent halakhist zeroes in on a relevant passage in the Gemara to fill the lacuna where no definitive decision has ever been rendered.

Progressive Judaism has emphasized the pluralistic character of Halakhah throughout the ages. In this pluralistic tradition, and with all due respect and reverence for Rabbi Freehof, I must beg to differ with him. According to Halakhah, non-Jews are not required to observe the precepts of the Torah, but only the seven Noahide precepts that are incumbent on all human beings. A non-Jew is not commanded to protest, and certainly is not subject to punishment if he does not. In the passage from the Gemara cited by Rabbi Freehof, the righteous who "obeyed the commandments from *Alef* to *Tav*" and should have protested were Israelites.[3] On the verses "He issued His commands to Jacob, His statutes and rules to Israel. He did not do so for any other nation; of such rules they know nothing" (Ps. 147:19–20), the medieval Spanish commentator Abraham Ibn Ezra (1089–1164) wrote: "The reason He gave His Torah only to His nation is that He separated them to be His treasured people." The Sages expounded the precept "reprove your fellow but incur no guilt because of him" (Lev. 19:17) as an injunction "to reprove an Israelite who does not conduct himself properly."[4] It is unjust to punish non-Jews for failing to observe commandments that were given exclusively to the Jews.[5]

INDIVIDUAL RESPONSIBILITY PRECLUDES COLLECTIVE PUNISHMENT

My disquiet with Rabbi Freehof's responsum is founded not merely on formal halakhic grounds, however, but chiefly on its ethical ramifications.

The Talmud discusses the apparent contradiction between two biblical verses: "He . . . visits the iniquity of parents upon children and children's children" (Exod. 34:7) and "parents shall not be put to death for children, nor shall children be put to death for parents" (Deut. 24:16). According to the rabbis, the first verse refers to descendants who follow in their fathers' evil ways and are punished in consequence of their own wickedness; whereas the second passage refers to children who are not sinful (BT Berakhot 7a). Worthy and upright children are not punished for their parents' misdeeds. Rabbi Jose ben Ḥanina held that Moses' decree of hereditary punishment was revoked by the prophet Ezekiel, who declared, "The person who sins, he alone shall die (Ezek. 18:20)" (BT Makkot 24a). The general thrust of these talmudic passages leads to the conclusion that we must determine the complicity of the relatives of the suspected criminal before punishing them.

"Resident Gentiles" Must Receive Fair Judicial Treatment

The Arabs of the territories may be deemed to fall into the halakhic category of *ger toshav*—a gentile who observes the seven Noahide commandments, including that to abstain from idolatry (BT Avodah Zarah 64b; Maimonides, Laws of Forbidden Intercourse 14:7–8), and consequently is permitted to live in Eretz Yisrael. The Palestinians are such Noahides, in accordance with the determination by Rabbenu Tam (grandson of Rashi) and others that Christians are not idolaters (Tosefot on Sanhedrin 2b) and with Maimonides' ruling that Moslems are monotheists.[6] Although not all authorities agree, we can rely on Rabbi Abraham Isaac Kook, who held that "the Ishmaelites [Arabs] are not idolaters and fall into the category of resident gentile, and may be settled in the Land of Israel" (i.e., may own land and buildings and live in them). He noted that there are various reasons why this ruling is correct and solidly based, in particular that we are dealing with "an entire people that has abandoned idolatry and has taken upon itself to keep the seven moral laws assigned to non-Jews."[7]

If we accept the Arabs as resident gentiles, not only do they have the right to live in Eretz Yisrael, we are duty bound to avoid judicial discriminations against them (Maimonides, Laws of Kings 10:12). This means that the homes of Arab suspects may not be destroyed if the Israeli authorities do not also blow up the homes of Jews accused of murder and terrorist activities.

As much as we might like to believe that the year-long moratorium, during which no Arab homes were destroyed was the result of the Israel Defense Forces' studying Halakhah, a more plausible explanation, verified by sources within the Defense Ministry, is that the Government was unwilling to blow up the homes of members of the "Jewish underground."[8] Since the military authorities were not allowed to blow up the homes of Jews accused of murdering an Arab girl or planning terrorist acts, they apparently felt constrained to discontinue this form of punishment for suspected

Arab terrorists. It was indirectly and unwittingly that the authorities came to obey this moral requirement of the Halakhah.

Perhaps we could take a first step toward rapprochement with the Palestinians if we heeded Rabbi Kook's prophetic declaration about the Arabs who are destined to live alongside and among us: "There is absolutely no justification for any people to limit the rights of another without a general higher purpose. The prophets of Israel were right when they asserted, 'Have we not all one Father?' (Malachi 2:10)."[9]

Why Was the Policy of Demolishing Houses Reinstituted?

On April 19, 1985, the security forces demolished the house in the Gaza District of a terrorist who had been killed earlier that day in a terrorist attack. Why, we might ask, did the military government blow up houses in Gaza, but not in Judea and Samaria? It is noteworthy that after the terrorist murder of a Jerusalem taxi-driver, about the same time, the suspects' homes in Judea were not demolished.

The only plausible explanation is that it was Defense Ministry policy not to blow up the houses of settlers in Judea and Samaria who belonged to the "Jewish underground" of that period and who were tried for and convicted of murder and other violent acts. Accordingly, the military government did not demolish Arab houses in these districts, but only in Gaza, where no Jews accused in that case lived.

The house-demolition policy in Judea and Samaria was modified after the prisoner exchange of May 1985, when 1150 terrorists, including 879 who had been tried and convicted in Israeli courts, were set free in return for 13 Israelis. About 600 of the released terrorists were allowed to return to their homes in Israel and the territories. The Israeli public was shocked by the deal, especially in light of the concurrent terrorist assaults and the fact that those released were allowed to return to their homes and move freely throughout the territories (see chapter 16). Evidently influenced by the change in the public mood, the security establishment decided to renew the practice of demolishing Arab houses in Judea and Samaria without applying the policy to Jewish terrorists as well. Within a short time, Arab houses in Judea and Samaria were being blown up again.

What is the rationale for blowing up houses? Punishment? Revenge? Deterrence? The suspected terrorists in these new cases were in detention; if convicted, they were sentenced to long prison terms. An enlightened judicial system views punishment as a means of deterrence and an instrument for protecting the public; it does not impose punishment for its own sake or to exact revenge. In criminal cases, even those that involve cruel and atrocious acts, we would never dream of punishing innocent relatives. So too, in the war we must wage against terrorism we should select methods that are both effective and moral.

The key question is this: Did the year-long moratorium on house demolitions have any effect on the curve of Arab terrorism? Had it been possible for Israeli governments to conduct a scientific statistical inquiry, taking all the variables into account, and compare periods when no houses were demolished with others when the demolition policy was implemented, we might have a better understanding of whether such punishment is an effective deterrent.

Two years after the end of the moratorium on demolishing houses, the Intifada (Palestinian uprising) broke out (December 1987). One result was an increase in the number of Arab homes demolished. During the decade 1987–1997, the Israeli authorities demolished 447 Palestinian homes and sealed off 294, to punish those convicted or suspected of violence against Israelis. During this period, 1346 Palestinians were killed by Israeli soldiers or civilians; 18 Israeli servicemen and 256 civilians were killed by Palestinian violence.[10] These statistics may not constitute conclusive proof, but they do seem to indicate that the demolition of homes is either irrelevant or ineffective as a deterrent to voiolence. Indeed, the ramifications of destroying dwellings appear to confirm the halakhic conclusions of this chapter.

14

Halakhah and the Intifada

THE YEARS OF VIOLENCE KNOWN AS THE INTIFADA (ARABIC for "uprising") were more than a violent confrontation between Israelis and Palestinians in the territories.[1] The crucial issue was Israel's status as an occupying power, a state of affairs at odds with our self-image as human beings and as Jews. We are the descendants of a people who, throughout the ages, adopted a moral stance regarding the relationship between the strong and the weak. Yet, we found ourselves ruling over a hostile civilian population.

How should we, as Israelis and as Jews, have responded to the riots, beatings, and bloodshed in Judea, Samaria, and the Gaza District? How should we have reacted to the killing of hundreds of Arab civilians and the wounding of thousands, many of them teenagers and women? (By contrast, relatively few Israeli soldiers and Jewish settlers have been killed or wounded.) Many Israelis found themselves in a state of spiritual shock. We looked to our political and religious leaders for guidance, but their answers dealt almost exclusively with security, with political and legal issues, to the exclusion of the ethical dimension. We searched in vain for a moral compass that would show us a way out of this quagmire. We sent our sons to use their rifles and batons as representatives of a hated occupation regime. What guidelines did we have to give them?

Our Jewish heritage and our conscience have the capacity to resolve our internal doubts about these issues. The Jewish people are the heirs of a 4000-year-old covenant, and the State of Israel was created to be the historical embodiment of this covenant. The state has the right and duty to protect its citizens. It must take measures of self-defense whenever life or property is threatened.

Nevertheless, this covenant between God and the Jews is conditional on Israel's observing the moral commandments. Moses and the Prophets repeatedly warned our ancestors that if they failed to fulfill their contractual obligation, "you will soon perish from the good land that the Lord is giving you" (Deut. 11:17); "and Israel shall be exiled from its soil" (Amos 7:17).

A corollary of the Jews' right to this land is the agonizing question of Israel's moral responsibility, in light of our Jewish heritage, toward a vanquished Palestinian population that has lived under our control for more than thirty years. The rabbinic authorities cited in this chapter provide both halakhic and moral guidelines. They emphasize the Jews' responsibility to non-Jews who live under their rule, spell out the Arabs' rights under Halakhah, and trace the paths we should follow toward peace.

THE ATTITUDE TOWARD INDIVIDUAL MEMBERS OF A HOSTILE POPULATION

A talmudic adage frequently cited by the Israeli in the street, and especially by members of the Knesset, is "if someone comes to kill you—kill him first" (BT Sanhedrin 72a). This ruling is based on a verse in the Torah: "If the thief is found while breaking in and is beaten to death, there is no bloodguilt in his case" (Exod. 22:1).

Some years before the outbreak of the Intifada, a former member of the Knesset asked Rabbi Ḥayyim David Halevy, the Sephardi Chief Rabbi of Tel Aviv, whether this principle also applies to the hostile population in the territories. The questioner wanted to know whether the talmudic ruling meant that Israeli Jews may view all Palestinians as if they were "breaking in," simply because they are members of a hostile population. If so, it would be permissible and perhaps even obligatory to regard them as having the permanent status of one "who comes to kill you."

Rabbi Halevy answered as follows:

> Quite astonishing is the foolish idea that we take such a view of a million and a half Arabs—of whom the overwhelming majority live their private lives quietly and peacefully, albeit they are somewhat hostile to and resentful of Israelis, whom they view as occupiers—because there are a few [terrorists] among them. The latter are undoubtedly an extremely small minority who attack us and come to kill us. Should we, because of that tiny minority, issue death warrants for a million and a half human beings?![2]

He concluded that

> It is not permitted to kill an individual even if he is a member of a hostile group, even extremely hostile, as long as this hostility is not expressed in deeds, because of individuals among them who commit murderous assaults but cannot be identified.[3]

This halakhic ruling has important implications for dealing with mass disturbances and the interrogation of suspected terrorists. Halakhah does not justify indiscriminate beatings and shootings that do not fall into the category of immediate self-defense. The sacred value of every individual, even if he or she belongs to a hostile group, must always light our path. In a democracy persons are judged according to their deeds, not their thoughts. Restraint is a fundamental element in all interpersonal relations, and all the more so in relation between nations and peoples.

TERRITORY FOR PEACE

A bitter dispute is being waged in halakhic circles as to whether Halakhah permits or prohibits relinquishing territory in exchange for peace.

Here I shall present the conclusions of one of the leading decisors in Israel today, Rabbi Ovadia Yosef, the former Sephardi Chief Rabbi. His acute argument is based on the assumption that genuine peace is impossible unless Israel withdraws from certain territories. If there is no peace, there will certainly be war, and this eventuality invokes the principle of saving lives.

Rabbi Yosef warns that rabbis should not be involved in determining the conditions or timing of such concessions. There are objective factors that only experts can interpret and then act on accordingly. All agree that this is the case when it comes to problems of medical Halakhah, where we must consult with a qualified physician. Who has the expertise to determine the conditions and circumstances for making peace with our neighbors?

Rabbi Yosef answers:

> If the military commanders, along with the government ministers, determine that this is a matter of saving lives, that if territories that are part of the Land of Israel are not returned there is the danger of imminent war with our Arab neighbors, and many would be devoured by the sword, Heaven forfend; but that if these territories were returned to them the danger of war would be removed and there would be prospects of lasting peace—it appears that all agree that it is permitted to return territories that are part of the Land of Israel to attain this goal, since nothing takes precedence over saving human life.[4]

This responsum cautiously blends a halakhic and moral stance with a pragmatic approach and understanding of *realpolitik,* a position that is shared by many in halakhic circles in Israel.

Rabbi Yosef was in fact echoing his predecessor, Rabbi Ben-Zion Uziel (Chief Rabbi of Israel, 1939–1953), who, when rabbi of Jaffa in 1921, told a gang of Arab rioters:

> We stretch out to you a sincere and true hand of friendship and say: Is not all the land before us? Let us cultivate it shoulder to shoulder, uncover its treasures, and live in it as brothers dwelling together in harmony. Know and believe that the Word of God will always be fulfilled. Make peace with us and we will make

peace with you. Together we shall all enjoy the Lord's blessings in His land in peace and tranquillity, love and fraternity.

Our cousins! When Abraham, our common father, the father of Isaac and Ishmael, saw that his nephew Lot was causing him problems and arguing that they could not live together, and instigated quarrels between the shepherds of the two flocks, he told him: "Let there be no strife between you and me, between my herdsmen and yours, for we are kinsmen" (Gen. 13:8). We too say to you, the land can bear all of us, can support all of us, so let us end the disputes between us. We, too, are kinsmen.[5]

We see that some of the greatest decisors have given us moral guidelines that make it possible for us live together with the Arabs over whom we rule and to have peace with our neighbors. Many fear that the peril latent in these guidelines outweighs the prospects of a peaceful solution. Nevertheless, they can serve as a moral compass for all who see them as the words of the Living God.

Israel has frequently demonstrated its valor in battle and has developed one of the best armies in the world. Today, however, another sort of valor is required.

Rabbi Abraham Isaac Kook expounded the daily morning benediction, "Blessed art Thou O Lord our God, King of the Universe, Who girds Israel in bravery," as follows:

Israel's valor is a special sort of valor, a valor that excels not in conquests that overrun others, subjugate them or destroy them, but a valor that is essentially associated with how individuals subjugate themselves. . . . The valor of forbearance is better than might, and self-control than conquering a city (after Prov. 16:32). This is the valor with which Israel is girded, which is appropriate to the standard of unsullied morality and to exalting man's value and advantage over the beasts.[6]

WHO IS AUTHORIZED TO DECIDE?

In July 1995, as negotiations between the Rabin government and the Palestinian Authority about redeployment of the Israel Defense Forces in the West Bank were proceeding, a group of rabbis affiliated with the Religious-Zionist establishment and the settlement enterprise in Judea-Samaria and the Gaza District published a ruling that Halakhah forbids dismantling army bases in the Land of Israel. Fierce criticism was directed at this step, on legal, political, social, and military grounds. How secure were its halakhic foundations?

The Rabbinic Council of Judea, Samaria, and Gaza ruled that it was forbidden to uproot any Jewish settlement in the Land of Israel and then added the novel concept that "a permanent army post is itself a full-fledged Jewish community." They did not bother to prove this from halakhic sources. Anyone who is familiar with a military base or outpost would be hard pressed to describe as a genuine community. The definition is even more inapt when the battalion commander is Druze or a majority of the soldiers are Circassian or Bedouin.

Over the generations, eminent decisors have not cited only those halakhic sources that are readily compatible with their outlooks; in their responsa and rulings they also dealt with (and refuted) opinions at variance with their own. The present crop of rabbis cited Nahmanides' opinion that the settlement of the Land of Israel is a Torah precept, and extended it to include army posts. They ignored the fact that most medieval and modern decisors do not accept Nahmanides' position. Maimonides, for example, did not include the precept of settling the land in his enumeration of the 613 commandments of the Torah. Nahmanides himself noted that according to Rashi, settling the land is not a Torah precept but a "promise" (commentary on Numbers 33:53 and Deuteronomy 5:1). Many eminent rabbis, including Rabbi Joseph of Trani and Rabbi Ḥayyim ben Attar, have disputed Nahmanides' view.

Does any group of rabbis have the halakhic authority to order young soldiers to refuse to carry out commands that are ultimately derived from an elected government? The rabbis asserted that they issued their ruling because of the danger that redeployment by the Israel Defense Forces would pose to human life and the survival of the state. But who is authorized to determine that this is a realistic assessment of the situation? Any group of fifteen people? Rabbi Ovadia Yosef has ruled that "if the leaders and commanders of the army, along with members of the government, determine that it is a matter of saving lives . . . it is permissible to return territory of the Land of Israel."[7] Rabbi Abraham Isaac Kook ruled that in an age when there is no king in Israel, the elected leaders bear responsibility for everything "associated with the general condition of the nation." Every leader "who arises in Israel has the status of a king, . . . especially in everything that has to do with leading the community." As he explains, "in everything associated with leading the community, whoever leads the nation . . . [assumes the functions of the monarchy]—that is, everything the nation requires in keeping with its time and status in the world."[8]

Rabbi Ḥayyim David Halevy ruled (following Rabbi Kook) that "we learn that even a king who is not enthroned by the Lord, but was crowned by Israel . . . has the status of a king and we are required to obey his orders." He emphasizes that "the obligation of obedience also applies to the instructions of any elected leader."[9] It is clear, then, that the rabbis who arrogated to themselves the authority to incite soldiers against their commanders were contravening the codified Halakhah.

Former Chief Rabbi Avraham Shapira, who drafted the ruling, holds that we are under a halakhic obligation to occupy the entire Land of Israel and may not leave any part of it to non-Jews. But one of his predecessors, the late Chief Rabbi Yitzhak Isaac Herzog, citing Rabbi Avraham ibn Daoud and Rabbi Joseph Caro, ruled that Arabs, both Muslims and Christians, may live in this country, even if they do not accept Jewish rule, because they are not idolaters.[10] Rabbi Kook went even further: "We should say that the Muslims are not idolaters and fall into the category of resident aliens and have the right to be settled in the Land of Israel."[11]

The rabbis who signed their names to this ruling should have given serious study to the position of all these Sages and should never have issued their flawed ruling.

A Flimsy Foundation

The issue of evacuating Jewish settlements in the territories is more than just a question of national security and politics. It has become a burning halakhic issue as well. In November 1993 the late Rabbi Shlomo Goren, who deemed himself to be the authoritative halakhic arbiter on such matters, issued a long halakhic ruling (subsequently published serially in the publication of the Forum of Rabbis in Judea, Samaria, and Gaza).

Among other things, Rabbi Goren forbade the government to evict settlers from their homes and called on Israeli soldiers to refuse to obey orders to evacuate settlements. If this ruling by the former Chief Rabbi was adequately grounded and carried his full prestige and authority with it, soldiers and civilians who accept his halakhic interpretations would find themselves in a bind should they receive an order from the army or government that contravenes from his opinion. A brief analysis, however, demonstrates that the ruling stands on very shaky ground. Throughout his career Rabbi Goren was known as an eminent scholar and brilliant decisor; but this document, one of the last he published (he died eleven months later), belies this reputation. Some of the arguments he advances in it are refuted by the very sources he cites in support of his case.

For a start, Rabbi Goren holds that the government of Israel must not violate the precept of settling the land; he cites Maimonides, in the Laws of Kings: "If the king decrees the abolition of some precept, he is not to be obeyed."

Here Goren is comparing the democratically elected government of Israel with a Davidic king of Israel, who must obey all the precepts of the Torah, including that to settle the Land of Israel. The modern government, too, he holds, has sovereignty over the Land of Israel, like the kings of old, and must also obey all the Torah commandments. Although this is the normative halakhic opinion, Goren claims elsewhere in this ruling that this same government is illegitimate and does not have the status of a Davidic king. He makes no attempt to resolve this contradiction, leaving his entire edifice resting on shaky foundations.

Next he rules that "one must not obey a military order that contravenes a Torah precept, for it is clear that the commandment to settle the Land of Israel is a serious one, because it is equal in weight to all the precepts in the Torah." Rabbi Goren bases this assertion on a mishnaic-era source that is mentioned in the ruling but is not quoted in full. In fact, this ancient source actually refutes Goren's ruling, since it is written there: "A person should always live in the Land of Israel, even in a city that has a gentile majority, and not outside the Land of Israel, even in a city that is inhabited entirely by Jews—which teaches that living in the Land of Israel is equal in weight to all the precepts in the Torah" (Tosefta Avodah Zarah 5:2). This Tosefta does not in fact support Rabbi Goren's thesis. It asserts the importance of living in the Land of Israel rather than in another country. Because there is no plan to evacuate settlements and force their residents to move outside Israel, but only to some other community in the Land of Israel, this and parallel passages are irrelevant to his argument. Surely Rabbi Goren acknowledged that all of the territory within the Green Line is also part of Eretz Yisrael.

Rabbi Goren also alleges the supreme importance of the commandment to settle the Land of Israel on the basis of the conclusion that it is "equal in weight to all the precepts in the Torah." This phrase, however, is not a halakhic definition but a common talmudic usage. Exactly the same thing is said of several other precepts, such as ritual fringes *(tzitzit)*, charity, and the prohibition of idolatry, each of which is said to be "equal in weight to all the precepts in the Torah."[12]

Another argument mobilized by Rabbi Goren in support of the call to refuse an order to evacuate settlements is the Deuteronomic injunction referring to the seven nations of ancient Canaan: "Do not let them settle" (Deut. 7:2). The Sages understood this to mean "Do not allow [gentiles] to take up residency in the land." Goren cites Maimonides' ruling in the Laws of Idolatry and concludes that "it is forbidden to sell land to a non-Jew in the Land of Israel." As he views the situation, "the purpose of evacuating settlements in Judea and Samaria is to hand over their lands to Arabs, which is a transgression doubled and redoubled. Certainly one may not compel a soldier to transgress so many severe prohibitions of the Torah."

Goren ignores the many halakhic rulings that "do not let them settle" applies only to idolaters, not to Palestinian Arabs. He does not even mention the rulings by his predecessors, Rabbis Kook and Herzog, that Arabs who are not idolaters may have the status of resident aliens and may own land, and should not be prevented from living in the Land of Israel. Rabbi Goren does not even try to refute these rulings. Hence his opinion remains one of many which can be accepted or rejected but which lacks conclusive authority.

Rabbi Goren also pays no attention to the rulings of eminent rabbis, such as that of Rabbi Yosef, that the commandment to save human life (pikkuah nefesh) takes precedence over all other precepts in the Torah, including the settlement of the Land of Israel, and that rabbis must not attempt to exploit halakhic rulings to dictate the conditions under which territories may be evacuated.

As further justification for his position, Goren notes that "the government does not depend on a Jewish majority but on Arab members of Knesset. . . . Its decisions have no authority or validity." He cites several halakhic sources that preclude Arab Knesset members from having jurisdiction over Jews. Various rabbis have alleged similar texts to reject the appointment of women to public positions in Israel, including membership in the Knesset; any nonreligious member of the Knesset could be disqualified on similar grounds. This method of disqualifying elected representatives on the basis of halakhic sources could lead to the absurdity of a rump legislature with only a handful of members, since one can find some halakhic impediment to the tenure of the vast majority of the ministers and legislators.

According to Goren, the Rabin government in office at the time was illegitimate and consequently was debarred from taking decisions not only about the territories but about any matter whatsoever. One may wonder how he allowed himself to accept his pension and funding for his yeshiva from this government.

Finally, Goren notes that we are enjoined to rend our garments when we see cities of the Land of Israel that have been destroyed and laid waste; this Halakhah, he says, has the same status as the injunction to "rend one's garments for parents who have passed away." From here Rabbi Goren somehow leaps to the conclusion that "destroying Hebron again would be in the same category as killing the fathers of the nation; in other words, . . . it falls under the rubric of *pikkuaḥ nefesh,* and the halakhic principle of 'let yourself be killed rather than transgress' applies."

This parallel is original with Goren. He offers no proof texts (for there are none) to support his contention that the category of saving life may be applied to some geographical entity. *Pikkuaḥ nefesh*—saving lives—means saving *human* life from the peril of death. It does not pertain to an inanimate object, not even a city in Israel. Obviously, then, the principle "let yourself be killed rather than transgress" cannot apply to "saving" any place, however important it may be.

Rabbi Goren grasped at flimsy halakhic straws in his attempt to undermine the government's policy and prevent the evacuation of settlements. There is some danger that persons who lack expertise in Halakhah may rely on his ruling without studying it and without discerning its moral implications. Rabbi Goren's halakhic writings may constitute fertile soil for the growth of other invalid halakhic rulings that justify violence to preserve the settlements. One may ask to what extent his delegitimization of the Rabin government ultimately served to legitimize violence against the prime minister. It is essential that all who deal with these matters remember the admonition of Avtalyon (first century B.C.E.): "Sages, be cautious in your words!" (Mishnah Avot 1:11).

15

The Attitude toward the Enemy

I HAVE NOTED MANY HALAKHIC RULINGS THAT PRESCRIBE A humane attitude toward enemies of the Jewish people and the State of Israel, even in wartime. In contrast, those issued by certain rabbis embody hatred and hostility.[1] They, too, base themselves on rabbinic sources, but arrive at antithetical conclusions.

JUSTIFICATIONS FOR HARMING WOMEN AND CHILDREN

Rabbi Shaul Yisraeli

On the night of October 14/15, 1953, a detachment of the Israeli army, under the command of Ariel Sharon, staged a reprisal raid against the Arab village of Kibya, some ten kilometers east of Ben-Gurion Airport in what was then Jordan; during the course of the action, about fifty Arab civilians were killed.[2] Rabbi Shaul Yisraeli analyzed this painful incident in the light of Halakhah and asked whether the Israeli soldiers had acted appropriately. He acknowledged the severe consequences of the raid: "The Arab village of Kibya suffered losses in property and life. Those killed included children and women."[3]

Nevertheless, he attempted to justify the action: "One night they attacked the Arab village of Kibya; there was proof that the murderous gangs came from there and were supported by its population.[4]" (He did not cite any proofs that the civilian population had supported the terrorists.)

To what extent must Jewish fighters endeavor to avoid harming civilians? Replied the rabbi:

> No military action that is a normal part of war—even though it may kill or injure children—is forbidden. As long as one is not intentionally operating against children, it is considered to be a punishment from Heaven, a situation in which children are certainly punished for the sins of their parents.

Despite what the Torah teaches about the value of the life of every human being, created in the Divine image, Rabbi Yisraeli held that there was no injunction that hostilities must spare children as long as there is no explicit intention to harm them. If the enemy's children are casualties of war, our soldiers are not to blame. It is divinely ordained punishment. Children are maimed and killed because of their parents' sins!

I must demur at this opinion of a learned rabbi, which is in fact a profanation of the Divine Name. Furthermore, precisely because it was widely circulated at the time and is still well known among halakhists, I am duty bound to state publicly that it contravenes the Torah and its spirit. One must not make light of such declarations, which can lead many people astray even after the lapse of more than forty years.

Rabbi Yisraeli's summary leaves no room for doubt:

> It follows that there is a place for reprisal actions and revenge against the enemies of Israel and that such action falls into the category of an obligatory war. Every disaster and injury that befalls the pogromists, their allies and their children—they themselves are responsible for them and must bear their own transgression. There is no obligation to refrain from reprisal actions lest the innocent be hurt, because we are not the cause. They themselves are, and we are innocent.[5]

Rabbi Yisraeli set no limits to his doctrine, which justifies the killing of civilians, even children, during battle. He provided the theological cover that their deaths are in any case ordained by Heaven as a punishment for the sins of adults.

The generation of the Holocaust, in which a million Jewish children were murdered, cannot tolerate such a warped doctrine of reward and punishment that applies not only to Arab children but could also prove a two-edged sword directed against Jewish children as well. The Torah teaches us that every human being is created in the image of God. Every human being, as a human being, has an intrinsic divine value that must not be dismissed lightly because of military operations.

Rabbi Shimon Weiser

About twenty years later, Rabbi Yisraeli's position was supported by Rabbi Shimon Weiser, who may actually have taken an even more extreme position in an exchange of letters with a soldier who asked him about the practical application of the doctrine of "purity of arms" (an Israeli idiom for soldiers' observing moral principles on the battlefield). The exchange dates from 1973—right before the Yom Kippur War—and speaks for itself.[6]

A soldier named Moshe wrote to his rabbi as follows:

There was a discussion [in my army unit] about "purity of arms." Then we argued about whether it is permitted to kill unarmed civilians, such as children and women. Or is it permissible to take revenge on Arabs, measure for measure, just as they murder without distinction? . . . In essence, perhaps the Arabs are in the category of Amalek . . . so that it is permitted to murder and wipe out their race!

A second problem: Is it permitted to risk one's life by allowing a woman to live?

Rabbi Weiser's reply was as follows:

Rabbi Simeon bar Yohai used to say: "The best among the Egyptians—kill him! The best among snakes—smash in his skull!" . . . However, . . . we have learned in a *baraita* that one does not lift non-Jews out of a pit into which they have fallen, nor does one lower them into a pit to kill them (BT Avodah Zarah 26a-b). That is, one need not save them from death, but one should not actively kill them. . . . In the opinion of the tosafists (loc. cit.), accordingly, we must distinguish between wartime and peacetime. Although in peacetime it is forbidden to kill non-Jews, . . . *in wartime it is a* mitzvah *to kill them.*[7]

The rabbi also provided a halakhic and theological basis for his answer:

The Jew is distinguished from a non-Jew as follows: Although the principle "if someone comes to kill you, kill him first" applies to a Jew, too . . . it holds only if there are grounds to suspect that he is coming to kill you. But with regard to a non-Jew in time of war it is assumed that this is the case, and one must always consider him to be someone who is coming to kill you, unless it is clear that he has no evil intent. It is this principle that determines the meaning of "purity of arms" according to Halakhah, not the non-Jewish sense that is currently the norm in the Israel Defense Forces and which to our regret has claimed no few victims.[8]

If there were any doubts about the implications of Rabbi Weiser's response, they were removed by the reply of the soldier who had submitted the original question, which the rabbi appended to his responsum when it was printed in a halakhic journal. The soldier summarized what he had learned from the rabbi's letter:

With regard to the letter itself I understand as follows: *In time of war, I am permitted and, what is more, am obligated to kill any Arab men or women I encounter, if there are any grounds for suspecting that they are aiding the war against us, directly or indirectly.* For my own part, I am obligated to kill them even if this will embroil me with military law. I think that this point about the "purity of arms" should be conveyed to educational institutions, at least the religious ones, to give them [the correct] perspective on this topic and keep people from being misled in the field of general "logic" on this of all topics, . . . so that our children will understand the path of our ancestors in a clear and unambiguous fashion.[9]

There is no doubt that the student's letter, published as the final word in this correspondence, embodies Rabbi Weiser's meaning. Clearly the rabbi endorsed the practical conclusions that the soldier drew from his halakhic ruminations.

As an observant Jew, Prof. Uriel Simon of Bar-Ilan University was outraged by this:

> Here we have reached a new and distorted form of willingness to sanctify God's name, set up as an antithesis to the illustrious ruling of the secular Israeli court in the Kafr Kasim case, namely, that soldiers must refuse to carry out an illegal order when, according to their best judgment and conscience, it is liable to lead to disaster and criminal action. . . . Every word that helps cheapen human life and makes light of the sanctity of life, especially when it comes from a rabbi, works inestimable damage. . . . He publicly states that one should dismiss the Geneva Convention, because it is "gentile," and utters no protest against the comparison of the Arabs to Amalek, a comparison that permits the student to ask the terrible question, "may one kill people who do not carry arms, such as children and women?" and which is left without a direct answer.[10]

Simon viewed Weiser's hard-line ruling as "a living illustration of the severity of the problem of the religious legitimacy of conscience as one element in halakhic decision-making and as its necessary complement."

In reply, Weiser did not claim that Simon had misunderstood him. He argued, instead, that his ruling was backed by the halakhic sources and precedents:

> My conclusion was that in wartime against non-Jews, each of them is considered *prima facie* to be someone who is coming to

kill you, so that the principle of "if someone comes to kill you, kill him first" applies to him. This was not written according to my own thoughts and outlook only, but on the basis of a discussion of halakhic sources and the drawing of conclusions from them. . . . I have learned that Rabbi Avidan, the chief chaplain of the Central Command, reached a similar conclusion in a pamphlet published by the military rabbinate of the Central Command.[11]

Rabbi Lt. Col. Avraham Avidan

Rabbi Weiser mentioned his reliance on a halakhic ruling issued by the chief chaplain of the Army Central Command, Rabbi Lt. Col. Avraham Avidan. In 1974, Rabbi Avidan edited an official Army publication, which included his article "Purity of Arms in the Light of Halakhah." In this article he asserted, *inter alia,* as follows:

When our forces encounter civilians in war, pursuit, or a raid, as long as there is no certain evaluation that those civilians cannot harm our forces, killing them is permitted and even required by Halakhah. In no case should one trust an Arab, even when he gives the impression of being a cultured human being.

In wartime, when Israeli forces are attacking the enemy, they may and in fact are required by Halakhah to kill even good civilians, that is, civilians who seem to be good. This was the case about which the Sages said, "the best among non-Jews—kill!" One must not trust a non-Jew that he will not harm our forces. . . . The law that applies to those who assist the enemy or a terrorist is the same as that for the enemy or terrorist himself. . . . That is, the very fact that he provides assistance to the enemy turns him into a hostile object, who is considered to be an enemy who may be killed.[12]

Here Avidan repudiates the humane spirit of Halakhah. Every Jew, all the more so a rabbi, should be punctilious about respecting the sanctity of every human life, instead of outlawing women and children. Newspaper responses to the appearance of Rabbi Avidan's pamphlet reflected the internal contradiction in his arguments:

The conclusion is that "killing enemy civilians in wartime is permitted and even required by Halakhah, as long as there is no certain evaluation that those civilians cannot harm our forces." Since, however, in every case one must not trust an Arab, it follows that a certain evaluation that an Arab cannot do harm is never possible, and accordingly the rule is always to kill them.[13]

Another absurd argument is that assisting the enemy turns a person into an enemy who may be killed. This line does not distinguish among various forms of helping an army. Did the chaplain mean to say that a child who offers a piece of candy to an Arab soldier is helping the enemy and falls into the category of an enemy who may be killed? Such an argument turns the entire civilian population into military auxiliaries who may be killed.

Avidan seems to offer one ray of light when he states that there are cases in which one should not behave according to the general principles presented in his article. It is permissible to kill civilians only if

> there are no special and specific political conditions that require one not to harm civilians, even in the conditions described above. Sometimes the propaganda and political effect for which the operation was planned is its most important achievement.[14]

Evidently what disturbs the rabbi is not the loss of innocent life but the diplomatic damage and negative propaganda that might result from the killing of noncombatants. He is not interested in the commandment "Thou shalt not murder" but only in "What will the gentiles say?" Where is Halakhah's insistence on morality and humanity, underscored by Rabbis Uziel and Kook? Is a rabbi supposed to concern himself with propaganda effects, or with morality?

In the wake of the storm caused by the pamphlet, the Army spokesman released the following statement:

> There is no resemblance between the contents of this pamphlet and the practice and norm in the Israel Defense Forces. Not only

does the Army educate its soldiers not to harm civilians; not only is this stated in the standing orders and applied in practice—the Army has suffered many casualties precisely because of stringent compliance with the sacred law that one must avoid injuring civilians at all costs.[15]

In the end, the pamphlet issued by the military rabbinate was withdrawn at the order of the then Chief of Staff, Lt. Gen. Mordechai Gur.

The Ideological Basis for Animosity toward Arabs

How is it possible to understand such extremist views held by rabbis, opinions that permit the killing of Arab women and children in the name of the holy Torah?

There seem to be two ideological bases, at least, for this attitude: (1) hostile opinions about non-Jews in the rabbinic classics and (2) contemporary ideologies that give a theological imprimatur to the hostile attitude.

Hostile Opinions in the Rabbinic Classics

Because Halakhah is pluralistic and variegated, its texts offer many statements that manifest enmity toward non-Jews, alongside many others that demonstrate sympathy for the nations of the world. Rabbis with a predisposition to xenophobia can cite passages that they extract from their original context:

The best among the gentiles, in wartime—kill![16]
You [the Jews] are called "human"; but non-Jews are not called "human."[17]
Non-Jews are comfortable with licentiousness.[18]
When there is no war between us and non-Jews, . . . one does not cause their death; but it is forbidden to save them if they are

dying, for example if you see one of them fall into the sea you do not fish him out, as it is said: "You shall not stand passively beside your brother's blood"—but he is not "your brother."[19]

Rabbinic decisors with a philosophical bent can rely on the system of Judah Halevi in *The Kuzari,* which postulates a hierarchy in the universe, ranging from mute stones up through plants and animals and on to human beings. On a higher rung still stands the paragon of humanity—the Jews.[20]

If one were to ignore the context, the dozens of opposing viewpoints, and the explanations by commentators over the generations, one might rely on such passages disparaging or denying the humanity of non-Jews.

Contemporary Xenophobic Ideologies

One can find ostensible justification for enmity toward Arabs not only in the words of the Sages of antiquity but also in ideological tracts written by contemporary rabbis, including some deemed to be among the leading Torah scholars of our generation.

Rabbi Yaakov Ariel

Rabbi Yaakov Ariel, currently the Chief Rabbi of Ramat Gan, has dealt with the halakhic and religious meaning of peace. From biblical days until the present, much has been written about the supreme importance of peace and its superiority to war and conflict. Rather than follow in the footsteps of the Sages, however, Rabbi Ariel makes so many stipulations about the nature of peace with our neighbors that for all practical purposes it becomes a mirage.

The passages that follow were written in the late 1970s, during the peace negotiations with Egypt:

For the sake of genuine peace, which includes a spiritual and moral revolution, inward and outward, perhaps it is worth paying a high price. For such a peace, we should consider, with all due caution and responsibility, making far-reaching concessions and compromises.[21]

Here Ariel implied that such a "genuine" peace will not be on the horizon before the coming of the Messiah; what we may expect now is only an incomplete and truncated peace. This view fueled his criticism of the peace process:

> If a peace like this would bring us closer to the goal we yearn for—universal peace, which is genuine, stable, and just—all would be well. But let us compute profit against loss: abandoning territory in exchange for the breaching of spiritual boundaries—which imperils the survival of the Jewish people, in the feeble and weak climate that exists today in Israel—represents retreat more than progress. There is serious apprehension that in the absence of security-related pressure the idealistic tension that still exists here and there in people's hearts would slacken. A grave danger of internal disintegration would threaten Israeli society, which, in the brief period of the ingathering of distant and long-settled diasporas, has not yet had time to consolidate itself and stabilize.[22]

To Rabbi Ariel, the absence of the tension caused by national and physical insecurity—one result of an incomplete peace—would be cause for mourning. Here a rather dubious utilitarianism takes the place of an ancient Jewish value: peace.

It is forbidden—alleged the rabbi—to try to bring the Messianic Era and peace closer by means of agreements between human beings. No: ours is an eschatological age,

> the beginning of the redemption, the footsteps of the messiah. . . . The facts speak for themselves. . . . Every passing day necessarily brings us closer to the future that was foreseen by the prophets of Israel.[23]

This belief has particular implications for the Palestinians, who are compelled to find a place in Ariel's theological vision:

Every observant Jew believes in the settlement of all the People of Israel in all its land and in the renewal of its days as of old, the building of the Temple, the re-establishment of the Davidic Kingdom, and the restoration of the system of justice as of old. The foreign residents of our land, who perhaps with no special guilt took possession of it when it was desolate, will at some point have to determine their destiny, of their own free will, whether to become converts to Judaism out of conviction, permanent residents, or temporary residents—and even if [the Arabs] decide of their own volition to emigrate to another country they will see Jerusalem as their spiritual capital and the source of their traditional inspiration.[24]

Is this indeed the faith of every observant Jew? I am quite sure that many would demur at these views.

Rabbi Ariel makes his political intentions regarding the Arabs living throughout the Land of Israel perfectly clear:

We are against their forcible expropriation and discrimination. However, ethical honesty requires us to tell them the truth and not delude them. Ethics requires us not to lie and not to make promises to them that we will not be able to keep, in the near or distant future. Precisely in the name of unsullied morality, in the name of universal peace and justice, in order to prevent unnecessary mutual bloodletting, to rectify the moral injustice of the attitude towards the Jewish People over thousands of years with which humanity has corrupted itself, and in order to raise its moral level, I believe that we must stand up for the right of the entire Jewish People to settle throughout the Land of Israel, as one of the conditions of peace, of which the most important is the recognition in principle of our right to our land.[25]

Despite his promise not to discriminate against or expropriate Arabs, Rabbi Ariel's words clearly allude to "voluntary transfer" ("if they decide of their own volition to emigrate to another country") for the sake of universal peace and justice—but quite against the principles of biblical and rabbinic justice and morality.

Rabbi Zvi Yehuda Kook

Rabbi Zvi Yehuda Kook was the son of Chief Rabbi Avraham Yitzhak Kook, but he was not his spiritual heir—at least not with regard to the present topic. Rabbi Zvi Yehuda (as he was known) served for many years as the head of the Mercaz Harav Yeshiva in Jerusalem, exerting great influence on his students and admirers and becoming the spiritual father of Gush Emunim.

Rabbi Zvi Yehuda maintained that Jewish control of the entire territory of the Land of Israel was not only essential, as a matter of security, but a veritable Torah commandment. It was not a matter for calculations of defense or foreign policy or for utilitarian debates. It was not a decision left to human choice but a heavenly imperative:

> It is an obligation from the Torah that we be the rulers of this land of ours and not, heaven forbid, any of the nations of the world. . . . We are required by the Torah to conquer our land. Because all of the Torah is eternal, this precept too obligates us throughout the generations. Conquest means war. Conquest means selfless dedication.[26]

In his view, it is impossible to fulfill our duty of settling the entire Land of Israel peacefully, as the result of direct or indirect negotiations; only conquest will do. The precept of conquering the land in our own time is promoted to the category of the most severe prohibitions—murder, idolatry, and incest—which we are enjoined not to violate even on pain of death.

> With regard to the commandment to conquer the Land of Israel, the obligation is imposed on us and we are enjoined to enter a state of war, in order to fulfill it, even if we be killed. This is a special precept and as such is on a par with all the rest of the Torah . . . namely, that the entire land, its borders and straits, be in our hands and not those of some other nation. This commandment is a national affair. Blessed be He who has made us live . . . [in a time] when we rule our land and we are the landlords here, not the gentiles.[27]

Hence, the precept of conquest is made of equal importance with the three traditional absolute prohibitions. But it is distinguished from the latter, which require that a Jew passively submit to martyrdom rather than breach them. In conquest, a Jew must be active every day of his or her life.

To eliminate any doubt, Rabbi Zvi Yehuda ruled that the foregoing is not merely a theoretical declaration but has practical consequences. Compliance will necessarily lead to the implementation of the Divine program. This goal can be attained only by armed struggle:

> The principal mitzvah is conquest—war. This is a matter for the entire Jewish People. . . . This is authentic Halakhah.[28]

In his lectures and writings, Rabbi Zvi Yehuda provided a theological basis, which bordered on the mystical, for his charge to conquer the Land:

> The legacy of the Land of Israel comprises "the sworn promise to the fathers and the conquest by the sons." All the settlements of today are individual sparks from our father Abraham's passage through the land. . . . Our father Abraham prepared our conquest by means of the Divine Source, the commandment "arise and walk about the land" (Gen. 13:17). We were commanded to conquer and there is a way to conquer. This is a precept in every generation. Today, the First Cause, Who announced the generations from the start, has ordained matters so that we have the tools that permit the fulfillment of this precept. The time has come for the eternal, Heavenly, spiritual oath to couple with the conquest by the sons and its sequel, namely, "that we not leave it desolate" and not "in the hands of another nation," . . . but only in our own hands, the hands of the godly nation.[29]

It is not surprising that his sermons at the Mercaz Harav Yeshiva and his published writings made Rabbi Zvi Yehuda the spiritual mentor of Gush Emunim and other nationalist religious groups. One cannot know to what extent they acted as they did as a direct result of his influence or simply invoked his sermons to justify their own leanings. There is no doubt that the rabbi laid solid foundations for the ideology of those who work to realize a Greater Land of Israel for Jews by teaching that the right of settlement is derived from the authority of the Torah and Divine ordinance.

This ideology of exclusive Jewish ownership of the Land of Israel and the justification of occupying it by military conquest complements Rabbi Ariel's view that a true and lasting peace is impossible. Both opinions serve to justify the hostile attitude toward the Arabs of the territories, who for hundreds of years have been living on land that does not belong to them, and toward the neighboring countries that support the the Palestinians. Such views, when maintained by leading rabbis, provide an ideological underpinning for the actions of religiously observant settlers. According to these rabbis' halakhic rulings, the settlers' "conquest of the land" falls under the rubric of a precept not to be breached even at the cost of one's life—actions for which there is no alternative, not even peace.

THE HUMANIST APPROACH

The Secular Court's Ruling in the Kafr Kasim Case

We should compare the halakhic rulings cited above with the verdict of the secular Israeli courts in a very similar issue: the infamous Kafr Kasim case.

In October 1956, at the start of the Sinai Campaign, a curfew was clamped on the Arab-populated areas adjoining the Jordanian border, including the village of Kafr Kasim. When residents, unaware of the curfew, returned from their fields that evening, a Border Police detachment opened fire on them without warning. More than forty civilians were killed, including women and children.[30]

The battalion commander and ten of his soldiers were court-martialed. In October 1958, the military court (its president was

District Court Judge and later Supreme Court Justice Benjamin Halevy, sitting with his reserve rank of colonel) convicted them and sentenced them to various terms of imprisonment. An appeal was submitted to the Supreme Court. Let us examine portions of the rulings of these two courts.

Halevy began his verdict with the following words: "No man, including someone who is serving in the military or police, has the right to kill or give orders to kill another human being, except in exceptional cases that are defined in the law."[31] Furthermore: "It is a general rule that a soldier is forbidden to kill an unarmed person without cause and trial."[32]

As for a soldier's argument that he had no choice because his commander had ordered him to shoot the civilian, Halevy wrote that such an order would be "a patently illegal order" that a soldier need not obey; moreover, he would "bear criminal responsibility for the consequences of implementing it."[33]

The military court promulgated an ironclad rule: "There are laws of war that every commander in the Israel Defense Forces must respect and obey. One of them is the ban on murdering civilians who are not taking an active part in the hostilities."[34] Compare this with Rabbi Avidan's halakhic ruling that sanctioned the killing of Arabs who assist the enemy army, even though they take no active part in the fighting.

Ruling on the soldiers' appeal, the Supreme Court laid down the principle that "a democratic state must establish legal safeguards so that the weapons it entrusts to its army to protect the state will not be misused against the laws of the state."[35] Here we hear the opinion that firm boundaries must be set so that the military and its personnel observe the laws of the state.

Is it reasonable to expect every private to know how to distinguish a legal order from an illegal order or a patently illegal order? Must every soldier and officer acquire a legal education before going into battle? The justices ruled that although they cannot be required to fight with the military lawbook in their pocket, it may be expected that "a reasonable soldier can identify a patently illegal order." How can he do this without studying lawbooks? The justices replied that "the legal provisions in the statutes are intended to stimulate the moral and humane conscience of our soldiers." In fact, the answer had already been stated definitively, in a phrase that still resounds in Israeli society, by Halevy in his original verdict: An illegal order is one in which the illegality "pierces the eye and outrages the heart, if the eye is not blind and the heart not sealed or corrupt."[36]

Both Halevy and the Supreme Court referred soldiers to their ethical and human conscience, which a believing person can view as the gift of God. The contrast between the ethical humanism of the military and civil courts and the views of the rabbis cited above is striking. We can be proud of the former, but the remarks of the latter, uttered by those who are supposed to teach the Torah in Israel, are disappointing and disgraceful.

Rabbi Shlomo Goren

One religious leader who advocated the humane position was the late Rabbi Shlomo Goren. Despite his hawkish position on the Land of Israel, Rabbi Goren, drawing on midrashic and halakhic texts, offered quite a different view at the start of his volume of responsa on the laws of war.[37] Here is his treatment of two issues.

"The Works of My Hands Are Drowning in the Sea"

Rabbi Goren discussed a famous midrash:

> [When the Egyptians were drowning in the sea], the ministering angels wanted to sing praises to the Holy One Blessed Be He. The Holy One Blessed Be He said to them: "The works of My hands are drowning in the sea and you would sing My praises?!" (BT Sanhedrin 39b)

Rabbi Goren inferred from this that "those who go into battle are commanded to fight with all their heart and soul against the enemy, but not to rejoice in this."[38]

Not only should we should refrain from rejoicing at the fall of our enemies—an emotion that seems perfectly natural and is celebrated in the literature of nations throughout human history—but the manner in which one fights must also be without blemish:

> Despite the explicit Torah commandment to wage war, we are enjoined to have mercy on the enemy, too, and not to kill even in wartime, except when self-defense is imperative for conquest and victory, and not to harm a noncombatant population. It is certainly forbidden to harm women and children who are not taking part in the war.[39]

If we read this carefully, we see that Rabbi Goren prohibited killing not only enemy civilians but also enemy soldiers if it is not absolutely necessary to kill them in battle—a humanity that is at odds with the rulings of other decisors.

But doesn't this approach contradict the Torah commandment as enunciated by Maimonides?

> It is a positive commandment to utterly destroy the seven nations, as it is stated: "you must proscribe them" (Deut. 20:17). Anyone who encounters one of them and does not kill him has violated a negative commandment, as it says (Deut. 20:16): "you shall not let a soul remain alive" (Laws of Kings 5:4).

Maimonides concluded this section of his code with the reservation that "their memory [of the seven nations of ancient Canaan] has already been lost." According to the Mishnah, "long ago Sennacherib, king of Assyria, came and mixed up all the nations" (Mishnah Yadayyim 4:4). Thus, today, as in Maimonides' time, this commandment is no longer applicable. Rabbi Goren stated as much in a subheading: "One must not harm a noncombatant population and one may not learn from the wars of antiquity." He explained that in the matter of

> those obligatory wars that we were explicitly commanded by the Torah to wage in antiquity, in which "you shall not let a soul remain alive"— . . . one must not learn from them, heaven forbid, about other wars and our own time. . . . We are commanded by

the Torah to follow in the ways [of the Holy One Blessed Be He] and to have compassion for His creatures, as it is written: "His mercy is upon all His works" (Ps. 145:9).[40]

King David Was Not Allowed to Build the Temple because of His Cruelty in War

To ground his position on the ethics of warfare, Rabbi Goren cited a passage from Maimonides as to why King David was not allowed to build the Temple:

> We have found that he was cruel. . . . It is stated clearly in the Book of Chronicles that God did not allow him to build the Temple and that he was not worthy in His eyes to do so because he killed so many people. He said (1 Chron. 22:8): "But the word of the Lord came to me, saying, 'You have shed much blood and fought great battles; you shall not build a House for My name, for you have shed much blood on the earth in My sight.'"[41]

Rabbi Goren asserted that Maimonides understood the verse literally. In other words, although David fought against non-Israelite idolaters, he was not deemed worthy to build the Temple because he behaved cruelly in these wars. "Even though David's wars were wars of the Lord against idolaters, some measure of cruelty nevertheless adhered to him and made him unfit to build the Temple."[42]

To buttress his argument, Rabbi Goren cited Nahmanides' comment on the verse "when you go out as a troop against your enemies, be on your guard against anything evil" (Deut. 23:10):

> The verse cautions against a time when sin is widespread. It is well known among the customs of troops that go out to war that . . . the most upright person in his nature becomes cruel and wrathful when the troop goes out against the enemy. Accordingly, Scripture warns him, "be on your guard against anything evil." [43]

From the case of King David one may draw an *a fortiori* inference about the national leaders and military commanders of our own day. The mandate to avoid cruelty and bloodshed is equally valid in our own generation and has actually increased in importance in this age of sophisticated weaponry. Nahmanides' words should be inscribed on the banner and in the heart of every officer and soldier in the Israel Defense Forces. All the more so should his principles guide every minister in an Israeli government who sends soldiers into battle.

To sum up, Rabbi Goren reached a position very close to that of the humanist respondents cited above. He relied on ancient and medieval rabbinic sources only, not on more recent texts or modern decisors, and certainly not on contemporary scholars of Judaics, law, or history. He wrote purely as a halakhic decisor.

Furthermore, we must give extra weight to his remarks because of his expertise in the Halakhah of military matters and warfare, which he cultivated as the first chief chaplain of the Israel Defense Forces.

I believe that Rabbi Goren's humane views reflect an enlightened approach to Halakhah. His opinion about the ethics of combat is even more important in light of its contrast with those of other rabbis of our generation and his own hawkish views on territorial issues.[44]

WHO IS THE GREATEST HERO?

We must decide which approach is correct according to evolving Halakhah: the humane views of Rabbis Abraham Isaac Kook, Ben-Zion Uziel, Ovadia Yosef, Ḥayyim David Halevy, Shlomo Goren, and others, or the vicious opinions of Rabbis Shaul Israeli, Shimon Weiser, Avraham Avidan, Yaakov Ariel, and Zvi Yehuda Kook? Halakhah is pluralistic; when confronted by conflicting decisions, a Jew may choose in such matters. A human being who lives in accordance with evolving and ethical Halakhah should have no trouble deciding which approach is correct here.

With regard to the inner struggle of an individual with his own nature, the Sages declared: "Who is a hero? A person who subdues his evil inclination." And with regard to the struggle between an individual and his or her enemy, they said: "Who is the greatest hero of all? . . . One who turns his enemy into his friend."[45]

According to the Torah and to a progressive view of Halakhah, making peace is the greatest bravery of all—greater than holding on to every square inch of the land. As for the argument that it is impossible to make peace because there is no one with whom to negotiate, let alone make peace, the Midrash has already answered that, making the Lord say that "if you bow your will so as to make your enemy into your friend, I promise that I will make your enemy into your friend."[46]

Is it not incumbent upon every believing Jew to rely on Him who makes peace on high? If we work in concert with Him, we must believe that "He will make peace for us and all Israel."

16

Ransoming Captives

IN 1983 AND AGAIN IN 1985, ISRAEL EXCHANGED THOU-
sands of Arab terrorists for a handful of captured Israeli soldiers.
This was not an exchange of prisoners of war, common after the
termination of hostilities. It was a trade—some say extortion—in
which a handful of Israeli soldiers were set free in return for thousands of terrorists who had been duly convicted in courts of law of
terrorism, murder, and other serious offenses.

The public's reaction to the trade was generally ambivalent: Relief and joy at the soldiers' release from captivity and rescue from
mortal peril, on one hand, wrestled with bewilderment and anxiety
at the freeing of thousands of terrorists and murderers, on the
other.

This contrast between fear for a captive's life and concern
about the implications of paying an outrageous ransom is reflected
in Halakhah as well. From one perspective, Maimonides emphasized the great importance of this precept:

> There is no precept greater than the redemption of captives,
> since a captive falls into the category of the hungry and thirsty
> and naked and is in danger of death. Those who close their eyes
> to redeeming him transgress . . . "do not stand passively beside
> the blood of your fellow" (Lev. 19:16) and nullify the precept of
> . . . "Love your fellow as yourself" (Lev. 19:18) (Laws of Gifts to
> the Poor 8:10).

Rabbi Joseph Caro made the matter even more acute and emphasized the urgency of release: "Every moment one puts off

redeeming captives, where it is possible to do so sooner, is like shedding blood" (*Shulḥan Arukh, Y.D.* 252:3).

If redeeming captives is so vital a precept, it seems to be our duty to do so at any cost. Yet, the Mishnah holds that "captives should not be ransomed for more than their value, as a precaution for the general good" (Mishnah Gittin 4:6). In the Gemara the Sages propose two reasons for this prohibition: the "penury of the community" that might be reduced to destitution by paying the ransom, and "so as not to encourage them to kidnap more" hostages and extort even larger sums. Rabbenu Nissim Gerondi (1310–?1375) added the gloss "so that the gentiles will not exert themselves and kidnap many [Jews] because they can sell them so dearly" (on BT Gittin 45a). According to Maimonides, this is "so that the enemy will not pursue [other victims in the future] to take them captive " (Laws of Gifts to the Poor 8:12).

Consequently, most decisors have ruled that despite the great importance of rescuing captives, it is forbidden to pay an exorbitant ransom. The unreasonable payment may indeed save today's captives, but perhaps at the price of the freedom or even life of other victims in the future. Thus, the great *mitzvah* of redeeming captives has a limit: One must not pay ransom for a prisoner today in an amount that is liable to endanger other persons later on.

Some eminent decisors disagree with this conclusion, especially when the captive faces imminent death or has the means to pay his own ransom. The discussion focuses chiefly on a difficult moral dilemma: Do we save one Jew without considering the consequences? Or must we consider the possible implications of the sum paid for the welfare of other Jews? The value of saving human life troubled our Sages in the Middle Ages just as they troubled the Israeli teams that negotiated with the terrorist organizations. Some rabbis ruled that in such cases any price may be paid. Nahmanides, however, rejected the opinion that when there is reason to fear for the captives' lives, "one redeems them for whatever sum can redeem them." Instead, he ruled that even in a life-or-death situation, one may pay a ransom only "within the bounds of the regulation."[1] According to Rabbi Elijah ben Samuel of Lublin, "one does not redeem [a person] for more than his value" even if he is about to be killed.[2]

Rabbi Meir ben Gedaliah, the Maharam of Lublin (1558–1616), ruled that

> If it is because they want to kill him, no decisor has written a dissenting opinion that if they are going to kill him one must redeem him even for more than his value. . . . Thus the conclusion is that even those who will be killed are not to be redeemed for more than their value.[3]

In the halakhic debate as to the reasonable price to be paid for the redemption of a captive—for example, his value in the slave market—in the sixteenth century, Rabbi David ben Zimra (the Radbaz) wrote that the criterion should be the actual situation in the world. We should examine the practices of other nations. He ruled that it was not proper to redeem Jewish captives "for more than captives of other nations." He cautioned that to do so would motivate enemies to focus their attacks on Jews, "especially since it is already well known that Jews ransom captives even though they have nothing of their own, and they would certainly raise their price very high."[4] This is the lesson learned in our own day by the world powers, who in the past readily agreed to hijackers' demands to release terrorists and only later began to follow in Israel's footsteps and fight against terrorism, refusing to submit to extortion.

Our rabbis ruled as they did on the basis of bitter personal experience, since their communities were surrounded by hostile gentiles who thirsted for their blood and money.

There is the famous case of the great decisor Rabbi Meir ben Baruch, the Maharam of Rothenburg (1215–1293), who led a mass exodus of Jews from Germany, hoping to reach the Land of Israel, but was caught and thrown into prison in 1286. In 1288, the Jews offered the Emperor Rudolph of Habsburg a ransom of more than 20,000 pounds of silver—a truly astronomical sum in those days.

The rabbi would not permit the Jews to complete this deal and ransom him for such an exorbitant price, fearing that other rulers in the future might be tempted to detain eminent rabbis and extort huge sums for their release. Rabbi Solomon Luria described the case as follows:

> I have heard that the Maharam of Rothenburg, of blessed memory, was held in the fortress of Ensisheim [in Upper Alsace] for a number of years. The prince demanded a large sum from the communities and they were willing to ransom him. But he would not let them do so; for, he said, "one does not redeem captives for more than their value."[5]

The result was that the great rabbi languished in prison for the last seven years of his life.[6]

How can we apply these halakhic principles to the redemption of captives in our own time? First of all, we must confront the difficult choice between the immediate danger to the prisoners and the potentially disastrous future results of paying an exorbitant price. In antiquity the ransom extorted was pecuniary; but today the price demanded is the release of terrorists and murderers, which only increases the danger to all of us.

According to Halakhah, we must do everything to fulfill the great and meritorious precept of ransoming Jewish captives and use all available means to do so. Nevertheless, there is a limit: We may not endanger others by releasing these terrorists. We must consult with experts in antiterrorism and ask whether submitting to this extortion will only whet the terrorists' appetite for hostage taking and whether paying so high a price will encourage the terrorists to take more prisoners with the aim of freeing their comrades from Israeli prisons. Are we exposing all or some of the Israeli public to mortal danger by releasing murderers who are likely to return to their old ways and kill more Jews? If the experts answer these questions in the negative, we can ransom our captives at any price. If their answer is in the affirmative, however, we must not pay such a high price and endanger others.

The choice between the two approaches—ransoming captives at any price or protecting the community—must take account of the cruel reality of our own time, just as our Sages did in theirs.

In the years that have passed since this chapter was first written, many of the terrorists released in 1983 and 1985 have returned to their old ways. Many of them assaulted property and people, murdering Israelis and others.

These distressing facts add another dimension and historical perspective to this issue.

17

"Halakhic" Justifications for Murder

Rabbinic Responsibility for a Massacre

On Friday morning, February 25, 1994, Dr. Baruch Goldstein, a resident of the Jewish town of Kiryat Arba on the outskirts of Hebron, entered the Isaac Hall in the Tomb of the Patriarchs (known to Muslims as the Ibrahimi Mosque), where the Muslim Ramadan service was taking place. Wearing his army reservist's uniform with its captain's bars, he was neither stopped nor suspected, even by the Arabs at prayer. Positioning himself behind the congregation, he raised his Galil assault rifle and emptied four magazines into the backs of the worshippers, killing twenty-nine and wounding perhaps twice as many before he was overpowered and killed by one or more of the Arabs.

Only at first sight was this appalling massacre the action of a single person. It is true that Baruch Goldstein carried out his murderous rampage alone; but he would not have committed twenty-nine murders without ideological and social backing. Goldstein, a physician who violated the Hippocratic Oath and shot down defenseless worshippers in a holy shrine, was nurtured by a warped and distorted faith that many shared with him.

We all think we know where this poison came from. Goldstein was a fervent supporter of the late Meir Kahane. He absorbed his mentor's racist doctrines, which pretend to be derived from halakhic sources, and put them into practice.

In Kahane's book *Know Your Judaism (in Truth)* he could find the following rabbinic gems: "Only non-Jews are cruel" (Maimonides, *Mishneh Torah*, Laws of Gifts to the Poor 10:2); "You [Israel] are called 'human'; but non-Jews are not called 'human'" (BT Baba Metzia 104); "'You shall not take vengeance or bear a grudge against your countrymen' (Lev. 19:18)—but you may take vengeance or bear a grudge against a non-Jew" (*Sifra* ad loc.). Kahane's book presents these and other passages, twisted out of context, as God-given imperatives. It is no wonder that the disciple carried out his master's dictates.

Nevertheless, the massacre would not have taken place had Goldstein not been able to rely on the support of the milieu in which he lived—a sympathy manifested by the way in which many residents of Kiryat Arba, including well-known rabbis, reacted to the massacre. Not only did they refuse to condemn the murderer's actions; some lauded him and called him a "martyr" and a "righteous man."

The reactions of these residents of the Jewish suburb of the City of the Patriarchs, most of whom are not shackled by Kahane's doctrines, were based on a halakhic and ideological infrastructure built up over the decades by leading rabbis. This platform continues to provide the settlers with theological backing in their confrontations with Arabs and with successive Israeli governments.

In 1953, a retaliatory raid on the village of Kibya[1] (discussed in chapter 15) resulted in the deaths of Arab civilians—men, women, and children. Rabbi Shaul Yisraeli, a member of the Chief Rabbinate council, justified the children's death as "a punishment from Heaven, . . . in which children are . . . punished for the sins of their parents." Some twenty years later, this view was seconded by Rabbi Shimon Weiser ("although in peacetime it is forbidden to kill non-Jewish civilians, . . . *in wartime it is a* mitzvah *to kill them*") and Rabbi Avraham Avidan ("in wartime, . . . even good civilians [may be killed]"). Rabbi Yaakov Ariel pronounced that the Arabs could convert, accept the status of resident aliens, or decide "of their own free will" to emigrate to another country. Rabbi Zvi Yehuda Kook maintained that today the commandment to occupy and settle the Land of the Israel has the same status as the most serious of the negative prohibitions—those against bloodshed, idolatry, and incest.[2]

Exhortations of this sort by eminent rabbis, expounded in the ostensible name of Halakhah and Torah, constitute the ideological basis of the right-wing settlement movement Gush Emunim. They are liable to have an influence on every Torah-observant Jew, as we saw in the settlers' reactions to the Hebron massacre.

But Halakhah is pluralistic and provides the settlers with every possibility to turn their backs on those who preach hatred. For example, they could heed Rabbi Abraham Isaac Kook's humane ruling concerning Arabs: "We should say that the Muslims are not idolaters and fall into the category of resident aliens and may be settled in the Land of Israel." Similarly, the late chief rabbi Yitzhak Isaac Herzog ruled that non-Jews who are not idolaters should not be prevented from settling in the Land of Israel, even though they have not stood before a Jewish religious court and formally accepted the seven Noahide commandments.

If those who honor the Torah had accepted these and other halakhic rulings by eminent rabbis—rulings that advocate a humane approach toward non-Jews—our spiritual and political situation in this country would be very different today.

THE ASSASSINATION OF THE PRIME MINISTER

We have seen that halakhic rulings can have great influence on acts of violence. Yigal Amir, the convicted murderer of Prime Minister Yitzhak Rabin, was apparently influenced by these teachings. The following is an excerpt from the dialogue between Amir and the magistrates' court judge at his arraignment:

> **Amir:** There is a *p'sak halakhah* [halakhic ruling] that it is permitted to kill someone who gives away part of the Land of Israel.

According to Halakhah, the moment a Jew hands over *[moser]* his people and land into the hand of a gentile, we are obligated to kill him.

Judge: What rabbi taught you this Halakhah?

Amir: No one taught this to me. I have studied Talmud all my life. . . . There are 613 commandments in the Torah.

Judge: Have the Ten Commandments been nullified?

Amir: The Ten Commandments have not been eliminated. But there is a Divine commandment that is higher than "thou shalt not murder": saving life. It is the same as when you kill the enemy in war. There is a higher purpose and therefore it is permitted. If the Prime Minister declares that he is not responsible for the security of 2 percent of the population [the settlers in the territories] and shakes the hand of the arch-murderer [Arafat] and frees terrorists from prison . . . he is not my prime minister.[3]

In the eyes of the assassin, and those of like mind, two halakhic indictments were invoked to justify the murder of Prime Minister Rabin. These two capital charges are those of *moser* and *rodef* ("pursuer").[4]

Moser

A *moser* is someone who informs on a fellow Jew or hands him over to gentiles. Maimonides states that the prohibition of informing on or delivering up a Jew to the enemy applies to both individuals and their possessions (Laws of Damage and Destruction 8:9–10).

Only a twisted mind would interpret this precept as applicable to the decisions of the democratically elected head of government of a sovereign Jewish state. No minority group of Israelis, wherever they live, may arbitrarily decide that an agreement concluded by the government violates the law against handing over a Jew to the enemy. No individual or group can decide on behalf of the entire country who is the enemy and who is a *moser*. This is the exclusive prerogative of the elected government and the courts. To do so is not only a misinterpretation of Halakhah but also a distortion of the judical process in which an individual or group arrogates to itself the roles of prosecutor, judge, and executioner all in one.

Rodef

The late Prime Minister was also accused of being a *rodef*. Maimonides defines this criminal as "one who is pursuing another person to kill him. All Jews are obligated to save the pursued individual, even at the cost of the life of the pursuer." He adds that "if they can save the pursued by wounding one of the limbs of the pursuer, they should do so and not kill the latter" (Laws of Murder and Preservation of Life 1:7).

One of Amir's fellow yeshiva students testified that he had asked the head of their yeshiva whether this law of *rodef* is applicable in our day. The rabbi did not answer, but pointed instead to the open Talmud volume on his study stand and left the room. The student approached the stand and saw that the book was open to Tractate Sanhedrin 49a, which deals with the issue of killing a pursuer.

This passage is based on the biblical story of Asahel. This swift-footed Asahel, the younger brother of Joab, the commander of King David's army, pursued Abner, who had commanded the army of King Saul and was now upholding the royal pretensions of Saul's surviving son Ish-bosheth. The veteran Abner told the young Asahel to stop chasing him or he would have to strike in self-defense. When Ashahel refused and persisted in his pursuit, Abner thrust backwards with his spear and killed him. Joab later killed Abner to avenge his brother's death (2 Sam. 2:8–3:27).

The talmudic passage is a protocol of Joab's trial before King Solomon, many years later:

> Then Joab was brought before the court and King Solomon questioned him. "Why did you kill Abner?
>
> Joab replied: "I was the avenger of the blood of my brother, Asahel."
>
> Solomon interrogated him further: "But Asahel was a pursuer [*rodef*]!
>
> Joab: "Even so, Abner should have saved himself at the cost of one of [Asahel's] limbs.
>
> Solomon: "Yet perhaps he could not do so." (Rashi: Abner was unable to aim precisely to hit one of his limbs).

Joab retorted: "If Abner could aim exactly at the fifth rib [where the gall bladder and liver are located—hence a certainly fatal blow], could he not have aimed at one of his limbs?"

Thereupon Solomon concluded: "Let's drop the incident of Abner."

The yeshiva students and their rabbi were studying the question whether it is permissible to kill a pursuer and the judgment upon someone who executes the killer of the pursuer. Such studies must have been of more than academic interest to those contemplating assassination of a leader whom learned rabbis had indicted as a *rodef.*

Pulsa Denura

Where, then, did Amir derive the loathsome view that a "lofty goal," which is "a Heavenly injunction," may justify violating the commandment "Thou shalt not murder"? We do know about one particular document that was distributed in some synagogues on the Day of Atonement in 1995 and gleefully read out on television by an activist on the extreme right. Its heading is *Pulsa Denura* (an Aramaic expression that Rashi glosses as "lashes of fire"). The term appears in several talmudic legends—for instance, the description of the punishment of the angel Gabriel (BT Yoma 77a)—and, in more moderate form, in the responsa literature of the sixteenth through the twentieth centuries.[5]

The document in question, however, is neither folktale nor prayer (as it was sometimes described by the media). Rather, influenced by "practical kabbalah" or witchcraft, it is a text of black magic and excommunication, a death-curse directed at a particular person, in this case the late Prime Minister, as we learn from the following text:

With regard to Yitzhak son of Rosa, known as Rabin, permission is given by the destroying angels to send a sword against that wicked man. The angels of destruction, who are the emissaries from below, have no permission to be merciful to him and forgive him for his sins. For this reason let any good he may have done in this world be forgotten . . . so he may be killed because he misleads the holy nation and hands over the Land of Israel to our enemies. . . .

There is no escaping the echo of this monstrous death sentence in the assassin's declaration that it is an obligation to kill a Jew who hands over his people and land to the enemy. Is this similarity merely happenstance? Or is this kabbalistic curse one small tile from the mosaic of distorted "Halakhah" that underlay this atrocious crime?

SUMMARY

We may conclude that the questionable attempts to give supposed halakhic support to relatively "minor" acts of violence like stoning vehicles, wild demonstrations against archaeologists, damaging the shops and homes of those who peacefully carry on their own way of life, and blocking main traffic arteries can and have escalated into deeds with catastrophic results. Israelis have been told to respect the feelings of these pious persons, who claim to be acting in accordance with Halakhah.

There is much beauty and wisdom in our halakhic tradition, which has guided the people of Israel and kept them alive throughout the millennia. But when these words are twisted and distorted they can be very dangerous. All teachers of Torah should remember the stern warning of Avtalyon, the teacher of Hillel and Shammai: "Sages, give heed to your words, lest you incur the penalty of exile to a place of evil waters, and the disciples who come after you drink thereof and die, so that the name of Heaven is profaned" (Mishnah Avot 1:11).

V

The Status of Women

If she were required to perform a positive commandment that is time-dependent, it is possible that while she was fulfilling [God's] commandment her husband would tell her do his own bidding. If she performed the command of the Creator and neglected her spouse's command, woe to her from her husband. But if she complied with her husband's command and set aside the command of her Creator, woe to her from her Creator.

DAVID ABUDARHAM (fourteenth century)

Not only is there no ban on women's voting for an elected assembly and participating in all matters connected with the organization of the state, it is a mitzvah *for them to participate in every way, just like men.*

RABBI CHAIM TCHERNOWITZ (twentieth century)

Over the last century and a half, the status of women has advanced greatly in most parts of the world. Some say that in this period their status has progressed more than in all earlier human history. Women have received the right to vote and be elected to public positions, and have served in many senior posts, including prime minister of Israel, India, Great Britain, Turkey, Norway, and Pakistan. In the liberal professions, academia, the arts, and the business world, too, many women have reached the highest rungs.

Nevertheless, it must be admitted that women have not attained absolute equality in all walks of life.

What about the halakhic status of women? Has there been similar progress in this realm? Do decisors of the present day advance the status of women in accordance with the approach of the Sages of antiquity? For our Sages banned marrying a woman against her will and found the authority to prevent a husband from divorcing a woman against her will, to make life easier for women who required *yibbum* or *halitzah, agunot,* and women who were discriminated against for other reasons.

Yet, in contrast to the daring and humane approach of our Sages, who looked for solutions to the difficult condition of being a woman, the contemporary rabbinic establishment is frequently stringent without any basis. Liberal halakhic solutions advanced by the talmudic Sages, great medieval decisors, or eminent rabbis of the last two centuries are too bold for the taste of certain contemporary rabbis who occupy positions of power.

In this section we shall consider various issues to determine whether Halakhah really bars women from serving as members of religious councils, participating in funerals, saying kaddish for their relatives, and serving in the armed forces. We shall endeavor to determine whether the attitude of the establishment rabbis reflects the spirit of Halakhah of antiquity.

18

Is a Woman Permitted to Hold a Public Position?

IN THE MID-1980S, THE RELIGIOUS ESTABLISHMENT IN Israel proclaimed that as a matter of Halakhah, women may not serve on religious councils.[1] It never published the ostensible halakhic rationale for this ban. Nor has the Chief Rabbinate ever made a detailed presentation of its case so that the general public could know the grounds of its ruling that a woman may not hold public office.

Whatever the reasons were, the refusal by the Minister of Religious Affairs in 1986 to approve the first such appointment, that of Leah Shakdiel to the Religious Council of Yeroham, an outlying town in the northern Negev, was nothing new. There were precedents that seem to have escaped the eye and memory of the religious establishment. Most prominent was the bitter contention, in both Palestine and the Diaspora, in 1920, on the eve of the first elections for the Assembly of Delegates (the representative assembly of the Jews of Palestine under the British mandate). The Ultra-Orthodox and Orthodox parties made every effort to deny women the right to vote and run for office. The resulting tempest sparked a sharp halakhic dispute, which, as we shall see, is relevant to the contemporary problem of the appointment of a woman to religious councils.

ARE WOMEN FORBIDDEN TO HOLD OFFICE?

Leading rabbis in Eretz Yisrael and the Diaspora adduced many halakhic passages to prove that Halakhah permits or bars women from voting or holding public office.

One source cited by the prohibitionists was the mishnaic-era Halakhah that understands the verse "you shall set a king over yourself" (Deut. 17:15) to mean "a king and not a queen" (*Sifre*, Shofetim 157). On the basis of this exegesis, Maimonides ruled that

> A queen is not to be entrusted with power, as it is stated, "[you shall set] a king over yourself"—and not a queen. Similarly, with regard to all positions in Israel, only a man may be appointed to them (Laws of Kings 1:5).

Some rabbis have cited this ruling to prove that a woman may not be appointed to any position whatsoever. Among them was Rabbi Israel Zev Mintzberg of Jerusalem (1872–1962):

> It is absolutely forbidden by the Torah to appoint a woman to any civil position of authority over the public, even if the entire community agrees—as in the case of the Founding Assembly that passed a law giving women the right to be elected.[2]

Other prominent rabbis asserted that Halakhah does not bar a woman from serving as an elected representative. Rabbi Chaim Hirschensohn (1857–1935; in New Jersey from 1904) maintained that the stricture that power may be entrusted to "a king and not a queen" applies only to the Davidic monarchy and is irrelevant for other public positions.[3]

Rabbi Ben-Zion Uziel also found grounds to permit the election of women, despite Maimonides' ruling:

> This halakhah applied only to appointments made by the Sanhedrin; in our question, however, it is not a matter of appointing but of receiving. By means of elections the majority of the

community expresses its opinion, agreement, and confidence in those who are elected. In such a case, even Maimonides acknowledges that there is no prohibition whatsoever.[4]

DOES CUSTOM BAN THE APPOINTMENT OF WOMEN?

David Danino, who served as a member of the Knesset representing the National Religious Party and as head of all the religious councils throughout the country, once declared that women had never served on a religious council and never would do so. Wittingly or unwittingly, his statement reflected a well-known conservatism that opposes all change merely because it is innovation. According to another of the antifeminists in the 1920 controversy, Rabbi Dr. Bernhard Reiter of Rotterdam:

> In the annals of the medieval decisors and later rabbinic authorities, nothing is known about the election of women. It never appeared on the agenda in any Jewish community in any period during the thousands of years of our exile. If our ancestors were not prophets, they were at least the sons of prophets.[5]

By contrast, Rabbi Chaim Tchernowitz (1871–1949; at the Jewish Institute of Religion in New York from 1923) rejected out of hand the idea that women could be disqualified from serving in a public position because there was no precedent for their doing so:

> It is quite irrelevant to rely on custom with regard to a matter that was not prevalent; the question of general elections to a political organization did not exist until the present. What is more, the custom [of male office-holders only] is not one that was adopted intentionally.[6]

Should Female Candidates Be Disqualified because "Women Are Frivolous"?

Some rabbis cited the talmudic adage often rendered as "women are frivolous" (BT Shabbat 33b) as grounds for ruling that women could not vote or be elected to public office. Rabbi Uziel, by contrast, noted that if we were to bar women on these grounds,

> We would also have to delete from the voting rolls those men who are weak-minded, who will always be with us. But reality slaps us in the face and shows us that in the past as well as in the present, women may have the same learning and knowledge as men to conduct negotiations, to buy and sell, and to manage their affairs in the best way possible. . . . The Sages' remark that they are "frivolous" has an entirely different meaning.[7]

A reading of the entire talmudic passage at issue reveals that during the Hadrianic decrees against observance of Judaism, Rabbi Simeon bar Yoai decided not to expose his wife to danger by having her bring provisions to him in his hiding place, because "women are *unstable*" and liable to break under torture and reveal the hiding place. This is the "entirely different meaning" to which Rabbi Uziel referred.

To Preserve Domestic Harmony

For whatever reason, Rabbi Abraham Isaac Kook never issued a halakhic opinion on this subject. He did, however, produce an ethical treatise in which he averred that if women were to participate in elections and public life they might come to argue with their husbands, upsetting domestic harmony:

> If we ask women to enter the political forum and entangle them in making known their opinions on matters of elections and

policy in general, then . . . as a result of the confusion of views and disagreements, domestic harmony will be destroyed.[8]

Rabbi Hirschensohn replied that anxieties of this sort cannot be used to deny women their rights and obligations: "If we are afraid of this, we must also deny suffrage to sons and brothers, so as to avoid quarrels among them, and extend this right only to the *pater familias.*"[9]

Rabbi Uziel added:

In truth there is no place here for discord, because the difference of views can be expressed in any form and no person can stifle his views and opinions. But family love that is based on working together is strong enough to emerge unscathed by such differences of opinion.[10]

DISCUSSIONS OF SECULAR MATTERS BUT NOT OF TORAH

After the storm around the Leah Shakdiel case, the religious establishment retreated somewhat and offered her a compromise: she could serve as a member of the religious council and participate in discussions of profane matters, such as administrative and financial arrangements; but whenever the discussion turned to matters of Torah and Halakhah, she would have to leave the room. Is there any halakhic basis for this proposal?

In an analogous case, Rabbi Moshe Feinstein was asked whether women could participate in Torah study sessions, just as they participate in discussions of profane matters.

There were meetings of a society to which men and women come to discuss and debate and decide its profane matters. It was decided that, at every meeting, one member would teach some passage from the *Shulhan Arukh* or the ethical literature. . . . As for the women, can they be there during the study session, as they are there during the discussions and debates about profane matters, or do they have to go into another room?

In addition to agreeing implicitly that men and women could sit together and discuss profane matters, Rabbi Feinstein issued a categorical response with regard to the Torah study sessions:

> Questions of Torah and ethics are not inferior to profane matters. . . . There is no reason for them to leave during the Torah study, because women too must know the laws of the Torah and it is beneficial for them to hear words of Torah, law, and ethics.[11]

A *Mitzvah* for Women

It follows from the foregoing discussion that there is no unequivocal ban on women's serving on religious councils. Every ruling against can be matched by one for, issued by rabbis of equal eminence who found good reasons for permitting. The rabbis in the latter group, including a Chief Rabbi of Israel, are representatives of an Orthodoxy that does not usually extend full equality of rights and obligations to women in the synagogue and public life, as the non-Orthodox do as a matter of course.

Given that there is no absolute halakhic ban, the vigorous opposition to the appointment of women to public office may be explained by two factors: (1) Those who hold the reins of organized religion cling to a particular conception of women and maintain that women's roles should be limited to the kitchen, the women's gallery, the bedroom, and the nursery; accordingly they must be excluded from discussions that involve finances or Torah. (2) Politicians are always looking over their shoulders at the Ultra-Orthodox, who of course reject the very possibility of women's equality. This approach disqualified Golda Meir as a candidate for mayor of Tel Aviv. Later, when the Labour Party nominated her to succeed Levi Eshkol as prime minister, however, the Ultra-Orthodox made no objection.

We also see that there is no basis to the religious establishment's long and fierce opposition to the inclusion of women in the electoral colleges that select local and national chief rabbis. In this case, too, the Chief Rabbinate never published a detailed opinion to explain why a woman could not serve in such a public position, and eventually caved in on the issue.

I can do no better than close with the opinion of Rabbi Tchernowitz, which is applicable today no less than when he gave it:

> Not only is there no ban on women's voting for an elected assembly and participating in all matters connected with the organization of the state, it is a *mitzvah* for them to participate in every way, just like men.[12]

19

Women and Service in the Israel Defense Forces

MOST PARTICIPANTS IN THE PROTRACTED PUBLIC DEBATE about the military conscription of women in Israel start from the erroneous assumption that the Torah forbids Jewish girls to serve in the army. If we examine the halakhic arguments adduced as the basis for exempting Orthodox young women from military service, we will find that they are not necessarily supported by the ancient texts and rabbinical rulings over the generations.

"IN AN OBLIGATORY WAR ALL GO FORTH TO BATTLE"

The Mishnah in Tractate Sotah expounds the passage in Deuteronomy that enumerates those who are exempt from going out to war—"anyone who has built a new house but has not dedicated it, . . . anyone who has planted a vineyard but has never harvested it, . . . anyone who has been betrothed to a wife, but who has not yet married her" (Deut. 20:5–7). Afterward, the Mishnah stipulates that these excuses are valid only when national survival is not at stake:

What has been said [that some do not go forth to war] applies to a war of choice; but in an obligatory war all go forth, even the bridegroom out of his chamber and the bride out of her bridal canopy (Mishnah Sotah 8:7).

Maimonides, too, rules that in such an obligatory war, even the bride must go out from her canopy (Laws of Kings 7:4).

What Is the Role of Women in War?

Rabbinic opinion is divided as to what role women play in obligatory wars. Rabbi David ben Zimra (the Radbaz, died in Safed in 1573), commenting on Maimonides' dictum, explains that women were not in the habit of participating in battles; but "it is possible that in an obligatory war the women provided water and food to their husbands, and that is the custom among Arab women."[1] Rabbi Samuel Strashun (died in Vilna in 1872) ruled that women are indeed limited to noncombatant roles but provide support to all soldiers, not just their husbands:

The implication is the women too go forth to war, and this is something new. Perhaps they go out only to cook and bake and the like for the male soldiers.[2]

Israel Is in a Situation of Obligatory War

One of Maimonides' definitions of an obligatory war is one to "save Israel from an enemy who attacks it" (Laws of Kings 5:1)—a phrasing borrowed from Numbers 10:9: "when you are at war in your land against an enemy who attacks you." This, unfortunately, is an apt description of the situation in Israel today: attacks by terrorists and the unremitting threat of hostilities with the countries in our region that still consider themselves to be at war with us. According to Rabbi Yissakhar Halevy Levin:

> In the present conditions, when the Land of Israel is surrounded on all sides by savage foes and almost every settlement is like a frontier town, even those who are not on the front lines must know how to defend themselves and are almost always in a situation of obligatory war.[3]

In this situation of having to defend ourselves against those who attack us, it seems to follow from the authorities cited above that women are required to participate in the military effort, at least as noncombatants, since by doing so they release soldiers for combat duty. Today, many women soldiers are instructors in various courses, some of them teaching combat-related skills. These women are essential to the Israel Defense Forces, and their contribution to Israel's security is beyond any doubt.

HALAKHAH DOES NOT DISTINGUISH BETWEEN OBSERVANT AND SECULAR YOUNG WOMEN

There is no basis for any distinction between religiously observant and nonobservant young women. In fact, Halakhah makes no distinction between observant and nonobservant Jews with regard to their obligations—whatever is forbidden is forbidden to all, and whatever is permitted is permitted to all.

The reason that observant young women, but not their secular cousins, are exempt from the draft derives from considerations of parliamentary coalition-making, not Halakhah.

MORALITY AND SECLUSION IN THE HOME

The argument that Jewish tradition requires Jewish women to seclude themselves within the confines of home and family is based on a rather far-fetched homiletic interpretation of a verse in Psalms, traditionally rendered as "the king's daughter is all glorious within" (Ps. 45:14) and understood to mean that a woman should seek honor and recognition only inside the home.

The late Rabbi Shaul Yisraeli, a member of the Chief Rabbinate Council, accepted the ruling of Rabbi David ben Zimra, cited above, that women must provide food and water to the army:

> Providing water and food and the like in time of war is a matter of saving lives and falls into the category of [averting] certain physical loss, which take precedence over the traditional understanding [of the verse in Psalms].[4]

It is likely that Rabbi Samuel bar Isaac, a Palestinian *amora* of the fourth century, was accurately describing the status of women in his age when he remarked that "it is the way of women to sit at home and the way of men to go out to marketplace and learn wisdom from other people" (Genesis Rabbah 18:1). The situation today, however, is quite different. The vast majority of Jewish women, religious and nonreligious, are active in the marketplace, the office, and the university, and even as domestics in other peoples' homes. The exemplary woman of valor of the Book of Proverbs, who supports her family both in the marketplace and at home, is much closer to the way we live today.

No one has demonstrated that the army has a worse influence on the moral conduct of young Jewish women than any other social setting. Those who advance such an argument must be very careful not to transgress the severe interdiction on tale-bearing and slander against the many Jewish women who have served, do serve, and will faithfully serve the Jewish people and the State of Israel.

IT IS FORBIDDEN TO USE THE TORAH FOR EXTRANEOUS PURPOSES

It appears that a few young women who declare that "reasons of religion and conscience" or "a religious way of life" do not allow them to serve are impelled by other motives, such as fear, an unwillingness to accept the discipline of army life, or the desire to get a head start in the labor market or at the university.

There is no halakhic basis for enjoying extra rights because of one's beliefs or observance of the *mitzvot*. Exploiting one's observance to avoid the civic obligations incumbent on everyone and to gain the advantage of two years in the workplace or academia means receiving a reward in this world for performing a *mitzvah*.

Of course there is an alternative, in the form of one or two years of National Service in socially beneficial tasks such as teaching in outlying towns, serving as youth-group counselors, and working in hospital auxiliaries. Since it is voluntary, however, only some Orthodox (and no Ultra-Orthodox) girls sign up. The onus of their nonservice is ultimately on the rabbis and religious parties, who have frightened the young women and their families about the calamities that will befall them in National Service, even if they live at home. The religious parties have consistently opposed the idea of making such civilian work on behalf of the country compulsory.

20

A "Women's Gallery" in the Cemetery

AS IN A COMPLICATED PASSAGE OF THE TALMUD, THERE ARE various versions concerning the sequence of events in the town of Migdal Ha'emek several years ago. Did the local rabbis bar women from attending burials, as was reported at first? Or was the correct version the one later enunciated by the local rabbi, namely, that it was the community at large that requested that men and women be separated in the cemetery, whereas he merely acquiesced in requiring this segregation?

Whatever the precise circumstances, all the reports agreed that the residents were on the verge of panic, following a string of premature deaths of men in the community. This led the local rabbinate to apply a procedure mentioned in the Zohar, in the hope of averting calamities in the future.

This was not the only such case in recent years. Not long ago, a woman approached me and complained that the members of the burial society in her town, Beit Shemesh, forbade women to stand with men during the graveside eulogy and forced them to stand outside the awning, even in driving rain or scorching sun. Although this custom is not rare in Israel, the general public has no idea of its source. What *is* the reason for the separation of women and men in the cemetery? Is there any support for the custom in Halakhah and Jewish tradition?

Women "Brought Death into the World"

In the Talmud, we read that women participated in funerals: "In a place where it was the custom for women to follow the bier, they do so; to precede the bier, they do so" (BT Sanhedrin 20a). In some places women walked ahead of the pallbearers, and in others after them. In both cases, however, they participated in funerals.

The Jerusalem Talmud reports on a dispute related to the above custom: Some maintained that "women walk first [right behind] the dead and the men after them"; others, that "men [walk] first and the women after them." The Gemara explains that those who held that women must precede the men believed that women "brought death into the world"; those who maintained that the men must walk ahead of the women did so to protect "the dignity of Jewish women and keep the men from looking at them" (JT Sanhedrin 2:4), since "it is disgraceful for women to have men look at them."[1]

Consider the two reasons the Sages offered for the location of women in funeral processions: (1) women brought death into the world and precede the men; (2) the dignity of Jewish women must be preserved, so they walk after the men. We can understand the second approach. But why should women walk after men "because they brought death into the world"?

The Angel of Death Is among the Women

Rabbi Joseph Caro is more stringent on this matter than the Talmud: "Women should be prevented from following the bier to the cemetery" (*Shulḥan Arukh, Y.D.* 359:2). His reason for this absolute ban is that "if they go, they cause evil to the world; so it is appropriate to prevent them."[2] In addition to the passage in the Jerusalem Talmud cited above, Rabbi Caro also refers us to the

Zohar, the central text of Jewish mysticism, as the source of his ruling.

The key passage in the Zohar reads as follows:

> The majority of people do not die before their time, but only those who know not how to take heed to themselves. For at the time when a dead body is taken from his home to the place of burial, the Angel of Death [places himself among] the women. Why the women? Because that has been his habit since the time that [in his original form as the primeval serpent] he seduced Eve, through whom he brought death upon the world. Hence, when he takes a man's life, and the males are accompanying the dead body, he mingles himself on the way [to the cemetery] among the women, and has then the power to take the life of the sons of men. He looks on the way at the faces of those who come within his sight, from the time they carry the dead body out from his house to the place of burial until they return to their homes. It is on their account that he brings about the untimely death of many people.[3]

Now we can understand what the rabbi of Migdal Ha'emek meant when he said that there had been untimely deaths that should be prevented in the future. When the reason for a disaster is known, it behooves religious leaders to take preventive steps. The Zohar not only warns against the lurking peril but also proposes a way to avert it:

> What is the remedy that protects against [the angel of death]? When the dead body is carried to the place of burial, a man should turn his face in another direction and leave the women behind him. Should the latter pass in front [of him], he should turn round so as not to face them. Similarly, when they return from the place of burial he should not return by the way where the women are standing, and he should not look at them at all, but should turn in a different way.[4]

The Zohar warns against the lethal danger that women pose to men in the cemetery. The serpent that seduced Eve, leading to the

expulsion from the Garden of Eden and the death of all human beings, has metamorphosed into the angel of death, who is liable to
slay men by hiding among the daughters of Eve during funerals.
This is the rationale for separating women and men in the cemetery and for the ban on women's even going to the cemetery.

DECISORS WHO ALLOW WOMEN TO PARTICIPATE IN FUNERALS

In contrast to the prohibitions cited above, there are rulings that
do allow women to participate in funeral processions. Rabbi Jacob
ben Samuel, the head of the religious court in the city of Susmir in
the seventeenth century, challenged the Zohar and argued that it
contradicts the passage in the Babylonian Talmud indicating that
women did participate in funerals. He could find no justification
for separating men and women in the cemetery. As for the problem
that men may look at women in the cemetery, he ruled that "because it is a time of grief, one need not be apprehensive about sexual thoughts"; that is, when people are mourning the death of a
loved one, a man is not likely to have lustful thoughts if he looks at
a woman, and accordingly there is no problem.[5]

Thus, he refuted the two reasons advanced for separating
women from men in the cemetery. Even if we were to accept the
fundamental notions that underlie the prohibitions, we must insist
that the idea that the angel of death hides among women during a
funeral, in order to attack men, is a rank superstition. In the Middle Ages this idea may have been believed as a way of explaining
sudden and unexplained deaths; but it has no significance for enlightened Jews today.

Another ruling rebuts the edict issued by the rabbi of Migdal
Ha'emek. If it is the custom in a certain place for men and women
to stand together during a funeral, the members of the burial society cannot prevent them from doing so. We can learn this from a
ruling issued by Rabbi Isaac bar Sheshet of Algeria (1326–1408) in
response to a question about whether the peculiar custom of the

city of Saragossa (Spain), where women wailed and beat drums, should be put down: "Because they do this in honor of the dead, the custom should not be abolished." He even rebuked the questioner, Rabbi Amram ben Meruam: "I have asked you a number of times already not to be so punctilious about changing their customs in such matters, if you wish to be at peace with them."[6] It would be appropriate for every rabbi in Israel to follow this ruling.

All the passages cited here demonstrate that there is no solid basis for the notion that female mourners may not stand alongside the bier during a funeral. On the contrary, there is rabbinic permission for them to do so. Anyone who believes in this superstition about women and the angel of death in the cemetery may act accordingly in his or her private life, but must not impose such customs on others who reject these superstitions.

21

Delaying a Funeral Until the Daughter of the Deceased Arrives

A WOMAN WHO LIVES IN TEL AVIV WAS NOTIFIED THAT HER mother had passed away in Montevideo, Uruguay. She was told that the local rabbi had decided that the funeral would take place the next day. The daughter informed the rabbi, via her relatives in Montevideo, that she could not arrive by then because the trip from Israel to South America takes thirty-six hours. She pleaded that the funeral be delayed for several hours so that she could be present. The rabbi absolutely refused, citing two reasons:

1. The funeral could not be delayed, out of respect for the dead.
2. A dead person must not be left unburied to accommodate a daughter's presence at the funeral, even though it is permissible to wait for a son, so that he may say kaddish at the graveside.

The rabbi was asked to provide halakhic precedents for his ruling but refused to do so. Missing her mother's funeral caused great anguish to the woman, the eldest daughter of the deceased.

Does Halakhah truly stipulate that in such circumstances she may not attend her mother's funeral?

The key questions relate to the reasons cited by the rabbi:

1. Is it permissible to delay burial, and in what circumstances?
2. Is there a halakhic basis for discriminating against a daughter and in favor of a son as grounds for delaying burial? The Mishnah discusses the question of delaying burial as follows:

Anyone who allows his dead to remain unburied transgresses a negative commandment; but if he left him unburied out of respect for him, to bring a coffin and shroud, he does not transgress [the prohibition of deferring burial] (Mishnah Sanhedrin 6:5).

In such a case, according to the Tosefot, "the dead may be left unburied for several days if it is a matter of his own dignity."[1]

In his fourteenth-century code, the *Arba'ah Turim,* Rabbi Jacob ben Asher confirmed the mishnaic ruling and added another reason: to bring in professional mourners.[2] Rabbi Joseph Caro, in the *Shulḥan Arukh,* after citing the *Tur* and other authorities, added a new reason: "If they left him unburied so that relatives could arrive, it is permitted."[3] In his commentary on the *Arba'ah Turim,* Rabbi Joshua Falk (1550–1610) cited all these rulings and emphasized that "this also applies to waiting for relatives."[4]

Rabbi Jehiel Michel Epstein (1835–1905) ruled that

The ban on leaving a body unburied applies only when it is done out of disrespect. . . . If one leaves the body unburied to honor the dead, to prepare the shroud, or so that many persons can come to the funeral . . . one does not transgress this prohibition, because it is not disrespectful.[5]

From all of these sources we learn that the rabbis forbade delaying burial only if doing so would dishonor the deceased. Already in the Talmud we find a distinction between different reasons for delaying burial. Interment may be postponed to preserve the dignity of the dead person and to bring needed appurtenances for the burial. Rabbi Joseph Caro explicitly ruled that one could wait for the arrival of relatives, since this too is out of respect for the deceased. Rabbi Epstein even permitted a postponement to enable a large crowd to attend the funeral.

Clearly, it is not forbidden to delay burial if the reason is to honor the dead person. There is a long line of rulings that interment may be postponed to allow time for relatives, and not only relatives, to arrive. It is unfortunate that the distinguished rabbi of Montevideo did not provide halakhic grounds for his ban. None of the sources about delaying burial that I have checked draw a distinction between male and female relatives. Nor have I found any precedent that burial may be delayed only to allow the son of the deceased to be present to say kaddish at the graveside. (On a woman's right to say kaddish, see the next chapter.)

Indeed, over the generations the rabbis have kept expanding the halakhic principle that burial may be delayed out of respect for the dead person. Initially, the only instances cited were to acquire a coffin and shroud; later, the arrival of professional mourners was deemed sufficient grounds; still later, the arrival of relatives; and finally, a large crowd of acquaintances and strangers. If all of this is allowed as a mark of respect for the deceased, how much the more should it be permitted in the present case, when the presence of her oldest daughter at the funeral would certainly be to the honor of the dead woman. The rabbi who refused the daughter's request to postpone the funeral for several hours so that she could be present contravened the ruling that "the dead may be left unburied for several days if it is a matter of his own dignity." As a matter of Halakhah and decency, the funeral should have been delayed until the woman could arrive from Israel.

If there were precedents for the rabbi's unfortunate ruling, he should have cited them and published the halakhic grounds for his refusal to accede to the family's request to honor their late mother. If in fact he had no good reasons for wounding the family in this way, he should apologize to the woman he prevented from attending her mother's funeral and beg forgiveness from the family, in accordance with the ruling of Maimonides: "Even if he hurt his fellow only in words—he must appease him and urge him until he forgives him" (Laws of Repentance 2:9).

22

The Right of Women to Say Kaddish

Despite women's struggle to better their status in many religious matters, there seems to be a feeling of despair that many things cannot be changed. This, in any case, was the complaint I heard from a woman shortly after her father had passed away. The burial-society functionary did not permit her to say the mourner's kaddish at his funeral, even though she was her father's only child. Instead, he turned to one of the men present, who had barely known the deceased, and asked him to recite the kaddish at the graveside. The woman asked me:

> In what way was this man, who was not close to my father and mumbled the kaddish by rote, preferable to a daughter who is mourning bitterly for her father? Why am I forbidden to say kaddish? In a few days we will have the memorial service marking thirty days since his death and will go to the cemetery for the unveiling of the headstone. Am I permitted to say kaddish in my father's memory then?

REASONS FOR PERMITTING A DAUGHTER TO SAY KADDISH

Is there a halakhic precedent for a woman's reciting kaddish for her parents? The famous decisor Rabbi Jair Bacharach of Worms

(1638–1701) was asked about a case in Amsterdam of a daughter who said kaddish. He mentioned the case of a man who had died

> without a son and left instructions before his death that every day during the twelve-month mourning period, ten men should study Torah in his house for payment and that after the session his daughter would recite kaddish. The community rabbis and leaders did not protest. There is no proof against this, because a woman too, is commanded to sanctify the Divine Name. . . . [Furthermore,] we have reason to conjecture that a daughter, too, may bring benefit and comfort to the soul of the deceased, because she is indeed his offspring.[1]

Rabbi Bacharach cited four reasons for allowing the daughter to say kaddish:

1. It was public knowledge that the daughter was saying kaddish for her father, but the rabbis and community leaders expressed no objection. Their lack of reaction may be taken as at least tacit consent.
2. There is no halakhic proof that a woman may not say kaddish.
3. The recitation of kaddish derives from the commandment to sanctify the Divine Name, which is incumbent upon women as well. It follows, then, that a woman too should say kaddish.
4. Her saying kaddish benefits the soul of her late father, since she is his child.

REASONS TO FORBID A DAUGHTER TO SAY KADDISH

In the face of all these reasons, Rabbi Bacharach nevertheless forbade Jewish women to recite the kaddish:

For we may fear that the force of the Jews' customs—and they too are Torah—will be weakened and everyone will build his own platform on the basis of his own conjectures.[2]

For him, the need to buttress Jewish customs and frustrate individual initiatives outweighed the other points, including the fact that the recitation of kaddish is a positive commandment that women too must fulfill, because it is not time dependent.[3]

Somewhat later, Rabbi Jacob Reischer (1670–1733) ruled in a similar case that a daughter could say kaddish when there was a minyan in the home of the family, but "in the synagogue, one should certainly not allow her to say kaddish at all."[4] In other words, a distinction is to be drawn between reciting kaddish in the synagogue, which is not allowed, and reciting it in a private home, which is permitted.

Rabbi Jacob Emden (1697–1776), by contrast, ruled that a woman could not say kaddish anywhere. Nevertheless, he found a way to accommodate her: "If she wishes, whenever there are prayers in the synagogue or in a *minyan* she should take care to listen to the recitations of kaddish and to answer 'amen' with full devotion."[5] The best solution that Rabbi Emden could offer, then, was that a woman should be satisfied with the limited role of answering "amen" when the men said kaddish. Other rabbis have followed his lead.

Rabbi Ephraim Zalman Margalioth of Brody (1760–1828) issued a similar ruling. He based the ban on women's saying kaddish on the prevalence of immoral conduct in his generation.

It is likely that she would try to make her voice sweet. . . . But it is right and proper that every God-fearing and pious woman, married or unmarried, not sing aloud when there is a man present; only her lips should move and her voice not be heard at all, for perhaps a man who heard her would have improper thoughts—and improper thoughts about sin are worse than the sin itself.

He, too, proposed an alternative:

> In order to benefit her father, she should be meticulous to go to the synagogue at the times of prayer and listen to the recitation of kaddish and answer "amen." . . . He Who knows inner thoughts will know the content of her heart—that were she a man, she would recite the kaddish in public.[6]

Here we have the well-known idea that a woman is the source of sexual seduction; if she recites kaddish in the presence of men, her sweet voice might arouse them to thoughts that are even worse than sin. This approach, which views all women as the daughters of Eve, who seduced Adam, has historical and literary importance, but it has no spiritual significance in our own day. It is doubtful whether any contemporary self-respecting woman could accept Rabbi Margolioth's advice that she make do with whispering "amen" after the men say kaddish aloud and trust that God will understand that this is the most she can do because she is only a woman.

"SOMETHING NEW AND STRANGE"

Rabbi Ḥayyim Hezekiah Medini (1832–1904), too, vigorously denied a woman the right to say kaddish for her father, on the grounds that it would be "something new and strange in the eyes of the masses." At the same time, he provided information about the spread of this custom:

> One of the Crimean Jews[7] wanted a daughter to say kaddish for her father, who had died without sons. . . . I replied that they are not entitled to change and make an innovation in the country. Even if this custom exists among the Ashkenazim, such a practice has never been heard of anywhere among the Sephardim.[8]

Many other scholars have found ways for women to observe this precept. Rabbi Joseph Elijah Henkin (1880–1973), one of the leading American decisors of the twentieth century, further widened the breach opened by his predecessors when he ruled that if a modest woman comes to pray in the women's gallery "and wishes to say kaddish in front of the women, when the men are saying kaddish in the men's synagogue, perhaps there is no reason to be strict [and forbid it]."[9] It has been reported, on the authority of the late Rabbi Joseph Dov Soloveitchik (1903–1993), that after the evening service it was the custom of the Vilna Gaon Kloiz (synagogue) in Vilna for the women to stand in the back of the sanctuary (there was no women's gallery) and recite kaddish out loud, whether alone or along with the men. This custom was also followed in other towns in Lithuania.[10]

About three hundred years ago, the argument was advanced that a woman is commanded to sanctify the Name of Heaven and, accordingly, should say kaddish, since this prayer is a sanctification of the Divine Name. From that time on we hear of more cases—in Amsterdam, the Crimea, Vilna, and other towns in Lithuania—in which women were permitted to say kaddish. At first, most of the permissive rulings allowed a woman to say kaddish only in a private minyan in the home of the deceased, when he had left only a daughter. Over time, Halakhah evolved and women were permitted to say kaddish in the synagogue as well. This permission can also be applied to the minyan at the graveside; accordingly, a woman may recite kaddish at her father's grave.

THE SPIRITUAL BASIS OF THE KADDISH

This right is anchored not only in law but also in the fact that she is a human being, created in the image of God and deserving equal rights in matters of religion—rights granted her not by flesh-and-blood rabbis but by her Creator.

The various halakhic rulings cited above are based not only on the status of women in Judaism but also on the function of the kaddish. In addition to the notions about the status of women and the need to preserve old customs and prevent innovation, which underlie some of these rulings, there are also beliefs about the function of the kaddish in maintaining a bond between the deceased and the bereaved relatives.

An outstanding example of this is found in a midrash cited by the thirteenth-century Rabbi Isaac ben Moses of Vienna, in his book *Or Zarua*. He related that Rabbi Akiba saw a man burning in hell. Nothing could deliver the man until Rabbi Akiba located his son in this world and taught him to recite kaddish. When the son said kaddish, "at that moment they immediately released the dead man from his torments." The dead man came to Rabbi Akiba in a dream and thanked him because "you saved me from the judgment of hell." Added Rabbi Isaac, "a son who says [kaddish] saves his father from torments."[11]

Some read this passage as meaning that only a son can benefit the father's soul by saying kaddish. According to Rabbi Bacharach, we should learn from this midrash that "the original recitation of the kaddish by orphans was by sons."[12] There is some benefit to be had from the recitation of kaddish by a daughter, he adds, but it certainly is not as effective as when it is recited by a son, who thereby extricates the father's soul from hellfire.

Does anyone today recite the kaddish for this reason? In fact, the superstitious element in this belief was rejected almost nine hundred years ago by the renowned mathematician and scientist Abraham bar Ḥiyya of Barcelona (died 1136):

> As for anyone who thinks that he will have some benefit from the deeds and prayers that his sons and coreligionists perform for his sake after his death—every scholar and savant considers these to be foolish thoughts and vain hopes.[13]

Is kaddish some magical formula that rescues the deceased from the torments of hell? In the sixteenth century, Rabbi Abraham Horowitz ruled that observing the commandments and doing good deeds, in accordance with the father's wishes, is better than reciting kaddish for the elevation of his soul:

> This kaddish is not a prayer that the son addresses to God for the sake of his father, to raise him up from the Underworld.

Rather, it is accounted a merit and *mitzvah* for the dead when his son sanctifies the Holy Name in public. How much the more so, then, when the son performs one of the Lord's precepts because he was enjoined to do so by his father, for action is surely great.[14]

In other words, four hundred years ago it was recognized that a person's continuance and eternity depend not only on words but primarily on his continued influence on his children, presumably including his daughters, to motivate them to observe the commandments and do charitable works.

When an only daughter lost her father, it was customary to hire men or yeshiva students to say kaddish instead of her. Rabbi Leopold (Jekuthiel Judah) Greenwald (1889–1955) was not pleased with the custom of hiring substitutes:

They do not know and do not understand that the kaddish was instituted precisely so that the mourner will say it, in order to learn a chapter in Judaism, to pour out his heart before the Lord, to amend his ways during that year. . . . But kaddish said by someone else . . . is not worth a cent, even if it is recited in Jerusalem or Hebron.[15]

THE RECITATION OF THE KADDISH ELEVATES THE SOUL OF THE DECEASED

Rabbi Greenwald was writing specifically about hiring people to recite kaddish in place of male mourners who find it difficult to attend services regularly; we can infer, however, that there is no spiritual value in having a stranger recite kaddish instead of a bereaved daughter, either. According to him, the kaddish is recited not only for the deceased but also for the mourner: "Not only does it elevate the soul of the deceased; it also elevates the soul of the person who recites it."[16]

Rabbi Binyamin Zev Jacobson ruled that reciting kaddish is significant only if the mourner says it in accordance with the intention of the deceased: "Only in this fashion does the kaddish, which is a prayer of the living, also become a prayer for the dead." To endow his words with value, "the son should lead the service with devotion and say kaddish not as the rote fulfillment of a precept but in order to sanctify the Divine Name in public and arouse the public to this sanctification.[17]

It is important to note the opinion of Rabbi Joseph Dov Soloveitchik, one of the greatest rabbis of our times, concerning the importance of the kaddish:

> Through the kaddish we hurl defiance at death and its fiendish conspiracy against man. When the mourner recites "Glorified and sanctified be the great name . . ." he declares more or less the following: No matter how powerful death is, notwithstanding the ugly end of man, however terrifying the grave is, however nonsensical and absurd everything appears, no matter how black one's despair is and how nauseating an affair life itself is, we declare and profess publicly and solemnly that we are not giving up, that we are not surrendering, that we will carry on the work of our ancestors as if nothing had happened, that we will not be satisfied with less than the full realization of the ultimate goal—the establishment of God's kingdom, resurrection of the dead, and eternal life for man.[18]

Reciting the kaddish has a profound spiritual significance for mourners, as we see from the rabbinic passages cited above. There is no doubt that it is just as important for a bereaved woman as for a bereaved man.

We can learn from the writings of two great Orthodox sages of our day that women may possibly have a share in this spiritual venture.

Rabbi Moshe Feinstein wrote in his responsa that "in all the generations it was customary that at times a poor woman would enter the *beit midrash* to receive charity or a woman mourner would enter to say kaddish."[19] He expressed no objection to this practice.

If it is indeed permitted for a woman to say kaddish, what are the ramifications of forbidding her to do so? According to Rabbi Aaron Soloveitchik,

> Nowadays, when there are Jews fighting for equality for men and women in matters such as *aliyot* [to the Torah], if Orthodox rabbis prevent women from saying kaddish when there is a possibility for allowing it, it will strengthen the influence of Reform and Conservative rabbis. It is therefore forbidden to prevent daughters from saying kaddish.[20]

The day may yet arrive when women's recitation of the kaddish will be not only be a liberal practice but may well become widely accepted by Jews of various degrees of traditional observance.

23

Is a Woman's Voice Sexually Enticing?

WE HEAR REPEATEDLY THAT GROUPS OF ULTRA-ORTHODOX worshippers have gone on a rampage and physically and verbally assaulted women who were praying at the Western Wall. Unfortunately, religious violence, though contrary to Jewish morality and the codified Halakhah, has become all too common in Israel.

Here we shall examine the pretexts offered for the behavior of the Ultra-Orthodox and their reasons for it, as they scream them in the ears of the women standing alongside the barrier of the women's section at the Western Wall plaza:

"You should not pray here at the Wall."
"Halakhah forbids a woman to hold a Torah Scroll."
"For shame! We protest: a woman's voice is sexually enticing."

ARE WOMEN REQUIRED TO PRAY?

Some of the Ultra-Orthodox assert that the women at the Western Wall disturb them and, moreover, that women are not required to pray. This position seems to be based on the general rule that women are exempt from the obligation to recite prayers whose time is fixed, as is stated in the Mishnah: "Every positive commandment whose observance is time dependent—men are obligated and women are exempt" (Mishnah Kiddushin 1:7).

In his commentary on this Mishnah, Maimonides explains that "this refers to the precepts that a person must perform at a defined time; and when it is not that time, the obligation is canceled." For example, the recitation of the morning service is not mandatory for women, as it is for men.

In the fourteenth century, Rabbi David Abudarham provided the following explanation for the exemption granted women from time-dependent positive commandments:

[The reason is that] a woman is subordinate to her husband and must fulfill his needs. If she were required to perform a positive commandment that is time dependent, it is possible that while she was fulfilling that commandment her husband would tell her to do his own bidding. If she performed the command of the Creator and neglected her spouse's command, woe to her from her husband. But if she complied with her husband's command and set aside the command of her Creator, woe to her from her Creator. Accordingly, the Creator exempted her from His commandments, so that she should live in harmony with her husband.[1]

Few modern women see themselves as subordinate to their husbands in this way. They participate fully in the religious life of the community and cannot accept Abudarham's rationalization of their incapacity to fulfill all the commandments. Hence, this reason is no longer valid.

The first opening for a small measure of equality for women in matters of prayer and the commandments was found long ago, even before Abudarham. Rabbi Isaac Halevi, who was Rashi's teacher, ruled that women should not be prevented from fulfilling time-dependent precepts from which they are ostensibly exempt, such as the Four Species and living in the Sukkah on Sukkot:

If they wish to accept the commandments themselves, they may do so and we do not protest. . . . If she wished to fulfill a positive commandment, she may do so and there is no question here of a benediction uttered in vain.[2]

Hence, women may pray even if Halakhah does not require them to do so—and this permission applies at the Western Wall as well.

May a Woman Hold a Torah Scroll?

One of the complaints made by the Ultra-Orthodox was that the women had held a Torah scroll and read the weekly portion from it. With regard to the public reading of the Torah, the Talmud states that "all may go up [to read the Torah] to make up the standard number of seven, even a minor and even a woman." This principle is hedged immediately, however: "But the Sages said that a woman should not read from the Torah because of the honor of the community" (BT Megillah 23a).

In talmudic times, each person called was expected to read his or her own portion. Rabbi Jacob Emden (eighteenth century) accordingly understood the addendum as referring to a situation in which there are seven men present who know how to read from the Torah, so that the standard number of readings can be completed without calling a woman. In this case, women are not called up. (The problem is that if a woman were called, a bystander might think that there are not seven knowledgeable men present, which would bring disgrace on the community by implying that the local educational system is deficient.) The statement that "all may go up [to read the Torah]," he added, refers to a situation in which there are fewer than seven men present who know how to read from the Torah, but there is a woman who does know how.[3] In such a situation, a woman may be called to the Torah if she knows how to read from it, in order to make up the mandatory number of seven.

In the thirteenth century, Rabbi Meir of Rothenburg affirmed that in certain situations a woman may read from the Torah. As for the Sages' injunction "that a woman should not read from the Torah because of the honor of the community," he ruled that "where it is impossible [to call seven men], the honor of the community must be set aside."[4]

Originally, only the first person called recited the benediction before the Torah *(asher bahar banu mi-kol ha'ammim)*, and only the last person called recited the benediction after the Torah *(asher natan lanu torat emet);* the five persons called between them recited no benediction. Later, the rabbis decided that all those called should recite both benedictions; nevertheless, the opening benediction recited by the first reader and the closing benediction by the last reader retained a higher status. Thus, Rabbi Joseph Caro noted that because "there is a rabbinic regulation that all those called recite the benedictions, a woman and a minor may read, even if they are first or last; and because they read they certainly recite the benedictions."[5] In other words, he takes it for granted that a woman may read from the Torah and recite the corresponding benedictions.

These are only a few of the many halakhic rulings that permit women to be called up to and read from the Torah. The Ultra-Orthodox at the Western Wall may have been broadly hinting that all or many of the women were ritually impure on account of menstruation and therefore were not allowed to hold a Torah scroll (and, since the reader must grasp the handles of the Torah while reciting the benedictions, they certainly could not read from it). They seem to have forgotten a passage in the Babylonian Talmud: "Rabbi Judah ben Beteira used to say: 'Words of Torah cannot become ritually impure'" (BT Berakhot 22b). On the basis of this, Maimonides ruled that "all those who are ritually impure, even menstruating women and even non-Jews, may hold a Torah scroll and read from it, because words of Torah cannot become ritually impure" (Laws of Torah Scrolls 10:8).

A Woman's Voice Is Sexually Enticing

Some objected to the women's prayer because it was conducted within hearing distance of the Ultra-Orthodox men praying at the wall. These opponents cited a passage in the Babylonian Talmud (BT Berakhot 24a): "Samuel said, a woman's voice is sexually enticing [literally, a woman's voice is (like her) nakedness] as it says: 'For your voice is sweet and your appearance is comely'" (Song of Songs 2:14). Rabbi Joel Sirkes (1561–1640) explained that this biblical praise of a woman's voice and appearance implies that they are attractive to men.[6]

Some authorities hold that men are forbidden to listen to a woman singing, particularly during prayer. According to Rabbi Joshua Falk, "that a woman's voice is like her nakedness and that they said that it is forbidden to pray in her presence—this is a universal ruling that applies to all women [including one's wife]."[7]

In our day, some say that it is forbidden to hear the voices of women who are chanting the prayers in the women's gallery in the synagogue.[8] Rabbi Mordecai Jacob Breisch of Zurich ruled that it was forbidden to hear a woman singing even over the radio.[9]

On the other hand, Rabbi Aaron de Toledo held that there was no such prohibition, as long "as it is not erotic and one does not intend to get pleasure from her voice, when she sings hymns to the Lord . . . [The prohibition does not apply to one] who is not intending to get pleasure from her voice."[10]

The greatest German rabbis of the nineteenth and twentieth centuries, Esriel Hildesheimer, Samson Raphael Hirsch, and Jehiel Jacob Weinberg, all permitted women to sing hymns at the Sabbath table along with men.[11]

Hence, we see that there is a dispute between those who forbid and those who permit. The key point is the intention of the listeners. If the Ultra-Orthodox have no intention of getting pleasure from the singing voices of the women who are praying when they approach the barrier between the men's and women's sections, there is certainly no impediment to their own prayer.

WOMEN'S EQUALITY

After presenting all these arguments on both sides of the question, we must add an important principle that is implicit in our tradition but has truly blossomed only in the modern age, namely, women's equality in almost every area of life. Today, women can attain the most senior positions: surgeon, army officer, newspaper editor, prime minister, supreme court justice, state comptroller, and so on. It seems that the currents in our tradition that point toward the advancement of women require that absolute equality be granted to Jewish women in matters of prayer as well, both in the synagogue and at the Western Wall.

VI

The Ultra-Orthodox

Seclusive Ultra-Orthodoxy is the option of flight, weakness, and writing off the majority of the people and is . . . a prescription for failure. It is a fact that the vast majority of the secular *and even* antireligious *adult population is a* product of the Ultra-Orthodox path *and fell away from it in the recent generations of secularism.*

AMUDIM, THE JOURNAL OF THE
RELIGIOUS KIBBUTZ MOVEMENT (1979)

In recent years, the power of Ultra-Orthodox groups in Israel has increased as a result of success in the polling booth and clever coalition bargaining, their high birth rate, and the swelling of their ranks by the "newly religious." This does not seem to endanger Israeli democracy, because on the surface these achievements have all been won through legal means.

Nevertheless, as we shall see in the present section, a byproduct of these achievements, and perhaps one of the causes of the Ultra-Orthodox success, is the unceasing religious violence, threats, and pressures on non-Orthodox, Orthodox, and even other Ultra-Orthodox groups. In Israel today there is an unremitting atmosphere of intimidation and religious coercion.

Most distressing is the fact that precisely those who claim to be the guardian of the fortress of Halakhah are those who desecrate the Torah, both its letter and its spirit, through their violent demonstrations, inappropriate methods of recruiting young Jews to join the Ultra-Orthodox fold, and other actions. We should make plain that not only do their actions violate the laws of the state and undermine the foundations of democracy, but they also contravene Halakhah, in whose name they are ostensibly acting.

24

Desecrating the Sabbath in Order to Sanctify It

Ultra-Orthodox demonstrations in Jerusalem, a phenomenon almost as old as the State of Israel, fit into a larger picture of violence by members of that community. Although such violent demonstrations are evidently in pursuit of political gains, leaders of the Ultra-Orthodox community always adduce the halakhic concepts of preserving the Sabbath and observing the Torah to explain them.

Does Halakhah really sanction such violent demonstrations? To answer this question we must consider three issues:

1. Do the demonstrations by the Ultra-Orthodox themselves constitute desecration of the Sabbath?
2. If so, is it permitted to desecrate the Sabbath in order to preserve its sanctity?
3. Do these demonstrations expand the circle of Sabbath observance among non-Orthodox Jews?

Unfortunately, there is no escaping the conclusion that the Ultra-Orthodox campaign to defend the Sabbath in Jerusalem and elsewhere in Israel involves public desecration of the Sabbath. The battle to increase Sabbath observance has actually increased Sabbath desecration. Violence has become an inseparable part of the

Sabbath demonstrations and a normal method of applying massive pressure to achieve the objectives of the Ultra-Orthodox leadership with regard to many other issues. On weekdays, too, there have been violent disturbances to protest archaeological excavations or "pornographic" pictures on bus shelters, assaults on peaceful citizens who were minding their own business, and even the desecration of graves.

A survey of the media indicates how deeply rooted in these circles is the use of violence as a means of persuasion. Not only have bottles and rocks been hurled at policemen in downtown Jerusalem from time to time; the "sport" of stoning traffic on the Ramot road went on for four full years. Nor has this Sabbath violence been limited to the capital. On the mall in Haifa, too, a large group of Ultra-Orthodox ruffians beat up three journalists who had come to observe a mass prayer rally.

In the spring of 1984, the rabbi of Petah Tikva, speaking at the end of a mass rally on behalf of Sabbath observance, called for action against the public desecration of the Sabbath by a local coffee house. The result, according to media reports, was that Ultra-Orthodox demonstrators "ripped off the metal door and forced their way inside. Fistfights quickly developed and blows were exchanged. . . . During the disturbances, windows were broken, tables overturned, and bottles smashed."[1]

In addition to contravening the laws of the state, these and similar acts also involved forbidden labor on the Sabbath. According to Halakhah, if there were two witnesses present who warned that they were about to desecrate the Sabbath, the perpetrators were liable to death by stoning (Maimonides, Laws of the Sabbath 1:2).

The years of Sabbath riots on the Ramot road in suburban Jerusalem gave rise to sad thoughts concerning our ability to live as equal citizens in a free Jewish state, despite our differences. In any case, the Chief Rabbinate and official religious establishment stood aside and generally maintained perfect silence on this matter. Do they realize that "silence is tacit acknowledgment" (BT Yevamot 87b)?

Particularly worrisome is the attitude of one of the leaders of Neturei Karta, Rabbi Moshe Hirsch, as reported on Israel Radio in

September 1979. Rabbi Hirsch offered halakhic arguments that ostensibly justify the use of force to preserve the nature of the Sabbath as he understands it. He also offered a "halakhic solution" to the crisis. Let us investigate the halakhic basis of this rabbi's arguments.

"ZEALOTS ATTACK HIM"

Rabbi Hirsch found support for the violence on the Ramot road in a well-known Mishnah: "If a man stole a sacred vessel or cursed by means of witchcraft or had sexual relations with a [gentile] woman—zealots may attack him" (Mishnah Sanhedrin 9:6). The Sages held that even though the Torah does not stipulate the death penalty for those guilty of these misdeeds, those who are zealous for the Lord have permission to assault and kill them.

Throwing stones at passing cars on the Ramot road is quite remote from the cases mentioned in the Talmud and by later codifiers. What is more, Rabbi Hirsch seems to have forgotten or purposely suppressed an important element in the license granted to zealots. According to the Gemara, this justifiable zealousness must be a spontaneous and unplanned act: "Rabbi Ḥisda said: If someone comes to ask [whether he may assault someone who has profaned the sacred] we do not instruct him to do so" (BT Sanhedrin 82a).

That is, there is no permission to harm or attack a Sabbath desecrator if the zealousness is not a spontaneous emotional outburst. The carefully planned activity organized in Ultra-Orthodox neighborhoods far from the Ramot road, such as Me'ah She'arim, was not spontaneous by any standard and could hardly satisfy the halakhic criterion that licenses those zealous for the Lord to give vent to their pent-up feelings.

DESECRATING THE SABBATH TO PREVENT DESECRATION OF THE SABBATH?

Rabbi Hirsch, other Ultra-Orthodox leaders, and their followers who hurled stones and bottles at vehicles and people clearly believe that they may desecrate the Sabbath in order to keep others from desecrating the Sabbath. No one has ever stated the source of this license—probably for the simple reason that it is not to be found anywhere in the codified Halakhah. Not only are these actions by the Ultra-Orthodox crimes against the laws of the state, they are also severe violations of the Sabbath.

It is permitted to desecrate the Sabbath for only one reason— to save lives; that is, saving human life *(pikkuaḥ nefesh)* takes precedence over observance of the Sabbath. The underlying principle is "desecrate one Sabbath for his sake so that he may observe many Sabbaths" (BT Yoma 85b). In other words, desecrating the holy Sabbath to save a human life aims in fact at augmenting its holiness through the observance of the Sabbath and other precepts in the future.

The desecration of the Sabbath by the Ultra-Orthodox in Jerusalem, by contrast, does not and cannot increase the prospects of Sabbath observance in the future or augment its sanctity. In fact, it has quite the opposite effect because it leads to further radicalization of the nonreligious population as well. Instead of educating the nonreligious population and helping them experience the wonderful value of Sabbath observance, the Ultra-Orthodox zealousness and extremism repulse them and push them further away from Jewish tradition.

"TWO WHO LAID HOLD OF A *TALLIT*"

Rabbi Hirsch and the Ultra-Orthodox Council in Jerusalem offered a miracle solution to the quarrel over the Ramot road. The solution was based on seeing the road as falling into the category of the disputed Mishnaic *tallit:* "Two people laid hold of a *tallit* [i.e., a prayer shawl or cloak] and one says . . . 'it's all mine,' and the other says, 'it's all mine'" (Mishnah Baba Metzia 1:1). In such a case, the Sages ruled, the *tallit* was to be torn in half and divided fifty-fifty. The Ultra-Orthodox rabbis wanted to apply this halakhic principle as follows: For two weeks the residents of Ramot would be allowed to travel on the new road that passes by the Ultra-Orthodox neighborhood of Kiryat Sanz; for the next two weeks, they would travel by the old road, which passes by the Orthodox neighborhood of Sanhedria. In this way they would split the experience of Sabbath desecration with a religious neighborhood that had so far remained aloof from the violence. If the road is the *tallit,* who were the two claimants holding on to it? The Ultra-Orthodox from Kiryat Sanz, the residents of Ramot, or the religious residents of Sanhedria? What sort of partition is being proposed? Is it not rather more like the solution proposed by King Solomon to the two harlots who asserted maternity of a single child—namely, that the child be cut in two? The implementation of such a division is so absurd that we need speak of it no further.

Some would have us ignore the facts and swallow the Ultra-Orthodox contention that the violence is an anomaly in their struggle, that their demonstrations are usually calm and orderly. Even so, we must ask whether Halakhah permits demonstrating and waging violent campaigns, as the Ultra-Orthodox have repeatedly done on the Sabbath. Not only the violent attacks related above, but also many of the actions associated with the demonstrations themselves are forbidden by Halakhah. For example, one of the rabbinic dicta that might impinge on the Sabbath demonstrations is that adults may not walk quickly or run on the Sabbath. Maimonides phrased this as "you should not walk on the Sabbath as you do on weekdays" (Laws of Sabbath 24:4; compare the annotation by Rabbi Moses Isserles to *Shulḥan Arukh O.H.* 301:1).

Even when they are not running, the way in which the Ultra-Orthodox speak is a violation of the Sabbath. According to Maimonides, "you should not speak on the Sabbath in the fashion you speak on weekdays" (ibid.). According to the press, these demonstrations are regularly accompanied by shouts of "Shabbes!

288 / Evolving Halakhah

Shabbes!" and curses against the municipality, the police, and cinema-goers. Such loud and uncouth speech is utterly forbidden on the Sabbath.

In fact, and as a general rule, all disputes are forbidden on the Sabbath. According to the prominent twentieth-century decisor Rabbi Israel Meir Kagan of Radun, known as the Ḥafetz Ḥayyim (1838–1933), "the Zohar and the kabbalists warned strictly against any dispute on the Sabbath, Heaven forbid."[2] Yet the rabbis of the Ultra-Orthodox community, who should know Halakhah intimately, provoked a severe quarrel every Sabbath. By so doing, they violated the ruling of Rabbi Ḥayyim Joseph David Azulai (1724–1806): "On the Sabbath it is strictly forbidden to stir up quarrels or to get angry and it is twice as severe as when done on a weekday."[3]

These rabbinic prohibitions stand in utter contrast to the nature of protests in which demonstrators push against police barricades and chase nonreligious youth on the Sabbath. Such behavior is forbidden even during the week; how much the more so on the holy Sabbath! It is hard to understand why the chief rabbis and the Chief Rabbinate Council, an official state body, never issued a pronouncement calling on the observant to refrain from demonstrations that profane the Sabbath.

It is equally hard to understand how a pious Jew, who maintains that Torah is his profession, can fail to understand that he must distance himself from every form of Sabbath desecration. Evidently the Ultra-Orthodox rabbis, eminent Torah scholars, do not tell their students that such is their obligation.

Have the Ultra-Orthodox nevertheless found a halakhic precedent that gives them a license to desecrate the Sabbath to prevent Sabbath desecration by others? If they have such permission, they should publish it for all to read. Both their silence and intensive halakhic research indicate, however, that there is no such ruling anywhere in the rabbinic literature.

It is an ironclad rule that extremism on one side leads to radicalization on the other. We must take sorrowful note of an intensification of antireligious violence, such as the vandalizing of a synagogue in south Tel Aviv and the cutting off of the sidecurls of a boy in Jerusalem.

The periodical of the religious kibbutz movement (Hakibbutz Hadati) published a forlorn evaluation of the results of the zealots' approach:

> Seclusive Ultra-Orthodoxy is the option of flight, weakness, and writing off the majority of the people and is . . . a prescription for failure. It is a fact that the vast majority of the *secular* and even *antireligious* adult population is a *product of the Ultra-Orthodox path* and fell away from it in the recent generations of secularism.[4]

If the Ultra-Orthodox circles continue on this path, they will manage only to stir up the generation that has not yet rebelled against Judaism and send it running into the arms of radical secularism.

Particularly astonishing and disappointing is the fact that the Ultra-Orthodox approach utterly ignores the supreme precept to love one's fellow Jews, as stated by Maimonides: "Every man is commanded to love each and every Jew as himself, as it is stated, 'Love your neighbor as yourself'" (Laws of Beliefs, 6:3).

We sorely miss the perspective of Rabbi Abraham Isaac Kook, who discerned sparks of holiness in the secular Zionist enterprise and endeavored to draw all the nonobservant toward the Jewish religion with "golden ropes." His approach was based on a profound faith in the value of each and every Jew as such, even if he or she does not observe the *mitzvot*. His words are important to the Ultra-Orthodox in Me'ah She'arim and to all of us, whenever we are embroiled in potentially catastrophic quarrels like that on the Ramot road: "Even from the profane, the sacred may be revealed, and even from libertine freedom the cherished yoke."[5] This approach, which finds something positive in all Jews and attempts to bring them closer, rather than repel them, is what we need if we are to survive the worsening crisis between the religious and nonreligious sectors in Israel.

25

Religious Violence against a Progressive Congregation

ON THE EVENING OF SIMḤAT TORAH IN 1986, THE MEM-
BERS of the Kol HaNeshama Progressive Congregation in the Baka neighborhood of Jerusalem—men, women, and children—were dancing with the Torah scrolls in accordance with the custom of that festival. Without warning, the official state-salaried Orthodox rabbi of the neighborhood and several companions forced their way into the building and began yelling about the desecration of the Torah and the Divine Name. The members of the congregation and their rabbi asked the uninvited guests to participate in the festivities. The response was a stream of abuse and an attempt to snatch away a Torah scroll and take it out of the building.

The rabbi of Kol HaNeshama, Levi Weiman-Kelman, filed a complaint with the police against the neighborhood rabbi and his companions for trespassing and desecrating a place of worship.

The storm eventually died down, and the rabbi sent an apology of sorts to Rabbi Weiman-Kelman, after which the latter withdrew his complaint. Nevertheless, this sad incident still bears reviewing, even now.

The neighborhood rabbi did not address his letter of apology, written under the threat of criminal charges, to the victims of his assault—Rabbi Weiman-Kelman and his congregation—but to "all the residents of Baka and the area." Its content left no doubts as to his views:

> I address you in the name of our Holy Torah, which forbids all violence, and express my regret if anyone from the Kol HaNeshama Congregation, led by Rabbi Weiman-Kelman, was hurt by my presence and words there. [The author wrote the word *rabbi* in smaller letters.] . . . I personally will do nothing to disturb the congregation.

It is hard to understand these words as a direct apology. It is most doubtful whether it can be viewed as fulfilling the Halakhah as stated by Maimonides:

> One who injures his fellow or curses his fellow or steals something from him, and so on, is never forgiven until he gives his fellow what he owes him and appeases him. . . . Even if he merely teased his fellow verbally, he must appease him and urge him until he forgives him (Laws of Repentance 2:9).

One cannot be sure whether it was a sincere desire to appease Rabbi Weiman-Kelman and his congregants and win their forgiveness that moved the rabbi of Baka to write his letter, or whether he acted in response to the strong pressure exerted by the neighborhood administration and the complaint filed with the police. Rabbi Weiman-Kelman, on the other hand, followed the dictates of Halakhah and showed himself "easy to forgive and hard to anger": he forgave his colleague and withdrew the complaint.

In this entire incident, the worst attack on freedom of religion was not in the Baka neighborhood but in the reactions and apathy of the religious establishment. In an interview broadcast on Israel Radio, Rabbi Mordechai Eliyahu, then the Sephardi Chief Rabbi, expressed his indirect approbation of the Orthodox violence against those who had been celebrating Simḥat Torah in Baka:

> I think it is the right of people who live in the neighborhood to protest the desecration of the honor of the Torah when they see a

Torah scroll and naked or half-naked people dancing [with it]. This is disrespect for the Torah. It is the right of the public to protest. If they protested in a civil way, it was their right to do so.[1]

Rabbi Eliyahu had received a detailed report on the incident. We may accordingly assume that he considers the epithets hurled in the synagogue—words like *lewdness, heretics,* and *brothel*—along with the shoving, snatching of a Torah scroll, and striking of the rabbi, to be a civil and dignified form of protest. There is no doubt that most Israelis of all stripes rejected Rabbi Eliyahu's position. It is also clear that in this case, Halakhah is on the side of the majority of the Israeli public.

Rabbi Eliyahu advanced the strange and provocative claim that members of Kol HaNeshama who were dancing with Torah scrolls were "naked" or "half-naked." Concepts of nudity and modesty vary from generation to generation and from society to society, and this holds true for Jewish tradition as well. Anyone who has ever attended services in a Progressive synagogue in Israel will be hard pressed to understand what Rabbi Eliyahu meant, unless this is how he refers to any human being—especially a woman—who wears a garment that does not cover the elbows.

As a matter of both Halakhah and ethics, it was incumbent upon the official rabbinate to issue an unequivocal condemnation of the hooliganism in Baka. Instead, the day after the incident we heard Rabbi Shlomo Goren state over the radio that he was opposed to violence against the non-Orthodox for two reasons: (1) "because I believe that violence will not attain the objective and bring salvation, spiritual or physical, to the Jewish People," and (2) "I am afraid that violence, indeed any physical assault on someone, merely strengthens him." The former Chief Rabbi's opposition to violence was not based on Halakhah or ethics, nor was it a matter of principle. His rejection of violence against non-Orthodox Jews was purely pragmatic and utilitarian: not only does force not achieve the desired goal; it may even help the opponent gain strength. As our Sages said, "from a negative rule one can infer the positive" (*Sifra,* Shemini 1:5). If Rabbi Goren or those who share his views concluded that violence would indeed serve their goals, would it then be permissible or even mandatory to employ it?

We must regret that the rabbinate did not emulate the path of a Jerusalem rabbi who, in a similar situation, behaved quite differently. Rabbi Levi ben Ḥabib, born in Spain about 1484, was named rabbi of Jerusalem in 1524. In that capacity he was once asked about two Jews who entered a particular synagogue two Sabbaths in a row and accused the worshippers of augmenting the service with additional psalms. One of them denounced the custom, which he rejected as invalid: "One of them protested loudly and mocked them, saying, 'this addition is like the prayer of the Karaites.'"[2] When the time for the afternoon service came, it was discovered that someone had defaced the controversial prayerbook.

In his responsum, Rabbi Levi ben Ḥabib sharply castigated the Jew who had done such a thing in a synagogue on the Sabbath. Such a person

> desecrates the Divine Name and commits a great transgression.
> . . . He has interfered with the service of Heaven . . . and made
> light of the dignity of Heaven and the dignity of the Torah. . . .
> Accordingly, one should in no way shield him . . . since it is fit-
> ting for him to be ashamed. . . . Let him come to the synagogue
> [in which he committed this act] and ask forgiveness from our
> God, may He be praised, and from His Torah.[3]

With regard to the ostensible "ideological" grounds that justified the deed, the fifteenth-century Jerusalem rabbi wrote:

> Whoever said that the custom of reciting those hymns is like the
> custom of the Karaites and sectarians merits punishment, since
> one must not say of a custom of believers and the children of be-
> lievers that it is a custom of sectarians.[4]

Rabbi Levi ben Ḥabib's vigorous reaction to the desecration of a prayerbook on the Sabbath should be studied by the rabbis of the contemporary establishment. Allegations of heresy and sectarianism could not justify desecration of a holy place four hundred years ago, nor can they do so today.

26

The Cult of the Newly Ultra-Orthodox

IS IT APPROPRIATE TO REFER TO EVERY PERSON WHO HAS adopted Orthodoxy as a penitent *(ba'al teshuvah)?* At first sight, the expression seems to be appropriate. Maimonides states that someone who, having transgressed any of the Torah commandments, does penance and repents of his or her sin is deemed a "penitent." If he withstood the temptation of a renewed opportunity to commit the same transgression "and turned away and did not commit it because of his repentance, . . . he is a full penitent" (Laws of Repentance 1:1 and 2:2). It follows that every Jew, scrupulously observant or otherwise, may be a penitent with regard to some commandment that he or she transgressed and then regretted having violated.

But this is not what the term means to the heads of yeshivas and the thousands of young people who have begun to be meticulous in their observance of the precepts related to ritual behavior, adopted Orthodox dress, and enrolled in the special yeshivas that cater to those with no prior background. The general public has the impression that these young people have changed their entire way of life and are focusing on observing all the commandments, both toraitic and rabbinic. Is this indeed the case? Are they in fact penitents with regard to all of the commandments? It seems that there are at least three important precepts that the "missionizing" yeshiva deans do not inculcate in their new recruits: combining Torah observance with earning a living, respect for one's parents, and military service.

Torah and Labor

Most of these newly hatched yeshiva students spend all their time learning Torah and do not work to support themselves. According to Maimonides:

> Anyone who entertains the notion that he will study Torah instead of working and be supported by charity has desecrated the Divine Name, disgraced the Torah, and extinguished the light of religion, . . . because it is forbidden to gain benefit from Torah study in this world. . . . They also enjoined: do not make of it a crown in which to glory or a spade with which to dig (Laws of Torah Study 3:10).

Maimonides stated unequivocally that all students are commanded to combine Torah with labor and to work to support themselves. Rabbi Joseph Caro demurred at Maimonides' extreme formulation and would permit scholars to receive remuneration for teaching Torah; all the same, he concurred with Maimonides' general orientation, writing that "that a person should not throw off the burden of working and be supported by society in order to learn, but should study a craft that can support him."[1] Only if he cannot maintain himself in this fashion may he accept an income supplement from the community. In the *Shulḥan Arukh*, Rabbi Caro ruled that a Jew should go to the synagogue and house of study in the morning, but afterwards "he should go to his business, since any Torah study that is not accompanied by labor eventually comes to naught and leads to sin" (*O.H.* 156:1).

According to Rabbi Moses Sofer, known as the Ḥatam Sofer (1762–1839), the general rule that Torah study must be combined with labor has even greater force in the Land of Israel:

> In the Holy Land . . . working the land is itself a precept—to settle Eretz Yisrael and grow its sacred produce. With regard to this, the Torah commanded, "you shall gather in your grain" (Deut. 11:14)— . . . on account of the commandment. You might as well say, I will not put on *tefillin* because I am studying

Torah. In this case, too, you may not say, I will not gather the grain because of Torah study. It may be that other crafts, too, that are connected with maintaining human society are also included in this commandment.[2]

Heads of yeshivas would do well if they required their students to engage in some trade or learn some vocation that promotes the settlement of the Land of Israel and maintains human society, instead of influencing them to give up their university studies or quit their jobs and detach themselves from their former surroundings.

HONORING ONE'S PARENTS

The media frequently report about "newly religious" teens and young adults who have broken with their parents as a result of their new piety, thereby transgressing the Torah precept, one of the Ten Commandments, to honor one's father and mother. Is it permissible to turn one's back on one's parents in order to secure the newfound piety and Torah study? In the thirteenth century, the anonymous author of *Sefer Haḥinnukh* answered this question as follows:

> It is fitting for a man to acknowledge and treat with lovingkindness the person who treated him with goodness; he should not be a scoundrel, an ingrate who turns a cold shoulder [to him]—for this is an evil quality, utterly vile before God and mankind. A person should realize that his father and mother are the cause of his being in the world; hence it is proper for him to honor them and give them every benefit he can.[3]

Halakhah does not stop at declarations of intentions; it applies these principles to newly religious persons who return to the house of their nonobservant parents. Such a person must not reprove them for their failure to observe commandments; children must take account of their parents' sensitivities in this matter. The *Shulḥan Arukh* rules:

If he saw his father transgressing Torah precepts, he should not say to him, "you have transgressed Torah precepts," but rather, "Father, in the Torah it is written thus and so," as if he were asking him and not admonishing him (*Y.D.* 210:11).

True, it is codified Halakhah that "studying Torah is greater than honoring father and mother" (BT Megillah 16b; *Shulḥan Arukh, Y.D.* 210:13), but this principle was never intended to detract from the obligation to honor one's parents. According to the seventeenth-century Rabbi Hezekiah da Silva, the idea behind the ruling was that a son may leave home and travel to a far-off place in order to study Torah. However, if he studies close to his parents' home—the usual situation in Israel today—he must first "honor his father and [after that] return to his Torah."[4]

Hence, it is incumbent on the yeshivas to inform their new students of the manifold significance of this commandment, about which Rabbi Simeon bar Yoai, one of the greatest Mishnaic Sages, said: "Honoring father and mother is so great a precept that the Holy One blessed be He preferred it over His own honor" (JT Pe'ah 1:5).

MILITARY SERVICE

Many of the new yeshiva students we are discussing here have already served in the Israeli army. Now, to further the process of their break with the outside world, social and psychological pressure is exerted to get them to request to be released from reserve duty and be more like those born into Ultra-Orthodoxy, who have never served in the Israel Defense Forces.

Rabbi Ḥayyim David Halevy, the Sephardi chief rabbi of Tel Aviv, defended this conduct even in wartime, after the abatement of the fiercest fighting. According to him, yeshiva students should return to study in safety while others remain at the front:

Even though it is still a time of emergency and war, yeshiva students return to their houses of study to engage in the study of the Torah. Through their merit the Lord will protect those who fight at the front, so they may be victorious and return home safe and sound.[5]

This approach contravenes the principle that it is forbidden to gain any benefit from the study of Torah, since the yeshiva students are sitting safely in the yeshiva, far from the inferno of battle, and letting their peers risk their lives to protect them.

A modern Jew certainly prefers the rulings of the Talmud and Maimonides, which are oriented toward the entire polity and emphasize the moral position. In Tractate Sotah, where the Mishnah deals with the obligation to serve in the army and wage wars, it is made plain that all the exemptions mentioned in the Torah apply only to a war that is not essential for the nation's survival:

> What has been said [that some do not go forth to war] applies to a war of free choice; but in an obligatory war all go forth, even the bridegroom out of his chamber and the bride out of her bridal canopy (Mishnah Sotah 8:7).

Maimonides ruled in similar fashion.

The operative question, then, is whether Israel today is in the situation of obligatory war? One of the Maimonides' definitions of an obligatory war is one to "save Israel from an enemy who attacks it" (Laws of Kings 5:1)—a phrasing borrowed from Numbers 10:9: "when you are at war in your land against an enemy who attacks you." This, unfortunately, is an apt description of the situation in Israel today: attacks by terrorists and the unremitting threat of war with countries in our region that still consider themselves to be at war with us.

In the present situation, when we are involved in a war to defend the Jewish people against its enemies, every citizen must do his or her part, especially those with military training. Halakhah makes no distinction between observant and nonobservant Jews with regard to their obligations.

What do these three precepts have in common? The workplace, the university, the home of nonobservant parents, and the army are all settings in which these yeshiva students are liable to be exposed to influences and value systems that are antithetical to the seclusive philosophy of the yeshiva. Perhaps this is why the yeshiva heads do not teach their students all the ramifications of the observance of these commandments.

Thus we see that many of the newly Orthodox do not fully observe these three commandments. They are no different from many other Jews who have not yet done penance for all the sins they have committed. How, then, should we refer to these people? Perhaps the appropriate term is to be "Ultra-Orthodoxized"—to join the cult of the newly pious. This is not merely a matter of semantics. Calling a phenomenon by the right name can frequently help us view it in the proper perspective.[6]

27

Religious Tolerance among Jews: A Critique of Rulings by Rabbi Moshe Feinstein

ONE OF THE FUNDAMENTAL POSTULATES OF LIBERAL Halakhah is that mutual tolerance is a prerequisite for Jewish unity and a peaceful and harmonious society. Unfortunately, many declare, in the name of Halakhah and Jewish tradition, that tolerance of non-Orthodox Jews is out of the question. When I served as head of the Council of Progressive Rabbis in Israel, I once invited a well-known Orthodox academic, Dr. Eliakim Ellinson, to speak on a topic he had researched. He felt that he could not accept the invitation, however, citing certain halakhic impediments embodied in rulings by Rabbi Moshe Feinstein. Since I was confident that the professor was a true scholar of impeccable intellectual honesty, I decided to analyze the sources cited in Rabbi Feinstein's responsa, the halakhic basis for the professor's declining our invitation. The letter-responsum that I sent the professor, repeating the invitation to address us at a future conference, follows:

Dear Professor,

As you may recall, last summer I invited you to speak on the laws of personal status to the Council of Progressive Rabbis in Israel, during a symposium to be held at the guesthouse of Kibbutz Shefayim. You replied that you were not allowed to lecture to this group, because of a ruling that forbids this, issued by one of the greatest decisors of our day, Rabbi Moshe Feinstein, then the president of the Orthodox Rabbinical Council of America. You derived this ruling from several decisions published in his collected responsa, *Iggerot Moshe*. In what follows I will supplement these with several other responsa that seem to bear on our topic and provide a basis for discussing the ruling.[1]

Your question appears to be as follows: Is a religiously observant professor permitted to deliver a lecture on the laws of personal status to a group of Progressive rabbis at a kibbutz guesthouse?

Since you say that you submit to the authority of Rabbi Feinstein, I will endeavor to confine my analysis to his responsa and accept, for the purpose of the argument, his fundamental assumptions about the absolute authority of certain texts. Nor will I challenge his wholesale delegitimization of non-Orthodox rabbis and institutions, even though much could be said on these points as well.

Four conclusions relevant to our topic are prominent in his responsa: (1) Non-Orthodox rabbis are heretics. (2) One may not accept a position in a non-Orthodox synagogue or institution. (3) One may not participate in a prayer service in a non-Orthodox synagogue. (4) A God-fearing individual who associates with the non-Orthodox is in jeopardy of leaving the Orthodox fold.

NON-ORTHODOX RABBIS ARE HERETICS

Again and again, Rabbi Feinstein refers to Conservative and Reform rabbis as "denying the Torah." Thus, for example, he writes about those who studied at the (Conservative) Jewish Theological Seminary:

> They are rabbis in their synagogues, and their philosophy is to discard and make light of some Torah precepts. This derives from their denial that the Torah is of Heavenly origin—the attitude of a learned heretic. ... They are presumed to be heretics who reject the Torah and are disqualified from testifying in a rabbinical court.[2]

Another responsum deals with "the post that His Honor [the questioner] accepted among heretics to serve as principal of a religious school for young boys and girls."[3]

In yet another responsum, Rabbi Feinstein declares unequivocally that

> All of the Reform are disqualified from testifying [in a religious court] because they deny that the Torah is from Heaven, for even though there are no witnesses to their transgressing all the precepts of the Torah, the very designation "Reform" attests that they are heretics.[4]

Here Rabbi Feinstein is arguing that there is no need for witnesses to prove that all non-Orthodox rabbis are heretics. Be that as it may, the implications of this wholesale indictment are limited to a few matters, such as testimony before a religious court, marriage, and conversion. They have no bearing on whether one may deliver a ninety-minute talk to rabbis who are "heretics."

Furthermore, it is no great tragedy if I make no attempt to refute the questionable allegation that all non-Orthodox rabbis are heretics. Rabbi Feinstein has merely placed us in the honorable company of the many eminent rabbis who have been accused of similar derelictions down through the ages. Here I will mention only a few of them.

BANNING RABBIS THROUGH THE CENTURIES

SA'ADIAH GAON (882–942)

Sa'adiah Gaon was accused of heresy in a writ of excommunication issued by the exilarch (the head of the Babylonian Jewish community) David ben Zakkai and by Rabbi Kohen-Zedek:

> Sa'id el-Fayyumi [i.e., Sa'adiah], the bloody and wicked man, . . . a churl, the son of a nobody: . . . let everyone know that he is a madman and evil, like this heretic. . . . Now, immediately excommunicate and ban all who read Sa'id el-Fayyumi, the destroyer of Israel . . . and all who go to his court and are judged by him and all who are in his camp.[5]

Sa'adiah Gaon did not take this lying down, but castigated his accusers in the same coin.

MAIMONIDES (1138–1204)

In the thirteenth century, after the death of Maimonides, several French rabbis, led by Rabbi Solomon ben Abraham of Montpelier, in Provence, banned his writings. Some of them found elements of sectarianism and heresy in *The Guide of the Perplexed* and *The Book of Knowledge* (the first volume of the *Mishneh Torah* code).[6] These rabbis excommunicated all those who studied or taught Maimonides' philosophical works. The Maimonideans proclaimed a counter-ban against their opponents. The direct or indirect result was that the above-mentioned works were burned by the church in Montpelier in 1232, as we learn from Maimonides' son, Rabbi Abraham:

> The works of the rabbi, my father, his memory for a blessing, *The Guide of the Perplexed* and *The Book of Knowledge,* were burned by one party in Montpelier and the group of ministers who helped them because they disagreed with their beliefs and disclosed the falsity of their opinion. The Christians certainly assisted them.[7]

Rabbi Zacharias Frankel (1801–1875)

In 1873 Rabbi Frankel, the head of the Rabbinical Seminary in Breslau and author of a ground-breaking monograph on the Mishnah (published in 1859), had the merit of being indicted by Rabbi Esriel Hildesheimer: "With regard to the book by that apostate Frankel, . . . one should not treat it as holy; burning it may even be a meritorious deed."[8]

Rabbi Esriel Hildesheimer (1820–1899)

Nor was Rabbi Hildesheimer, the head of the Berlin yeshiva that later bore his name, immune to similar allegations. In that same year (1873), Rabbi Hillel Lichtenstein (1815–1891), a leader of hard-line Hungarian Orthodoxy, described Rabbi Hildesheimer in the following words:

> Doctor Hildesheimer . . . —his way is always to hunt for pure souls and chop down goodly plants [a talmudic metaphor for heresy]. His disposition is only to uproot the Torah and fear [of the Lord] and to increase heresy and unbelief in Israel.[9]

Rabbi Lichtenstein also quoted from a letter written by Rabbi Ḥayyim Sofer (1821–1886), the head of the religious court in Munkács:

> That "wicked man Hildesheimer" is the horse and chariot of the Evil Inclination. His bravery and success are not natural, but because the guardian angel of Esau rides on him. . . . The Lord will not forgive them if they do not call public convocations to excommunicate and ban the man, . . . whose entire path is that of impurity and heresy.[10]

RABBI DAVID ZEVI HOFFMANN (1843–1921)

Rabbi Hoffmann, Hildesheimer's student and successor as head of the Berlin Rabbinical Seminary, won great acclaim for his talmudic studies. But when Rabbi Samson Raphael Hirsch (1808–1888) was asked his opinion of Hoffmann's monograph *Mar Shmuel,* published in 1873, he replied, "Dr. Hoffmann's book contains rank heresy!"[11]

RABBI MOSHE FEINSTEIN (1895–1986)

The venerable tradition of hurling accusations of heresy at great rabbis continues in our own time. Rabbi Feinstein, too, was the target of indictments no less severe than those he directed at Progressive rabbis. Some of his Ultra-Orthodox colleagues found him guilty of no less heinous "deviations"!

One of his most severe critics, Rabbi Yomtov Halevi Schwartz of the Nahalat Yakov Synagogue in Queens, New York, published a volume challenging more than 180 of the responsa collected in *Iggerot Moshe.* Rabbi Schwartz accused Rabbi Feinstein, among other offenses, of "leading the masses astray most atrociously by permitting many serious prohibitions."[12] He went on to explain that Feinstein misled the masses "with regard to the prohibition of a married woman, by permitting a woman to remarry after receiving an invalid *get"* and also "[annulled the marriage of] a woman whose husband was impotent, without a *get."* Feinstein, he charged, "had misled [people] to eat unkosher foods by ruling that it is permissible for old people to eat meat in the homes of their apostate children." Rabbi Feinstein was impeached for other sins, too, many of them no less severe than heresy and unbelief.

An Ultra-Orthodox *beit din* in New York issued a ruling against Rabbi Feinstein's Tiferet Yerushalayim Yeshiva:

> With regard to the admixture of secular studies in a yeshiva and factory for producing rabbis, in the matter of Rabbi Moshe Feinstein's yeshiva, the Metivta Tiferet Yerushalayim, we declare that this seminary is a forbidden place and in the category of schools under a ban, Heaven save us. . . . The publications of the institution that is run by the author of the book *Iggerot Moshe* are apt to cause the present and future generations to commit sins *of sectarianism, heresy, and the uprooting of religion, Heaven forfend.*[13]

Here we see Rabbi Feinstein hoisted on his own petard, accused by other Orthodox rabbis of "transgressions" resembling those for which he upbraided non-Orthodox rabbis. As the Sages noted, "a man is measured by the same standard that he uses to measure others" (BT Sotah 8b, Megillah 12a). Or, in the words of the fourth-century *amora* Rava, "the fletcher slain by an arrow receives retribution from his own handiwork" (BT Pesaḥim 28a).

The long annals of denunciation for heresy, from Sa'adiah Gaon through Moshe Feinstein, are ample proof of the sterility of this approach, which prefers *ad hominem* attacks to constructive dialogue and debate.

ONE MAY NOT ACCEPT A POSITION IN A NON-ORTHODOX SYNAGOGUE

This is the second ruling in *Iggerot Moshe* that is relevant to the present topic. Rabbi Feinstein was replying to a questioner who had been offered a "teaching position with the Conservatives":

> With regard to the post that His Honor accepted among heretics to serve as principal of a religious school for young boys and girls . . . — and with even greater force, if the [school] is in the same building [as the Conservative synagogue] it is clear that it is forbidden to accept such a post.[14]

In another responsum on a similar topic, but where the school and synagogue were some distance apart, Rabbi Feinstein permitted the questioner to take the job:

> As long as the teachers are allowed to teach as they should, with no changes, and the school is in a separate location and not in their synagogue, there is no prohibition on accepting [the job].[15]

In yet another question about the permissibility of accepting a job as teacher and principal of the religious school of a Conservative synagogue, Rabbi Feinstein expressed grave reservations—"the spirit of the rabbis is not comfortable with this"—but nevertheless ruled that it was permissible to do so:

> But one cannot say that it is forbidden to be the principal and teacher in a school of theirs, if one is allowed to teach the Lord's Torah and pray in the correct manner.[16]

On the other hand, he ruled that the sexton of a Conservative synagogue could not serve as a teacher and lecturer in an Orthodox synagogue.[17]

There seems to be a certain inconsistency in these responsa. Rabbi Feinstein's rulings are evidently influenced by the time, place, questioner, and specific circumstances.

In another case, having to do not with employment but with the rental of premises for an Orthodox elementary school in a building owned by Conservative or Reform congregations and adjacent to their synagogues, the rabbi responded with a certain degree of ambiguity (as he frequently did): "The spirit of the rabbis is not comfortable with these two places, even though one cannot say that there is a clear and explicit prohibition."[18] Rabbi Feinstein's response does indicate that in this matter, at least, the heterodox are preferable to Christians, since in a parallel case he absolutely forbade renting space for a yeshiva adjacent to a church.[19]

In two rulings about ritual slaughterers who were associated with Conservative synagogues—one served as the sexton and the other applied for a job as cantor—Rabbi Feinstein ruled that such an affiliation disqualifies a man from serving as a ritual slaughterer, because "it is clear that one cannot trust his slaughtering."[20]

In most cases of a contractual relationship with a Conservative synagogue, Rabbi Feinstein prohibited; only in a minority of cases did he permit. Yet, the stringent rulings deal with regular employment by a non-Orthodox synagogue and cannot serve as a precedent for a single lecture to be delivered at a kibbutz to the Council of Progressive Rabbis. The site is a neutral venue, not one of our synagogues—even though Rabbi Feinstein did sometimes permit contact with a non-Orthodox synagogue. Nor are we offering you a permanent or even a temporary position, but inviting you to deliver a single lecture. In my humble opinion, the implications of Rabbi Feinstein's responsa are that it is permissible to deliver a lecture to our rabbis; certainly it is not forbidden to do so.

ONE MAY NOT PARTICIPATE IN A PRAYER SERVICE IN A NON-ORTHODOX SYNAGOGUE

This ruling was issued in response to a questioner who asked whether it was permitted to attend a wedding in a Conservative synagogue. The wedding dinner was to be held in a different hall, "but the ceremony will be in the synagogue [sanctuary] at a time when there are no prayer services." The officiating rabbi will be Orthodox "and their rabbi will not be present at all."

Rabbi Feinstein permitted this arrangement because "many Torah-observant people will attend and no one will think that they are going to pray there."[21] He reiterated that it is forbidden to pray in a non-Orthodox synagogue and "be one of the of Conservatives and pray in their synagogues, alongside women."[22] Yet, not only did he permit the wedding dinner to be held in the hall of the Conservative synagogue, he explicitly allowed an Orthodox rabbi to conduct the ceremony in the sanctuary itself and sanctioned the presence there of observant Jews. To this liberality he attached a stringent condition, however: that the rabbi not be inside the synagogue sanctuary at the hour of prayer services.[23]

In this case, as in others, it is not forbidden to enter a non-Orthodox synagogue, even for a religious ceremony, as long as one does not participate in public prayers there.

The implications for you, dear professor, are clear. The hour set for your lecture will not be close to the time of our prayers. Hence, according to the author of *Iggerot Moshe,* there is no prohibition.

AN ORTHODOX JEW WHO ASSOCIATES WITH THE NON-ORTHODOX IS IN JEOPARDY OF LEAVING ORTHODOXY

This fourth idea is a central thread of *Iggerot Moshe.* In the aforementioned case of an observant Jew who had been offered a job as principal of a Conservative religious school, Rabbi Feinstein was ambivalent:

> Even though the observant Jew will sometimes have a beneficial influence on others, the contrary is more likely, because sectarianism, Heaven forbid, is attractive, and [according to the Talmud, the biblical admonition] "'keep yourself far away from her' (Prov. 5:8) refers to sectarianism" (BT Avodah Zarah 17a).[24]

One can discern Rabbi Feinstein's fear of ideological and spiritual competition between Orthodoxy and other movements. He is aware of the lurking peril posed by the unremitting influence of a non-Orthodox institution, which may lead a person to desert to the other side and stop being Orthodox.

Rabbi Feinstein was also ambivalent about the cases of a teacher and principal in a Conservative religious school:

> For there is also a benefit, because the children of the Conservatives, too, must learn the Divine Torah and may perhaps grow up to Torah and *mitzvot* as kosher Jews.

This is the positive side; but there is also a danger waiting to ambush the principal:

> There is reason to be apprehensive that he himself might be drawn after them, because this would lead to proximity and association with the heretics. . . . Even if he is strong-minded, one must fear that others too will allow themselves [to enter into such a relationship] but will not be so steadfast in their beliefs.[25]

When he grants permission to conduct a wedding ceremony in a Conservative synagogue, he also sounds a warning note:

> In any case, one ought to distance oneself from their synagogue as much as possible. In particular, people learn from an important person, such that we may fear that others will mistakenly say that that important person too, is on good terms with [the non-Orthodox] and their synagogue.

This notion that an eminent person is liable to make what is *treif* appear kosher and mislead innocent believers recurs many times. Nevertheless,

> Because it is not prohibited, but there is only a precaution of maintaining extra distance and a slight apprehension of error, even an important person may act leniently, where he deems the need to be great.[26]

This ruling may well apply to you, dear professor. You could be a factor that "might influence others for good"[27] if you came to speak to our rabbis on your field of expertise, the laws of personal status. Perhaps, though, you believe that it would pose an even greater danger for you? To quote Rabbi Feinstein: "The contrary is more likely, because sectarianism, Heaven forbid, is attractive."[28] Only you can decide which of the two possibilities is correct. If you feel there is a danger of your being attracted to "sectarianism," you certainly are forbidden to come lecture to us.

In this case, you need not be apprehensive that you might lead others astray, since the lecture will not take place in a synagogue, nor will there be any Orthodox people present who might be deceived into thinking that you are—Heaven forbid!—intimate with Progressive Jews. Nevertheless, if you believe that a lecture about "marriage not according to Jewish Law" might make a significant contradiction and enlighten us, and perhaps even get us to amend our ways, it may be your *obligation* to accept my invitation.

In any case, in these circumstances Rabbi Feinstein would have ruled leniently and left the final decision to you, as he did for one of your colleagues:

> Accordingly, if your eminence believes that it is necessary . . . —because you are on the spot and know that it will not lead to any error—then you certainly may do it.[29]

Ultimately, you, too, are on the spot and the decision is yours.

WHERE WE TRULY DIFFER

The preceding analysis of the rabbinic responsa leads to the conclusion that there is no explicit prohibition that bars an Orthodox professor from delivering a lecture to our rabbis. In fact, there are a number of lenient rulings associated with our synagogues, from which one may draw an analogy that permits the matter at hand. Ultimately, the decision depends not on a ruling by Rabbi Moshe Feinstein, but only on you.

Rabbi Feinstein is lenient in such matters, despite his sharp language and grounds for stringency. This, in fact, is the argument advanced by Rabbi Yomtov Schwartz and others. One who is predisposed to the severe view should consult authorities who are strict about this question, such as Rabbi Eliezer Waldenberg[30] and Rabbi Meshulam Rothe,[31] whose extremely harsh rulings against the opening of the Reform rabbinical seminary in Jerusalem may have some bearing on the matter at hand. Those who prefer a liberal ruling can consult *Iggerot Moshe* or other decisors, including the many Orthodox professors and rabbis who lecture at our seminary and synagogues on a regular basis.

There is a much more serious problem here, however. Despite Rabbi Feinstein's halakhic brilliance and his broad knowledge of worldly matters and contemporary problems, which sometimes led him to issue enlightened and liberal rulings—for example, waiving the requirement of token circumcision for a pre–Bar Mitzvah convert who had been circumcised in infancy[32]—the responsa in *Iggerot Moshe* frequently reflect intolerance, suspicion, and separatism. Sometimes these are expressed in fierce hostility towards other movements in Judaism. Why is this so? Is it motivated by zealousness to defend the Torah, as Rabbi Feinstein understands it? Is he afraid that Orthodox Jews may be snatched away by other movements—notably Conservatism, whose allures are clearly much stronger—or of the influence of these movements on Orthodoxy in general?

There is reason to believe that Rabbi Feinstein's hostility is rooted in the disparity between his worldview and conception of Halakhah and those held by the ideologues of our movement. There is no doubt that we profoundly disagree with regard to Divine revelation, the concept of the God-given Torah, the source of authority in Halakhah, the evolution of Halakhah and its pluralistic nature, and many other topics. All these questions merit serious and comprehensive attention. Here, though, I can merely touch on the last two.

Progressive Judaism sees Halakhah—and Judaism as a whole—as an evolving system, in which changes take place from generation to generation. The vast majority of our rabbis certainly identify with the statement by Prof. Yitzhak Gilat:

> [Issues from the past] teach us about the link between Halakhah and the factors and conditions of real life in every generation, a link that was expressed in the desire to respond to the needs of the hour and of the nation. This response was not the result of inattention to the principles and historical continuity of Halakhah, but of a re-examination of Halakhah and the application of the accepted methods of exegesis.[33]

Furthermore, our movement views Halakhah as a system that is fundamentally pluralistic, today as in the past. In the words of Prof. Jakob J. Petuchowski:

> There were many models within Halakhah, both with regard to its history—that is, as a result of the emergence of stages in its evolution—and with regard to the co-existence of different schools within each of these stages.[34]

One may assume that Rabbi Feinstein would reject out of hand such notions concerning the evolution of Halakhah and its pluralistic nature, these keystones of our philosophy, which support the legitimacy of change in Halakhah and of differences among Jews as to their approach to the commandments, and permit tolerance for the views of others. Rabbi Feinstein, and the Orthodox world in general, see Halakhah as static, monolithic, and invariant. Our liberal worldview may very well threaten the pillars of the Orthodox philosophy. Liberal Jews, who consider pluralism and diversity to be a welcome phenomenon in Judaism, can and must be tolerant of Jews who act differently than they do, in accordance with their own beliefs and views. This is not the case with some Orthodox Jews, who believe they have a monopoly on truth and reject the very possibility that liberal Jews can observe Halakhah in their own way. We are heretics in their eyes. It is unfortunate that the lessons of history have not been internalized by them, since the annals of Halakhah teach that our Sages knew how to disagree with their colleagues even while evincing (for the most part) respect for them and their approach.

MAY YOU TEACH US?

But to return to our starting point: Is it permissible for an Orthodox professor to deliver a lecture on Jewish marriage law to the Israel Council of Progressive Rabbis on a kibbutz? We have seen that the rulings of Rabbi Moshe Feinstein and the principles that underlie his decisions do not forbid it and may even be read as permitting it.

It should of course be noted that this conclusion is based on responsa dealing with similar topics and not with the precise question before us here. Hence, we can never be certain whether Rabbi Feinstein would indeed have permitted you to lecture before the Rabbinical Council on a kibbutz, since you did not address this particular question to him.

By the same token, though, we cannot know whether Rabbi Feinstein believed that you are permitted to serve on the faculty of Bar Ilan University![35]

I hope to hear from you soon and initiate a genuine dialogue.

Yours,
Moshe Zemer

When the professor returned from a sabbatical in North America, we did meet to discuss the foregoing letter. During our conversation, which lasted for many hours, he checked and studied the sources I had quoted, raised questions, and answered my objections. In the end, he turned to me and declared: "I accept your invitation to deliver a lecture to your Council of Rabbis. Your conclusions are in line with the rulings of my master and teacher, Rabbi Moshe Feinstein."

To our great sorrow, the distinguished professor died suddenly before he could address us. Alas for those who are lost and irreplaceable!

28

Archaeology as a *Mitzvah*

THE LAST TWO MONTHS OF 1992 AND THE BEGINNING OF 1993 were marked by repeated Ultra-Orthodox demonstrations against archaeological excavations of ancient burial sites in Jerusalem, especially the salvage dig at the site of a new highway interchange in the northern suburbs of the city. Although these protests were ostensibly staged in the name of the Jewish religion and against archaeological excavations, no Orthodox rabbi ever published a reasoned halakhic ruling to justify such extremism. The chief rabbi of Jerusalem, Rabbi Yitzhak Kolitz, issued a ban on removing bones from burial caves, but, in a departure from the usual practice of decisors, he did not cite any of the halakhic sources on which he based his ruling. Hence, we may legitimately wonder whether the codified Halakhah really does prohibit the transfer of bones from archaeological sites for reburial in a Jewish cemetery.

In the time of the Second Temple (starting in the fifth century B.C.E.), bones were moved out of ancient burial caves dating from the time of the First Temple to facilitate the expansion of Jerusalem. The Tosefta (Baba Batra 1:11) states that "a tomb that has been surrounded by the city on all four sides, on three sides, or on two opposite sides, and more than fifty cubits away, is not to be moved; but if less than that it may be moved." This means that the Jerusalemites of antiquity used to remove bones from ancient burial caves when the growth of the city left them surrounded by urban development on several sides and within fifty cubits (about one hundred feet). The Tosefta adds that "all tombs may be moved except for the tomb of the king and the tomb of the prophet," and some say that they, too, were moved.

Despite the prohibition on exhuming a body and reburying it elsewhere, stated in the Jerusalem Talmud (JT Mo'ed Katan 2:4), the Babylonian Talmud does permit transferring human remains from an "unauthorized grave," that is, where a body has been buried without the consent of the owner of the ground, or from "a grave that is a public nuisance" (BT Sanhedrin 47b). In his commentary on Maimonides, Rabbi Joseph Caro held accordingly that "a grave that is a public nuisance, [that is, if] someone is buried in a place that is a public thoroughfare . . . it is permitted to move it because it is a public nuisance."[1]

The codified Halakhah permits transferring human remains in other circumstances as well, such as exhumation for reburial in the Land of Israel or in a family plot. It is also permitted and even deemed meritorious to transfer bones from a grave that cannot be preserved, that is, one where there is a danger of landslide, flooding, or destruction. In such cases, transferring the bones is permitted and may even be required.

In both theory and practice, the salvage excavations of the burial tombs in the French Hill neighborhood of northern Jerusalem, which sparked the late 1992 protests, fell into the category of removing the dead from a grave that could not be preserved. The license to do so can be traced to a ruling by Rabbi Isaac ben Moses of Vienna (1190–1260), who permitted the remains of a deceased person to be moved if "they would not be adequately preserved in this grave and one may fear that the [non-Jews] might remove it or that water might seep into the grave. . . . Then it is certainly a meritorious action to move him, to avoid pain and disrespect to the dead."[2] Many later decisors have followed his lead.

In 1728, Rabbi Abraham Yitzhaki, the Chief Rabbi of Jerusalem, permitted the Sages of Safed to move some of the graves in the ancient cemetery of that town to permit repair and expansion of the sewer line that passed through it. He based his permission on the risk that these were graves that would not be preserved, so that moving the bodies would prevent disrespect to the dead.[3] In the eighteenth century, Rabbi David Oppenheim ruled that it was permissible to move all of the graves that had been uncovered during the excavation of foundations for a synagogue. This ruling is unique in that it permitted the removal of the graves and the construction of the new synagogue on the foundations of the old synagogue. It was based on precedents of the Sages, who permitted the removal of an unauthorized grave but *required* the removal "of a grave that is in the way so that it does become a public nuisance."[4]

Rabbi Elijah Guttmacher (1795–1874) permitted the Jewish community of Neustadt on the Warthe to relocate all the graves in its cemetery to a new location to permit expansion of the synagogue that stood next to it. He relied in part on Rabbi Oppenheim's precedent.[5]

Leading Hungarian rabbis of the nineteenth century issued similar rulings. Rabbi Moses Sofer permitted the transfer of the bodies from old cemeteries "that cannot be preserved and where flooding may be expected."[6]

Cases similar to the building of the French Hill interchange have been considered by other eminent scholars. Rabbi Moses Schick permitted a community to transfer bones from a cemetery through which a railroad was going to be built.[7] When Rabbi Samuel ben Ezekiel Landau of Prague was asked about a highway that the governor of the city planned to cut through the Jewish cemetery, he replied: "On this matter they must make an effort and spend as much as they can . . . to have the highway rerouted, but if this would cost more than they can afford and it is impossible to divert the highway around the graves, then in my humble opinion it would be better to move the graves to a place where they can be preserved. . . . It is even a meritorious action to do so."[8]

Similarly, Rabbi Mayer Lerner of Altona, Germany (1857–1930), ruled that all the graves could be moved from a cemetery when the authorities "had definitely resolved to widen the street and run it through the Jewish cemetery."[9]

These rabbinic responsa are only a few of many lenient rulings on the subject. The halakhic sources demonstrate that archaeologists' salvage excavations of graves that are about to be destroyed by the construction of buildings or roads fall under the halakhic rubric of "removing bones from a grave that will not be preserved." Had the Ultra-Orthodox studied these and other halakhic precedents, they would have come to the conclusion that the archaeologists' acts were permissible.[10]

The archaeologists handed over sixteen ossuaries for reburial. There seems to be a halakhic basis for this: the *Shulḥan Arukh* states that "no benefit may be derived from a coffin that has been emptied. If it is made of stone or ceramic, it should be shattered; if of wood, it should be burnt" (*Y.D.* 363:5). In the nineteenth century, however, Rabbi Jehiel Michel Epstein ruled that it is not obligatory to destroy an ossuary; one need only "be sure that no one derives benefit from it."[11] According to this ruling, the French Hill ossuaries did not have to be destroyed or reburied. It was enough to prevent anyone from deriving benefit from them.

But what is the forbidden benefit of a coffin? The consensus of opinion is that it must somehow involve re-use. Does this restriction prevent archaeologists from preserving and studying ossuaries? Chief Rabbi Benzion Uziel permitted autopsies and postmortem dissection for the purpose of medical study and research, and he ruled that this did not constitute deriving benefit from the dead.[12] One may rule similarly that it is permitted to hand over ossuaries to archaeologists for observation, research, and study.

We may thus conclude that there was no halakhic justification for the violent demonstrations against the excavations. The archaeologists were not violating any halakhic prohibition. On the contrary, they were acting according to the letter and spirit of Jewish law by preserving those ancient grave sites.

29

Circumcising a Corpse

WHEN A RECENT IMMIGRANT FROM THE SOVIET UNION was killed in a traffic accident in the northern Israeli town of Nahariyya in 1991, his corpse was circumcised before burial. This was done on the instructions of the local rabbi and with the approval of the Chief Rabbinate, which declared that "Halakhah requires that a man be circumcised posthumously if he was not circumcised while alive." The rabbinate did not specify which sections of the law require removing the foreskin of the deceased. All of us, not only new immigrants who are unfamiliar with the Jewish religion, deserve a persuasive explanation for such an act.

In fact, there is no halakhic principle that requires postmortem circumcision of a Jew. What, then, was the basis for the rabbinate's ruling? The *Shulḥan Arukh* stipulated that a posthumous circumcision be performed on an infant who died before he could be circumcised: "An infant who died before reaching eight [days] is to be circumcised at his grave . . . but one does not make a benediction over the circumcision" (*Y.D.* 263:5).

Why should an infant be circumcised posthumously? We can find three reasons for this procedure in the sources:

Rabbenu Asher ben Jehiel (known as the Rosh, d. 1327) quotes Rabbi Nahshon Gaon about a male infant who succumbs before he is a week old. The custom was to circumcise and name him before burial so that Heaven would have mercy on him at the Resurrection of the Dead and his father would recognize him.[1]

The crux of this rationale is that infant boys are named when they are circumcised; after the dead child is circumcised and given a name, the father will know he had a son named such-and-such and will recognize him at the time of the Resurrection. In a similar vein, if the child were not circumcised the father might think the resurrected boy was not his, but the child of non-Jews. As Rabbi Joseph Caro summarized it, the child is given a name "as a memorial, so that Heaven will have mercy on him and he will be restored to life in the Resurrection of the Dead" (*Shulḥan Arukh, Y.D.* 263:5). Even if we accept the beliefs on which this rationale is grounded, it is irrelevant to the circumcision of an adult who has borne a name for many years.

In his commentary on Maimonides' *Mishneh Torah,* Rabbi Meir Hakohen (fourteenth century) wrote that it was customary to remove the foreskin from a dead infant because of the "provision for miscreants."[2] The nature of this "provision" is explained by the following midrash:

> Rabbi Levi said: In the future world Abraham will sit at the gate of Gehinnom [Hell] and will not allow a circumcised Israelite to descend into it. What will he do about those who sinned too much? He will remove the foreskin from infants who died before they could be circumcised, attach it to [the adult sinners], and then send them down to Gehinnom (Genesis Rabbah 48:8).

According to this legend, the Patriarch Abraham stands sentry at the gates of Hell and makes sure that circumcised Jews are not carried into its depths—except for the gravest sinners among them. So that these wicked people can be punished, he detaches the foreskins of infants who died uncircumcised and attaches them to the sinners, thereby "undoing" their circumcision and making them "eligible" to enter Hell.

The great Sage Rabbi Ezekiel Landau of Prague (1713–1793) challenged this custom: "Perhaps the reason for removing the foreskin is only the 'provision for miscreants' and it is not in keeping with the dignity [of the deceased]."[3] If the posthumous circumcision is not in keeping with the dignity of the deceased and is conducted only because of a legend that has no real anchorage in

Jewish belief and in reality, what is the significance of the requirement to circumcise the corpse?

Similarly, Rabbi Moses Sofer, the Ḥatam Sofer of Pressburg (1762–1839), one of the strictest rabbinic authorities of the last two centuries and a mainstay of stringent Orthodoxy, stated unequivocally that "cutting off the foreskin of the deceased . . . is no more than excising a piece of odious flesh and does nothing to rectify the person." He adds however, that "it is nevertheless meritorious to do so because of the 'provision for the miscreants of Israel.'"[4] Accordingly, anyone who dismisses this provision as a nonbinding legend will see no obligation to circumcise a corpse, because the operation is only the excision of a piece of loathsome flesh, does no benefit to the deceased himself, and is not conducive to his dignity.

A third reason advanced for posthumous circumcision is to remove the dead man's shame. Rabbi Joseph Caro notes that "it was customary to circumcise a child who died before he reached eight days . . . in the cemetery in order to remove his shame—he should not be buried in his foreskin, because it would be shameful for him."[5] Today the question seems to be, Which is the greater humiliation—burial with one's foreskin or posthumous circumcision?

As we have seen, the custom of posthumous circumcision was originally applied only to infants; I have located no source that even discusses circumcising adults after death. Furthermore, the reasons for the custom derive from a belief system that is incompatible with the worldview of contemporary enlightened Jews. Notions that circumcision will facilitate family reunification at the time of the Resurrection or that Father Abraham would use the foreskins of dead infants to condemn Jewish sinners to the tortures of Hell may have some folkloristic and historical interest, but they command little credence today. Someone who accepts these beliefs may act accordingly but may not impose them on those who reject them.

If the foregoing were not enough to demonstrate that there is no halakhic mandate to perform post-mortem circumcisions, we find that Rabbi Elijah, the Gaon of Vilna (1720–1797), after citing all of the above sources, concludes that even in the case of infants, "as a matter of Halakhah, circumcision is not required."[6] No authoritative halakhic decisions contradict this conclusion. And despite the

statement issued by the burial society in Nahariyya, there is no halakhic impediment to burying an uncircumcised Jew in a Jewish
cemetery. Certainly there is no requirement to bury such a person in
a non-Jewish cemetery—in fact, it is forbidden to do so.

The biblical commandment of circumcision, incumbent on all
Jewish males, applies only to the living. It is a well-known principle
that the dead are exempt from all the commandments, as we are
taught by Rabbi Johanan: "When a man dies he becomes free of
the Torah and the commandments" (BT Shabbat 30a). It is difficult to comprehend how there could be a requirement to remove
the foreskin from a corpse, given that the halakhic aversion to desecrating the dead is so strong that the rabbinate opposes postmortem examinations for purposes of medical research. On this
matter, the late Chief Rabbi Ben-Zion Uziel ruled that there is no
desecration of the dead when a procedure is intended for medical
purposes and to save human life, "where the desecration is done for
the needs of the living, to save lives."[7] This license would not apply
to circumcising a corpse.

By emphasizing the superstitious side of Jewish tradition and
not explaining it to new immigrants who were deprived of any ac-
quaintance with the sanctity and profound thought of our tradition, the religious establishment will only distance these new
citizens (as well as their more veteran fellow Israelis) from the Jewish religion. If this is how the rabbinate treats the dead, how will it
handle the personal status of those who are the children of mixed
marriages and the problem of converting members of this wave of
immigrants, when these issues become pressing matters?

Actions such as this, performed with the consent of the Chief
Rabbinate, the supreme spiritual authority in the State of Israel,
can only make the Jewish religion despicable to many Jews. They
teeter ominously on the verge of desecration of the Divine Name,
as Maimonides ruled: "There are other things that fall into the category of desecration of the Divine Name, as when a learned Sage
and pious man acts in a way that causes people to murmur about
him. Even though these deeds are not transgressions, he has nevertheless desecrated the Divine Name." (Laws of the Fundamentals
of the Torah 5:11).

VII

Medicine

The Torah warned us about preservation of life because God graciously created the world to benefit His creatures so that they may be aware of His greatness and may serve Him by observing His commandments and Torah.

RABBI MOSES RIVKES (seventeenth century)

If we do not permit an autopsy it will never be possible to study this and we will not find a treatment for all who are sick today as well as those who will come down with such a disease in the future. This is certainly a case about which it was said, "live by them, the Torah said, not die by them."

RABBI BEN-ZION UZIEL (TWENTIETH CENTURY)

Everyone, whether secular, Orthodox, or Ultra-Orthodox, requires modern medical care at some time or other. Some of the Ultra-Orthodox, though, have attempted to bind physicians with restrictions derived from belief rather than from science. This pressure might be venial were it applied only to Orthodox hospitals and the treatment of religious patients. The Orthodox establishment, however, working through the religious parties and Knesset legislation, endeavors to impose its views on everyone and to set restrictions based on their view of Halakhah on all hospitals and physicians.

The sanctity of life, which is a gift of the Creator, is a guiding principle for physicians no less than it is for Halakhah. Perhaps the large number of Jewish physicians in Israel and the Diaspora is a direct result of the great value that Jewish tradition ascribes to human life. In any case, Halakhah stipulates that physicians themselves, as experts on illness and treatment, are those who decide when certain precepts may be set aside in order to save human life. It is impossible to determine the moment of death, in order to permit organ transplants, without calling in a physician.

In the following chapters we shall see that there is no necessary contradiction between medicine and Halakhah, especially progressive Halakhah.

30

A Dialogue on Autopsies

AT THE BEHEST OF THE RELIGIOUS PARTIES, THE KNESSET passed legislation that places drastic restrictions on postmortem examinations. Ultra-Orthodox circles led the public to believe that there is a stark contrast between codified Halakhah and the demands of modern medicine. A believer, it is asserted, must be willing to allow a number of human beings to die rather than violate certain dictates of the Torah. In response to this view, two friends of long standing, Prof. Raphael Walden, head of the department of surgery at Tel Hashomer Hospital, near Tel Aviv, and I, each with his own approach, sat down together and analyzed the halakhic sources, reviewed the attitude of modern medicine, and endeavored to clarify whether there really is such an antithesis between the needs of medical science and the principles of Judaism.[1]

IS THERE A CONTRADICTION BETWEEN MEDICINE AND THE TORAH?

Dr. Walden: One of the most difficult moments in my professional life is when I suffer the agonizing failure of having a patient die. At that moment I am prey to mixed feelings: profound grief and frustration over the loss, on one hand, but on the other hand a fierce desire to know exactly how and why it happened. Did I make a mistake? Did I do everything possible? Was the failure in the diagnosis or in the treatment? And, most important of all, what can I learn from this tragedy to keep it from recurring tomorrow?

This is why I turn to the family of the deceased and gently ask their permission to perform an autopsy. In these moments it is only natural that I am confronted by their feelings of bereavement. When the request is made of the Ultra-Orthodox, however, I encounter not only an understandable sense of loss but also anger and panic at the very possibility that a postmortem examination might be performed. These people are convinced that it is absolutely forbidden to perform an autopsy, for so their rabbis have ruled. As a religious person I find myself in a difficult dilemma. The procedure may help me acquire vital information that can save lives in the future, but its performance is prevented by the claim that an autopsy "is against the Torah." In my innocence I thought that I was fulfilling the great precept of *pikkuah nefesh,* saving human life; instead, I am castigated as a destroyer of Israel who would desecrate the dead person and wreak havoc with the feelings of his or her relatives.

Rabbi Zemer: One of the most distressing aspects of life in Israel is that Judaism and its precepts are often presented in a fashion that makes them appear obscurantist and fanatical, opposed to progress and development. Does the codified Halakhah really outlaw autopsies? The debates over this question have a long history, and the decisors have rendered various and even contradictory opinions. But the concept that underlies the entire dispute derives from the statement in the Torah that "You shall keep My laws and My rules, by the pursuit of which man shall live" (Lev. 18:5).

In several places, the Sages emphasized that observance of the commandments is intended to serve life and the living; consequently they expounded this verse as meaning "live by them, not die by them" (*Sifra* ad loc.; see also BT Yoma 85b and BT Sanhedrin 74a). To the best of my understanding, the purpose of autopsies is to learn from particular cases in the hope of discovering something that will make it possible to save human lives in the future. If so, we can decide without hesitation that there is no ban on postmortem examination and that performing them is a classic example of *pikkuaḥ nefesh*.

Rabbi Lord Immanuel Jakobovits, the former Chief Rabbi of Britain, ruled as follows:

> Just as with the injunction to desecrate the Sabbath where there is danger to human life,[2] even when the peril is extremely doubtful, the rule is that "one who acts with alacrity is praiseworthy, one who stops to ask a question sheds blood, and the person who is asked is blameworthy" (based on *Tur O.H.* 328), such is the case in this matter too, in my humble opinion. Because the only justification for permitting autopsies is to save human life, accordingly it is not *optional* but *obligatory* and meritorious. . . . Hence [rabbis] are commanded to announce and preach to the public that autopsies may be performed whenever there is the slightest question of danger to human life, so that those who prevent [autopsies] will not be like shedders of blood, and so that the rabbis will not fall under the rubric "the person who is asked is blameworthy," standing idly by the blood of their fellows.[3]

This ruling is based on the assumption that autopsies do indeed serve the objective of saving human life. Is this in fact the case?

Dr. Walden: Postmortem examinations serve several purposes. Historically, the most important aim was to learn human anatomy. This is a vital part of the education of future physicians. Without detailed knowledge of the structure of the body, medical studies have no foundation. Today, however, most postmortem examinations are conducted not to train medical students but to derive knowledge from concrete cases. They constitute the essential monitoring and control mechanism of every medical system. Without them, serious errors of diagnosis and treatment are liable to recur, and many patients who could have been saved will pay for these mistakes with their lives. Even today we do not understand all the mechanisms of diseases that kill tens of thousands each year in our country, such as heart attacks and cancer.

The knowledge we gain from an autopsy is another step that brings us closer to understanding the course of human illness.

Autopsies frequently turn up findings that had not been suspected while the patient was alive and that cast a new light on the clinical picture. In the case of hereditary ailments, one can arrive at important conclusions concerning close relatives. What we learn from autopsies is frequently published and becomes available to the entire medical community, so that everyone, not only patients of the attending physician, benefits from the accumulated experience. Autopsies are essential for all, not just physicians. No doubt some physicians would rather have their mistakes buried quietly. But pathology steps in and makes us conduct a meticulous and piercing review. Would we allow professionals in other, less vital fields to work without feedback and supervision? After all, here we are speaking about human life!

Rabbi Zemer: That puts me in mind of the position of the late Sephardi Chief Rabbi, Ben-Zion Uziel, which supports the stance of modern medicine. In 1935, Rabbi Uziel ruled that autopsies and anatomical dissection of cadavers are certainly permitted. He wrote as follows:

> With regard to the present issue—dissection of cadavers to learn medicine and be able to heal other human beings—it follows with certainty that it is absolutely permitted. There is no doubt that all those Sages of the past who were also expert physicians had to examine corpses in order to learn and gain experience and were not deterred by the ban on disgracing the corpse. . . . If an autopsy is not performed on this body because of some prohibition involved, one will never be done and this knowledge will always be hidden from us, and cause the certain death of a number of persons. . . . But in the case of a familiar disease whose secrets are not known to physicians, and they wish to take this opportunity to learn about it by means of a postmortem examination; and all the more so where it is not possible for Jewish doctors to learn medicine other than by dissecting cadavers— and this would certainly endanger life because there will always be sick people, all of whom need medical treatment: [in these cases] it is certainly and unquestionably permissible to perform an autopsy.[4]

The ruling by Rabbi Uziel and other lenient decisors is based on the assumption that there is no substitute for autopsies and anatomical dissection. But today, in the wake of major technological advances and noninvasive techniques—X-rays, ultrasound, CT scans, isotopes, and so on—aren't there other ways besides autopsies to investigate the causes of illness and death so that the knowledge can be applied to the treatment of others?

There Is No Substitute for Autopsies

Dr. Walden: No. Despite all the advances that medical science has made, there is still no substitute for postmortem examinations and anatomical dissection. The human body, the pinnacle of creation, is so complex that no mechanical model could provide adequate knowledge of its structure. As for determining the cause of death, every effort was made to discover the cause of the illness while the patient was still alive—but the treatment failed nevertheless. Even when the cause of death is ostensibly known, we often turn up unexpected findings during an autopsy. Postmortem examinations are even more important in cases of sudden death or when the clinical picture was never clear. In some Western countries, one criterion for the quality of a hospital is its autopsy rate; if some minimum percentage of postmortem examinations are not performed the hospital is not allowed to train residents.

Rabbi Zemer: It is interesting that Rabbi Uziel reached the conclusion that there is no substitute for dissection and autopsies as far back as 1935: "For there is no other way. If we ban all dissection of corpses we will never be able to learn this science, which can be learned only be seeing."[5] In another place he states that

> if we do not permit an autopsy it will never be possible to study this condition and we will not find a treatment for all who are sick today as well as those who will come down with such a disease in the future. This is certainly a case about which it was said, "live by them, the Torah said, not die by them."[6]

Nevertheless, some Orthodox sources maintain that it is possible to rely on research based on dissections performed abroad. I have heard that no autopsies are performed at Shaare Tzedek Hospital in Jerusalem; yet, the medical staff is nevertheless on a high level. What do you think of such arguments?

Dr. Walden: Just as people are different from one another, so too living conditions and the causes of disease differ from population to population. For example, research about liver disease in Sweden is certainly very interesting, but many of its conclusions cannot be applied to patients in Israel. Environmental and genetic factors, as well as local diagnostic and therapeutic conditions, distinguish the population of Israel from that of other countries. When human life is at stake, it is utterly impossible to rely on data gathered in other conditions and from other populations in the hope of drawing proximate analogies.

Hospitals in Israel where autopsies are not performed can benefit from the accumulated experience of nearby institutions. Their physicians regularly attend meetings and lectures where the results of pathologic investigations are reported on.

As a matter of principle it seems to me that the idea that the corpses of observant Jews must not be touched and that information crucial to saving human life may be derived only from the dissection of non-Jews or nonobservant Jews is a distorted and immoral attitude. I see this as a distressing manifestation of parasitism and a mentality that is inappropriate for a sovereign Jewish state and the responsibility that all Jews bear for one another.

Rabbi Zemer: Jewish tradition, too, is opposed to making a distinction among Jews and does not assign them to higher and lower castes. There is no doubt that Halakhah applies this egalitarianism with regard to *pikkuaḥ nefesh* and does not allow the responsibility to be shunted onto others. Rabbi Joseph Caro enunciated this principle in the *Shulḥan Arukh:* "When one desecrates the Sabbath for a patient who is dangerously ill, one endeavors to do it, not by means of non-Jews or children and women, but by adult Jews who aware of what they are doing" (*O.H.* 328:12).

Maimonides placed even stronger emphasis on the responsibility of those well versed in Halakhah to set an example: "When such things must be done they are to be done . . . only by rabbis and scholars" (Laws of the Sabbath 2:3).

Dr. Walden: If great rabbis have ruled that autopsies are permitted, why is there such fierce opposition to them?

Rabbi Zemer: All the rulings I have quoted so far were by rabbis with whose leniency on this subject I can identify. But it cannot be denied that there are complex halakhic problems that lead other rabbis to be much more strict and to ban postmortem examinations. The permissive decisors had to make strenuous efforts to rebut the objections and stringencies of the other camp. If we set aside the political aspects of the question—which are of greater weight, as we know, than the halakhic perspective—both parties to this argument can allege sources and precedents to buttress their arguments. Ultimately, the great decisors on both sides are guided by their worldview when they select and interpret precedents.

A decisor opposed to autopsies, such as Rabbi Yitzhak Arieli, can enumerate a large number of prohibitions that he believes rule out the procedure. His list includes the following: "Disrespect and desecration of the dead, the pain of the dead, the suffering of the soul, the ban on deriving benefit from the dead, causing ritual impurity to relatives of a dead *kohen,* and protracting the interval between death and interment when the bereaved are exempt from the positive commandments."[7] Note, however, that other rabbis have found ways to resolve all the problems raised by Rabbi Arieli (some we have mentioned already; others will come up later in our conversation).

Tell me, though, what responses do you meet with when you talk with the grieving survivors?

Dealing with the Bereaved Family

Dr. Walden: Asking the family of the deceased for permission to perform an autopsy is an extremely painful scene. In addition to their shock and grief, many instinctively flinch when this subject is raised. This phenomenon is common to all—Jews and non-Jews, religious and secular. Among Ultra-Orthodox Jews in Israel, however, this reaction is enhanced by the lurking suspicion that the physician has impure motives. Wicked libels, with no basis in reality, keep circulating, to the effect that physicians benefit personally from autopsies. There are stories about lavish research grants supposedly extended by institutions overseas because certain examinations can be conducted in Israel but not elsewhere. Recently I even encountered the absurd allegation that Israel exports organs to other countries.

How is it that families who entrusted the lives of their loved ones to physicians, for better or worse, and accepted their professional opinion as long as the patient was alive, suddenly lose their confidence in them? Even the most extreme Ultra-Orthodox circles generally leave the determination of what constitutes *pikkuah nefesh* to the discretion of the physicians and their accumulated experience. Once they have done so it is permitted and even mandatory to violate almost all the prohibitions in the Torah—except for bloodshed, idolatry, and forbidden sexual relations—to carry out the prescribed course of treatment. Why, then, after the patient has died, do they no longer accept the physician's word that the information to be derived from an autopsy could help other patients whose lives are at risk?

We physicians are very much pained by the atmosphere of incitement and humiliating suspicion that emanates from much of the Ultra-Orthodox sector. I cannot escape the feeling that underneath it all is a crying misunderstanding of the development of medicine in our day and that the approach to applying Halakhah belongs to bygone centuries.

Particularly upsetting is the fact that those at the focus of the conflict are relatives whose loved ones are still lying before them. In some Western countries, autopsies are not performed without permission from the next of kin, except in criminal cases. We accept that principle here, too, and that is how we operate in practice. But there is a vast difference between the climate in Israel and that abroad. In Europe and North America, families usually consent when the attending physician requests permission to perform an autopsy. There is no atmosphere of incitement against us. Most people understand that both the family and the general public will benefit from a more precise determination of cause of death. In Israel, by contrast, many view autopsies as desecration of the corpse and consider physicians to be heartless ghouls who would benefit from the misfortunes of others.

After the Knesset passed the Anatomy and Pathology Law, another burden was piled on the grieving family. Relatives must now provide their consent in writing. Many persons probably understand the importance of the matter and would agree if they could do so quietly, but now that they must take some kind of initiative and assume responsibility, they hold back.

Today, as in the past, we do not perform postmortem examinations without the approval of the surviving relatives. We can only regret the loss of vital information that might benefit other patients whose lives hang in the balance.

THERE IS NO NEED FOR RELATIVES TO CONSENT

Rabbi Zemer: The requirement that relatives consent to an autopsy is a political demand, not one based on the codified Halakhah. For those who are lenient on the whole subject, the Anatomy and Pathology Law places another heavy and unnecessary burden on the shoulders of the bereaved family, who are already quite at a loss. According to these halakhic authorities, the family in fact has no halakhic status to permit or forbid an autopsy. According to Rabbi Uziel, "We must not even begin to imagine that the body of the deceased is in some fashion inherited by his heirs, like the other property that comes into their possession."[8] Furthermore, "This depends neither on the desire of the deceased nor the consent of his heirs. No person may permit disfigurement and desecration of his body and image, . . . because the body belongs to no one."[9]

For the anti-autopsy camp, by contrast, members of the family have no right to agree even if they so wish. According to Rabbi Arieli, "although members of the family have no authority to permit an autopsy, Halakhah allows them to prevent one."[10] Similarly, the well-known decisor Rabbi Eliezer Waldenberg ruled uncompromisingly that "no waiver by the relatives is of any benefit for the purpose of permitting an autopsy."[11]

In the view of those who permit autopsies, there is no need for the family to give its consent, and in fact the survivors have no status in the matter, because it is a question of *pikkuaḥ nefesh*, saving human life. Those who ban autopsies are equally unwilling to leave the decision to the relatives. It follows, then, that there is no halakhic sanction for laying this difficult decision at the door of the grieving family.

As for the allegation that you and your colleagues treat the dead disrespectfully, the halakhic topic is extremely complex. In brief, anything done to a corpse with the intention of desecrating or destroying it—such as not leaving it unburied—is considered disrespect for the dead. Some rabbis hold that an autopsy and the removal of organs and tissues are indeed degrading and disrespectful. But what counts here is the intention. This is what determines whether the action is lacking in respect. As you put it yourself, your intention is to heal the living, not—Heaven forbid—to defile the dead. Rabbi Eliezer Berkovits gave cogent expression to this principle

> The general rule . . . is that disrespect for the dead applies precisely when something is done disrespectfully because we have no concern for their dignity, but whatever is done to serve the needs of the living is not disrespectful to the dead.[12]

Rabbi Uziel ruled unequivocally that it is the physician's intention that determines the nature of the procedure:

> We learn that whenever the disgrace is not intentional, there is no prohibition, and all the more so when the disgrace is done on behalf of the living to save lives. . . . According to Halakhah it is

permitted to perform an autopsy and this is neither disgracing the corpse nor gaining forbidden benefit.[13]

This enlightened and humane approach, deeply rooted in Jewish tradition, is what should guide all of us—physicians, rabbis, and legislators—when we must deal with the vital topic of autopsies.

31

Abortion Is Not Murder

AS ORIGINALLY PASSED IN 1977, THE TERMINATION OF Pregnancy section of the Penal Law included a clause that permitted abortion when family or social circumstances made birth of the child inadvisable. Subsequently, the Ultra-Orthodox parties launched a campaign to repeal this section. When, in the heated parliamentary debate that ensued, Knesset members of the religious parties were guilty of inaccurate statements of halakhic concepts, one could perhaps be understanding, realizing that that is the way of politics. One could not ignore it, however, when the Rebbe of Gur, a member of the Council of Torah Sages, presented his view of the abortion law in *Hamodi'a,* the daily newspaper of the Ultra-Orthodox Agudat Yisrael party, and wrote as follows:

> If the law is not amended [to prohibit these abortions], Agudat Yisrael cannot be a partner to *the murder of fetuses* and for Agudat Yisrael to remain in the coalition would be tantamount to partnership in the murder of fetuses.[1]

The rebbe, Rabbi Simcha Bunim Alter, was a distinguished scholar and was held to be an expert in Halakhah. Accordingly, we must relate seriously to his words and investigate whether, according to Halakhah, abortion is indeed tantamount to murdering the fetus.

A FETUS IS NOT A PERSON

An examination of the sources reveals that there is no halakhic basis for Rabbi Alter's allegation or similar arguments advanced by Knesset members representing the religious parties. We begin with the Mishnah, which permits abortion if the fetus is endangering the mother's life:

> If a woman is having a difficult labor [and there is fear for her life], the fetus must be cut up while it is in the womb and removed limb by limb, because her life has priority over its life (Mishnah Oholot 7:6).

This principle holds as long as the fetus is unborn. However, the Mishnah continues,

> If most [of the fetus] has emerged, it may not be touched, since the claim of one life cannot override the claim of another life (ibid.).

Thus, Halakhah holds that as long as the fetus is inside the mother, it does not have the status of a human being. Rashi makes this quite plain:

> As long as the fetus has not emerged into the air of the world it is not a person and it may be killed to save the mother (Rashi on Sanhedrin 72b, s.v. *yatze'ah rosho*).

Rabbi Meir Abulafia (1180–1245) concurred: "As long as [the fetus] is inside, it is not a person and the Torah does not protect it."[2] So did Rabbi Menaḥem Hameiri (1249–1306): "One may cut up the fetus inside her womb . . . because it is not considered to be a person, since it has not yet emerged into the air of the world."[3]

This doctrine of the medieval commentators paved the way for later decisors to rule leniently and permit abortion in certain cases. For example, Rabbi Joseph ben Moshe of Trani (1568–1639) ruled that abortion involves "no suspicion whatsoever of destroying souls."[4]

He was followed by Rabbi Jacob Emden (1697–1776), who permitted abortion "as long as [the fetus] has not emerged from [the womb], even if it is not a question of saving the mother's life but only to save her from distress, because it causes her great pain."[5] This ruling has served as a precedent on which later decisors relied to permit an abortion on account of the mother's emotional state.

Because a fetus is not considered to be a person, the concept of murder does not apply as long as it has not emerged into the air of the world.[6] We must accordingly conclude that the Rebbe of Gur was not delivering a halakhic ruling when he stated publicly that the clause in the abortion law permitting abortions for socioeconomic reasons was tantamount to the murder of fetuses. He must have been writing in his role as the rabbinic mentor of one faction within the Agudat Yisrael party; his declaration in *Hamodi'a* had more to do with this political function than with serious halakhic debate.

THE UNHOLY ALLIANCE OF RELIGION AND POLITICS

The Rebbe of Gur and his colleagues on the Council of Torah Sages never demonstrated that there was something amiss only with the "social" clause of the abortions law[7] and that it is halakhically permissible to participate in a coalition that permits abortions in the circumstances enumerated by other sections of the law, such as pregnancy in women who are below the age of consent (seventeen), past forty, or unmarried.

Why, in these cases, was membership in the coalition not a matter of being accessories to feticide? The great decisors of the past did not agree about the conditions and situations in which abortion is permitted or forbidden. Unfortunately, the Council of Torah Sages and the Chief Rabbis have not performed their duty as teachers and enlightened us concerning the halakhic validity of each section of the law. Instead, they mounted the barricades against the section that benefited the weaker strata of society, which are most in need of the relief offered by the law. Enlightened decisors who follow the path of evolving Halakhah could have relied on Rabbi Emden's ruling and expanded the circumstances in which abortion is permitted so as to help suffering women whose pregnancy is causing them great social and psychological pain.

The unholy alliance of religion and politics does no honor to the Torah and does not bring our people closer to the traditions of our ancestors. We need moral spiritual guidance—not fraudulent political slogans like "murder of fetuses."

It is not called spilling one's seed because eventually the sperm will be inserted into the womb for the purpose of conception. He is following the instructions of the physicians and doing it to fulfill the precept [of procreation].[6]

Rabbi Isaac Jacob Weiss of Manchester, England, ruled that the intention, not the act, determines whether the treatment is permitted. Accordingly, he ruled that if a husband's intention is to help his wife conceive, he may donate his sperm, "because his sole intention is to fertilize and in addition he is fulfilling the precept to be fruitful and multiply."[7]

Does the rabbinate follow those who permit or those who ban? Its publications do not provide an answer to this question.

The rabbis have also disagreed about how long a childless couple must wait before they undergo such treatment. Rabbi Shalom Mordecai Schwadron, a leading Sage in Galicia, was inclined to agree to treatment if stringent conditions were met. "But even in this case I gave permission only if ten years had passed and she had not given birth, which would be grounds for divorce."[8]

On the other hand, Rabbi Eliezer Yehuda Waldenberg, a member of the Supreme Rabbinical Court in Jerusalem, has confirmed that some rabbis permit a woman to undergo such treatment even though ten years have not passed, if competent physicians have determined that it is absolutely impossible for her to be impregnated by her husband in the normal way.[9] The notice in the newspapers does not state the rabbinate's position on this issue, either.

IS THE CHILD A *MAMZER?*

There is no doubt, however, that the rabbinate rejects the use of sperm donated by a man other than the woman's husband. Many questions come into play here. Would insemination with the sperm of another man be tantamount to adultery or harlotry? If a woman does undergo such treatment, is she forbidden to her husband, in accordance with the law of the unfaithful wife? If a child is born from sperm donated by another man, is it a *mamzer?*

Among the earlier decisors who issued a narrow ruling on this question was Rabbi Judah Leib Zirelson of Kishinev: "The sperm within her body from another Jewish man is forbidden per se and the child produced by it is a *mamzer.*"[10] According to Rabbi Hadaya:

> A woman who is defiled by the sperm of a man other than her husband, when this occurs willingly and with forethought . . . —any woman who is defiled in this fashion is forbidden to her husband. . . . From this it follows, too, that the child is a *mamzer.*[11]

However, most decisors believe that there is no infidelity here because there is no sexual intercourse. Accordingly, the woman is not forbidden to her husband, and the child is not a *mamzer.* Some 400 years ago, Rabbi Joel Sirkes (1561–1640) ruled, in an analogous case, that "because there was no forbidden intercourse, the child is legitimate, even if she became pregnant from the sperm of another man."[12]

Regarding a woman who had been impregnated in the bath, Rabbi Judah Rosanes (1657–1727) ruled that "without doubt she is not forbidden to her husband, because there was no forbidden intercourse here."[13]

Most rabbis through our own day have followed these rulings. Rabbi Moshe Feinstein, one of the leading rabbinic authorities of the later twentieth century, was unequivocal:

> It is clear that in the absence of intercourse, a woman is not forbidden to her husband. The prohibition of an unfaithful wife to her husband is the result only of the illicit intercourse and not of the sperm of another man. . . . The child is kosher because *mamzerut* exists only when it was conceived through intercourse.[14]

The consensus of rabbinic opinion from the Middle Ages until the present is that there is no infidelity if there is no sexual contact. And if there is no forbidden intercourse, the child is not a *mamzer*.

On this question we do know the rabbinate's position and its motives for banning third-party sperm donations. In an interview that Chief Rabbi Avraham Shapira granted to a journalist, he explained that "there are serious concerns about *mamzerut* when a married woman receives sperm donated by another man."[15] Evidently the Chief Rabbinate decided to reject the preponderance of liberal rulings that there is no adultery or *mamzerut* in such a case, and preferred to adopt the more narrow view.

When it has been proved that a man is sterile and there is no hope that he can ever impregnate his wife, there is no justification for the rabbinate to condemn the couple to perpetual childlessness.

THE CASE OF A NON-JEWISH DONOR

The rabbinate explicitly forbids a Jew to donate his sperm to hospitals. Furthermore, it does not permit a woman to receive sperm donated by a non-Jew. On the other hand, Rabbi Feinstein ruled thus:

> One should permit [artificial insemination] with the sperm of a non-Jew. Because the child will be Jewish there are no problems, as he will not be considered to be related to his non-Jewish father.[16]

Following this line, he ruled that if the sperm comes from a sperm bank, at least in the Diaspora, "one need not fear that the sperm came from a Jew, because most comes from non-Jews."[17] Rejecting this lenient approach, Rabbi Eliezer Waldenberg ruled that "taking sperm from a non-Jew for this purpose is the greater abomination many times over." In his view, the procedure solves no problems and in fact creates new ones, because "even with sperm from a non-Jew [the woman] is forbidden [on its account] to her husband and the child is blemished"[18]—the child is not a *mamzer*, but its lineage is blemished.

The matter is indeed complex and could not be explained in the rabbinate's brief press release. Nevertheless, the Chief Rabbinate Council knows how to initiate interviews with the media and publicize its position and reasons. If it has not done so, evidently the rabbinate prefers not to issue a ruling and make its position public.

The last item in the notice states that Jews may not make decisions about artificial insemination on the basis of what is written in the media. Instead, "each and every person must ask a rabbi." But there is a serious problem here: Either the Chief Rabbinate has issued mandatory instructions or guidelines to every rabbi, or it allows each rabbi the freedom to decide, relying on halakhic precedents. We may well ask if they are allowed to rule in accordance with the pluralistic spirit of Halakhah over the generations.

If the Rabbinate has issued detailed guidelines, it has not published them. If every rabbi can rule according to his understanding of the issue and follow the lenient or strict decisors of the past, as he sees fit, it is extremely probable that some local rabbis will allow couples to act in ways that contradict the Rabbinate's halakhic ruling as published in the press.

Such autonomy would not be welcomed by the religious establishment, which advocates an authoritarian hierarchy, even though the annals of halakhic legislation prove that Halakhah has been essentially pluralistic. One of the factors that has modified the circumstances with which Halakhah must cope today is modern science and its discoveries.

The talmudic Sages emphasized the supreme importance of the precept to "be fruitful and multiply" and the contribution that children make to a happy marriage. If the rabbis of our day were to attribute the same weight to these principles as did their predecessors, perhaps they would not issue rulings that pile up the obstacles and ban the procedure. On the contrary, they would be flexible and encourage barren couples to take advantage of what modern medical science has to offer so they can fulfill the very first commandment given in the Torah: "Be fruitful and multiply and fill up the earth"—which, in the words of *Sefer Haḥinnukh,* "is a great *mitzvah,* thanks to which all the other precepts are observed."[19]

33

To Smoke or
Not to Smoke:
A Jewish Question

SMOKING HAS BECOME A JEWISH PROBLEM, NOT JUST A universal health issue. Congregations all over the world have prohibited this practice on synagogue premises. In Israel, the Knesset has passed legislation that limits tobacco use in public premises and workplaces and restricts cigarette advertising.

Rabbis have addressed smoking almost from the day of tobacco's introduction to Europe. Rabbi Ḥayyim Benveniste (1603–1673) described the great pleasure derived from tobacco and how many people became addicted to it. Smokers, he averred, knew no pleasure that could match it. Even when smokers were putting themselves in danger because the authorities had outlawed smoking, there were those who took the risk of lighting up "clandestinely, between the oven and the cookstove." Additional evidence of widespread tobacco dependency is provided by his description of pious Jews during the last minutes before the end of the Sabbath, after a full day of abstinence—a phenomenon familiar today as well:

> On the holy Sabbath, as the day grew late and the shadows of evening were lengthening, their eyes surveyed the darkness and watched the stars. As soon as three were visible many smoked before Havdalah.[1]

Until a few years ago, the hazardous nature of smoking was not on the public or the Jewish agenda. On the contrary, some rabbis believed that smoking was beneficial and had therapeutic properties. According to Rabbi Jacob Emden (1697–1776):

Tobacco is a healthful substance for the body. . . . Its natural action is important in helping to digest food, cleanse the mouth, separate the humors, and help the movement of essential functions and blood circulation, which are the root of health. . . . It is indeed beneficial to every healthy man, not only because of the pleasure and enjoyment it affords, but because it preserves one's health and medical fitness.[2]

Eventually, the rabbinic attitude toward smoking changed. At the turn of the twentieth century, the opposition was based not on considerations of health, but of propriety. Rabbi David Zevi Hoffmann, head of the Hildesheimer Rabbinic Seminary in Berlin, told a questioner that even on weekdays "it is forbidden to smoke in a synagogue because of the sanctity of the place." He added another reason for this prohibition: "It is known that the gentiles are very punctilious and forbid smoking in their houses of worship. Hence it would be a desecration of the Divine Name, God forbid, if we permitted smoking. Accordingly it is clearly forbidden."[3]

The mounting medical evidence about the health dangers of smoking, which became public knowledge in the 1960s, brought most rabbis to the conclusion that not only is it devoid of benefit, it may be dangerous and even lethal. In this context they dealt with two major issues: the danger to nonsmokers (passive smoking) and the danger to the smokers themselves.

DANGER TO NONSMOKERS

Rabbi Moshe Feinstein forbade the widespread practice of smoking in yeshivot. He would not relate to the medical evidence, on the grounds that the deleterious effect of smoking had not been conclusively proved. Nevertheless, he prohibited smoking if it disturbed others who were studying in the same room, whether or not it was injurious to their health. He rejected the argument that smoking helped students concentrate. He ruled that leaving the study hall to take a puff outside would be time stolen from the study of Torah. He also dismissed the contention that since the room is already full of smoke, each smoker adds only an insignificant amount. Rabbi Feinstein replied that each smoker is responsible for his portion of the smoke in the room and therefore for the discomfort of all those present who suffer from his habit.[4]

Rabbi Eliezer Waldenberg of the Israel Chief Rabbinate Council went a step further and forbade a person to smoke in his own home if the smoke would bother or harm his guests or members of the family, and especially children who might be present.[5]

DANGER TO SMOKERS

Rabbinic respondents have been divided as to whether the available medical evidence is sufficient to ban smoking because it is life-threatening and as such clearly impermissible. Rabbi Feinstein would concede only that since "there is a supposition that one may become ill from [smoking cigarettes], one ought to be cautious."

He was unwilling to forbid smoking as banned by the Torah, however, for two reasons:

1. Tobacco is in very wide use and has become an entrenched popular practice. The Talmud states about such a habit, "since the multitude are accustomed to it, 'the Lord will protect the foolish'" (BT Shabbat 129b, quoting Psalms 116:6).
2. "We must especially note that some of the great Torah scholars of past generations and the present day were and are smokers."

We may and should *advise* against taking up the habit, he said, and in particular should keep children from starting to smoke. Nevertheless, in his opinion, the Torah does not forbid offering a light or matches to a smoker.[6]

The Sephardi Chief Rabbi of Tel Aviv, Rabbi Ḥayyim David Halevy, subsequently disagreed with this last ruling. A youngster asked him whether he must obey his father who sent him out to buy a pack of cigarettes. Rabbi Halevy responded:

> In view of the fact that physicians have universally warned against the great danger of smoking to human health, and since, in my opinion, it is forbidden by the Torah, which commands, "You shall carefully preserve your lives" (Deuteronomy 15:4), . . . you are not permitted to buy him cigarettes. Furthermore, whenever you see him with a cigarette in his mouth, . . . say to him, "Father, it is written in the Torah, 'You shall carefully preserve your lives,' and smoking is very harmful"—in the hope that he will understand, overcome his urge, and give up the habit.[7]

One of our generation's foremost experts on medicine and Halakhah, Rabbi Eliezer Waldenberg, has accepted the findings of medical experts and asserted that "smoking is the number one killer of humanity." Disagreeing with Rabbi Feinstein's position, he declared "that there is no reason to be complacent . . . and rule that, because smoking is widespread" there are no grounds for prohibiting it. Rabbi Waldenberg cited the medical evidence that "cigarette smoking is the main cause of death from cancer. . . . Hence it is certainly absurd to turn a blind eye on all this and blithely to conclude that [in a case like this] 'The Lord will preserve the foolish.'"[8]

Scientific evidence has proved conclusively that smoking is dangerous and even lethal. The United States Surgeon General's Report, issued annually, now consists of more than thirty heavy volumes that scientifically demonstrate the danger of smoking to every organ of the human body. Nonetheless, United States law requires only a minuscule reference to this report as a warning of the danger to health in the omnipresent smoking advertisements sponsored by the tobacco industry. The same is the case in Israel, where cigarette packages bear a tiny Health Ministry warning. Yet, smokers continue to smoke and adolescents willingly addict themselves, despite the fact that in Western countries smoking is responsible for more deaths each year than gunshot wounds, terrorism, and AIDS combined. Aroused public opinion and antismoking legislation have only just begun to deal with the epidemic proportions of the problem.

Despite the widespread social condemnation of their practice, many smokers today view their habit as a strictly private matter and insist that no one has the right to interfere or tell them to stop. Many contemporary rabbis reply to this by quoting Maimonides: "The Sages forbade many things that involve mortal danger. Anyone who does these things and says, 'I am endangering myself and what does it matter to others,' or 'I don't care' is to be flogged [by the rabbinical court]" (Laws of Murder and Preservation of Life 11:5). According to Halakhah, human beings have stewardship over the bodies given them by their Creator, not ownership, and may not jeopardize their own lives.

To whom, then, do our bodies and lives belong? In his glosses on the *Shulḥan Arukh,* Rabbi Moses Rivkes (d. 1671/72) stated that "the Torah warned us about preservation of life because God graciously created the world to benefit His creatures so that they may be aware of His greatness and may serve Him by observing His commandments and Torah."[9]

What operative conclusions may we draw from these rabbinic rulings? There is almost universal agreement that this habit endangers life; hence, banning it is a matter of *pikkuaḥ nefesh,* saving human life. The consensus of halakhic opinion may be summarized as follows:

1. Smoking near anyone who may be disturbed or harmed by smoke is prohibited.
2. It is forbidden to harm oneself by smoking. Accordingly, smokers who cannot break the habit "cold turkey" must make every effort to cut back gradually or receive professional help until they are weaned of their addiction.
3. It is forbidden for children and adolescents to begin or to become accustomed to smoking. Adults may not help or encourage them to acquire the habit.

4. Encouraging smokers in their habit, by offering them a cigarette or light, is prohibited.
5. Elected officials and spiritual leaders should sponsor serious educational campaigns to convince the public of the extreme danger of smoking.

The gradual evolution of rabbinic thought about smoking reflects the nature of Halakhah as a developmental and dynamic process that takes account of the discoveries of medical science. The halakhic view of smoking has progressed from the eighteenth-century rabbinic dictum that "tobacco is healthful for the body" to the present-day opinion that "smoking is the number one killer of mankind."

34

"It Is Forbidden to Delay Death"

A FORTY-YEAR-OLD MAN WAS SUFFERING FROM AMY-otrophic lateral sclerosis, which is characterized by progressive paralysis of the muscles. In the terminal stage, the patient could no longer swallow or use his muscles. He was in extreme discomfort and pain. The prognosis was certain and irreversible. The patient's attorney appealed to the Tel Aviv District Court for an injunction to bar his physician and hospital from connecting him to a heart-lung machine. The injunction was granted. I was asked whether that decision was contrary to Halakhah. My reply was as follows:

In Jewish tradition there is a serious conflict between two spiritual values. One value is the sanctity of life, of every human life. To save human life one may transgress all the commandments of the Torah except three prohibitions: those against murder, illicit sexual relations, and idolatry.

The other value is that of concern and compassion for the suffering of human beings, who are created in the image of God. Halakhah allows many precepts to be set aside in order to alleviate such suffering and preserve human dignity.

Sometimes preserving a person's life also means prolonging his or her unbearable suffering. There are situations in which death provides the only relief from this suffering.

The term *euthanasia* covers several different kinds of activity that lead to a patient's death. Here we shall consider only the form that fits the initial question: passive euthanasia, which is not usually considered to fall into the category of euthanasia in the classic sense. At the same time, however, we shall touch on two other forms that can shed light on our case.

The Talmud relates that the maidservant of Rabbi Judah the Prince prayed for his recovery from a severe illness. When she realized how much he was suffering, however, she prayed instead that he be released from his agony. Finally she disturbed his disciples while they were praying, and the brief interruption in their entreaties made it possible for his soul to depart to its eternal rest (BT Ketubot 104a).

Rabbi Nissim ben Reuben Gerondi (Spain, d. 1380) commented on this: "There are times when one should ask for mercy for the ill that he may die; such as in the case where he is suffering greatly and there is no hope that he may recover and live, as in the case of Rabbi Judah the Prince and his maidservant" (commentary on BT Nedarim 40a).

Another example is the midrash about a very old woman who wished to depart from this world. Rabbi Jose recommended that she refrain from going to the synagogue for three consecutive days. The result was that she fell ill and died (*Yalkut Shimoni,* Proverbs, 943).

These sources deal with situations in which there is no physical contact with the dying person. But what does Halakhah say specifically about these three questions?

1. Is it permissible to hasten the death of a patient whose death is imminent?
2. Is it better to postpone the end of life or to remove an impediment to death in order to hasten the end?
3. In what situation are we to act in accordance with the halakhic principle of refraining from action *(shev ve-'al ta'aseh)?*

The Talmud and halakhic codes state that persons whose death is imminent (the Hebrew term is for such a person is *gosess*) are regarded as living persons in all respects. Nothing may be done that might hasten their death. It is forbidden to wash such patients, remove pillows from underneath them, or place them on the ground.

It is also forbidden to close their eyes, "for whoever closes the eyes with the onset of death is a shedder of blood." Nor may the keys of the synagogue be placed under their head so that they may depart (*Shulḥan Arukh, Y.D.* 339:1).[1]

Each of these acts is forbidden because the slightest movement of the patient may hasten death. As the Babylonian Talmud put it: "This action may be compared to a flickering flame; as soon as one touches it, the light is extinguished" (BT Shabbat 151b). All these actions fall into the category of *harigah bayadayim,* "killing with the hands"—or, in modern parlance, active euthanasia.

The restriction holds even in cases where the dying person would be deprived of only a few minutes of life. The Talmud rules that if a wall falls on a person on the Sabbath, any action required to clear away the debris and extricate the victim is permitted, even when such efforts will prolong his life only by a matter of moments (BT Yoma 85a). Every moment of human life is immeasurably precious.

What might be called passive euthanasia appears in two forms:

The first is utterly passive, refraining from action *(shev ve-ʿal taʿaseh)*—the logical contrary of active euthanasia. This usually refers to the situation before intravenous feeding is begun or a patient is attached to a heart-lung machine.

Rabbi Solomon B. Freehof wrote a responsum in 1969 about a terminal patient who had suffered a series of strokes. With the family's consent, two physicians, one of them the patient's son, decided to hasten the end by withdrawing all intravenous medications and fluids. Rabbi Freehof consented, but suggested that a better approach would have the hospital adopt the practice whereby each day's intravenous feeding required a direct order by the attending physician. Thus if, on a particular day, the doctor simply refrained from ordering intravenous feeding, no one would be taking any action, and the talmudic dictum that refraining from direct action is preferable *(shev ve-ʿal taʿaseh ʿadif*—BT Eruvin 100a) would certainly apply.[2]

The second form of passive euthanasia does involve an action of sorts, namely, removing any impediment to death. In his annotations to the *Shulḥan Arukh,* Rabbi Moses Isserles ruled that it is permissible to eliminate anything that may be hindering the departure of the soul, such as the noise of wood being chopped or salt on the patient's tongue. The rabbis viewed this not as a positive action, but only as the removal of the impediment (*Y.D.* 339:1).

In his commentary on the *Shulḥan Arukh*, Rabbi Zvi Hirsch ben Azriel of Vilna explained this permission: "It is forbidden to delay his death and one must not put salt on his tongue to keep him from dying. . . . Thus they did not act properly in the first place when they put the salt on his tongue, so it is permitted to remove the salt from his tongue."[3]

According to the seventeenth-century Rabbi Jacob ben Samuel of Seusmer (Dyhernfurth), Prussia, "it is forbidden to delay the soul's departure and the demise of the terminal patient. One must not use medication in order to prolong the dying process."[4]

His younger contemporary Rabbi Jacob ben Joseph Reischer (1670–1733), however, maintained that a physician or apothecary who knows that a medication will delay the dying process for even a few moments is permitted to administer it to the patient. This action is similar to clearing away the debris on the Sabbath to add a few minutes to the victim's life.[5]

We find a basis for this second form of passive euthanasia, the withdrawal of life support, among modern Israeli decisors. Rabbi Baruch Rabinowitz, the Chief Rabbi of Holon, Israel, held that the permission to remove an impediment to death is an important part of medical practice today:

> In most cases, when efforts are made to save the patient he is connected to various sorts of equipment to provide oxygen and medications to his body. As long as his body is connected to this equipment he can continue to live—what physicians call "vegetative life"—for a very long time. We, however, are not able to distinguish between vegetative life and rational-emotional life. The question therefore arises: Are we permitted to disconnect the patient from the machines as long as he shows signs of life? The physician has, it is true, already despaired of restoring the patient to natural and spontaneous life, but this artificially sustained life can continue. Is it permitted for the doctor to put an

end to it? That is the problem that we encounter in the hospital every day. Many doctors ask what they should do, because the moment they disconnect the patient, he dies. Is this not a form of active killing? . . .

The above-mentioned halakhah, which distinguishes between shortening the life of a *goses* and removing the impediment that delays the departure of the soul [death]—that is, the artificial prolongation of the life of a dying person—gives us a clear answer to the question. The apparatus is delaying death artificially. After the physician has reached the conclusion that there is no further possibility of natural life in the person and that he is indeed moribund, a *goses,* the action of the machine is merely preventing the departure of his soul and artificially prolonging the state of dying. Hence, the person must be disconnected from the machine and left in a natural state until he dies.[6]

According to Rabbi Ḥayyim David Halevy, the Sephardi Chief Rabbi of Tel Aviv, "not only is it permitted to disconnect him from a respirator, it is even mandatory to do so, because the person's soul, which belongs to God, has already been taken by his Maker. For as soon as the respirator is removed he will die."[7]

As we see, both medieval and modern decisors rendered halakhic rulings substantially in agreement with the verdict of the Tel Aviv District Court.

There can be no better way to conclude this chapter than by quoting Justice Haim Cohn:

The golden rule of biblical law, "Thou shalt love thy neighbor as thyself," was interpreted by the talmudic jurists as imposing a duty to choose for one's fellow the most "beautiful" death possible (BT Sanhedrin 45a, 52a-b). In practice, the application of the rule was originally confined to choices among several possible modes of [judicial] execution. . . . Both the reasoning behind the talmudic rule and its comprehensive language allow it to be applied more generally to every situation in which a person (usually the physician) is faced with a choice between two kinds of death to be caused to his fellow—one agonizing and protracted, the other relatively easy, swift, and humane. This most fundamental of all divine commands (Genesis Rabbah 24:7, in the name of Rabbi Akiba) exhorts us to conduct ourselves, especially in the face of death, in such a manner as may be dictated by sincere love for the dying person. . . .

The Midrash relates that the Torah scroll of Rabbi Meir had a variant text of the conclusion of the creation story of Genesis: "And God saw everything that He had made and behold it was very good." What was it that God, seeing all of His creation, beheld to be very good? It was death. Rabbi Meir's version read *vehinneh tov mot,* and behold good is death (Genesis Rabbah 9:5).[8]

Justice Cohn concludes:

Might it be that surveying the whole of His magnificent creation, a merciful God consoled himself with how good and comforting it was that having created man, He had created death to rescue man from life?"[9]

VIII

Burial

We support the non-Jewish poor along with the Jewish poor and visit the non-Jewish sick along with the Jewish sick and bury the non-Jewish dead with the Jewish dead, for the sake of peace.

BT GITTIN 61A

[The body of the non-Jewish woman in her grave] disturbs her Jewish neighbors. . . . . In her death she is disturbing others and causing them pain.

RABBIS OF RISHON LEZION (1983)

In every age and society, death gives rise to grievous thoughts of loss and bereavement, which are reflected in the religious tradition of that society. So too in Jewish tradition.

Nevertheless, with regard to the difficult issue of burial, we can find in our tradition not only a translation from the sense of mourning to the language of action and catharsis, but also an expression of views about matters that have no necessary connection with mourning rites, such as attitudes toward non-Jews, superstitions, anxieties, and attitudes toward certain strata of society.

In this section, we shall see that imposing psychological forces are mobilized to settle the problem of the burial of a non-Jewish woman in a Jewish cemetery. We shall also consider several superstitions associated with burial, which warn us of the perils associated with caring for the deceased. We shall juxtapose

Halakhah with opinions and beliefs that explain the development of peculiar customs. We shall attempt to state the attitude of Halakhah to these phenomena as well as the position of evolving Halakhah.

35

For the Sake of Peace

THERESA ANGELOVICH WAS A GENTILE WOMAN WHO CAME on *aliya* with her Jewish husband and lived in Israel for many years. When she died in 1983, she was buried in the municipal Jewish cemetery of Rishon Lezion, where she had lived. Shortly thereafter, when it was discovered that she had never converted to Judaism, the local rabbinate, with the approval of the Chief Rabbinate Council, issued a halakhic ruling that her body must be exhumed from the local cemetery.[1] As we shall see, this ruling was erroneous and misleading to the public at large. The codified Halakhah regarding the burial of non-Jews—and Jewish law in general—is much more multifaceted, dynamic, and flexible than the narrow approach of the Rishon Lezion rabbis. In this chapter, we shall attempt to answer the important questions raised by this ruling.

IS IT REALLY FORBIDDEN TO BURY A NON-JEW ALONGSIDE A JEW?

The implication of the ruling by the Rishon Lezion rabbis is that a non-Jew may not be buried alongside a Jew. Yet, the earliest halakhic text on the topic, a *baraita* in the Babylonian Talmud, expresses a positive attitude about acts of kindness by Jews toward non-Jews:

We support the non-Jewish poor along with the Jewish poor and visit the non-Jewish sick along with the Jewish sick and bury the non-Jewish dead with the Jewish dead, for the sake of peace (BT Gittin 61a).

Correct relations between Jews and non-Jews must be based on the principle of "for the sake of peace," which is also the rationale behind these precepts.

About nine hundred years passed, and Rashi, in his commentary on this *baraita*, pared back the ruling by adding the reservation "but not in Jewish graves"; in other words, we must see to the burial of non-Jews, but not alongside Jews. The fourteenth-century commentator Rabbenu Nissim Gerondi (d. 1380) added a reason for this limitation: "One should not bury [non-Jews] alongside a Jew, since one must not bury the wicked next to the righteous."

Over the centuries, evidently, a circumscribing exegesis had been applied to the broad liberal basis of the *baraita* in Tractate Gittin. Nevertheless, most of the decisors of subsequent generations did not accept this interpretation and did not promulgate an explicit halakhic ban against burying a non-Jew alongside a Jew. The great codifiers—Maimonides in the twelfth century (Laws of Kings 10:12), Rabbi Moses of Coucy in the thirteenth century (*Sefer Mitzvot Gadol,* Positive Commandments, no. 163), and Rabbi Joseph Caro in the sixteenth century (*Shulḥan Arukh, Y.D.* 367:1)—all bring down the Halakhah from Tractate Gittin with no restrictions on where a non-Jew may be buried. Rabbi Jacob ben Asher (thirteenth–fourteenth centuries) in his *Arba'ah Turim* (*Tur Y.D.* 367), and Joseph Caro in his commentary on that work, the *Beit Yosef,* both refer to the view of Rashi and Rabbenu Nissim, but their actual halakhic rulings do not include this caveat. Whereas the *Tur* and the *Shulḥan Arukh* ban the burial of the wicked alongside the righteous, they do not mention any prohibition on burying a non-Jew next to a Jew (*Y.D.* 362:5).

The bottom line is that until the time of the *Shulḥan Arukh,* in the sixteenth century, there was no fixed rule against burying a non-Jew in a Jewish cemetery. Evidence for this is provided by the writings of three nineteenth-century rabbis. Rabbi Meir

Friedmann ("Ish-Shalom," 1831–1908) summed up his exhaustive study of the issue with the statement that "there is no prohibition here. It is in fact a meritorious action to bury a non-Jew in a Jewish cemetery."[2] His colleague Rabbi Isaac Hirsch Weiss (1815–1905), the author of *Dor Dor ve-Dorshav* (a history of the Oral Law), ruled that not only was there no prohibition, it was "in fact an obligation and precept to bury him with the Jewish dead for the sake of peace, and 'for the sake of peace' is itself a *mitzvah*."[3] Rabbi Weiss added, however, that this ruling was a matter of theoretical, not practical, Halakhah.

In one of his responsa, Rabbi Esriel Hildesheimer displayed commendable intellectual honesty when he candidly acknowledged that although on the emotional level he did not feel that one should bury a non-Jew alongside a Jew, this sentiment could not stand up to criticism:

> According to my personal feelings and those of many thousands of believers and children of believers, it is certainly true [that the interment is forbidden], but anyone who challenges this has grounds for disagreeing. . . . It all depends on whether there is a prohibition on burying a non-Jew in a Jewish cemetery.[4]

Note that Rabbi Hildesheimer does not cite an explicit prohibition.

DOES HALAKHAH REQUIRE THE EXHUMATION OF A NON-JEW BURIED IN A JEWISH CEMETERY?

We have seen that the codified Halakhah, through the time of Rabbi Joseph Caro, did not bar the burial of non-Jews alongside Jews; many later decisors, however, did. This prohibition applied before the fact; that is, it was valid before the interment of a non-Jew in a Jewish cemetery. But did these rabbinic rulings also apply after the fact and require the exhumation of a corpse if it had already been buried in a Jewish cemetery?

It is a curious fact that when the Rishon Lezion rabbis ruled that Theresa Angelovich should be reburied elsewhere, they did not cite a single halakhic precedent to support their case. On the other hand, one can quote many halakhic rulings that forbid or express strong reservations about the exhumation of a gentile from a Jewish cemetery.

Rabbi Eliezer Deutsch (1850–1916) of Hungary cited the codified halakhah concerning the burial of the wicked alongside the righteous—if the deceased has already been buried, the body must not be exhumed: "Similarly in the case of a non-Jew buried alongside a Jew, after the fact one is in any case not required to exhume the body."[5] In the same case, Rabbi Avraham Isaac Glick ruled that "it seems, in my humble opinion, that the Burial Society is not required to make any effort to remove [the gentile woman] from there."[6] Rabbi Judah Leib Zirelson of Kishinev, when asked about a Muslim who had been buried some distance from the graves of children in a Jewish cemetery, ruled that "as for removing the body from the grave, Jews must not do this, since such an action on our part would be totally contrary to the principle of peaceful relations."[7]

When the case of a doubtful convert was referred to Rabbi Moshe Feinstein, he ruled that the woman in question was certainly not Jewish. As to exhuming her body, however, he told the rabbi who asked the question that he was not "obliged to wage a great battle":

> Accordingly, [your] only obligation is to caution the Torah-observant to leave instructions not to be buried nearby. . . . As for those who are not Torah-observant and do not care about this, [you] need only remonstrate. . . . But you are not obliged to wage an open battle against the transgressors.[8]

It is unfortunate that the Chief Rabbis did not heed that eminent decisor's counsel to avoid disputes but instead attempted to impose their view on Jews who do not accept their authority.

DOES "FOR THE SAKE OF PEACE" OUTWEIGH OTHER PRINCIPLES?

The precept of burying non-Jews is one of a series of rabbinic regulations intended to establish social harmony and prevent quarrels.

The local rabbis in Rishon Lezion and the Chief Rabbinate Council ignored the basic tenet "for the sake of peace" and could find no peaceful halakhic solution, despite the many halakhic precedents. Accordingly, they bear direct and indirect responsibility for a situation that totally undercuts this principle and seems to be the antithesis of "peaceful relations." There is no doubt that a solution can be found in the context of Halakhah and Jewish ethics, in the spirit of Maimonides' ruling:

> With regard to non-Jews, the Sages enjoined that we visit their sick and bury their dead with Jewish dead and support their poor along with Jewish poor, on account of peace. For it is written: "The Lord is good to all and His mercy is upon all His works" (Ps. 145:9); and it is written: "Its [the Torah's] ways are pleasant ways and all its paths are peace" (Proverbs 3:17) (Laws of Kings, 10:12).

PERMISSIVENESS IS PREFERABLE

While the High Court of Justice was considering the Angelovich case—it eventually ruled that her body should remain for all time in its grave in the cemetery in Rishon Lezion—six residents of the town, whose relatives were buried in that cemetery, petitioned to be added as parties to the suit. They based their petition on the contention that because Torah Law forbids the burial of non-Jews in a Jewish cemetery, if Angelovich's body remained in its grave they would be compelled to transfer their relatives to some other Jewish cemetery where there were no non-Jews.

We have already seen (in the previous section) that Halakhah does not require the exhumation of a non-Jew buried in a Jewish cemetery. The question now is whether it requires the exhumation of Jews buried near a non-Jew. There are both historical and halakhic answers to this.

A survey of the history of Jewish communities covering about five centuries found many cases in which non-Jews were buried in Jewish cemeteries, in circumstances similar to those of the Angelovich case. Usually the heads of the community acquiesced, at least after the fact, in the burial of non-Jews there. There is no evidence that a Jewish community ever tried to remove Jewish bodies from a Jewish cemetery because of their proximity to the grave of a non-Jew. The list begins in the year 1515 in Eblona (Italy) and continues through the twentieth century in Europe, the United States, and Israel.[9]

Over the generations, rabbis and decisors were repeatedly asked about the burial of non-Jews in Jewish cemeteries. Rabbi Judah Leib Zirelson of Kishinev instructed a rabbi from Yalta that it was permitted to bury dead Subbotniki, or Sabbatarians—members of a Russian sect who follow many Jewish customs and rituals but do not convert to Judaism—in a special plot in the city's Jewish cemetery. He added that the plot should be about two meters away from Jewish graves and should be fenced off.[10] We have already noted another responsum in which Rabbi Zirelson ruled that it was a meritorious act to leave the corpse of a Muslim soldier in its grave in a Jewish cemetery. In this case, too, he suggested building a fence around the grave.[11] In none of these rulings, or many others, is there any suggestion that Jewish bodies be removed from cemeteries in which non-Jews had been buried.

In 1903, a boy whose father was Jewish and mother Christian was buried by the Neologue Burial Society in the Jewish cemetery in Temesvár (Transylvania). Rabbi Benet (Berachiah) Schick, the local Orthodox rabbi, was vigorously opposed to this and appealed to the leading rabbis of the generation, including David Zevi Hoffmann and Eliezer Deutsch. He received forty-two carefully argued halakhic responsa. Not a single one held that Jewish remains should be transferred from the cemetery in Temesvár, even though the grave of the non-Jewish child was in no way separated from the others and was not fenced off.[12] All the rabbis agreed, tacitly or otherwise, that the body could stay where it was.

These many precedents indicate that there is no halakhic basis for the notion that Jews must be moved out of a Jewish cemetery because their graves are adjacent to non-Jewish graves.

It seems likely that the six petitioners referred to above were influenced by the halakhic ruling published by the Rishon Lezion rabbis. Because the rabbis could find no explicit halakhic basis for their ruling that the body of Theresa Angelovich must be exhumed, their only alternative was to rule—with the approval of the Chief Rabbinate Council—that any Jews buried nearby must be moved elsewhere. They declared that "if the trespasser is not removed, it will be necessary to move the Jews who are buried nearby. . . . A Jew who is buried alongside a non-Jewish grave must be removed from there."

Ignoring the question whether this ruling was designed to add to the pressure to exhume Angelovich's remains, we shall try to clarify whether it has any halakhic basis.

The rabbis provide several references from the halakhic literature to support their ruling: "See the responsum of the Ḥakham Zevi, cited by the Maharsha on *Yoreh De'ah* 363." Someone who consults the commentary on the *Shulḥan Arukh* by the Maharsha—Rabbi Solomon Eger (1786–1852)—will find the following ruling: "It is permissible to move him so that he not remain buried alongside the grave of a non-Jew." In other words, reburial is permitted but not required.

It is curious that the rabbis did not quote Rabbi Zevi Hirsch Ashkenazi (known as the Ḥakham Zevi, 1660–1718) directly. In the case of a Jewish lad who had been buried in an agricultural field, where his grave would be plowed over and sown, he was asked to rule whether the remains could be exhumed and reburied in a Jewish cemetery.[13] Absolutely nothing in this responsum can be used to support the idea that Jewish bodies can or must be disinterred from a Jewish cemetery.

The Rishon Lezion rabbis also alleged support for their ruling by Rabbi Moshe Feinstein: "In practice in *Iggerot Moshe,* Volume 3:247, he suggested that a Jew who is buried among non-Jews be transferred to a Jewish cemetery." This reference, too, is misleading, since the case referred to a Jew buried in a Christian cemetery. Because of the crosses on the tombstones there, Rabbi Feinstein permitted exhumation of the remains for reburial in a Jewish cemetery, ruling that "one may and must remove the body from a non-Jewish cemetery."

The situation in Rishon Lezion was quite different: the rabbis would have required the exhumation of Jews from a Jewish cemetery. In other words, the Chief Rabbis approved a ruling that was not supported by precedents; the main thing was to impose their will.

It should be noted that in practice, the rabbis' ruling did not apply to the petitioners, who deemed themselves bound by it. They had ruled that if the non-Jewish woman were not exhumed, it would be necessary "to move all the Jews buried near this grave, so that there be a space of at least eight cubits [about twelve feet] between their graves and her grave." Yet, none of the petitioners were concerned by this stipulation, since the distance between Theresa Angelovich's grave and the nearest of their relatives was more than forty feet!

So much for the quandary facing the petitioners. There remains a halakhic question concerning those few Jews who are buried within twelve feet of Theresa Angelovich's grave. Although their families did not comply with the rabbinic ruling that they must move their dear ones and did not petition to the High Court of Justice, the rabbinate, on its own initiative, asserted its responsibility for these graves.

I was invited by the Angelovich family and their lawyer to meet with the two Chief Rabbis of Rishon Lezion and the attorneys for the petitioners in an attempt to find a halakhically acceptable compromise. The rabbis maintained that there was only one solution: to transfer Theresa Angelovich's remains to a separate section of the cemetery. I suggested a solution, based on the codified Halakhah, that would permit leaving the body where it was. My solution drew on the opinion of eminent and strict rabbis, who had ruled that a non-Jew, once buried, can be left undisturbed if a fence that is ten hands' breadths (about three feet) high is built around the grave. This was the ruling of such eminent decisors as Rabbi Abraham Isaac Glick (nineteenth century),[14] Rabbi Eliezer Deutsch,[15] and Rabbi Moshe Feinstein.[16]

I thought it might be possible to persuade the Angelovich family to agree to this solution, especially since there is halakhic sanction for incorporating the fence into the tombstone. Had the rabbinate been inclined to leniency in this matter, it could have relied on the opinion of Rabbi David Sperber (nineteenth–twentieth centuries), who ruled that in such a case, all that required "is a barrier of sorts, not an actual barrier, and this is enough. . . . Accordingly one can say that given the custom of mounding the earth above every grave, this too is enough."[17] In other words, an obvious fence is not required, and even the normal form of arranging the grave may be enough. This is an unquestioned halakhic solution that all parties, strict and lenient rulers, should have been able to accept, allowing Theresa Angelovich to rest in peace "on account of peace" (BT Gittin 61a).

The rabbis' response was that they had already considered my solution, in consultation with the Chief Rabbinate Council, and concluded that it was not possible. When I asked my colleagues from Rishon Lezion to indicate what was wrong with this established halakhic solution, they replied that they had to remove the Christian woman from her grave because of the threats of zealots from Bene Berak, Me'ah She'arim, and Williamsburg (New York). When I asked whether this was a valid halakhic argument, they did not respond.

Thus, we once again witnessed a situation in which the Orthodox rabbinic establishment, which asserts its exclusivity in matters of Halakhah, recoiled from applying lenient precedents to solve a serious problem. In the Angelovich case, as in many others, the rabbinate preferred to hew to the strict line even when this has no solid basis in Halakhah, and lamely excused the inflexibility of its ruling on the grounds that it is threatened by Ultra-Orthodox zealots who restrict its leeway.

Halakhah and Jewish tradition are too important to be left to the exclusive custody of the Orthodox rabbinate, whose members are unable or unwilling to apply the talmudic principle that "it is preferable to be lenient" (BT Beitzah 2b). They ought to act in accordance with Rashi, who interprets this dictum as follows: "It is better to teach us the force of a permissive decisor because he relies on his halakhic tradition and is not afraid to be lenient." [18]

It is most unfortunate that the narrow interpretations of the religious establishment distance many good people from the Torah. Particularly distressing is the fact that such stringencies are unnecessary and are not based on halakhic sources. Rashi, at the end of the passage just cited, warned against such decisors: "But the force of those who forbid is no proof, since anyone can be stringent, even about something that is permitted." [19]

Our country needs rabbis who have the courage and knowledge to rule in the spirit of the great rabbis of the past who showed that leniency is preferable.

Undesirable Proximity in the Cemetery

Later, the Israeli public was shocked when it was discovered that Theresa Angelovich's grave was empty. Ultimately, two Ultra-Orthodox men were convicted of stealing her body and dumping it in a Muslim cemetery in a nearby town.

What motivated them to dig up her grave in the dark of night? Only God, "the just judge, Who tests the thoughts and the mind" (Jer. 11:20), can answer this question. We may conjecture, however, that they were influenced in part by the rabbinate's ruling that her body must be exhumed and reburied. To our sorrow, it must be noted that this ruling was based in part on superstition.

The reasons cited by the rabbis included a passage from *Klei Yakar*, the Pentateuch commentary by Rabbi Samuel Laniado (died 1610), which recounts "the pain caused to the dead by undesirable neighbors" and describes the physical existence of the corpse in the grave:

> Even after the soul is sundered from the body part of the soul remains on the body of the deceased and even on his bones,

guarding him, and hears when people come to pray at the graves of the righteous.[20]

According to this belief, the dead in their graves can hear and suffer physical pain because their souls remain in some fashion attached to their remains. As a result, those buried nearby can disturb their last rest. The rabbis of Rishon Lezion ruled that the corpse of Theresa Angelovich "disturbed her Jewish neighbors. . . . In death she is disturbing others and causing them pain."

This idea derives from a view that was common in the Middle Ages. In *Sefer Ḥasidim,* Rabbi Judah the Pious (twelfth century) wrote about a righteous scholar who had been buried next to someone less meritorious. It seems that the righteous man came to the city fathers and complained that he had been buried in a place where the stench and smoke bothered him. "They placed stones to serve as a barrier between the grave of the righteous man and that of the wicked man. After that he no longer appeared to them in their dreams."[21]

In the fifteenth century, Rabbi Jacob Moellin disclosed why the wicked must not be buried next to the righteous:

> The reason is that what is decreed behind the Heavenly veil is revealed to the righteous man. . . . But when a wicked person is [buried] near him they do not reveal this to the righteous man, so that the wicked man will not hear too.[22]

Beliefs like this were common among our medieval ancestors and are still widespread in Ultra-Orthodox circles today. Well-known modern rabbis have enlisted similar notions to prove that it is dangerous to bury a non-Jew next to a Jew. In a ruling about a non-Jewish woman buried in a Jewish cemetery in Hungary, Rabbi Ḥayyim Eleazar Shapira quoted the passage from *Sefer Ḥasidim,* which he supplemented with another reason, namely, that the renowned sixteenth-century kabbalist Isaac Luria (known as the Ari) "wrote in *Sefer Hayḥiudim* that one should not walk over graves that are near to the graves of non-Jews, so that the evil spirits not adhere to one, Heaven forbid." He proceeded to explain that when Jewish graves are "adjacent to those of non-Jews, their Jewish children or loved ones who heed the warning of the Ari" would have to avoid visiting their relatives' graves, so as not to be contaminated by the defiling spirits.[23]

In this context, one can understand the assertion by the rabbis of Rishon Lezion that moving Theresa Angelovich's remains to another place would be to her benefit, too:

> Moving her would also benefit her, because certainly it is bad for her that in her death she is disturbing others and causing them pain. . . . Nor is this an insult to her. On the contrary, putting an end to the pain of the dead buried alongside her would be accounted to her merit.

One can understand this argument by the rabbis only in the light of the beliefs outlined above, which many Ultra-Orthodox Jews truly and sincerely believe. They are entitled to their own beliefs, as long as they do not impose them on others.

But enlightened Jews of the modern age certainly prefer to view the survival of the human soul as involving its return to the Creator, the works it leaves behind, and its influence on relatives and friends, irrespective of the physical location of the corpse in its tomb. In the words of Ecclesiastes: "And the dust returns to the ground as it was, but the spirit returns to God Who bestowed it" (Eccles. 12:7).

BURYING THE GOOD NEXT TO THE WICKED

Theresa Angelovich, a non-Jew who joined her fate to that of the Jewish people, is not the only one who has suffered at the hands of Ultra-Orthodox zealots. When their "cousins" in Jerusalem vandalized the grave of Rabbi Morton Berman (1899–1986) in the Mount of Olives cemetery, they attempted to justify their deed in posters that were plastered on walls in the Me'ah She'arim neighborhood of Jerusalem: "The Reform villain has been banished outside the camp. . . . According to Halakhah, the wicked must not be buried alongside the righteous." The zealots did not enumerate the sins of the late rabbi, who had passed away at a ripe old age, as full of good deeds as a pomegranate is with seeds. In their eyes, his greatest sin may have been that he was an enthusiastic Zionist—following a long line of Reform rabbis, including Abba Hillel Silver, Stephen S. Wise, and Judah Leib Magnes—who put his Zionism into practice when he walked away from his pulpit at a large synagogue in Chicago in 1957 to make *aliya* with his family. For the vandals, the title "Reform rabbi" was epithet enough to condemn him posthumously. On the other hand, they offered no support for their statement that the deceased buried in proximity to Rabbi Berman had all been "worthy and righteous men."

Do these Ultra-Orthodox hooligans represent Halakhah and Judaism? When it comes to the question of burying certain people near others, Halakhah is not nearly as unequivocal as they assert.

According to the *Shulḥan Arukh:*

One must not bury a wicked man alongside a righteous man, nor even a very wicked man next to a slightly wicked man; nor does one bury a righteous man, and all the more so an ordinary man, alongside a saint. (Note [added by Rabbi Moses Isserles, whose annotations indicate the Ashkenazi practice]: but a penitent may be buried next to a completely righteous man) (*Y.D.* 362:5).

Rabbi Joel Sirkes (sixteenth–seventeenth centuries) nevertheless read in this a certain restriction on where a penitent may be buried: "The implication is that one does not bury a penitent near a saint."[24] Rabbi Joshua Falk Katz added "a moderately wicked person" to the list of those subject to burial restrictions.[25]

It is extremely doubtful whether all of these categories and gradations can be identified precisely. And if it were possible to do so, every burial society and community would need a cemetery of infinite size if it wanted to leave an appropriate buffer between the graves of the multiple categories of deceased persons.

372 / E<small>VOLVING</small> H<small>ALAKHAH</small>

We should note that Maimonides, unlike the other authorities cited above, does not include a single one of these prohibitions in his halakhic rulings, and his silence speaks volumes.

Rabbi Samuel Engel (1853–1935), the head of the religious court in Radomisl (Ukraine), dealt with demands that a wicked person not be buried alongside a righteous person and that a space be left between the graves in every cemetery. In reply, he argued that "each time they would have to buy a new cemetery, which is quite unfeasible." But the very idea is unnecessary, he contended: even where the deceased person had been truly wicked, death and burial atoned for his sins. And if some suspicion persisted about his iniquity, "one can answer that we consider [the deceased person] to be worthy, because he certainly had thoughts of repentance before he died." [26]

Clearly, then, there were Orthodox communities that did not insist on separating graves for one reason or another. Rabbi Jehiel Jacob Weinberg quoted Rabbi David Zevi Hoffmann of Frankfurt to the effect "that in Germany it has become customary to bury those who desecrate the Sabbath and commit other sins in the same row with observant Jews."[27]

Somewhat earlier, Rabbi Esriel Hildesheimer of Berlin cited a rabbi from Leipzig who said, with regard to the prohibition against burying the wicked alongside the righteous, that "today we do not insist on this so much."[28] It is clear that a similar situation exists in the vast majority of cemeteries in Israel. No one seems interested in changing it, even if it were feasible.

36

Burial and Superstition

THAT SONS DO NOT FOLLOW THEIR FATHER'S BIER TO THE CEMETERY

A young man asked me about the funeral of his late father. While the young man was in Europe, he received the sad news of his father's death. With great difficulty the son managed to get back to Israel and reach Jerusalem before the funeral. But the representative of the burial society firmly insisted that he could not accompany his father on his last journey. When the son asked why, it was explained that the holy custom of Jerusalem is that sons do not follow their father's bier to the cemetery. This in fact is what happened. The son was not permitted to take part in his father's interment.

The son asked several persons about the reasons for this astonishing custom, which kept him from being present at his own father's burial, but no one could give him a satisfactory answer. When he turned to me I was able to answer him more or less as follows:

Rabbis and scholars agree that the custom is derived from the Zohar, the most important text of the kabbalah, which tells of a demon named Na'amah (the daughter of the infamous Lilith, Adam's first wife):

Now this Na'amah . . . goes out and arouses men and grows warm from them in their dreams, and in the lust of the dream has relations with them. . . . From that lust she conceives and brings forth various other types of [demons] into the world (Zohar, III, 76b–77a).

This account builds on a passage in the Talmud, reported in the name of Rabbi Jeremiah ben Eliezer, that Adam, when excommunicated after the expulsion from the Garden of Eden, "begat spirits and goblins and [female] demons." The Gemara explains that these are the fruit of nocturnal emissions (BT Eruvin 18b).

According to Prof. Gershom Scholem, the Jerusalem funeral custom derives from a medieval superstition:

The succubi (female demons) use a man's seminal emissions to conceive and bear evil spirits. In the later kabbalah, the demons that are born to a man from such a coupling are considered to be his illegitimate children. When the man dies these "children" come to accompany their late "father" [to his grave] and demand their share of his estate. This is the source of the custom, followed in Jerusalem and other places since the seventeenth century, that forbids flesh-and-blood children to accompany their father to the cemetery, for fear that the demons, their "step-siblings," might harm them.[1]

Academic scholars of kabbalah are not the only people aware of the source of this custom. So too are the halakhic decisors, including Rabbi Ovadia Yosef, the former Chief Rabbi:

In the case of a man who emits sperm in vain or even under duress, . . . even though the remnants of the drops that are emitted in vain are not fit to cause conception, evil spirits and demons are produced from them. . . . When the begetter of these evil spirits dies and his sons and daughters follow him [to the cemetery], they are accompanied by these evil spirits who surround [the deceased] and cause him great distress. This is why they proclaimed a ban that offspring of the deceased not follow him, as a way of preventing the deceased from [suffering] this great distress.[2]

Despite Rabbi Yosef's explanation that the custom is based entirely on belief in these strange spirits, and despite his acknowledgement that "as a matter of theoretical Halakhah sons do follow the bier," he ruled in favor of the custom. Nevertheless, he held that if the sons are vigorously opposed and demand to accompany the deceased, they must not be prevented from doing so. He recommended that a scholar go up to the mourners and

> inform them, gently and kindly, of the custom of the Holy City of Jerusalem, whose foundation is in the holy mountains, and especially that this custom is meant for the good of their deceased father.[3]

I told the young man: If you share the belief in demons who are present at the funeral and might harm you or cause pain to your late father, you ought to accept this custom. On the other hand, most of those who know its source believe that it is merely a superstition based on the idea of evil spirits and has no spiritual significance in our own time. Not only is there no absolute prohibition on following one's father to his grave, Halakhah holds that after the death of a parent the sons must walk "in front of the bier until he is buried" (*Shulḥan Arukh, Y.D.* 348:16). Such, too, was the ruling of the late Chief Rabbi Ben-Zion Uziel (in contrast to that of Rabbi Yosef):

> Here it is stated explicitly that it is meritorious and even an obligation for sons to accompany their father's coffin until burial. . . . [Anyone who prevents this] is merely causing disputes in Israel and the Sages are not pleased with him.[4]

We see, then, that mourners' spiritual need to accompany their loved ones is anchored in Halakhah. Those who believe in the menace of evil spirits may act in accordance with their belief, but they ought not to impose it on others. This applies to burial societies, too.

BURIAL IN COFFINS

Burial in a shroud only, without a coffin, is widespread in Israel. This is a matter of custom. There is no halakhic prohibition on the use of coffins. If this practice is only a custom, should it have the force to prevent coffin burials altogether?

We all know that coffins are used in military funerals in Israel, even when the deceased has died of illness. The military sections are integral parts of cemeteries where burial in coffins is not otherwise allowed. There are also some communities in Israel—such as Kfar Shemaryahu—where people are buried in coffins. We see then that the custom of burying without coffins is not followed exclusively.

In fact, the custom is not based on an unambiguous obligation. The assertion that we must implement the statement "dust you are and to dust you shall return" (Gen. 3:19) literally, by burying the dead in direct contact with the ground, has no solid basis. In his will, Rabbi Judah the Prince asked to be buried in the Land of Israel in a coffin, "and may my coffin have a hole in it" so that his body would come into contact with the earth (JT Kil'ayim 9:3). A similar ruling was handed down by Rabbi Shabbetai ben Meir Hakohen (1621–1662), in his *Siftei Kohen* commentary on the *Shulḥan Arukh* (*Y.D.* 362:1). Another rabbi who preferred burial in coffins was the second-century Sage Rabbi Jose ben Kisma, who instructed his students to bury him in a coffin deep in the soil of the Holy Land (BT Sanhedrin 98a).

Thus, it seems that there is no halakhic basis for the refusal by the rabbinate and the burial societies to allow the use of coffins; it is merely a custom. We have already seen that contradictory customs may co-exist. Nor is there anything in Halakhah mandating that the deceased be carried out on a stretcher and buried only in a shroud. There are great variations in burial customs, depending on the time, place, and individual involved. It is certainly permitted to bury a Jew in a coffin.

Afterword

The halakhic sources presented in this book demonstrate that in various ages, rabbinic decisors found ways to relieve the ills that beset their people. Not a few of these troubles had stemmed from the inflexible rulings of stringent rabbis.

Many decisors took account of the situation in which the Jews were living. The people simply were not able to satisfy all the demands of Halakhah because of the difficulty of making a living and other daily stress and strife. Thus, for example, the School of Hillel enacted the Provision of the Penitent so that a thief would be able to repent. Maimonides saw this regulation as a precedent and relied on it to allow an Egyptian Jew to emancipate and marry his non-Jewish slave woman. In these cases, the rabbis employed halakhic methods based on logic. They knew the nature of their people and preferred the lesser evil.

However, there were also situations where no solution could be found in accordance with simple logic; then rabbis had to look for a more radical response. Thus, for example, Hillel the Elder came up with an extremely tendentious and far-fetched exegesis in order to purify children from Alexandria. Rabbi Judah the Prince was forced to modify the very halakhic basis of the laws of the Sabbatical Year in order to save the people from starvation.

In the Middle Ages, too, and through our own century, eminent decisors, including Rabbi Moses Isserles, Rabbi D. Z. Hoffmann, and many others, boldly assumed responsibility and permitted serious prohibitions. Some decisors foresaw catastrophic results from the forcible imposition of a Torah precept, even to the point of causing desecration of the Divine Name.

The question arises: Did these rabbis recognize that they were engaging in legal fictions and giving tendentious and at times radical interpretations to the codified Halakhah? They were wise men, and there is no doubt that they knew precisely what they were doing. This is the way of Halakhah. Great Sages recognized the fact that their predecessors in earlier generations had acted in precisely the same way in order to save Jewish souls.

The annals of Halakhah indicate that a rabbi and decisor who wanted to cope with the problems of his generation had to satisfy at least four requirements: profound knowledge of halakhic sources, sensitivity to the suffering of his fellow Jews, a fierce desire to help them, and the courage to decide and act. Many grave problems were solved by rabbis endowed with these traits, as we have seen throughout this book. For the most part, they were able to rely on the many halakhic precedents that permitted change.

Perhaps it is impossible to solve all the severe halakhic problems of our age according to these methods. Consequently, I have examined of the writings of certain twentieth-century rabbis who sketched out directions for halakhic decision making according to particular criteria and standards. These can serve us as a sort of bridge between the approach of the Sages of old and the needs of the present age.

Finally, we have seen that not only is it permitted to enact new regulations and innovate in order to repair the wounded souls of our brethren, it is also the imperative of the hour. Decisors and rabbis must cope with the situation of our generation, just as was stated by Rabbi Joseph Albo more than five hundred years ago:

> Certain general principles were only briefly alluded to in the Torah, so that the Sages of every generation may work out the newly emerging particulars.[1]

Bibliography

Note: An asterisk indicates that the work is in Hebrew (or Aramaic).

Aaron de Toledo. *Divrei efetz.* Saloniki, 1798.*

Abraham bar Ḥiyya. *Higgayon Hanefesh.* Ed. S. J. Rappoport. Leipzig, 1865.*

Abraham, Samson ben Jacob Abraham. *Responsa Or Hayashar.* Amsterdam, 1769.*

Abramsky, Yeezkel, et al. *The Battle to Save the Rabbinate in Israel and the Danger Posed by the Candidacy of Rabbi Shlomo Goren.* N.p., 1973.*

Abravanel, Isaac. *Commentary on the Pentateuch.* Jerusalem, 1964.*

Abudarham, David. *The Complete Abudarham.* Jerusalem, 1963.*

Abulafia, Meir. *Yad Ramah.* Saloniki, 1798; repr. Jerusalem, 1971.*

Adani, Shlomo. *Melekhet Shlomo.* Vilna, 1905.*

Adret, Solomon ben Abraham. *Responsa of the Rashba.* Vienna, 1812.*

Agus, Irving. *Rabbi Meir of Rothenburg.* New York, 1970.

Albo, Joseph. *Sefer Ha-Ikkarim—The Book of Principles.* Ed. and trans. Isaac Husik. Philadelphia, 1930.

Amudim, the Journal of the Religious Kibbutz Movement. Elul 5739 (1979).*

Ariel, Yaakov. "Morality, Religious Faith, and Peace Policy." *Niv Hamidrashiyah* 13 (1978–1979).*

Arieli, Yitzhak. "The Problem of Autopsies." *No'am* 6 (1963).*

———. "The Problem of Autopsies." *Oral Law* 6 (1964).*

Arik, Meir. *Responsa Imrei Yosher.* Munkacs, 1913.*

Aristotle. *Nicomachean Ethics.* Trans. W. D. Ross, rev. J. O. Urmson. In *The Complete Works of Aristotle,* ed. Jonathan Barnes. Princeton, 1984.

Asher ben Jehiel. Commentary on the Talmud. Included in standard edition thereof.*

Ashkenazi, Zevi Hirsch. *Responsa Ḥakham Zevi.* Jerusalem, 1970.*

Avidan (Zemel), Avraham. *In the Wake of the Yom Kippur War: Meditations, Halakhah, and Research.* IDF Central Command, IDF Rabbinate, 1974.*

Avot de-Rabbi Nathan (The Fathers According to Rabbi Nathan). Ed. Solomon Schechter. Vienna, 1887.*

Azulai, Ḥayyim Joseph David. *Sefer Avodat Hakodesh.* Jerusalem, 1913.*

Babylonian Talmud with Variant Readings: Tractate Keteubot. Ed. Moshe Herschler. Jerusalem, 1972.*

Babylonian Talmud with Variant Readings: Tractate Yevamot. Ed. Avraham Liss. Jerusalem, 1986.*

Bacharach, Jair. *Responsa Ḥavvot Ya'ir.* Lemberg, 1896.*

Bar-Ilan University Responsa Project, 5th version, 1997.*

Barth, Julian H., and Moshe Zemer. "The Congenital Eunich, a Medical-Halakhic Study." *ASSIA, the Journal of Jewish Medical Ethics and the Halakhah* 2, no. 2 (1995): 44–50.

Bat-Adam, Rahel. "The Vocation of Zionism Today: Winning Partners." *Shedemot* 52 (1974): 61–69.*

Beit Talmud. Ed. Isaac Hirsch Weiss and Meir Ish-Shalom. Vienna, 1884.*

Ben-Yehudah, Eliezer. *Dictionary of the Ancient and Modern Hebrew Language.* Ed. N. H. Tur-Sinai. New York and Jerusalem, 1959–1960.*

Benveniste, Ḥayyim. *Sheyarei Knesset Hagedolah.* Izmir, 1734.*

Berkovits, Eliezer. *Conditions in Marriage and Divorce.* Jerusalem, 1967.*

———. *Halakhah: Its Authority and Role.* Jerusalem, 1981.*

———. *Not in Heaven: The Nature and Function of Halakhah.* New York, 1983.

———. "Clarification of the Halakhah on Autopsies." *Sinai* 69 (1971).*

Bettan, Israel. "Marriage of a Cohen to a Divorcée," *Yearbook of the Central Conference of American Rabbis* 53 (1943).

Bleich, J. David. "The Conversion Crisis: A Halakhic Analysis." *Tradition* 11, no. 4 (1971).

———. "Communication," *Tradition* 12 (3-4) (1973).

———."The Conversion Crisis." *Contemporary Halachic Problems* 1. New York, 1977.

Breisch, Mordecai Jacob. *Responsa Ḥelkat Ya'akov.* Jerusalem, 1951.*

Caro, Joseph. *Beit Yosef* on the *Arba'ah Turim.* Included in standard edition thereof.*

———. *Kesef Mishneh* on the *Mishneh Torah.* Included in standard edition thereof.*

———. *Shulḥan Arukh* (with standard commentaries). Jerusalem, 1973.*

Chief Rabbinate Council. "Permanent Regulations Relating to Personal Status in Israel." Jerusalem, 1950.*

———. *The B'nai Israel: Halakhic Rulings and Sources to Clarify their Legal Status and Origins.* Jerusalem, 1962.*

Chorin, Aaron, et al. *Nogah ha-tzedek.* Dessau, 1818.*

Cicero, Marcus Tullius. *De officiis.* Trans. E. M. Atkins. Cambridge, 1991.

Cohn, Haim H. "Faithful Exegesis—in Both Senses." *Petaḥim* 4, no. 40 (1977).*

———. *Human Rights in Jewish Law.* New York, 1984.

———. "The Duty to Live and the Right to Die: On the Dichotomy of Divinity and Humanity in Jewish Law." In *Euthanasia,* ed. Amnon Carmi. Medicolegal Library II. Berlin, 1984: 31–67.

Committee on Jewish Law and Standards of the Rabbinical Assembly of America. "Memorandum on Waiving the Requirements of Formal Halitzah." New York, 1970.

Corinaldi, Michael. *Ethiopian Jews: Identity and Tradition.* Jerusalem, 1989.*

David ben Zimra. Commentary on the *Mishneh Torah.**

———. *Responsa of the Radbaz*. Warsaw, 1882–1883; repr. Jerusalem, 1972.*

Dembitzer, Ḥayyim Nathan. *Sefer Kelilat Yofi*. Cracow, 1888.*

Dessler, Eliyahu Eliezer. *A Letter from Eliyahu*. Bene Berak, 1964.*

Deutsch, Eliezer. *Responsa Peri Hasadeh*. Banihod, 1913.*

Deutsch, Gotthard. Untitled responsum. *Yearbook of the Central Conference of American Rabbis* 29 (1919); quoted in Walter Jacob, ed., *American Reform Responsa*.

District Court Verdicts 17, Military Tribunal MR/57/3, the Judge Advocate General vs. Maj. Shmuel Melinki and 10 others. Tel Aviv, 1959.*

Divrei Haknesset 40, no. 38. Fifth Knesset, Third Session, August 17, 1964. Jerusalem, p. 38.*

Don-Yihya, Shabbetai. *Rabbi Ben-Zion Meir Hai Uziel: His Life and Doctrine*. Jerusalem, 1955.*

Eilenburg, Issachar Dov. *Responsa Be'er Sheva*. Warsaw, 1890; repr. Jerusalem, 1969.*

Elijah ben Samuel. *Responsa Yad Eliyahu*. Amsterdam, 1712; repr. Bene Berak, 1983.*

Elijah ben Shlomo Zalman. *Bi'ur HaGra* on the *Shulḥan Arukh*. Included in standard edition thereof.*

Ellenson, David H. "The Development of Orthodox Attitudes to Conversion in the Modern Period." *Conservative Judaism* 36, no. 4 (1983).

———. *Tradition in Transition*. Lanham, New York, and London, 1989.

———. *Rabbi Esriel Hildesheimer and the Creation of a Modern Jewish Orthodoxy*. Tuscaloosa and London, 1990.

———, and Robert N. Levine. "Jewish Tradition, Contemporary Sensibilities, and Halakhah: A Responsum by Rabbi David Zvi Hoffmann." *Journal of Reform Judaism* 30, no. 1 (winter 1983): 49–56.

Ellinson, E. G. *Marriages Not According to the Rites of Moses and Israel*. Tel Aviv, 1976.*

Elyashar, Jacob Saul. *Responsa Simah La'ish*. Jerusalem, 1888.*

———. *Responsa Olat Ish*. Jerusalem, 1898.*

Emden, Jacob. *Glosses and Novellae* on the Talmud. Included in standard edition thereof.*

———. *Mor u-ketziah*. Altona, 1761.*

———. *Responsa of the Ya'avetz*. Lemberg, 1884.*

———. *Siddur Beit Yaakov*. Lemberg, 1904.*

Encyclopaedia Judaica. Jerusalem, 1971.

Engel, Samuel. *Responsa of the Maharash*. Warsaw, 1936.*

Epstein, Baruch Halevy. *Torah Temimah*. Tel Aviv, 1956.*

Epstein, Ḥayyim Fischel. *Teshuvah Sheleimah*. Piotrkow, 1913.*

Epstein, Jehiel Michel. *Arukh Hashulan*. Jerusalem, 1987.*

Falk, Joshua. *Derishah u-Perishah*, commentary on the *Arba'ah Turim*. Included in standard edition thereof.*

Falk, Ze'ev. *Halakhah and Practice in the State of Israel.* Jerusalem, 1967.*

Feinstein, Moshe. *Iggerot Moshe.* New York, 1959–1974; Bene Berak, 1981–1985.*

Frankel, David. *Korban ha-eidah* on the Jerusalem Talmud. Tel Aviv, 1949.*

Freehof, Solomon B. *A Treasury of Responsa.* Philadelphia, 1963.

Freiman, Avraham Ḥayyim. *The Order of Betrothal and Marriage.* Jerusalem, 1964.*

Fried, Netanel Hakohen. *Responsa Penei Meivin.* Munkács, 1913.*

Friedman, Mordechai Akiba. *Jewish Polygamy in the Middle Ages.* Jerusalem, 1986.*

Friedman, Tuvia. "Conversion in Israeli Law." *Shalhevet* 27 (1983).*

Gagin, Shalom Moshe Hai. *Responsa Yisma Lev.* Jerusalem, 1878.*

Galante, Moses. *Responsa.* Venice, 1608.*

Gershom ben Judah. *Responsa of Rabbenu Gershom Me'or Ha-golah.* Ed. Shlomo Eidelberg. New York, 1956.*

Gilat, Yitzhak D. "On the Formation of Halakhah," *Ha'ummah* 7, no. 4 (1969).*

——. "A Court Makes a Condition to Uproot a Torah Precept." *Bar-Ilan Annual* 7–8. Ramat Gan, 1970.*

——. "The Influence of Reality on Halakhic Distinctions." *Molad* 3, no. 14-15 (1970).*

——. "Halakhah's Link to Reality." *Studies in Problems of Culture, Education, and Society* (1972).*

——. *Studies in the Development of Halakhah.* Ramat Gan, 1992.*

Glick, Abraham Isaac. *Responsa Yad Yitzak.* Satmar, 1902.*

Goldman, Aaron Halevi. *Responsa Divrei Aharon.* Jerusalem, 1981.*

Gumbiner, Abraham. *Magen Avraham* on the *Shulḥan Arukh.* Included in standard edition thereof.*

Gordis, Robert. "A Dynamic Halakha." *Judaism* 28 (1967).

Goren, Shlomo. *Halakhic Opinion on Personal Status.* N.p., 1971.*

——. *Halakhic Ruling Concerning the Brother and Sister.* Jerusalem, 1973.*

——. *Responsa Meshiv Milamah.* Jerusalem, 1983.*

——. "The Integrity of the Land in the Light of Halakhah." *Hazofeh,* June 22, June 28, July 12, 1985.*

Green, Y. "Artificial Insemination." *Assiya* 40 (1985).*

Greenberg, Simon. "And He Writes Her a Bill of Divorce." *Conservative Judaism* 24, no. 3 (1970).

Greenwald, Jekuthiel Judah. *Compendium of Mourning.* Jerusalem and New York, 1973.*

Grodzinsky, Ḥayyim Ozer. *Aiezer.* Vilna, 1932–1939; repr. Tel Aviv, 1974.*

Guttmacher, Elijah. *Responsa Aderet Eliyahu.* Jerusalem, 1984.*

Guttmann, Jehiel Michel. *Examination of the Mitzvot.* Breslau, 1931.*

Guttmann, Julius. *Religion and Science.* Trans. S. Asch. Jerusalem, 1955.*

Hadaya, Ovadiah. *Responsa Yaskil Avdi*. Jerusalem, 1931–1958.*

Hakohen, Meir Simah. *Or Samea on the Mishneh Torah*. Jerusalem, 1978.*

———. *Responsa Or Samea. Jerusalem, 1981.*

Hakohen, Moshe ben Shalom. *Ve-heishiv Moshe*. Jerusalem, 1968.*

Halevi, Judah. *The Kuzari: An Argument for the Faith of Israel*. Trans. Hartwig Hirschfeld. New York, 1964.

Halevy, Ḥayyim David. *Responsa 'Aseh Lekha Rav*. Tel Aviv, 1976–.*

Ḥazzan, Elijah. *Responsa Ta'alumot Lev*, vol. 2, Leghorn, 1893; vol. 3, Alexandria, 1903.*

Hebrew Encyclopedia. Jerusalem, vol. 6, 1967; v. 26, 1974.*

Heinemann, Isaac. *Rationales of the Commandments in Jewish Literature* 2. Jerusalem, 1956.*

Heller-Feldman, Yehoshua. "Conversion and Converts." *Daf le-tarbut* 151 (1984).*

Henkin, Joseph Elijah. "A Daughter's Saying Kaddish." *Hapardes* 37, no. 6 (1963).*

Herzog, Yitzak Isaac Halevy. *Responsa Heikhal Yitzak*. Tel Aviv, Jerusalem, 1960–1972.*

———. "The Rights of Minorities according to Halakhah." *Teumin* 2 (1981).

Heschel, Abraham Joshua. *Israel, an Echo of Eternity*. New York, 1969.

Hildesheimer, Esriel. *Letters*. Ed. Mordechai Eliav. Jerusalem, 1966.*

———. *Responsa of Rabbi Esriel*. Tel Aviv, 1969.*

Hirschensohn, Chaim. *Responsa Malki Bakodesh*. St. Louis, 1921.*

Hoffmann, David Zevi. *Responsa Melammed Le-ho'il*. Frankfurt, 1926–1927.*

Horowitz, Abraham. *Yesh Nohalim*. Sidalkov, 1835.*

Ibn-Shimon, Raphael Aaron. *Nehar Mitzrayyim*. No-Amon (Cairo), 1908.*

Isaac bar Sheshet. *Responsa of the Ribash*. Lemberg, 1805.*

Isaac ben Moses. *Or Zarua*. Zhitomir, 1862.*

Isaac ben Reuben of Barcelona. *Sefer Derekh Mitzvotekha (Azharot)* Susa, Tunisia, 1920.*

Ishbili, Yomtov ben Abraham. *Novellae of the Ritba*. New York, 1966.*

Ish-Horowicz, Moshe. "Theodicy as Evidenced by Early Rabbinic Discussions of the Flood." Doctoral dissertation, University of Manchester, 1987.

———. *Halakhah: Orthodoxy and Reform*. London, 1989.

Isserles, Moses. *Responsa of the Rama*. Ed. Asher Ziv. Jerusalem, 1971.*

Jacob ben Asher. *Arba'ah Turim*, including: Joseph Caro, *Beit Yosef;* Joel Sirkes, *Bayit Ḥadash;* Moses Isserles, *Darkhei Moshe;* Joshua Falk, *Perishah u-Derishah*. Jerusalem, 1985.*

Jacob ben Samuel. *Responsa Beit Yaakov*. Dyhernfurth, 1696.*

Jacob, Walter, ed. *American Reform Responsa*. New York, 1983.

Jacobs, Louis B. "Jewish Law: A Synthesis." In *Conservative Judaism and Jewish Law*, ed. Seymour Siegel. New York, 1977.

———. *A Tree of Life*. Oxford, 1984.

Jacobson, Yissakhar. *Netiv Binah.* Tel Aviv, 1964.*

Jakobovits, Israel (Immanuel). "The Problem of Autopsies in the Halakhic Literature and in Light of Contemporary Conditions." *Torah and Science,* 4, no. 2 (1974).*

Joseph ben Moses of Trani. *Responsa of the Maharit.* Constantinople, 1640.*

Judah the Pious. *Sefer Ḥasidim.* Ed. Reuven Margoliot. Jerusalem, 1960.*

Kagan, Israel Meir. *Mishnah Berurah.* Jerusalem, n.d.*

Kahane, Meir. *Know Your Judaism (Really): An Anthology of Sources.* Jerusalem, n.d.*

Karelitz, Avraham Yeshayahu. *Sefer Ḥazon Ish.* Bene Brak, 1959.*

Kasowski, Chaim Joshua. *Lexicon of Talmudic Language* 14. Jerusalem, 1965.*

———. *Concordance to Tannaitic Literature.* New York, 1968.*

———. *Concordance to the Talmud.* Jerusalem, 1971.*

Kasowski, Moshe. *Lexicon of Talmudic Language.* Jerusalem, 1980–1984.*

Klein, Isaac. "The Problem of *Chalitzah* Today." *Proceedings of the Rabbinical Assembly of America* 15. New York, 1951.

———. "The Marriage of a Kohen and a Giyoret," *Proceedings of the Rabbinical Assembly of America* 32. New York, 1968.

———. *Responsa and Halakhic Studies.* New York, 1975.

———. *A Guide to Religious Practice.* New York, 1979.

———. *Lexicon of Names in the Jerusalem Talmud.* Jerusalem, 1985.*

Kohen, Yeezkel. *The Conscription of Women and National Service: A Halakhic Inquiry.* Tel Aviv, 1979.*

Kook, Abraham Isaac Hakohen. *Responsa Mishpat Kohen.* Jerusalem, 1937; repr. 1966.*

———. *Letters of Rabbi Kook.* Jerusalem, 1962, 1985.*

———. *Siddur Olat Hare'iyah.* Jerusalem, 1963.*

———. *Responsa Ezrat Kohen.* Jerusalem, 1969.*

———. *Lights of Repentance.* Ed. by Yakov Halevy Filber. Jerusalem, 1977.*

———. *Ma'amrei Hare'iyah.* Jerusalem, 1984.*

Kook, Zvi Yehuda. *From the Redeeming Torah.* Jerusalem, 1983.*

Lampronti, Isaac. *Paad Yitzak.* Ed. S. Ashkenasy. Jerusalem, 1962 (first ed. 1750).*

Landau, Ezekiel. *Responsa Noda Biyehuda.* Vilna, 1899–1904.*

Landau, Samuel. *Responsa Shivat Ziyyon.* Warsaw, 1881; repr. New York, 1966*

Laniado, Samuel. *Klei Yakar.* Venice, 1656.*

Lau, Israel Meir. *Reponsa Yahel Yisrael.* Jerusalem, 1992.*

Lema, Moses. *Ḥelkat meokek.**

Lerner, Mayer. *Ḥayye Olam.**

Levi ben Ḥabib, *Responsa of the Ralba.* Lemberg, 1865.*

Levin, Yissakhar Halevy. "The Conscription of Women." *Torah and State* 5 (1953).*

Levinger, Jacob S. *Maimonides' Techniques of Codification.* Jerusalem, 1965.*

_____. *From Routine to Renewal*. Jerusalem, 1973.*

_____. *Maimonides as Philosopher and Codifier*. Jerusalem, 1989.

Lichtenstein, Hillel. *Responsa Beit Hillel*. Jerusalem, 1954.*

Lieberman, S. Zvulun. "A Sephardi Ban on Converts." *Tradition* 23, no. 2 (1988).

Lomza, Malkiel Zevi. *Responsa Divrei Malkiel*. Piotrkow, 1904.*

Luria, Solomon. *Yam shel Shelomo*. Stettin, 1861.*

Maimonides, Abraham. *Milamot Hashem*. Ed. Reuven Margoliot. Jerusalem, 1953.*

Margalioth, Ephraim Zalman. *Responsa Mateh Ephraim*. Berdaev, 1928.*

Margolioth, Moses. *Pnei Moshe* on the Jerusalem Talmud. Tel Aviv, 1949.*

Margulies, Mordecai. *Variations between Easterners and Jews of Eretz Yisrael*. Jerusalem, 1938.*

Mazikei Hadat. Ed. Abraham Schor. Jerusalem, 1920.*

Mazor Vitry. Ed. Shimon Ish-Hurwitz. Jerusalem, 1963.*

Medini, Ḥayyim Hezekiah. *Sede emed,* vol. 5. Tel Aviv, n.d.; vol. 6, Tel Aviv, 1963.*

Meir ben Baruch. *Responsa of Maharam Rothenburg*. Ed. Moshe Bloch. Budapest, 1895.*

Meir ben Gedaliah. *Responsa of the Maharam Lublin*. Warsaw, 1881.*

Meir ha-Kohen. *Hagahot Maimuniyot* on the Mishneh Torah. Included in standard edition thereof.*

Meiri, Menaḥem. *Beit ha-beirah* on Tractate Sanhedrin. Ed. Avraham Super. Jerusalem, 1965.*

Mekhilta of Rabbi Ishmael. Ed. Jacob Z. Lauterbach. Philadelphia, 1934.

Mekhilta of Rabbi Simeon bar Yohai. Ed. Yaakov Nahum Epstein and Ezra Ziyyon Melammed. Jerusalem, 1955.*

Midrash Rabbah. Ed. Moshe Aryeh Mirkin. Tel Aviv, 1957.*

Midrash Tanuma. Ed. H. Zundel. Jerusalem, 1962.*

Mielziner, Moses. *The Jewish Law of Marriage and Divorce*. New York and Cincinnati, 1901.

Miller, Joel. *Variant Customs of Jews in Babylonia and Eretz Yisrael*. Vienna, 1878; repr. Jerusalem, 1970.*

Mintzberg, Israel Zev. *Zot Ḥukkat Hatorah*. Jerusalem, 1920.*

Moellin, Jacob. *The Book of the Maharil*. Warsaw, 1874.*

Moses ben Baruch of Rothenburg. *Responsa of the Maharam of Rothenburg*. Ed. Moshe Bloch. Budapest, 1896.*

Moses ben Jacob of Coucy. *Sefer Mitzvot Gadol*. Jerusalem, 1973.*

Moses ben Nahman (Nahmanides). *Novellae*. Jerusalem, 1928.*

_____. *Nachmanides: Commentary on the Torah*. Trans. Rabbi Dr. Charles B. Chavel, Deuteronomy, New York, 1976.

_____. *Nahmanides on the Torah*. Ed. Ḥayyim Dov Chavel. Jerusalem, 1960.*

Moses Maimonides, *Anthology of Responsa by Maimonides*. Leipzig, 1859.*

———. *Mishneh Torah, a New Photostatic Edition Based on the 1580 Rome Printing.* Jerusalem, 1956.*

———. *Eight Chapters.* Jerusalem, 1962.*

———. *The Guide of the Perplexed.* Trans. Shlomo Pines. Chicago, 1963.

———. *Mishneh Torah* with standard commentaries. Jerusalem, 1963.*

———. *Responsa.* Ed. Jehoshua Blau. Jerusalem, 1986.*

———. *Sefer Hamitzvot.* Ed. H. Heller. Jerusalem, 1980.*

Movement for Progressive Judaism in Israel. "Platform of the Movement for Progressive Judaism in Israel." *Telem* 15 (1977).*

Obadiah of Bertinoro. *Commentary on the Mishnah.* Included in standard editions thereof.*

Palache, Ḥayyim. *'Einei kol ḥai.* Izmir, 1862.*

———. *Responsa Ḥayyim ve-Shalom.* Izmir, 1862–1879.*

Perla, Yeruham Fischel. *Commentary on Sefer HaMitzvot of Rabbi Sa'adya Gaon.* Warsaw, 1914.*

Pesikta Rabbati. Ed. Meir Ish-Shalom. Vienna, 1880.*

Petuchowski, Jakob Joseph. "Plural Models within Halakhah," *Judaism* 12 (1970: 77–89.

———. *Heirs of the Pharisees.* New York, 1970.

Plato. *Protagoras.* Trans. W. K. C. Guthrie. Harmondsworth, 1956.

Proceedings of the Rabbinical Assembly of America 15. New York, 1951.

Proceedings of the Rabbinical Assembly of America 32. New York, 1968.

"Protokolle der Rabbiner-Conferenz gehalten zu Philadelphia." In *Yearbook of the Central Conference of American Rabbis* 1 (1891).

Rabinowitz, Baruch. Lecture at a symposium on "Establishing the Moment of Death and Transplantations." *Assia* 1 (1979).*

Rabinowitz, L. I. "A Family That Has Been Assimilated Has Been Assimilated." *Ha'umah* 31 (1971).*

Reischer, Jacob. *Responsa Shevut Yaakov.* Lemberg, 1861.*

Responsa ha-Ribash. Vilna, 1879; repr. New York, 1954.*

Riskin, Steven. "Conversion in Jewish Law." *Tradition* 14, no. 2 (1973).

Rivkes, Moses. *Be'er Hagolah* on the *Shulḥan Arukh.* Included in standard edition thereof.*

Rosanes, Judah. *Mishneh Lamelekh* on Maimonides' *Mishneh Torah.* Included in standard edition thereof.*

Rosenzweig, Franz. "The Builders." In *On Jewish Learning.* New York, 1965.

Rothe, Meshulam. *Kol Mevasser.* Jerusalem, 1955, 1972.*

Rulings of the Supreme Court of Israel. Ofer et al. vs. the Judge Advocate General, Ayin/58/279–283, 44 (1960).*

Sa'adiah Gaon. *Sefer Hagalui.* Ed. Abraham Harkabi. St. Petersburg, 1892.*

———. *Siddur of Sa'adiah Gaon.* Jerusalem, 1970.*

Samet, Moshe. *Who Is a Jew (1958–1988).* Jerusalem 1988.*

Schechter, Yosef. *Talmudic Lexicon.* Tel Aviv, 1962.*

Schick, Berachiah. *Dat ve-Din.* Temesvár, 1904.*

Schick, Moses. *Responsa of Maharam Schick.* Lemberg, 1884.*

Schulman, Hayyim Yitzhak. *Responsa Zera Yitzak.* Kidan, 1938.*

Schwadron, Shalom Mordecai. *Responsa of the Maharsham.* Satmar, 1926; repr. New York, 1962.*

Schwartz, Yomtov Halevi. *Responsa Ma'aneh La'iggerot.* New York, 1974.*

Sefer Hainnukh. Ed. Hayyim Dov Chavel. Jerusalem, 1988.*

Sefer Halakhot Gedolot. Ed. Esriel Hildesheimer. Jerusalem, 1972–1987.*

Septuaginta. Stuttgart, 1962.

Setton, Saul David. *Responsa Dibber Shaul.* Jerusalem, 1928.*

Shabbetai Hakohen. *Siftei Kohen* on *Shulhan Arukh.* Included in standard editions thereof. *

Shapira, Hayyim Eleazar. *Minat Eleazar.* Munkács, 1907–1937.*

Sharashewsky, B. *Family Law,* 3rd ed. Jerusalem, 1984.*

Shlomo ben Yitzhak, *Rashi's Siddur.* Ed. Solomon Buber. Berlin, 1912.*

_____. *Responsa of Rashi.* Ed. S. Elfenbein. New York, 1943.*

Shloush, David Hayyim. *Bnei Ami.* Jerusalem, 1977.*

_____. *Nidei Yisrael Yekhannes.* Jerusalem, 1988.*

Siegel, Seymour. "Ethics and the Halakha." In *Conservative Judaism and Jewish Law,* ed. S. Siegel. New York, 1977.

Sifre Deuteronomy. Ed. Meir Ish-Shalom. Vienna, 1864; ed. Finkelstein. New York, 1969.*

Silva, Hezekiah da. *Peri adash.* Amsterdam, 1730; repr. Prague, 1785.*

Silver, Daniel Jeremy. *Maimonidean Criticism and the Maimonidean Controversy, 1180–1240.* Leiden, 1965.

Simeon ben Zema Duran. *Zohar Harakia.* Constantinople, 1515.*

_____. *Responsa of the Tashbetz.* Lemberg, 1891.*

Simon, Uriel. "Religion, Morality, and Politics." *Bi-tefutsot Hagolah* 18 (1977).*

Sinclair, Daniel. "Trends in Rabbinic Policy in Relation to Insincere Conversions in Post-Emancipation Responsa." *Dinnei Yisrael* 16 (1991–1992).

Sirkes, Joel. *Bayit Hadash* on the *Arba'ah Turim.* Included in standard editions thereof. *

Sofer, Moses. *Novellae on the Babylonian Talmud.* Jerusalem, 1970.*

_____. *Responsa Hatam Sofer.* Jerusalem, 1970.*

Solomon ben Simeon Duran. *Responsa of the Rashbash.* Leghorn, 1742.*

Soloveitchik, Joseph B. "A Eulogy for the Talner Rebbe." In *Shiurei Harav: A Conspectus of Public Lectures of Rabbi Joseph B. Soloveitchik,* ed. Joseph Epstein. New York, 1974.

Sperber, David. *Responsa Afarkasta de'anya.* Satmar, 1940; repr. Jerusalem, 1981.*

Steinberg, Milton. *Basic Judaism.* New York, 1947.

Strack, Hermann L. *Introduction to the Talmud and Midrash.* Philadelphia, 1932.

Strashun, Samuel. *Glosses and Novellae of the Rashash* on the Talmud. Included in standard editions thereof.*

Talmudic Encyclopedia. Jerusalem, 1975–.*

Tanna de-Vei Eliyahu. Ed. Meir Ish-Shalom. Jerusalem, 1960.*

Tchernowitz, Chaim. "On the Election of Women." *Ha'ivri* 10 (1920).*

Toledano, Jacob Moses. "Conditional Marriage and the Annulment of Marriage." In *Otzar ha-Ḥayyim,* ed. Ḥayyim Ehrenreich. Romania, 1930.*

———. *Sefer Yam Hagadol.* Cairo, 1931.*

———. *Kunteres Meshiv Nefesh.* Cairo, 1936.*

Tosefta. Ed. M. Zuckermandel. Jerusalem, 1963.*

Trachtenberg, Joshua. *Jewish Magic and Superstition.* New York, 1970.

Tractate Soferim. Ed. Michael Hagar. New York, 1937.*

Treasury of the Gaonim. Ed. Baruch M. Levin. Haifa and Jerusalem, 1928–1931.*

Twersky, Isadore. *Rabad of Posquières.* Philadelphia, 1980.

Unna, Yitzhak. *Responsa Sho'alin ve-dorshin.* Tel Aviv, 1964.*

Unterman, Isser Yehuda. *No'am* 14 (1971).*

Urbach, E. E. "'Everyone who Preserves a Single Soul': The History of a Textual Variant—The Vagaries of Censorship and the Printing Trade." In *From the World of the Sages.* Jerusalem, 1988.*

Uziel, Ben-Zion Meir Hai. *Mishpetei Uziel.* Tel Aviv and Jerusalem, 1935–1965.*

———. *Piskei Uziel.* Jerusalem, 1977.*

Vaux, Roland de. *Ancient Israel.* London, 1961.

Waldenberg, Eliezer. *Responsa Tzitz Eliezer.* Jerusalem, 1985.*

Waldman, Menahem. *Anthology of Rabbinic Opinions about the Falashas.* Nir Etzion, 1982.*

———. "Rabbinical Opinions about the Jews of Ethiopia." *Teumin* 4 (1983).*

Washofsky, Mark. "Halakhah and Ulterior Motives: Rabbinic Discretion and the Law Of Conversion." In *Conversion to Judaism in Jewish Law,* ed. Walter Jacob and Moshe Zemer. Pittsburgh and Tel Aviv, 1974.

Weinberg, Jehiel Jacob. *Responsa Seridei Esh.* Jerusalem, 1977.*

Weiser, Shimon. "Purity of Arms: An Exchange of Letters." *Niv Hamidrashiyah* 11 (1974); ibid. 13 (1978–1979): 211–212.*

Weiss, Isaac Jacob. *Responsa Minat Yitzak.* London, 1955–1980.*

Welkin, Aaron. *Responsa Zekan Aharon.* 2nd ed. New York, 1951.*

Wolowelsky, Joel B. "Modern Orthodoxy and Women's Changing Self-Perception." *Tradition* 22, no. 1 (1986).

———. *Women, Jewish Law, and Modernity.* Hoboken, New Jersey, 1997.

World Rabbinic Council on Matters of Conversion. *The Scandal of Counterfeit Conversions.* Jerusalem, 1989.*

Yad Shaul, the Shaul Weingurt Memorial Volume. Ed. I. I. Weinberg and Menahem Biberfeld. Tel Aviv, 1953.*

Yalkut Shimoni. Ed. Bezalel Landau. Jerusalem, 1960.*

Yehudai, Moshe. "The Value of Non-Jewish Life in Halakhah." Master's thesis. Jerusalem, 1983.*

Yisraeli, Shaul. In *Torah and State* 4 (1952).

_____. "The Kibya Incident in the Light of Halakhah." *Torah and State* 5–6 (19531954).*

Yitzaki, Abraham. *Responsa Zera Avraham.* Izmir, 1733.*

Yosef, Ovadia. *Responsa Yabbia Omer.* Jerusalem, 1954–1976.*

_____. *Responsa Yeavveh Da'at.* Jerusalem, 1956–.*

_____. "Returning Territories of the Land of Israel in a Situation of Danger to Life *(pikkuah nefesh).*" *Oral Law,* 1980.*

Zemer, Moshe. "Rabbi Goren Performs a Reform Conversion." *Petahim* 4, no. 14 (1970).*

_____. "Mamzerut: Halakhic Background and a Progressive Approach." *Shalhevet* 7–8 (1971): 14–18.*

_____. "Mamzerut." *Central Conference of American Rabbis Journal* 19 (1972).

_____. "To Release or Not to Release?" *Shalhevet* 9 (1972): 30–32.*

_____. "The Rabbinic Ban on Conversion in Argentina." *Judaism* 37, no. 1 (1988).

_____. "Purifying Mamzerim." *Jewish Law Annual* 10 (1992): 99–114.

Zirelson, Judah Leib. *Responsa Atzei Halevanon.* Cluj, 1922.*

_____. *Responsa Ma'arkhei Lev.* Kishinev, 1932.*

The Zohar. Trans. Maurice Simon and Paul P. Levertoff. London, 1933.

Zussmanovich, Joseph. *Responsa Zera Hayyim.* Kidan, Lithuania, 1938.*

Zvi Hirsch ben Azriel. *Beit Leem Yehudah.* Polna, 1804.*

Notes

Part I

Chapter 1

1. Cf. Tosefta Ketubot 4:9 and JT Yevamot 15:3. See chapter 6 for an analysis of *mamzerut* in Halakhah.
2. See Yitzhak D. Gilat, "Halakhah's Link to Reality," p. 106.
3. See Gilat, "The Influence of Reality on Halakhic Distinctions," p. 285. On this and other questions I am indebted to Prof. Gilat for both his writings and oral comments.
4. Ibid., p. 285.
5. Among other leniencies, the rabbis permitted buying vegetables as soon as the Sabbatical Year was over (Tosefta Shevi'it 4:17) and importing vegetables from outside the Land of Israel during the Sabbatical Year itself (JT Shevi'it 6:4). See Gilat, "The Influence."
6. See Jehiel Michel Guttmann, *Examination of the Mitzvot*, p. 35.
7. See Gilat, "Halakhah's Link to Reality," p. 104.
8. *Responsa ha-Rama*, no. 125, pp. 488–495; translation based in part on Solomon B. Freehof, *A Treasury of Responsa*, pp. 113–117. All further translated passages from this responsum are based on the same source.
9. Quoted in Moses of Coucy, *Sefer Mitzvot Gadol*, Negative Precepts nos. 71–75
10. See Isserles' gloss on *Shulḥan Arukh* O.H. 339:9, which was apparently written in the wake of the incident discussed in this responsum: "[According to Rabbenu Tam] it is permitted to conduct a wedding [on the Sabbath] if [the groom] does not have a wife and sons. Perhaps the law permits them to enter the bridal canopy *[Sefer Mitzvot Gadol]*. Even though we do not follow this ruling, in any case we may rely on it when there is urgent need, since human dignity is important. For example, sometimes when they could not reach agreement about the dowry on Friday until the night, then the ceremony is conducted on the Sabbath night itself, because all the preparations have already been made for the feast and wedding and it would shame the bride and groom if they were not married then." Years later, another chief rabbi of Cracow wrote about the aftermath of this incident: "Evidently the members of the community did not agree with his ruling and thought it should be forbidden. . . . To establish a fence around the issue the scholars and community fathers

enacted that henceforth no wedding be celebrated on Fridays here in Cracow, until the present day, and if the matter is urgent it is conducted outside the city" (Rabbi Hayyim Nathan Dembitzer, *Sefer Kelilat Yofi* 17a, note).

11. *Responsa ha-Rama*, no. 19.

12. See Joseph Albo, *Sefer Ha-Ikkarim*, III 23, p. 203.

13. See Gilat, "A Court Makes a Condition to Uproot a Torah Precept," pp. 117–132; Eliezer Berkovits, *Not in Heaven*, pp. 57ff.

14. Another example: "It is permitted to [deliver the baby of a non-Jewish woman] for payment, on account of enmity" (BT Avodah Zarah 26a and elsewhere).

15. BT Gittin 51a–b, 61a; Tosefta Gittin 3, 19.

16. See Berkovits, *Halakhah*, p. 87. See also chapter 36.

17. BT Yevamot 87b–88a. See also Berkovits, *Halakhah*, pp. 150–151. The term *living widowhood* is a literal translation of the rabbinic Hebrew *al-menut hayyah*, the status of a wife abandoned without a *get*.

18. See Ze'ev Falk, *Halakhah and Practice in the State of Israel*, p. 26.

19. See also Rashi on Yevamot 90b, s.v. *a-da'ata de-rabbanan:* "It depends on the consent of the rabbis, for what he says is 'in accordance with the religion of Moses and Israel.'"

20. Ibid., s.v. "the rabbis expropriated it." The dictum that "whatever has been expropriated by the court has been validly expropriated" means that the *beit din* has the authority to remove assets from the possession of the owner and declare them ownerless, as if the owners themselves had done so. This is how the Sages could alter the purpose of the transfer of the ring from man to woman from marriage to an ordinary gift. In other words, retroactively they were never married.

21. Ibid., s.v. *amar leh*.

22. See Berkovits, *Halakhah*, pp. 151–155; Simon Greenberg, "And He Writes Her a Bill of Divorce," pp. 83–85.

23. See Jacob Moses Toledano, *Sefer Yam Hagadol*, E.H. 74.

24. Toledano, "Conditional Marriage and the Annulment of Marriage," p. 213. On p. 224 of that article, Rabbi Toledano conjectures that this responsum, which begins with the words "Joseph said," was written by Rabbi Joseph Hayoun of Lisbon. He then uses this identification to date the manuscript. Unfortunately, Rabbi Toledano offered no proofs for this identification or dating, and I believe they need to be reconsidered. It may nevertheless be possible that there was a historical and halakhic aspect to the dispute between Joseph and Samuel ben Halat.

25. See Toledano, *Yam Hagadol*, p. 128.

26. Ibid., p. 130.

27. Ibid., p. 132.

28. See Avraham Ḥayyim Freimann, *The Order of Betrothal and Marriage,* pp. 314–320.
29. Ibid., pp. 325–327.
30. Ḥayyim Palache, *Responsa Ḥayyim ve-Shalom* 2, *E.H.* 26. See also Freimann, *The Order of Betrothal and Marriage,* pp. 327–330.
31. Freimann, pp. 330–333.
32. See Raphael Aaron Ibn-Shimon, *Nehar Mitzrayyim,* p. 172a–b. See also Berkovits, *Conditions in Marriage and Divorce,* p. 161; Freimann, *The Order of Betrothal and Marriage,* pp. 337–345.
33. See Berkovits, *Halakhah,* chapter 4.
34. Ibid., pp. 153–154

Chapter 2

1. Maimonides, *Responsa,* vol. 2, No. 211, pp. 373–375.
2. Based on Mishnah Yevamot 2:8 and BT Yevamot 24b. The marriage might confirm the rumor that he had sexual intercourse with her while she was forbidden to him as a gentile. This rabbinic ruling is concerned with what people might think and say. See Rashi, s.v. *ha-nittan.* More than three centuries later, Joseph Caro codified the punishment for this offense in much harsher tones: "If one is caught with his female slave, they take her away from him, sell her, and distribute the sale price among the poor of Israel. The man is flogged, his head is shaved, and he is placed under the ban for thirty days" (*Shulḥan Arukh, E.H.* 16:14).
3. BT Gittin 55a.
4. As we shall see, this is a composite statement, composed of two Talmudic rulings.
5. BT Berakhot 54a.
6. BT Gittin 55a.
7. Leviticus 5:23.
8. Rashi on Gittin 55a, s.v. *mi-penei takkanat ha-shavim.*
9. Maimonides, Laws of the Sabbath 20:13; Laws of Forbidden Intercourse 12:11.
10. Idem, Laws of Forbidden Intercourse 14:19.
11. Idem, Laws of Repentance 7:6.
12. A check of the sources indicates that this phrase was not used before Maimonides. See Chaim Joshua Kasowski, *Concordance to the Talmud;* idem, *Concordance to Tannaitic Literature;* Bar-Ilan University Responsa Project, 5th version, 1997.
13. Leviticus 22:8.
14. Mishnah Yoma 8:1; BT Yoma 82a.
15. Eliezer Berkovits, *Not in Heaven: The Nature and Function of Halakhah,* p. 67.
16. Berkovits, *Not in Heaven,* p. 72. Justice Haim Cohn has called my atten-

tion to Rashi's commentary on BT Yevamot 79a, s.v. *ve-al yithallel shem shamayim:* "That the nations of the world will say this people are not fit to have relations with." Adds Justice Cohn: "It follows that it is a time to make a change in Halakhah even if only to improve the image of Judaism in the world" (letter to the author, September 1985).

17. BT Ḥullin 17a: "During the seven years of conquest [of the Land] they were permitted to eat unclean things, for it is written, 'and houses full of good things'; Rabbi Jeremiah ben Abba stated in the name of Rav that even sides of bacon were permitted!" Maimonides codified this in Laws of Kings 8:1: "When the vanguard of the army conquered a foreign land and settled in it, it was permitted for them to eat unkosher meat *(nevelot u-tereifot),* pork and similar foods, if they were hungry and could find only these forbidden foods. The same applied to drinking wine used for idolatrous libations *(yein nesekh).* We have learned from oral tradition that the Biblical phrase 'houses full of good things' includes sides of bacon and similar foods."

18. Maimonides, *Sefer Hamitzvot,* positive commandment no. 221; negative commandments nos. 263, 264; Laws of Kings 8:1.

19. Maimonides, *The Guide of the Perplexed,* 2:567.

20. "A sort of sin" renders the Hebrew *ke-'ein 'aveirah,* which was Prof. Jehoshua Blau's literal translation from Maimonides' original Judeo-Arabic. I should like to thank Prof. Blau for clarifying this and other aspects of the responsum.

21. The term appears again only in the eighteenth century, in Ezekiel Landau, *Responsa Noda Bi-yehudah, E.H.* 75.

22. In his introduction to the *Mishneh Torah,* s.v. *u-devarim halalu,* Maimonides writes that he has included all Talmudic statements (especially those from the Babylonian Talmud) that are "mandatory for all Israel." See Jacob Levinger, *Maimonides' Techniques of Codification,* pp. 88–89.

23. Laws of Divorce 10:14, based on Mishnah Yevamot 2:8 and BT Yevamot 24b.

24. Maimonides, *Responsa,* 353 and 372.

25. Although Maimonides does not always distinguish between the Hebrew terms *'aveirah* and *'avon,* the latter is generally reserved for a more severe category of wrongdoing (introduction to the *Mishneh Torah,* s.v. *u-devarim halalu).* For example, he uses *'avon* to categorize shaming a person in public (Laws of Beliefs 6:8), tale-bearing (termed "a great *'avon":* ibid. 7:1), slander (ibid. 7:2), and so on.

26. Deuteronomy 7:3–4 relates the Biblical prohibition on intermarriage with the seven nations of Canaan.

27. Maimonides, Laws of Forbidden Intercourse 12:11, 13.

28. Cf. Maimonides, *Responsa,* 353 and 372.

29. Mordechai Akiba Friedman, *Jewish Polygamy in the Middle Ages*, pp. 314–319

30. Maimonides compares this action with that of Ezra the Scribe (Ezra 10:10–44). Unlike Ezra, who ordered the foreign women expelled unconditionally, Maimonides offered a choice, as we have seen.

31. I am grateful to Justice Haim Cohn for suggesting this verse (letter to the author, May 18, 1994).

32. A check of the sources indicates that this phrase was not used before Maimonides. See Kasowski, *Concordance to the Talmud;* idem, *Concordance to Tannaitic Literature;* Bar Ilan University Responsa Project, 5th version.

33. *Avot de-Rabbi Nathan* 16:10.

34. Hermann L. Strack, *Introduction to the Talmud and Midrash*, pp. 93–98; Yosef Schechter, *Talmudic Lexicon*, p. 224, s.v. *middot*. While I was writing this book, my attention was called to the fact that nothing has ever been published about "the lesser evil" as a hermeneutic principle.

35. Letter to the author, May 18, 1994.

36. Plato, *Protagoras*, 358d.

37. Aristotle, *Nicomachean Ethics* V 3, 1131^{b}20–23.

38. Marcus Tullius Cicero, *De officiis*, III, 3.

39. Isaac ben Sheshet, *Responsa of the Ribash*, no. 171.

40. David ben Zimra, *Responsa of the Radbaz*, no. 472.

41. Most recently in Ovadia Yosef, *Responsa Yehavveh Da'at*, 5:49.

Chapter 3

1. Eliezer Ben-Yehudah, *Dictionary of the Ancient and Modern Hebrew Language*, ed. N. H. Tur-Sinai, p. 7880.

2. Aaron Chorin et al., *Nogah ha-tzedek*, incorporating *Responsa Derekh ha-kodesh, Ya'ir nativ, Kin'at emet*, and additional responsa.

3. Moses Sofer, *Responsa Hatam Sofer, O.H.* 28, 148, and 181; *Y.D.* 19 and 286. Incidentally, the adage "anything new is forbidden by the Torah in every place" actually puns on the Talmudic statement that prohibits eating grain from the current barley harvest before the *omer* (the first sheaves of barley) has been offered in the Temple on the second day of Passover (BT Rosh Hashanah 30b).

4. Sofer, *Responsa Hatam Sofer, Y.D.* 19.

5. Ibid., *O.H.* 101.

6. See chapter 6.

7. See chapter 5.

8. See Milton Steinberg, *Basic Judaism*, pp. 23–30. Similarly, Louis Jacobs distinguishes between a fundamentalist view of Halakhah and a nonfundamentalist view thereof (see Jacobs, *A Tree of Life*, pp. 236–248).

9. Brief submitted by the Chief Rabbinate of Israel to the High Court of Justice on 4 Av 5744 (August 2, 1984), HCJ 47/82, p. 3.

10. See Louis B. Jacobs, "Jewish Law: A Synthesis," in Seymour Siegel, ed., *Conservative Judaism and Jewish Law*, pp. 110–120.

11. JT Pe'ah 2:10. See also Jakob J. Petuchowski, "Plural Models within Halakhah."

12. Joseph Albo, *Sefer Ha-Ikkarim—The Book of Principles* 3:23, p. 203. Albo spells out the general principles, which are the hermeneutic rules propounded by the *tanna'im* for interpreting the Torah. Albo based his tenets on rabbinic sources such as the following: "Blessed be the name of the King, the King of Kings, the Holy One Blessed Be He . . . [who] gave us the Torah in writing in allusion, arcane and enigmatic, and expounded them in the Oral Law and revealed them to Israel. What is more, the Written Law is general and the Oral Law the details; and the Oral Law expansive and the Written Law concise" (*Midrash Tanhuma*, weekly portion of Noah, §3). Compare also JT Sanhedrin 4:2; *Pesikta Rabbati*, chapter 21, 101a. For an analysis of these sources, see Moshe Ish-Horowicz, "Theodicy as Evidenced by Early Rabbinic Discussions of the Flood," pp. 28–33; idem, *Halakhah: Orthodoxy and Reform*, pp. 37–38, 56. I would like to thank Dr. Ish-Horowicz for calling my attention to these sources.

13. Jacobs, "Jewish Law," p. 118.

14. Jacobs, *Tree of Life*, pp. 239, 242.

15. Ibid., p. 245.

16. Brief submitted to the High Court of Justice, HCJ 47/82.

17. Robert Gordis, "A Dynamic Halakha," p. 267.

18. Tosefta Yevamot 1:10–11 and parallel texts. See Yitzhak D. Gilat, "On the Formation of Halakhah," pp. 465–468.

19. See Joel Miller, *Variant Customs of Jews in Babylonia and Eretz Israel*; Mordecai Margulies, *Variations between Easterners and Jews of Eretz Israel*; see also Petuchowski, "Plural Models within Halakhah."

20. See Isadore Twersky, *Rabad of Posquières*, pp. 129–197.

21. Maimonides, *Mishneh Torah*, Laws of Idolatry 9:4 (in MSS); Tosefot on Sanhedrin 63b.

22. Included in Abraham Samson ben Jacob Abraham, *Responsa Or Hayashar*, No. 24.

23. Abraham Isaac Hahoken Kook, *Letters of Rabbi Kook* 1, letter 287. See also chapter 24.

24. See Abraham Yeshayahu Karelitz, *Sefer Hazon Ish*, Laws of the Sabbatical Year, §24.4, p. 149a.

25. See letters to the Jewish Agency, dated 29 Adar I 5714 (1954) and 2 Shevat 5715 (1955), cited in Menahem Waldman, "Rabbinical Opinions about the Jews of Ethiopia," p. 324.

26. See David Ḥayyim Shloush, *Bnei Ami*, "Laws Concerning Those of Doubtful Lineage," p. 142; see also Rabbi Shloush's lenient rulings in Michael Corinaldi, *Ethiopian Jews: Identity and Tradition*, pp. 224–225. See also chapter 9.

27. Eliezer Berkovits, *Not in Heaven*, p. 19.

28. Seymour Siegel, "Ethics and the Halakha," in Siegel, ed., *Conservative Judaism and Jewish Law*, pp. 125–126.

29. Ibid., pp. 128–130.

30. See Julius Guttmann, *Religion and Science*, p. 273.

31. See Franz Rosenzweig, "The Builders," in *On Jewish Learning*, pp. 72–92. Here I have given a somewhat broad interpretation of Rosenzweig's Ramarks.

32. John Rayner, vice-president of the Leo Baeck Rabbinical College in London, in an unpublished lecture delivered on June 24, 1985.

33. See Petuchowski, *Heirs of the Pharisees*, p. 174.

34. Ibid., pp. 176–177.

35. Ibid., pp. 177–179.

36. Judah Halevi, *The Kuzari* III 5, pp. 139–140.

37. Isaac Abravanel, *Commentary on the Pentateuch*, on Deut. 25:5.

38. Cited by Isaac Heinemann, *The Rationales of the Commandments in Jewish Literature*, vol. 2, p. 182.

39. The Israel Movement for Progressive Judaism has set forth several general criteria for *mitzvot:*

    "The Movement holds that the appropriate observance of the *mitzvot* requires intention, that is, after study, comprehension, and identification, and not as a matter of rote observance. This stance and our aspiration to renew the old and sanctify the new entail a dynamic attitude toward the commandments, in accordance with the following criteria:

    1. The rationales for the commandment and how it has evolved over the generations.
    2. People's ability to sanctify their lives through this commandment.
    3. People's ability to observe the commandment in light of the conditions of the time and place.
    4. Our responsibility toward the Jewish people as a whole.
    5. The absence of a contradiction between the commandment and the dictates of conscience.

    The Movement ascribes particular importance to the revival of the commandments that deal with relations between human beings, accompanied by their development and elaboration in practice and by emphasis on their religious significance for the individual and the community. This special importance stems from the complexity of interpersonal relations in modern society and from the particular needs of Israel society:

problems of social disparities, the ingathering of the exiles, the absorption of new immigrants, and the existence of a large non-Jewish minority in the state." (*Telem* 15 [1977], pp. 1–2).

Part II
Chapter 4

1. *Yedioth Ahronoth,* April 14, 1975.
2. Letter to the editor, *Maariv,* August 11, 1975.
3. See *Talmudic Encyclopedia,* 15:615ff.
4. Cf. Maimonides, Laws of Inheritance 3:7. See also the original opinion of Don Isaac Abravanel (p. 55).
5. See Walter Jacob, ed., *American Reform Responsa,* no. 183, pp. 419–425; Roland de Vaux, *Ancient Israel,* pp. 21–22, 37–38, 166–167.
6. Pines, II 603. See also Moshe Zemer, "To Release or Not to Release?" pp. 30–32.
7. Chief Rabbinate Council, "Permanent Regulations Relating to Personal Status in Israel." See B. Sharashewsky, *Family Law,* p. 570.
8. See Eliezer Berkovits, *Halakhah: Its Authority and Role,* pp. 143–149.
9. Maimonides accepts *ḥalitzah* by deception only in the present case; with regard to all others, he rules that "*ḥalitzah* by deception is invalid." See Laws of Yibbum and *ḥalitzah* 4:24. He also maintains that the precept of *yibbum* takes precedence over that of *ḥalitzah* (ibid., 1:2) and is opposed to coerced *ḥalitzah.* On the other hand, Rabbi Simeon ben Zemah Duran (the Tashbetz, 1361–1444), ruled that "in the case of *ḥalitzah* he is compelled even *a priori*" and cites a ruling by Rabbenu Asher (the Rosh), who wrote that "if we can deceive him into performing *ḥalitzah,* we deceive him." See *Responsa of the Tashbetz,* part 2, no. 180.
10. See Solomon ben Abraham Adret, *Responsa of the Rashba,* part 1, no. 1247.
11. Moses Galante, *Responsa,* no. 80, pp. 45a–46a.
12. *Shulḥan Arukh, E.H.* 165:2, gloss; see also *Responsa of the Rashba,* part 1, no. 1247.
13. *Shulḥan Arukh, E.H.* 157:2, gloss.
14. See Isaac Klein, "The Problem of *Chalitzah* Today," pp. 146–155. For a legal analysis, see Haim Cohn, "Faithful Exegesis—in Both Senses," pp. 42–48.
15. See Isaac Lampronti, *Paḥad Yitzḥak,* part 1, s.v. "brother," col. 417, no. 5.
16. See Ḥayyim David Halevy, *Responsa 'Aseh Lekha Rav* 1, no. 54.

17. See "Protokolle der Rabbiner-Conferenz gehalten zu Philadelphia," p. 120; Moses Mielziner, *The Jewish Law of Marriage and Divorce*, p. 58.

18. See "Verhandlunger der zweiten israelitischen Synode zu Augsburg," pp. 138–155, quoted in ibid., p. 58, and in *Yearbook of the Central Conference of American Rabbis* 1, p. 113. A similar resolution was passed by a conference held in 1869 in Leipzig (ibid., pp. 106–107).

19. See Klein, "The Problem of *Chalitzah* Today," pp. 146–150; Isaac Klein, *Responsa and Halakhic Studies,* pp. 13–21.

20. Ibid., pp. 153–154.

21. Ibid., pp. 146–150.

22. Ibid., pp. 152–153.

23. "Memorandum on Waiving the Requirements of Formal *halitzah* to the Committee on Jewish Law and Standards of the Rabbinical Assembly" (June 1970). Rabbi Sigal based his ruling on the inability of contemporary rabbinical courts to compel *halitzah* and the fact that today a widow may inherit her husband's estate. The "halakhic powers" vested in modern rabbis may be derived from the Sages' rulings about their authority to declare property ownerless, the dignity of human creatures, and the rabbis' power to "uproot a matter from the Torah." Note that Rabbi Sigal would retain the ceremony of *halitzah* for couples who request it, but ignore it for those not interested in going through this rite of release. He did not offer any precedent or halakhic basis for his "application of the rabbi's halakhic justification to waive the requirement of *halitzah*."

Chapter 5

1. Leviticus 21:7; BT Kiddushin 78a; Maimonides, Laws of Forbidden Intercourse 17:1; *Tur* and *Shulḥan Arukh, E.H.* 6:11.

2. In the Babylonian Talmud alone there are some ninety references to disqualified priests in six tractates. See Chaim Joshua Kasowski, *Lexicon of Talmudic Language* 14, pp. 464–465.

3. *Sefer Hahinnukh,* ed. Ḥayyim D. Chavel, precept 289, p. 373. The same reason is given for the prohibition of a *halalah* to a *kohen,* precept 290, p. 374. (In other editions of *Sefer Hahinnukh* these are precepts 266 and 267.)

4. Ibid., precept 291 [268], p. 376.

5. See Jacob Levinger, *From Routine to Renewal,* "The Renewal of the Sacrificial Service in This Age," pp. 112–137.

6. Rabbi Isaac Klein argued that the descendants of a *kohen* who married a divorcée must continue to observe all the special customs pertaining to kohanim "to promote peace." See Isaac Klein, *A Guide to Religious Practice,* p. 388.

7. Presumption (Hebrew *hazakkah*) is a status that remains valid until some

factor of weightier consequence comes and disestablishes it. See Yosef Shechter, *Talmudic Lexicon*, p. 131. *Ḥazakkah* provides the basis not only for the application of any Torah or rabbinic prohibition to a person presumed to have a certain status, but also for the imposition of severe punishments (see BT Kiddushin 80a; *Tur* and *Shulḥan Arukh, E.H.* 19:1). Thus, the prohibitions that apply to a presumed *kohen* according to the codified Halakhah are not canceled by the fact that he is not a certain *kohen*, but through the application of the aforementioned principle that halakhah is inherently moral (see above) and other principles.

8. See Israel Bettan, "Marriage of a Cohen to a Divorcée," pp. 84–86.

9. Isaac bar Sheshet, *Responsa of the Ribash*, No. 94.

10. Solomon Luria, *Yam shel Shlomo* on Tractate Baba Kama, 5, §35.

11. Abraham Gumbiner, *Magen Avraham* on the *Shulḥan Arukh, O.H.*, Laws of Passover 457:9.

12. Jacob Emden, *Responsa of the Ya'avetz*, part 1, no. 155.

13. Rabbi Moses Lema of Brisk (d. 1658) wrote in his commentary on the *Shulḥan Arukh* that "even if he found some untoward thing in her, such as someone gave testimony about her that obligates him to divorce her, he should not say 'I believe him' and divorce her at once, but should act with deliberation . . ." (*Ḥelkat Meḥokek, E.H.* 119:102).

14. Gershom ben Judah, *Responsa of Rabbenu Gershom Me'or Ha-golah*, regulation 4, p. 19.

15. Incidentally, this fact should inspire all rabbis to conduct an in-depth interview with couples before marriage and try to determine whether they are suited to each other and are sufficiently mature for marriage, and, if not, to refer them for counseling. Unfortunately, this is not the custom in Israel.

16. On the right to marry, see Haim H. Cohn, *Human Rights in Jewish Law*, chapter 8: "The Right to Marry and Raise a Family," pp. 80–86.

17. Tosefot on Yevamot 61a, s.v. *zonah*.

18. Yomtov ben Abraham Ishbili, *Novellae of the Ritba*: "It teaches us that she is included in the category of harlot not because she had intercourse but because the word *harlot* applies to any woman who is born a gentile" (on BT Kiddushin 78a).

19. Yehoshua Heller-Feldman, "Conversion and Converts," p. 3.

20. See Tuvia Friedman, "Conversion in Israeli Law," pp. 4–8.

21. Maimonides, *Responsa*, vol. 2, no. 293.

22. Ben-Zion Meir Hai Uziel, *Mishpetei Uziel*, part 1, *Y.D.* 14 (and see chapter 8). For other rulings that permit conversion for the sake of marriage, see Friedman, "Conversion in Israeli Law."

23. David Zevi Hoffmann, *Responsa Melammed Le-ho'il*, part 3, *E.H.*, no. 8. See J. David Bleich, "The Conversion Crisis," pp. 270–324. See also Bleich's letter in *Tradition* 12, nos. 3-4, pp. 163–167.

24. See David Ellenson, "The Development of Orthodox Attitudes to Conversion in the Modern Period," pp. 66–69; Ellenson and Robert N. Levine, "Jewish Tradition, Contemporary Sensibilities, and Halakhah: A Responsum by Rabbi David Zvi Hoffmann."

25. Isaac Klein maintains that in the present case the suggestion that after her conversion the woman continue to live with her husband without having a Jewish wedding is a further profanation of the Divine Name. See Isaac Klein, "The Marriage of a Kohen and a Giyoret," p. 222. In 1970, Rabbi Shlomo Goren, then the chief chaplain of the Israel Defense Forces, convened a religious court that converted Dr. Helen Seidman of Kibbutz Nahal Oz, even though it was known that her husband, Benjamin Seidman, was a *kohen*. Rabbi Goren never published his reasons for this conversion, which might have clarified whether he had indeed relied on Rabbi Hoffmann's lenient ruling (see chapter 8).

26. Judah Leib Zirelson, *Responsa Ma'arkhei Lev, E.H.*, no. 72.

27. Rabbi Zirelson found his authority in the Tosefot on Yevamot 61a, s.v. *zonah,* and in various commentators on Maimonides, Laws of Forbidden Intercourse 18:3.

28. Bettan, "Marriage of a Cohen to a Divorcée," pp. 85–86; Walter Jacob, ed., *American Reform Responsa,* pp. 435–436; *Proceedings of the Rabbinical Assembly of America* 32, p. 223.

29. See Jacob Moses Toledano, *Otzar ha-Ḥayyim,* p. 209.

30. See Ze'ev Falk, *Halakhah and Practice in the State of Israel,* p. 60.

31. The Knesset has passed several laws that explicitly pertain to common-law wives, including the Tenants' Protection Law (consolidated version) 5732–1972, title 6, §§20–25; the Inheritance Law 5725–1965, §55; and the State Service Law (Pensions) (consolidated version) 5730-1970.

32. Avraham Hayyim Freiman, *The Order of Betrothal and Marriage,* p. 397. Freiman reviews several rabbinic suggestions concerning concubinage; see pp. 395–396.

Chapter 6

1. *Ha'aretz,* April 7, 1971.

2. *Maariv,* April 9, 1971.

3. *Septuaginta,* vol. 1, p. 327; vol. 2, p. 554.

4. *Moses ben Nahman (Nachmanides): Commentary on the Torah,* Deuteronomy, p. 279.

5. Although these unions are forbidden *ab initio* (at the outset or before the fact), they are valid *post factum.*

6. Sixteen forbidden marriages are enumerated the Torah, to which the Sages added another ten, for a total of twenty-six (BT Yevamot 21a; Maimonides, Laws of Marital Relations 1, 6; *Shulḥan Arukh, E.H.* 15:1–26).

7. See E. G. Ellinson, *Marriages Not According to the Rites of Moses and Israel,* chapter 10; for an update on the situation see Z. Shohat, *Ha'aretz,* May 13, 1991: "Because of the problematic nature of personal-status law in Israel, many of the recent immigrants from the Soviet Union face problems of bigamy, halakhic illegitimacy, and living widowhood *(aginut)*." Others hold that usually there was no intent of forming a binding marriage through sexual intercourse, so they were never formally married in the eyes of Halakhah. See chapter 5, note 27.

8. The true names, file numbers, and minutes of the various rabbinic courts that dealt with the case are in my possession. For obvious reasons they are not divulged here.

9. According to Halakhah, an undoubted *mamzer* may marry another undoubted *mamzer,* but a doubtful *mamzer* may not marry anyone.

10. "Maimonides did not refrain from de-emphasizing laws of Talmudic origin, laws that have a severe halakhic nature, simply because they were based on scientific and philosophic premises with which he did not agree" (Jacob Levinger, *Methods of Halakhic Thought in Maimonides,* p. 121).

11. *Tur E.H.* 4; *Sefer Halakhot Gedolot,* end of the Laws of Marriage Contracts, p. 295.

12. Tosefot on Kiddushin 73a, s.v. *mai ika;* Rabbenu Asher, Kiddushin 4.7. See also *Sefer Halakhot Gedolot,* end of Laws of Divorce, p. 184. In note 66 there, the editor writes: "Not found in the extant text of the Jerusalem Talmud." A survey of Moshe Kasowski, *Lexicon of Talmudic Language* and *Lexicon of Names in the Jerusalem Talmud,* confirms that this legend is not found in any known manuscript of the Jerusalem Talmud.

13. There is a variation on this idea in BT Yevamot 78b, which distinguishes between a completely unknown *mamzer* who does not survive infancy and a "somewhat known" *mamzer,* whose taint does not continue past three generations.

14. See L. I. Rabinowitz, "A Family That Has Been Assimilated Has Been Assimilated," pp. 41–45. Rumor has it that before the Second World War certain Orthodox rabbis used to drop broad hints to known *mamzerim* that they would do well to emigrate to a community where they were not known and marry there. There is no confirmation of these rumors; what is more, the whole idea poses some difficulty, because the *mamzer* knows that he is not allowed to marry and the ban exists for him. In any case, there are almost no cases of halakhic illegitimacy among the Orthodox in the United States, because rabbis there intentionally avoid investigating the matter. See Louis B. Jacobs, *Tree of Life,* p. 275.

15. Shalom Mordecai Schwadron, *Responsa of the Maharsham,* 1:9. For an explanation of the legal fiction involved, see J. David Bleich, *Contemporary Halakhic Problems,* pp. 1, 162ff. A similar incident may provide the basis

for S. J. Agnon's novella "And the Crooked Shall Be Made Straight," in *Elu va'Elu* (Tel Aviv, 1960), pp. 61–127.

16. Rabbi Ḥazzan based his ruling on the testimony gathered by Rabbi Ventura in 1830 concerning the circumstances of Israel's conception and on Rabbi Amarillo's codicil to Israel and Simha's *ketubah*, which he deemed conclusive proof that the latter adjudged Israel to be an undoubted *mamzer*. azzan also found support in the succession of rabbis in Corfu and elsewhere who had affirmed the *mamzerut* of subsequent generations of the family. See Elijah Ḥazzan, *Responsa Ta'alumot Lev,* vol. 2, no. 6; vol. 3, nos. 1–5.

16 . Rabbi Ḥazzan and his party continued to disagree vigorously. They rejoined that even if Israel were cleared of his taint, his descendants were still *mamzerim,* because his wife Simha had herself been a *mamzeret*. Rabbi Amarillo, who had believed Israel to be an undoubted *mamzer,* would have married her only to a *mamzeret* or convert. Since Simha was not the latter, she must have been the former. This, they opined, was the meaning of the rabbi's appendix to their *ketubah,* in which both Israel and Simha were described as "children of fornication" whose "mother committed adultery" (Ḥazzan, *Ta'alumot Lev,* vol. 3, no. 1).

17. The Jerusalem party countered that Simha's mother had never been accused of adultery. Nor could Rabbi Amarillo have believed that Simha was a *mamzeret,* since he inscribed her name in the *ketubah* as "Simha bat Shabbetai Judah"—the daughter of her mother's husband. Rabbi Elyashar explained the uncomplimentary appendix to the *ketubah* as stemming from contemporary doubts about Simha's mother's morals. One may be suspicious of the status of the children of such a woman, in a general way, but not in the matter of *mamzerut*.

18. Jacob Saul Elyashar, *Responsa Olat Ish, E.H.,* Laws of Personal Status, 1a–6b.

19. Ibid., 6a–6b.

20. See Julian H. Barth and Moshe Zemer, "The Congenital Eunich, a Medical-Halakhic Study," in which a medical and halakhic basis for Rabbi Palache's ruling is established.

21. Dr. Julian H. Barth of the University of Leeds Old Medical School believes that he may not have been a eunuch. Rather, Abraham could have been a biological male with a hormone disorder that resulted in a malformation of his genitals.

22. Ḥayyim Palache, *'Einei kol ḥai,* 135a ff.; Jacob Saul Elyashar, *Responsa Simḥah La'ish,* no. 3; Shalom Moshe Hai Gagin, *Responsa Yisma Lev,* no. 13.

23. Jacob Moses Moshe Toledano, *Kunteres Meshiv Nefesh,* pp. 1–41.

24. Yitzak Isaac Halevy Herzog, *Responsa Heikhal Yitzḥak,* vol. 2, *E.H.,* nos. 17–19.

25. The witnesses to the marriage are a necessary condition and must be specifically designated as such by the groom: "In a marriage it is the witnesses who validate the act. Accordingly if there are both valid and invalid witnesses present, or relatives, and witnesses to the marriage were not specifically designated, the testimony of all of them is nullified and the woman has not been married" (Herzog, *Responsa Heikhal Yitzḥak,* §19). Rabbi Herzog relies on the statement by Rabbi Yomtov ben Abraham Ishbili (the Ritba), *Novellae,* on Kiddushin 43a and Gittin 18b, in the name of Rabbi Solomon ben Abraham Adret (the Rashba).

26. See Ellinson, *Marriages,* p. 179. Ellinson cites, among others, rulings by Rabbi Joseph Rosen of Dvinsk, Rabbi Joseph Elijah Henkin, and Rabbi Isser Yehuda Unterman.

27. Joseph Zussmanovich, *Responsa Zera Hayyim,* no. 11, pp. 308–309; included in Ḥayyim Yitzḥak Schulman, *Responsa Zera Yitzhak.*

28. Abraham Isaac Hakohen Kook, *Responsa Ezrat Kohen,* Laws of Marriage, nos. 38–39. See also Ellenson, *Marriages,* p. 181.

29. Shlomo Goren, *Halakhic Opinion on Personal Status;* idem, *Halakhic Ruling Concerning the Brother and Sister.* See also pp. 87–88.

30. Rabbi Meir disagrees. See also Tosefta Kiddushin 5:4 and the continuation of the debate among *amoraim* in JT Kiddushin 3:13.

31. The text of *al hanissim,* the special addition to the Amidah and Grace after Meals for Hanukkah and Purim, as found in the Siddur of Sa'adiah Gaon, p. 257. See M. Zemer, "Purifying Mamzerim." I wish to thank the trustees of Boston University for permission to use this material. See also idem, "Mamzerut: Halakhic Background and a Progressive Approach"; idem, "Mamzerut," pp. 33–37.

32. On March 27, 1991, the Tel Aviv District Rabbinical Court confirmed its ruling that the seven children of the father were *mamzerim,* because their mother had previously been married to and divorced from their father's brother and their relationship was consequently incestuous. The father claimed that he was an adopted child and had no genetic relationship to his "brother" or adoptive parents. To prove his case, the family asked Prof. Ephraim Gazit of the Sheba Medical Center to perform a DNA analysis, which showed conclusively that there was no biological connection between the "brothers" or between the father and his adoptive parents. But the court ruled, as stated, against the professor's testimony. See Y. Yarkoni, *Yedioth Ahronoth,* April 9, 1991, p. 25.

Chapter 7

1. Several different terms are commonly used in Hebrew to refer to this phenomenon, but what they have in common is that those covered cannot marry for some halakhic reason. The rabbinate maintains that there is no Jew who absolutely cannot marry, since a *kohen* can, for example, marry a woman who has never been married or a widow, and a *mamzer* can marry a convert. They are forbidden to marry only, perhaps, the person they love.

2. *Maariv,* July 27, 1971.

3. *Maariv,* August 3, 1971.

4. In December 1995, the incumbent minister of religious affairs, Shimon Shetreet, reported that there were only 2500 names left on the list (down from 5,200 when he first saw it), including *mamzerim*, adulteresses, and non-Jews who had used forged documents to be registered as Jews in Israel. In June of that year, there were public announcements concerning a reform in the methods whereby names would henceforth be added to the list, including a right of appeal. Little or nothing has been heard of this revolution since. (See the *Israel Yearbook and Almanac 1996,* pp. 263–264.)

5. A nazirite is a person who vows to abstain from partaking of grapes and their products, cutting his or her hair, and coming into contact with a corpse, for a specific period of time. See Numbers, chapter 6, and the Talmudic tractate Nazir.

6. The State Comptroller has condemned this phenomenon: "Information about the children of a person whose personal status was determined by a ruling by a rabbinic court must not be collected and archived. The children were not parties to the case, their arguments were not heard, and their legal status is not a matter for a request to register for marriage. Nor should information be gathered about persons who did not apply to register for marriage. Thus, for example, records must not be kept on the basis of information received from the Foreign Ministry or the Jewish Agency or any other body. Sometimes this information is not reliable. The person to whom it relates does not know about it and cannot refute it. The gathering of such information would turn the Ministry of Religious Affairs into a population registry in miniature. There is no legal basis for this and it offends the individual's right of privacy" (State Comptroller, *Annual Report No. 40,* p. 287).

Part III

1. Isaac Abravanel, *Commentary on the Pentateuch,* on Exod. 23:9, p. 216.
2. See Moshe Samet, *Who Is a Jew (1958–1988).*

Chapter 8

1. Dr. Seidman, who was a professor of genetics in Washington, D.C., came to Israel in the early 1960s. In Israel she met Benny Seidman, a member of kibbutz Naḥal Oz; they were married in a civil ceremony and settled there.
2. J. David Bleich, "The Conversion Crisis: A Halakhic Analysis," pp. 20 and 27.
3. Ibid., p. 34. See also Isser Yehuda Unterman, *No'am* 14, p. 5.
4. See *Oral Law* 13 (Jerusalem, 1971), p. 16.
5. Steven Riskin, "Conversion in Jewish Law," pp. 29–42.
6. See Meir Arik, *Responsa Imrei Yosher,* vol. 1, no. 176.
7. See Shlomo Goren, *Halakhic Ruling Concerning the Brother and Sister,* pp. 137ff. See also pp. 87–88.
8. In other words, a clear and reliable estimate.
9. See Riskin, "Conversion," p. 40, note. 1. Rabbi Goren never published a responsum or halakhic explanation justifying his conversion of Dr. Seidman.
10. See Moshe Feinstein, *Iggerot Moshe, Y.D.* 1, no. 157; *E.H.* 3, no. 4.
11. See *Oral Law,* p. 29.
12. On the other hand, Rabbi Yosef rejects the halakhic conversion of a person who lives on a secular kibbutz.
13. See David Zevi Hoffmann, *Responsa Melammed Le-ho'il,* vol. 2, *Y.D.* 87; emphasis mine.
14. Ibid. The remarks by Hoffmann are based on Maimonides, Laws of Forbidden Intercourse 14:2 See also p. 138.
15. Rabbi Hoffmann used an interesting syllogism to arrive at this conclusion. Throughout the history of halakhic legislation, the rule has been that there can be no valid conversion, even *post factum,* without acceptance of the commandments. Rabbi Hoffmann noted that informing the candidate about the commandments is not a prerequisite for conversion—an individual is deemed *(post factum)* to have converted even if the *beit din* did not acquaint him with the precepts of Judaism. As a result, someone who was circumcised and immersed without accepting the commandments can be accepted *post factum* as a convert. Rabbi Hoffmann's syllogism seems to run as follows:

Major premise: Awareness of the commandments is not a necessary condition for conversion.

Minor premise: Awareness of the commandments is a necessary condition for accepting the commandments.

Conclusion: Therefore, accepting the commandments is not a necessary condition for conversion.

In abstract terms, B is not a necessary condition for A; B is a necessary condition for C; therefore, C is not a necessary condition for A (where A is *post factum* conversion, B is awareness of the commandments, and C is acceptance of the commandments). One could argue that the minor premise in this syllogism (B is a necessary condition for C) is not self-evident.

Apparently Rabbi Hoffmann never had time to consider this case further, and his final opinion was never made clear. According to Prof. Saul Kripke of Columbia University, from the strictly logical perspective Rabbi Hoffmann's syllogism is indeed valid. See David Ellenson, *Tradition in Transition*, pp. 76–77.

16. See Hoffmann, *Reponsa Melammed Le-ho'il,* vol. 2, *Y.D.* §87; emphasis mine.

17. Rabbi Goren could rely on a series of lenient halakhic rulings about the acceptance of converts who seem to be converting not out of sincere religious belief but with some other end in mind. Hillel the Elder converted a non-Jew who explicitly stated that he wanted to convert "on condition that I become High Priest" (BT Shabbat 31a). Rabbi Ḥiyya accepted a non-Jewish woman who wanted to marry one of his students (BT Menaot 44a). The tosafists explain that "Hillel was confident that in the end he would have [converted] for the sake of Heaven," and the same was true of Rabbi Ḥiyya (Tosefot on Yevamot 24b). About such cases, Rabbi Joseph Caro noted that "from here we learn that everything depends on the judgment of the *beit din*" (*Beit Yosef, Y.D.* 268; see also Joshua Falk, *Derishah u-Perishah* ad loc.; Shabbetai Hakohen, *Siftei Kohen,* ad loc., §12). Compare the following halakhic rulings, all of which evince a favorable attitude toward conversion for the purpose of marriage: Hoffmann, *Responsa Melammed Le-ho'il, Y.D.* §83; Jehiel Jacob Weinberg, *Responsa Seridei Esh,* vol. 3, no. 50; Meir Simah Hakohen, *Responsa Or Sameah, no. 32; Yitzhak Isaac Halevy Herzog, Responsa Heikhal Yitzhak, E.H.,* no. 20; Ben-Zion Meir Hai Uziel, *Responsa Mishpetei Uziel,* vol. 1, *Y.D.* 14; Yitzhak Unna, *Responsa Sho'alin ve-dorshin,* vol. 1, *Y.D.* 45.

18. See "Protokolle der Rabbiner-Conferenz gehalten zu Philadelphia," p. 27, in Moses Mielziner, *The Jewish Law of Marriage and Divorce,* p. 59.

19. See Hoffmann, *Responsa Melammed Le-ho'il* 3, *E.H.,* no. 8.

20. See Judah Leib Zirelson, *Responsa Ma'arkhei Lev, E.H.,* no. 72. See chapter 5.

21. See the supplement to *Hazofeh* (June 19, 1970), p. 3, where A. Uri writes: "The question of whether she may marry a *kohen* was also before the religious court, which found interpretations by later authorities who were lenient on this matter and permitted marriage between a female proselyte and a *kohen.*" As stated, Rabbi Goren never told anyone what precedents he relied on and never provided grounds for any aspect of Dr. Seidman's conversion.

22. Riskin, "Conversion," p. 42, note 53.

23. See Hoffmann, *Responsa Melammed Le-ho'il, Y.D.,* no. 83.

24. Ibid.

25. See Feinstein, *Iggerot Moshe, Y.D.* 3, no. 105.

26. Ibid.

27. A third possibility is that Rabbi Goren and the religious establishment did not recognize the competence of the Progressive *beit din* and the fitness of its members. To this we can rejoin that—as we have seen—all conversions are valid *post factum,* whatever the identity of the members of the *beit din.*

28. These include Prof. Mark Washofsky, "Halakhah and Ulterior Motives: Rabbinic Discretion and the Law of Conversion"; Daniel Sinclair, "Trends in Rabbinic Policy in Relation to Insincere Conversions in Post-Emancipation Responsa." In fact, however, Maimonides' responsum deals not with conversion but with manumission. The former required circumcision, immersion, and accepting the yoke of the commandments in the presence of a competent *beit din.* Manumission required only that the owner free the slave. Conversion could be a protracted process. The *beit din* might or might not be helpful. Manumission was instantaneous. Furthermore, Maimonides made no reference to the issue of conversion in his responsum. Finally, Maimonides instructed the *beit din* in the young man's community to compel him to free his slave, but he said absolutely nothing about her being converted by this *beit din,* which would be expected if this were his understanding of his responsum. See chapter 2.

29. The responsum first resurfaced in *Melekhet Shlomo,* the comprehensive commentary on the Mishnah by Rabbi Solomon Adani (1567–1625). In the final edition of his work, written in 1621–1624, Adani refers to the responsum in his commentary on the mishnaic passage on which Maimonides based his ruling, in the *Mishneh Torah,* that a female slave may not marry her former master and suspected lover (*Melekhet Shlomo on the Mishnah,* on Mishnah Yevamot 2:8, s.v. *hanittan al hashifhah.*)

30. This responsum is found in the volume by his father, Ḥayyim Palache,

Hayyim ve-Shalom, E.H. 2, no. 108. The elder Rabbi Palache added a short imprimatur praising his son's responsum.

31. Laws of Divorce 10:14.

32. Among those who quoted Maimonides' decision in their responsa on intermarriage and conversion were Elijah Hazzan, *Responsa Ta'alumot Lev* 28; Meir Simhah Hakohen, *Responsa Or Sameah* 32; Hayyim Fischel Epstein, *Teshuvah Sheleimah, E.H.* 10; Shalom Mordecai Schwadron, *Responsa of the Maharsham,* vol. 6, no. 109; Hayyim Ozer Grodzinsky, *Ahiezer* 26; Ben-Zion Meir Yai Uziel, *Piskei Uziel,* nos. 59, 60, 63; Jehiel Jacob Weinberg, *Responsa Seridei Esh* 3:3; and Moshe ben Shalom Hakohen, *Ve-heishiv Moshe* 51.

33. Uziel, *Piskei Uziel* 63.

34. See Zemer, "Rabbi Goren Performs a Reform Conversion," pp. 39–41.

35. See Yehezkel Abramsky et al., *The Battle to Save the Rabbinate in Israel and the Danger Posed by the Candidacy of Rabbi Shlomo Goren,* pp. 16–18.

36. In 1989, the World Rabbinic Council on Matters of Conversion published a book entitled *The Scandal of Counterfeit Conversions,* which denounced the leniencies practiced by conversion tribunals in Israel and elsewhere. The moving force behind this council was Rabbi Haim Kreiswirth, president of the *beit din* of Antwerp and head of the Merkaz Hatorah yeshiva in that city. This volume, too, reprints my article on Rabbi Goren in full (pp. 60–64).

Chapter 9

1. Maimonides, *Responsa,* vol. 2, no. 448.

2. Some of the following rulings and statements refer to those who have been converted, while others refer to those who are in the process of conversion or wish to convert. See also the rulings of Hillel and Rabbi Hiyya, cited below.

3. BT Yevamot 24b.

4. Solomon ben Simeon Duran, *Responsa of the Rashbash,* no. 368.

5. Tosefot on Yevamot 24b, s.v. *lo bi-ymei David.*

6. BT Shabbat 31a.

7. BT Menaot 44a.

8. Joseph Caro, *Beit Yosef* on *Tur Yoreh De'ah* 268; cf. Shabbetai Hakohen, *Siftei Kohen* ad loc.

9. Modern commentators believe that the disease referred to is psoriasis, which is not dangerous but is extremely annoying and hard to cure. See *Hebrew Encyclopedia,* vol. 26, col. 766–767.

10. Tosefot on Yevamot 109b, s.v. *ra'ah.*

11. Tosefot on Kiddushin 70b, s.v. *kashim.* According to another passage in

the Gemara (BT Baba Metzia 59b), there are thirty-six or forty-six such injunctions.

12. *Mekhilta of Rabbi Ishmael,* Tractate *Nezikin,* chapter 18, pp. 137–138. Cf. note 1.

13. Maimonides, *The Book of the Commandments,* positive commandment no. 3. In *Sefer Hamitzvot.*

14. *Sifre Deuteronomy,* § 32.

15. Yeruham Fischel Perla, *Commentary on Sefer HaMitzvot of Rabbi Sa'adya Gaon,* positive commandment no. 19, p. 295. See also *Talmudic Encyclopedia,* vol. 1, col. 205, and vol. 6, col. 426.

16. Isaac ben Reuben of Barcelona, *Sefer Derekh Mitzvotekha (Azharot),* p. 16.

17. Simeon ben Zema Duran, *Zohar Harakia,* positive commandment no. 40.

18. The number of 613 *mitzvot* is stipulated in the Talmud (BT Makkot 23b). The methodology used to identify them in the text of the Torah, and the resulting specific enumerations, vary from commentator to commentator. Maimonides' list, for example, elicited vigorous criticism and a counter-list by Nahmanides.

19. Saul David Setton, *Responsa Dibber Shaul, Y.D.,* no. 3.

20. See Moshe Zemer, "The Rabbinic Ban on Conversion in Argentina," pp. 84–96.

21. Setton, *Dibber Shaul,* no. 2, which is identical with Aaron Halevi Goldman, *Responsa Divrei Aharon, Y.D.,* no. 40.

22. Ibid., no. 35.

23. *Shulḥan Arukh, Y.D.* 268:2; *Siftei Kohen* ad loc., §3, based on BT Yevamot 47a.

24. Goldman, *Responsa Divrei Aharon,* no. 35.

25. See S. Zvulun Lieberman, "A Sephardi Ban on Converts," pp. 22–25. The last proclamation, entitled "Reaffirming Our Tradition," was signed by the rabbis and presidents of the congregations of the Syrian and Near Eastern Jewish Communities of Greater New York and New Jersey at a special convocation convened for this purpose on June 3, 1984.

26. Mordecai Jacob Breisch, *Responsa Ḥelkat Ya'akov,* vol. 1, *Y.D.* 13.

27. Ibid., no. 14. See J. David Bleich, "The Conversion Crisis," pp. 282–283.

28. David Ellenson, *Tradition in Transition,* pp. 92–93.

29. Ibid., chapters 1-8; idem, *Rabbi Esriel Hildesheimer and the Creation of a Modern Jewish Orthodoxy.*

30. Maimonides, *Responsa,* vol. 2, no. 211. See chapter 2.

31. Herzog's meaning is that his authority to render this lenient decision is anchored in the ruling by Joseph Caro that "everything depends upon the discretion of the *beit din*" (see above, note 8, and chapter 8, note 17).

32. Yitzhak Isaac Herzog, *Responsa Heikhal Yitzhak,* vol. 1, *E.H.* 20:1, pp. 104–105.
33. Ibid., §2, p. 106.
34. Ibid., §21, pp. 108-109.
35. Ibid., §2, p. 109: Herzog repeated his anxiety about the validity of conversions in his day, in a manner very similar to that whenever he rendered a lenient ruling on the subject, and appeared to feel constrained to qualify that leniency with variations on the following caveat:

    > You should know that even though the law from the time of the Mishnaic sages is that *post factum* they are all converts (even if they did not accept the commandments), I have a very serious suspicion regarding the situation today. In the past in Israel, the violator of Jewish law was despised and persecuted by his people; therefore when a gentile came to accept Judaism, even though the primary reason that motivated him was marriage, he knew that his situation would be very difficult in Jewish society if he did not behave in accordance with the Torah. This is not the case in our day when so many are free [i.e., secular]; not only do they not have any difficulty because of this, but they stand at the head of our people and communities. Therefore, we should be suspicious whether they really accept the mitzvot, or whether for some reason, they promise with their mouth but not with their heart.

36. Jehiel Jacob Weinberg, *Responsa Seridei Esh,* vol. 3, no. 50.
37. Ben-Zion Meir Hai Uziel, *Responsa Mishpetei Uziel,* vol. 1, *Y.D.* 14.
38. Elijah Guttmacher, *Responsa Aderet Eliyahu, Y.D.* 87.
39. Maimonides, *Responsa,* vol. 2, no. 448.

Chapter 10

1. See Michael Corinaldi, *Ethiopian Jews: Identity and Tradition,* appendix 9, pp. 262–263.
2. David ben Zimra, *Responsa of the Radbaz,* vol. 4, §1290 (219).
3. Ibid., vol. 7, §5.
4. Ibid.
5. Letter to Solomon Judah Leib Rappoport, dated March 23, 1864, in Esriel Hildesheimer, *Letters,* p. 32.
6. *Hamagid,* no. 47 (December 7, 1864), p. 373.
7. Manifesto dated 3 Kislev 5682 (1921), cited by Corinaldi, *Ethiopian Jews,* p. 170. See also Menahem Waldman, *Anthology of Rabbinic Opinions about the Falashas,* pp. 36–37.
8. Letter to the Jewish Agency, dated 29 Adar I 5714 (1954), cited in Menahem Waldman, "Rabbinical Opinions about the Jews of Ethiopia," p. 324; idem, *Anthology,* p. 38.

9. Ibid.
10. Letter to S. Z. Shragai, a member of the Jewish Agency Executive, 2 Shevat 5715 (1955), in ibid., p. 40.
11. Ibid., p. 41. The letter was signed by Rabbis Shmuel Kipnis, Natan Selim, and Shmuel Ne'eri, and dated 6 Elul 5715 (1955), Jerusalem.
12. Ibid., p. 47.
13. Ibid.
14. Answer by the Chief Rabbinate, p. 4. Cited in Corinaldi, *Ethiopian Jews*, p. 225. For the grounds of the Chief Rabbinate's decision of 7 Sivan 5744 (1984), see ibid., appendix 7, p. 257.
15. Joseph Caro, *Beit Yosef, Y.D.* 264.
16. See David Ḥayyim Shloush, *Bnei Ami*, "Laws of Those of Doubtful Lineage," p. 142. See also idem, *Nidḥei Yisrael Yekhannes*.
17. HCJ 582/85. The court added that "this suggestion ought to be implemented as quickly as possible." Cited by Corinaldi, *Ethiopian Jews*, p. 29 and note 182.
18. Shloush, *Bnei Ami*, p. 142.
19. This section was originally written in August 1985, during the struggle by Ethiopian immigrants.
20. See Chief Rabbinate Council, *The B'nai Israel: Halakhic Rulings and Sources to Clarify Their Legal Status and Origins*, p. 2 (Hebrew).
21. Ibid., p. 22.
22. Ibid., p. 21.
23. See Ben-Zion Meir Hai Uziel, *Pisqei Uziel, E.H.* 68.
24. See Yitzhak Isaac Halevy Herzog, *Responsa Heikhal Yitzhak*, vol. 1, *E.H.* 13:4-17.
25. Ibid., 4–13.
26. See Chief Rabbinate Council, *The B'nai Israel*, p. 7.
27. Ibid., p. 8, directive issued by Chief Rabbi Yitzhak Nissim, president of the Chief Rabbinate Council (1962).
28. See *Divrei Haknesset*.

Chapter 11

1. In the Bible, the term *ger* refers to a sojourner in the land or to a stranger. At the end of the Second Temple Period, when conversion began to be practiced, the term was borrowed to designate a proselyte to Judaism, and the Biblical injunctions regarding fair treatment of the *ger* were then considered to apply to these converts.
2. Obadiah of Bertinoro, *Commentary on the Mishnah*, Baba Metzia 4:10.
3. Maimonides, *Responsa*, vol. 2, no. 293.
4. Ibid., no. 448.
5. Ibid.

Part IV

1. *Tanna de-Vei Eliyahu,* chapter 9, p. 48.
2. Judah Halevi, *The Kuzari,* I 114–115, pp. 78–79
3. Ibid., II 23–24. I wish to thank Prof. Aviezer Ravitzky for calling these passages to my attention. The other place in the *Kuzari* where the king bests the rabbi is when he notes that the Jews do not make *aliya* to the Land of Israel. Here too the rabbi tells the king that "you have found my disgrace."

Chapter 12

1. David Frankel, *Korban ha-eidah* on JT Nedarim 9:4.
2. Moses Margolioth, *Pnei Moshe* ad loc.
3. According to the MSS and the reading of Rabbi Menaem Hameiri (*Beit ha-behirah* on Tractate Sanhedrin, p. 168). There is a variant reading, however: "anyone who preserves a *Jewish* soul. . . ." See E. E. Urbach, "'Everyone Who Preserves a Single Soul': The History of a Textual Variant—The Vagaries of Censorship and the Printing Trade," pp. 561–577. Cf. Maimonides, Laws of the Sanhedrin 12:3.
4. Baruch Halevy Epstein, *Torah Temimah* on Deut. 21:7, note 53, p. 276.
5. Maimonides, *The Guide of the Perplexed,* III 40, vol. 2, p. 557.

Chapter 13

1. The biblical text seems to be referring to a sign of safe passage and refuge, rather than to a "sign of punishment" or "mark of guilt." Rashi explains that the mark is put on the foreheads of the righteous "to be a sign that they not be harmed by the destroyers" (on Ezek. 9:6). Rabbi David Kimchi (the Radak) offers a similar interpretation and compares the sign with the blood that the Israelites smeared on their doorposts in Egypt to ward off the Tenth Plague. (I wish to thank Ms. Rachel Yarden for drawing my attention to this point.) These commentators do agree, however, that punishment is to begin with the holy ones. Rabbi Freehof may have been referring to the much longer Talmudic exegesis of this passage in BT Shabbat 55a, which explicitly understands Ezekiel to be referring to *two* marks, one of ink and protection, the other of blood and guilt.
2. Letter to the author from Rabbi Dr. Solomon Freehof, March 12, 1984. I sent Rabbi Freehof my dissenting opinion. In accordance with his habitual generosity, he not only permitted me to publish his responsum along with mine, but also encouraged me to continue my independent halakhic inquiry in the path of the decisors of antiquity—as he had done

since the days when I was a young rabbinical student and he my guide in the principles of Halakhah. Unfortunately he never saw this note because he passed away in 1990, at the age of 97. May his memory be a blessing.

3. See *Sefer Ḥahinnukh*, positive commandment no. 218.

4. See *Tanna de-Vei Eliyahu* 18:41. I would like to thank Prof. Moshe Greenberg, who called my attention to this distinction in the halakhic literature. I quote from his letter of March 29, 1989: "The liability of someone who had the ability to protest and did not do so *is judged, according to the Sages, by Heaven and not by man;* it is a *moral* liability and not a *criminal* one to be punished by a court of law. . . . The Sages discuss the criminal liability of the *accomplices* to a crime—those who take an *action;* but judicial punishment was not meted out to those who failed to protest. Blowing up the houses of terrorists' relatives may be justified by civil law, not because the relatives did not protest, but because they sheltered or assisted the terrorist (if they did in fact shelter or assist him). The criminality of sheltering [a malefactor] is not recognized by the Torah even with regard to idolatry (Lev. 20:4–5): those who shelter one who worships Molekh—his family—are subject to excision by Heaven. . . . Thus far we have dealt with the law of one who shelters (or abets) whose culpability has been proven in a court of law. Blowing up the house of someone who has not been duly convicted of sheltering (or abetting) is not a matter of criminal law but an act of intimidation (deterrence), not in accordance with the rule of law, but pursuant to an emergency administrative decree about which one must always be vigilant" (all emphases in the original).

5. In the source, the midrash on "my holy ones" is distinct from that about the Patriarch Abraham and the people of Sodom, and there is no compelling reason to link the two. What is more, there are grave difficulties associated with basing halakhic rulings on *aggadah.* According to Rabbi Hai Gaon, "it is a general principle that we do not rely on *aggadah.*" Rabbi Saadiah Gaon held that "we do not rely on *aggadah.*" See *Treasury of the Geonim,* vol. 1, Tractate Berakhot 58b, p. 91, note 10; vol. 3, Tractate Pesaim 50b, p. 71, note 3. Maimonides noted that there are many contradictions in *midrashim* and *aggadot* so that we do not ask questions of them (see *Guide of the Perplexed,* end of introduction). I must also note that the Torah precept to reprove the miscreant is a positive commandment; see Maimonides, *The Book of the Commandments,* positive precept 205. The Sages held that persons are not punished for violating positive commandments—that is, for *not* doing what they ought to (BT Makkot 13b). In certain cases, the transgressor may be subject to flogging, but that provision does not apply to the issue at hand.

6. Maimonides, *Responsa,* vol. 2, no. 448.

7. See Abraham Isaac Hakohen Kook, *Responsa Mishpat Kohen,* no. 58.

8. *Ha'aretz* military correspondent, May 16, 1984.
9. Kook, *Letters,* Vol. 1, No. 89.
10. *Ha'aretz,* December 9, 1997.

Chapter 14

1. The "territories" refers to Judea, Samaria, and the Gaza District, which came under Israeli control as a result of the Six-Day War in 1967. They are variously referred to as "liberated" (by the Right), "conquered" or "occupied" (by the Left and the Arabs), or "administered" (the neutral term preferred by the Israeli government). In the media and general conversation, any or all of these adjectives are dropped.

    The *Intifada* began on Dec. 9, 1987, with Arabs throwing stones at Israeli soldiers in Gaza. It quickly spread to Judea and Samaria. The uprising continued until the signing of the Oslo Accords in September 1993 and the start of the peace process between Israel and the Palestinians.
2. Ḥayyim David Halevy, *Responsa Aseh Lekha Rav,* vol. 4, no. 2, pp. 34 and 38.
3. Ibid.
4. Ovadia Yosef, in *Oral Law* (1980), p. 14.
5. Shabbetai Don-Yihya, *Rabbi Ben-Zion Meir Hai Uziel: His Life and Doctrine,* pp. 75–77. See also Abraham Joshua Heschel, *Israel, An Echo of Eternity,* pp. 176–178.
6. Abraham Isaac Hakohen Kook, *Siddur Olat Hare'iyah,* vol. 1, p. 70.
7. Yosef, in *Oral Law.*
8. Kook, *Reponsa Mishpat Kohen* 144.
9. Halevy, *Reponsa Aseh Lekha Rav* 7:68.
10. Yitzhak Isaac Herzog, "The Rights of Minorities According to Halakhah," *Teḥumin* 2.
11. Kook, *Letters,* vol. 1, no. 89.
12. BT Nedarim 25a; BT Baba Batra 9a; BT Shevu'ot 29a.

Chapter 15

1. I would like to thank my friend and colleague Rabbi Moshe Yehudai, who called my attention to most of the sources cited in this section, which he mentioned in "The Value of Non-Jewish Life in Halakhah," his unpublished master's thesis, and especially the chapter "The Attitude toward Foreign Civilians and Combatants," pp. 212ff.; see also his bibliography, pp. 231ff.
2. "At 9:30 P.M. on 14 October [1953], soldiers from Unit 101 and an IDF paratroop unit crossed the border and attacked the village of Kibya. . . .

Houses were blown up during the operation and dozens of people were killed or wounded. Reports on the number of slain ranged from 42 to 56 persons. . . . The raid was conducted after several incidents in which infiltrators from Jordan had attacked Israeli citizens, culminating in the murders in Yahud," in which Arab infiltrators threw a grenade through an open window into a house, killing a mother and her two children, aged 1½ and 3 (*Documents on the Foreign Policy of Israel*, vol. 8 [Jerusalem, 1995], p. 357).

3. See Shaul Yisraeli, "The Kibya Incident in the Light of Halakhah," p. 71.
4. Ibid.
5. Ibid., p. 113.
6. See Shimon Weiser, "Purity of Arms: an Exchange of Letters," p. 29. This chapter was first written in 1988, shortly after the start of the *Intifada*.
7. Ibid., p. 30; emphasis mine.
8. Ibid., p. 30.
9. Ibid., p. 31; emphasis mine.
10. See Uriel Simon, "Religion, Morality, and Politics," pp. 8–13.
11. See Weiser, *Niv Hamidrashiyah* 13, pp. 211–212, note.
12. See Avraham Avidan (Zemel), *In the Wake of the Yom Kippur War: Meditations, Halakhah, and Research*, pp. 27–31 (Hebrew).
13. See *Haolam Hazeh*, no. 1915, May 15, 1975, p. 15.
14. See Avidan, *In the Wake of the Yom Kippur War*, p. 31.
15. See *Haolam Hazeh*, p. 25.
16. See *Tractate Soferim*, 15:7, pp. 280–281.
17. See BT Yevamot 61a, according to the text of Eliezer Goldstein, *Babylonian Talmud* 4 (Berlin and Vienna, 1925). See also *Babylonian Talmud with Variant Readings*, ed. Avraham Liss, 7:2, pp. 366–367, based on manuscripts and early printed editions.
18. BT Ketubot 11a, according to *Babylonian Talmud with Variant Readings*, ed. Moshe Herschler, *Tractate Ketubot* 1, p. 67, according to MS Venice 1520–1523.
19. Maimonides, Laws of Murderers and Preserving Life 4:11, according to the text in *Mishneh Torah, a New Photostatic Edition Based on the 1580 Rome Printing*.
20. Judah Halevi, *The Kuzari*, II 54.
21. Yaakov Ariel, "Morality, Religious Faith, and Peace Policy," pp. 210–211.
22. Ibid., p. 210.
23. Ibid.
24. Ibid., p. 211.
25. Ibid. In two conversations I had with Rabbi Ariel in 1990, he said that he considers the article to be journalism and therefore did not cite halakhic sources to buttress his arguments. Had he wished to, however, he

could have grounded them in Halakhah. He said that he continued to hold the views stated in the article.

26. Zvi Yehuda Kook, *From the Redeeming Torah*, p. 123.

27. Ibid., pp. 123–124.

28. Ibid.

29. Ibid., p. 225.

30. See *Hebrew Encyclopedia*, vol. 6, col. 524. Various sources give the number of victims as 43, 47, 49, and even 51.

31. See *District Court Verdicts* 17, Military Tribunal MR/57/3, the Judge Advocate General vs. Maj. Shmuel Melinki and 10 others.

32. Ibid., p. 91.

33. Ibid., p. 92.

34. Ibid., p. 93.

35. Ofer et al. vs. the Judge Advocate General, Ayin/58/279-283, *Rulings of the Supreme Court of Israel*, p. 411.

36. Ibid.

37. See Shlomo Goren, *Responsa Meshiv Milhamah* 1, §1, "The Ethics of Combat in the Light of Halakhah," pp. 1–40.

38. Rabbi Goren could have relied also on the midrashic exegesis of Proverbs 24:17–18: "If your enemy falls, do not exult; if he trips, let your heart not rejoice. Lest the Lord see it and be displeased, and avert His wrath from him." "God said: 'You are not better than I am. How? Israel merited to recite the Hallel all seven days of Passover, as they recite it all seven days of Sukkot, but they recite it only the first day. Why is this? Only because the Egyptians were killed and drowned in the sea. They are my enemies, yet I Myself dictated that 'if your enemy falls, do not exult'" (*Yalkut Shimoni*, §960).

39. See Goren, *Responsa Meshiv Milhamah* 1, p. 14.

40. Ibid.

41. See Maimonides, *Eight Chapters*, chapter 7.

42. See Goren, *Responsa Meshiv Milhamah* 1, p. 20.

43. Moses ben Nahman, *Nahmanides on the Torah*, p. 458.

44. See Goren, "The Integrity of the Land in the Light of Halakhah."

45. Mishnah Avot 4:1; *Avot de-Rabbi Nathan*, start of chapter 23, p. 75.

46. *Mekhilta of Rabbi Simeon bar Yohai*, weekly portion of Mishpatim, Exodus 23:4, p. 215. See also Rahel Bat-Adam, "The Vocation of Zionism Today: Winning Partners," pp. 61–69.

Chapter 16

1. Moses ben Nahman (Nahmanides), *Novellae*, on BT Gittin 45a.

2. Elijah ben Samuel, *Responsa Yad Eliyahu*, no. 43.

3. Meir ben Gedaliah, *Responsa of the Maharam Lublin*, no. 15.

4. David ben Zimra, *Responsa of the Radbaz*, vol. 1, no. 40.
5. Solomon Luria, *Yam shel Shelomo*, Tractate Gittin, 4:66.
6. The leading modern authority on the life and writings of Rabbi Meir of Rothenburg maintains that the emperor's intention was to compel the Jewish community to pay him direct taxes. The figure cited was quite arbitrary and was not the rabbi's ransom but a tax levy. The community leaders were willing to comply if the payment was accepted as ransom, but not as taxes. Rabbi Meir agreed to this. But the emperor refused the offer and insisted that the payment be accounted a tax. The result was that the rabbi died in prison. Even if this is the true version, rather than that of Rabbi Solomon Luria, the principle remains that individuals must not be rescued at the price of grave damage to the community. See Irving Agus, *Rabbi Meir of Rothenburg*, pp. 146–151.

Chapter 17

1. See chapter 16.
2. See chapter 16, pp. 255–256. The sources of the brief citations in the preceding paragraphs are given there.
3. *Davar*, November 7, 1995.
4. We should note that the rabbis of the various Orthodox educational institutions in which Yigal Amir studied over the years all disavowed responsibility for his views. Rabbi Mordechai Greenberg of the Kerem Be-Yavne yeshiva was quoted to the effect that "I do not believe that he absorbed the ideology behind his act in our yeshiva" (*Ha'aretz*, November 6, 1995). Rabbi Moshe Raziel, the head of the Higher Institute for Torah at Bar-Ilan University, maintained that Amir and other right-wing students of his institution did not receive any Torah-based guidance that might be interpreted as justifying murder.
5. See, for example, Issachar Dov Eilenburg, *Responsa Be'er Sheva* 48 (sixteenth century); Moses Sofer, *Responsa Ḥatam Sofer* 5, 124 and 7, 35 (nineteenth century).

Part V

Chapter 18

1. Under the Religious Services Budget Law (1949; amended 1967), every local authority must appoint a religious council to supervise the provision of public religious facilities for the local population—especially *kashrut* and ritual baths. The composition of each religious council must be ratified by the Minister of Religious Affairs. Forty-five percent of the members are nominated by the minister, 45 percent by the local authority, and 10 percent by the local rabbinate.

2. Israel Zev Mintzberg, *Zot Ḥukkat Hatorah,* p. 8.
3. Chaim Hirschensohn, *Responsa Malki Bakodesh,* vol. 2, no. 4, §3, p. 193.
4. Ben-Zion Meier Hai Uziel, *Piskei Uziel, H.M.* 54:1.
5. *Maḥzikei Hadat,* ed. Abraham Schor, vol. 2, no. 9, p. 1.
6. Chaim Tchernowitz, "On the Election of Women," p. 7.
7. Uziel, *Piskei Uziel, H.M.* 44:1.
8. Abraham Isaac Hakohen Kook, *Ma'amrei Hare'iyah,* vol. 1, p. 192.
9. Hirschensohn, *Responsa Malki Bakodesh,* vol. 2, no. 4, §7, p. 209.
10. Uziel, *Piskei Uziel, H.M.* 54:1.
11. Moshe Feinstein, *Iggerot Moshe, Y.D.* 2:109.
12. Tchernowitz, "On the Election of Women," p. 8. After the original version of this chapter was published as an article in *Ha'aretz,* Mrs. Shakdiel sent me a copy of the letter she had sent to the editors of the National Religious Party daily *Hazofeh,* which I cite here in part:

    "The secular readers . . . of *Ha'aretz* were able to read Reform Rabbi Moshe Zemer's profound halakhic analysis of the question of electing women to public positions, based on his research of contemporary rabbis who confirmed and negated their right. . . . All of this before the God-fearing readers of *Hazofeh* [the newspaper of the National Religious Party] had an opportunity to read a similar halakhic study of this issue. . . . The great Mizrahi rabbis [affiliated with the NRP] who were in favor of women serving in various public positions were quoted in *Ha'aretz*—but not in the newspaper of the National Religious Party. . . . And then you ask me why I and those like me have gone to pasture in alien fields!?" (Yeroham, October 16, 1986).

    The editors of *Hazofeh* did not publish her letter.

Chapter 19

1. David ben Zimra, Commentary on the *Mishneh Torah,* ad loc.
2. Samuel Strashun, *Glosses and Novellae of the Rashash,* on BT Sotah 44b.
3. Yissakhar Halevy Levin, "The Conscription of Women," p. 59.
4. Shaul Yisraeli, in *Torah and State* 4 (1952), p. 223, note 2. See also Yehezkel Kohen, *The Conscription of Women and National Service: A Halakhic Inquiry,* which includes some of these sources.

Chapter 20

1. David Frankel, *Korban ha-eidah* on JT Sanhedrin 2:4.
2. Joseph Caro, *Beit Yosef, Y.D.* 359.
3. *The Zohar,* Vayakhel, vol. 4, p. 161.

4. Ibid. 196b, pp. 161–162.
5. Jacob ben Samuel, *Responsa Beit Yaakov*, no. 72.
6. Isaac bar Sheshet, *Responsa of the Ribash*, no. 158.

Chapter 21

1. Rulings of the Tosafists, Tractate Sanhedrin, chapter 6, §100, p. 114a.
2. Jacob ben Asher, *Tur Yoreh De'ah* 357, in *Arba'ah Turim*.
3. Joseph Caro, *Beit Yosef*, ad loc.
4. Joshua Falk, *Derishah u-Perishah* ad loc.
5. Jehiel Michel Epstein, *Arukh Hashulhan, Y.D.* 357:2.

Chapter 22

1. Jair Bacharach, *Responsa Ḥavvot Ya'ir*, no. 222.
2. Ibid.
3. Note that even though kaddish is recited at daily services, which are time-dependent, recitation of the kaddish is not time-dependent: the rabbinic kaddish is recited by mourners at the end of any public study session.
4. Jacob Reischer, *Responsa Shevut Yaakov*, vol. 2, no. 93.
5. Jacob Emden, *Siddur Beit Yaakov*, vol. 1, p. 92.
6. Ephraim Zalman Margalioth, *Responsa Mateh Ephraim*, Laws of the Mourners' Kaddish, p. 51b, glosses on *Elef Lamateh*, §9.
7. The Krimchaks of the Crimea, where Medini served as rabbi.
8. Ḥayyim Hezekiah Medini, *Sede Ḥemed*, Anthology of Laws 6, Mourning, §160, p. 196.
9. Joseph Elijah Henkin, "A Daughter's Saying Kaddish," p. 6. Rabbi Israel Meir Lau objected to this leniency in his *Responsa Yahel Yisrael*, published shortly before his election to the Chief Rabbinate in 1992.
10. See Joel B. Wolowelsky, "Modern Orthodoxy and Women's Changing Self-Perception," p. 80, note 9. (See also below, note 17.)
11. Isaac ben Moses, *Or Zarua*, Laws of the Sabbath, §50, p. 12b.
12. Bacharach, *Responsa Ḥavvot Ya'ir*, No. 222.
13. Abraham bar Ḥiyya, *Higgayon Hanefesh*, Fourth Principle, p. 32.
14. Abraham Horowitz, *Yesh Nohalim*, introduction, p. 6a. The author was the father of the famous Rabbi Isaiah Horowitz, author of *Shenei Luḥot Haberit*.
15. Jekuthiel Judah Greenwald, *Compendium of Mourning*, chapter 5, §2, pp. 365–366.
16. Ibid., p. 365.

17. Quoted by his brother, Rabbi Yissakhar Jacobson, *Netiv Binah,* vol. 1, p. 368.
18. Quoted in Wolowelsky, "Modern Orthodoxy," p. 69, from Joseph B. Soloveitchik, "A Eulogy for the Talner Rebbe," p. 20. See also Wolowelsky, *Women, Jewish Law, and Modernity,* pp. 84–141.
19. Moshe Feinstein, *Iggerot Moshe, O.H.* 5, responsum 12.
20. Aaron Soloveitchik, *Od Yosef Beni Hai,* quoted in Wolowelsky, "Modern Orthodoxy," p. 93.

Chapter 23

1. David Abudarham, *The Complete Abudarham,* §3, p. 25.
2. See *Rashi's Siddur,* §267, pp. 127–128. See also *Responsa of Rashi,* ed. S. Elfenbein, §68; *Mahzor Vitry,* ed. Shimon Ish-Hurwitz, §359, pp. 413, 414. Sephardi decisors, however, do not allow a woman to recite the benediction in such cases.
3. See Jacob Emden, *Glosses and Novellae* on BT Megillah 23a.
4. Meir ben Baruch, *Responsa of Maharam Rothenburg,* no. 108.
5. See Joseph Caro, *Beit Yosef, O.H.* 282.
6. See Joel Sirkes, *Bayit Hadash, O.H.* 75.
7. See Joshua Falk, *Derishah u-Perishah, E.H.* 21.2.
8. See Netanel Hakohen Fried, *Responsa Penei Meivin.*
9. Mordecai Jacob Breisch, *Responsa Helkat Ya'akov* 1, no. 163.
10. See Aaron de Toledo, *Divrei Hefetz,* p. 113b, cited in Hayyim Hezekiah Medini, *Sede Hemed,* part 5, §100, rule 42, p. 282.
11. See Jehiel Jacob Weinberg, *Responsa Seridei Esh,* vol. 2, no. 8.

Part VI

Chapter 24

1. See *Yedioth Ahronoth,* March 11, 1974.
2. See Israel Meir Kagan, *Mishnah Berurah* 262:9.
3. See Hayyim Joseph David Azulai, *Sefer Avodat Hakodesh,* chapter 4, §152, p. 30b.
4. See *Amudim, the Journal of the Religious Kibbutz Movement* (Elul 5739 [1979]), p. 417; emphasis in the original.
5. See Abraham Isaac Hakohen Kook, *Lights of Repentance,* chapter 17, §3, pp. 159–160.

Chapter 25

1. Broadcast on Voice of Israel radio, October 26, 1986.
2. Levi ben Habib, *Responsa of the Ralbah,* no. 79.

3. Ibid.
4. Ibid.

Chapter 26

1. See Joseph Caro, *Kesef Mishneh* on the *Mishneh Torah,* ad loc.
2. See Moses Sofer, *Novellae on the Babylonian Talmud,* on BT Sukkah 36a, p. 54a.
3. See *Sefer Hahinnukh,* positive precept 27.
4. See Hezekiah da Silva, *Peri Hadash, Y.D.* 240:13. Da Silva refers us to the *Shulhan Arukh Y.D.* 246:18, where the ruling is that "if it is possible for the precept to be performed by others, he should not interrupt his learning; but otherwise he should perform the precept and then return to his studies." It is self-evident that the precept of honoring one's parents must be done by the individual.
5. See Hayyim David Halevy, *Responsa 'Aseh Lekha Rav,* vol. 1, no. 21.
6. This chapter is based on an article that first appeared in *Ha'aretz* on May 28, 1984. According to the newspaper's archives, this was the first time that the term *mithardim,* "the newly Ultra-Orthodox." had ever appeared in this sense.

Chapter 27

1. The responsa cited by the professor were as follows: Moshe Feinstein, *Iggerot Moshe, Y.D.* 2, nos. 6, 12, and 17; *E.H.* 1, no. 135; 2, end of no. 17; 3, nos. 3, 18, and 25; *O.H.* 3, no. 7. I myself have added the following: *Y.D.* 1, no. 139; 2, nos. 100, 106, 108. These seem to constitute a representative sample of Rabbi Feinstein's approach to the matter.
2. Feinstein, *Iggerot Moshe, E.H.* 1, no. 135.
3. Ibid., *Y.D.* 1, no. 139.
4. Ibid., *E.H.* 3, no. 3.
5. Sa'adiah Gaon, *Sefer Hagalui,* pp. 232–234.
6. Letter from Rabbi Hillel the Pious to Rabbi Isaac the Physician, *Anthology of Responsa by Maimonides* 3, p. 13b.
7. See Abraham Maimonides, *Milhamot Hashem,* p. 55. For more information about this controversy, see Daniel Jeremy Silver, *Maimonidean Criticism and the Maimonidean Controversy, 1180–1240,* especially chapter 9, pp. 148ff.
8. Esriel Hildesheimer, *Responsa of Rabbi Esriel, Y.D.* 238.
9. Hillel Lichtenstein, *Responsa Beit Hillel,* no. 13.
10. Ibid.
11. *Yad Shaul, the Shaul Weingurt Memorial Volume,* p. 242.

12. Yomtov Halevi Schwartz, *Responsa Ma'aneh La'iggerot,* title page.
13. *Da'at Hatorah* (New York, summer 1983), pp. 86–87; emphases in the original.
14. Feinstein, *Iggerot Moshe, Y.D.* 1, no. 139.
15. Ibid., 2, no. 106.
16. Ibid., no. 107.
17. Ibid., no. 108.
18. Ibid., no. 101.
19. Ibid., *Y.D.* 3, no. 77.
20. Ibid., *Y.D.* 2, no. 12.
21. Ibid., *O.H.* 3, no. 30.
22. Ibid.
23. See also *E.H.* 3, no. 17.
24. Ibid., *Y.D.,* 1, no. 139.
25. Ibid., no. 107.
26. Ibid., *O.H.* 3, no. 30.
27. Ibid., *Y.D.* 1, no. 139.
28. Ibid.
29. Ibid., *O.H.* 3, no. 30.
30. Eliezer Waldenberg, *Responsa Tzitz Eliezer,* part 5, introduction.
31. Meshulam Rothe, *Kol Mevasser,* part 2, no. 17.
32. Feinstein, *Iggerot Moshe, Y.D.* 3, no. 105. See also David Zevi Hoffmann, *Responsa Melammed Le-ho'il* 2, *Y.D.,* no. 82.
33. Yitzhak D. Gilat, "The Influence of Reality on Halakhic Distinctions," p. 288.
34. Jakob Joseph Petuchowski, "Plural Models within Halakhah." See also chapter 3, note 19.
35. See Eliyahu Eliezer Dessler, *A Letter from Eliyahu* 3, pp. 358–359. In 1951, Rabbi Dessler wrote that the leading rabbis of Hungary and Lithuania had opposed university studies leading to an academic degree. He mentioned the case of Rabbi Samson Raphael Hirsch, who began but did not complete university studies, acknowledging his error and recanting. Dessler received approval for this ban from Rabbi Avraham Yeshayahu Karelitz (the Ḥazon Ish). If yeshiva students are not allowed to *study* in a university, is it permissible for an observant professor to teach there?

Chapter 28

1. Joseph Caro, *Kesef Mishneh,* Laws of the Impurity of the Dead 8, 5–6.
2. Isaac ben Moses, *Or Zarua,* Laws of Mourning, §420.
3. Abraham Yitzhaki, *Responsa Zera Avraham, Y.D.* 21.

4. David Oppenheim, printed at the end of Jair Bacharach, *Responsa Ḥavvot Yaʾir*.
5. Elijah Guttmacher, *Responsa Aderet Eliyahu, Y.D.* 123
6. Moses Sofer, *Responsa Ḥatam Sofer, Y.D.* 353.
7. Moses Schick, *Responsa of Maharam Schick, Y.D.* 353.
8. Samuel Landau, *Responsa Shivat Ziyyon*, no. 62.
9. Mayer Lerner, *Ḥayye Olam*, §1.
10. In the summer of 1998, the leading Ultra-Orthodox decisor, Rabbi Yosef Shalom Eliashiv, did in fact issue a ruling that bones discovered in the path of a new trunk road in northern Jerusalem could be reburied at an adjacent site. His ruling sparked fierce and sometimes violent opposition in Meʾah Sheʾarim on the part of the groups most active in the anti-archaeology campaign.
11. Jehiel Michel Epstein, *Arukh Hashulḥan, Y.D.* 364:7.
12. Ben-Zion Meir Hai Uziel, *Piskei Uziel*, 32–33.

Chapter 29

1. Asher ben Jehiel, commentary on BT Moʾed Katan 3, §88.
2. Meir Sima Hakohen, *Hagahot Maimuniyot*, Laws of Circumcision 1.10.
3. Ezekiel Landau, *Responsa Noda Biyehuda*, 1st ed., *O.H.* 16.
4. Moses Sofer, *Responsa Ḥatam Sofer* 1, *O.H.* 147.
5. Joseph Caro, *Beit Yosef, Y.D.* 263, in the name of the *Kolbo*.
6. Elijah ben Shlomo Zalman, *Bi'ur HaGra* 263, §10.
7. Ben-Zion Meir Hai Uziel, *Mishpetei Uziel* 1, *Y.D.* 28.

Part VII

Chapter 30

1. Hebrew does not really distinguish between an autopsy or postmortem—the examination of a corpse to determine or confirm the cause of death—and anatomical dissection of cadavers. Nor do the halakhic texts treat them differently. In what follows, the identical Hebrew term *nittuaḥ le-aḥar ha-mavet* is sometimes rendered by one term or the other, as the sense seems to require.
2. The goal would be to discover fatal hereditary diseases or to discover why surgical intervention and drug therapy failed to save the patient's life.
3. Israel (Immanuel) Jakobovits, "The Problem of Autopsies in the Halakhic Literature and in Light of Contemporary Conditions," p. 64; emphasis mine.
4. Ben-Zion Meir Hai Uziel, *Mishpetei Uziel*, vol. 1, no. 29.
5. Ibid., no. 28, §4.
6. Ibid., no. 29, §1.

7. Yitzhak Arieli, "The Problem of Autopsies," *No'am* 6, p. 82.
8. Uziel, *Mishpetei Uziel,* no. 29.
9. Ibid., no. 28.
10. Arieli, "The Problem of Autopsies," *Oral Law* 6, p. 60.
11. Eliezer Waldenberg, *Responsa Tzitz Eliezer,* part 4, §14.
12. Eliezer Berkovits, "Clarification of Halakhah on Autopsies," p. 54.
13. Uziel, *Mishpetei Uziel,* no. 28.

Chapter 31

1. Cited in *Ha'aretz,* November 15, 1979; emphasis mine.
2. Meir Abulafia, *Yad Ramah.*
3. Menaem Meiri, *Beit ha-behirah* on Sanhedrin 72b.
4. Joseph ben Moses of Trani, *Responsa of the Maharit,* vol. 1, nos. 97 and 99.
5. Jacob Emden, *Responsa of the Ya'avetz,* vol. 1, no. 43. After this halakhic innovation, Emden added the common demurral that "further study is required," as is habitual with those who provide innovative halakhic answers but leave open the question of their validity in practice.
6. See BT Niddah 44a-b; Maimonides, Laws of Murderers 2:6.
7. In 1979, the Orthodox parties in the Knesset launched an assault on the "social" clause of the Abortion Law, which recognized the disadvantaged socioeconomic status of a woman's family (including low income and many children) as grounds for permitting her to have an abortion. The Knesset repealed this clause in 1980, when the coalition bowed to the Orthodox parties' threat to withdraw their support. The practical effect of the repeal was limited, however, since almost all the applications formerly approved under the "social" clause have since been approved pursuant to another section of the law, which permits abortions to safeguard the woman's psychological or emotional well-being.

Chapter 32

1. The notice appeared in several daily papers. See, for example, *Hadashot,* February 10, 1985.
2. For example, the published volumes of rabbinic rulings issued in Israel over thirty years include only three rulings about conversion and only a single case concerning conversion in order to marry a Jew. In a ruling by the Tel Aviv District Rabbinical Court, case 2022/45, the conversion and marriage of Samaritans was permitted, but no ruling was issued concerning conversion for the sake of marriage. See *Verdicts of Rabbinical Courts in Israel* 14(3) (n.p., n.d.), pp. 89–96; 14(4), pp. 97–99. There are many

hundreds of conversion files, but only a handful of them have ever been published, and the situation is similar with regard to other issues of personal status, such as halakhic illegitimacy.

3. Several cases were brought before regional rabbinical courts, but their verdicts were not officially published by the rabbinate or the Ministry of Religious Affairs. Nor is there any evidence that the Supreme Rabbinical Council adopted these rulings. See Y. Green, "Artificial Insemination," pp. 45ff (Hebrew).

4. Malkiel Zevi Lomza, *Responsa Divrei Malkiel,* part 4, no. 107.

5. Ovadiah Hadaya, *Responsa Yaskil Avdi,* part 5, *E.H.* 10, chapter 1, §4.

6. Aaron Welkin, *Responsa Zekan Aharon,* second ed., part 2, *E.H.* 97.

7. Isaac Jacob Weiss, *Responsa Minḥat Yitzḥak,* part 1, no. 50, §1, p. 103.

8. Shalom Mordecai Schwadron, *Responsa of the Maharsham,* part 3, no. 268.

9. Eliezer Waldenberg, *Responsa Tzitz Eliezer,* vol. 9, no. 51, pp. 258–259.

10. Judah Leib Zirelson, *Responsa Ma'arkhei Lev, E.H.* 73.

11. Hadaya, *Responsa Yaskil Avdi.*

12. Joel Sirkes, *Bayit Ḥadash* on *Tur Y.D.* 198.

13. Judah Rosanes, *Mishneh Lamelekh* on Maimonides' *Mishneh Torah,* Laws of Personal Status 15:4.

14. Moshe Feinstein, *Iggerot Moshe, E.H.* 1, no. 10.

15. *Ḥadashot,* February 10, 1985.

16. Feinstein, *Iggerot Moshe, E.H.* 1, no. 71.

17. Ibid., no. 10.

18. Waldenberg, *Responsa Tzitz Eliezer* 9, no. 51, pp. 258, 259.

19. *Sefer Haḥinnukh,* positive commandment 1, p. 55.

Chapter 33

1. Ḥayyim Benveniste, *Sheyarei Knesset Hagedolah, O.H.* 567.

2. Jacob Emden, *Mor u-ketziah, O.H.* 511

3. David Zevi Hoffmann, *Responsa Melamed Le-ho'il, O.H.* 15.

4. Moshe Feinstein, *Iggerot Moshe, H.M.* 2, no. 18.

5. Eliezer Waldenberg, *Responsa Tzitz Eliezer* 15, no. 39.

6. Feinstein, *Iggerot Moshe, Y.D.* 2, no. 49.

7. Ḥayyim David Halevy, *Responsa 'Aseh Lekha Rav,* vol. 6, no. 59.

8. Waldenberg, *Responsa Tzitz Eliezer* 15, no. 39.

9. Moses Rivkes, *Be'er Hagolah, H.M.* 427, §90.

Chapter 34

1. There was an ancient belief that placing the keys of the synagogue under the head of a dying person delayed his or her departure from this world.

The same belief attached to the other actions mentioned below under the second category of passive euthanasia. See Joshua Trachtenberg, *Jewish Magic and Superstition*, p. 175.

2. Walter Jacob, ed., *American Reform Responsa*, no. 77, p. 256.
3. Zvi Hirsch ben Azriel, *Beit Leḥem Yehudah on Shulḥan Arukh*, Y.D. 339:1.
4. Jacob ben Samuel, *Responsa Beit Yaakov*.
5. Jacob Reischer, *Responsa Shevut Yaakov*, vol. 3, no. 13.
6. Baruch Rabinowitz, lecture at a symposium on "Establishing the Moment of Death and Transplantation," pp. 197f.
7. Ḥayyim David Halevy, *Responsa 'Aseh Lekha Rav*, vol. 5, no. 39.
8. The Masoretic text of the verse reads, "and behold it was very good" *(ve-hinneh tov me'od)*. Rabbi Meir's text had a slight but crucial variant: "and behold death is good" *(ve-hinneh tov mot/mavvet)*.
9. Haim H. Cohn, "The Duty to Live and the Right to Die: On the Dichotomy of Divinity and Humanity in Jewish Law," pp. 31–67.

Part VIII

Chapter 35

1. Halakhic ruling issued by the chief rabbis of Rishon Lezion, Yehuda David Wolpe and Yosef Azran, July 20, 1983, and confirmed and adopted by the Chief Rabbinate Council on November 29, 1983.
2. *Beit Talmud*, ed. Isaac Hirsch Weiss and Meir Ish-Shalom, vol. 4, p. 70.
3. Ibid., p. 71.
4. Esriel Hildesheimer, *Responsa of Rabbi Esriel*, no. 259.
5. Eliezer Deutsch, *Responsa Peri Hasadeh*, part 3, no. 29.
6. Abraham Isaac Glick, *Responsa Yad Yitzḥak*, part 3, no. 296.
7. Judah Leib Zirelson, *Responsa Atzei Halevanon*, Y.D. 75.
8. Moshe Feinstein, *Iggerot Moshe*, Y.D. 160.
9. See Gotthard Deutsch, in *Yearbook of the Central Conference of American Rabbis* 29, pp. 80–85.
10. Zirelson, *Responsa Atzei Halevanon*, Y.D. 65.
11. Ibid., *Y.D.* 75. These rulings by Rabbi Zirelson are much more lenient than the stringent demands made by the Rishon Lezion rabbinate for a separation of eight cubits.
12. See Berachiah Schick, *Dat ve-Din*.
13. Zevi Hirsch Ashkenazi, *Responsa Ḥakham Zevi*, nos. 47 and 50.
14. Glick, *Responsa Yad Yitzḥak*, part 3, no. 296.
15. Deutsch, *Responsa Peri Hasadeh*, part 3, no. 29.
16. Feinstein, *Iggerot Moshe Y.D.* 2, no. 131; *Y.D.* 3, no. 146.
17. David Sperber, *Responsa Afarkasta de'anya*, no. 171.

18. Rashi, *BT Beitzah* 2b.
19. Ibid.
20. Samuel Laniado, *Klei Yakar*, p. 528, on 2 Kings.
21. Judah the Pious, *Sefer Ḥasidim*, §705.
22. Jacob Moellin, *The Book of the Maharil*, Laws of Rejoicing, p. 81a.
23. Ḥayyim Eleazar Shapira, *Minḥat Eleazar*, part 2, §41.
24. Joel Sirkes, *Bayit Ḥadash* on *Tur Y.D.* 362.
25. Joshua Falk, *Derishah u-Perishah* on *Tur Y.D.* 362.
26. Samuel Engel, *Responsa of the Maharash*, part 6, no. 3.
27. Jehiel Jacob Weinberg, *Responsa Seridei Esh*, part 2, no. 123.
28. Hildesheimer, *Responsa, Y.D.* 259.

Chapter 36

1. *Encyclopaedia Judaica*, vol. 5, col. 1530.
2. Ovadia Yosef, *Responsa Yabbia Omer*, part 4, *Y.D.* 27.
3. Ibid.
4. Ben-Zion Meir Hai Uziel, *Responsa Mishpetei Uziel*, 2nd ed., part 3, *Y.D.* 126.

Afterword

1. Albo, *Sefer Ha-Ikkarim*

Index

About JEWISH LIGHTS Publishing

People of all faiths and backgrounds yearn for books that attract, engage, educate and spiritually inspire.

Our principal goal is to stimulate thought and help all people learn about who the Jewish People are, where they come from, and what the future can be made to hold. While people of our diverse Jewish heritage are the primary audience, our books speak to people in the Christian world as well and will broaden their understanding of Judaism and the roots of their own faith.

We bring to you authors who are at the forefront of spiritual thought and experience. While each has something different to say, they all say it in a voice that you can hear.

Our books are designed to welcome you and then to engage, stimulate and inspire. We judge our success not only by whether or not our books are beautiful and commercially successful, but by whether or not they make a difference in your life.

We at Jewish Lights take great care to produce beautiful books that present meaningful spiritual content in a form that reflects the art of making high quality books. Therefore, we want to acknowledge those who contributed to the production of this book.

PRODUCTION
Bridgett Taylor & Marian Wallace

EDITORIAL & PROOFREADING
Jennifer Goneau & Bridgett Taylor

TEXT DESIGN
Sans Serif Inc.
Saline, Michigan

COVER DESIGN
Bridgett Taylor

JACKET & TEXT PRINTING AND BINDING
Lake Book, Melrose Park, Illinois

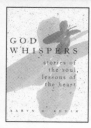
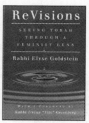

Spirituality

MY PEOPLE'S PRAYER BOOK
Traditional Prayers, Modern Commentaries
Vol. 1—The *Sh'ma* and Its Blessings
Vol. 2—The *Amidah*
Vol. 3—*P'sukei D'zimrah* (Morning Psalms)
Edited by *Rabbi Lawrence A. Hoffman*

Provides a diverse and exciting commentary to the traditional liturgy, written by 10 of today's most respected scholars and teachers from all perspectives of the Jewish world.

With 7 volumes published semiannually until completion of the series, this stunning work enables all of us to be involved in a personal dialogue with God, history and tradition through the heritage of the prayer book. "This book engages the mind and heart. . . . It challenges one's assumptions at whatever level of understanding one brings to the text." —*Jewish Herald-Voice*

Vol. 1: 7" x 10", 168 pp. HC, ISBN 1-879045-79-6 **$21.95**
Vol. 2: 7" x 10", 240 pp. HC, ISBN 1-879045-80-X **$21.95**
Vol. 3: 7" x 10", 192 pp. (est.) HC, ISBN 1-879045-81-8 **$21.95**

FINDING JOY
A Practical Spiritual Guide to Happiness
by *Dannel I. Schwartz* with *Mark Hass*

Searching for happiness in our modern world of stress and struggle is common; *finding* it is more unusual. This guide explores and explains how to find joy through a time-honored, creative—and surprisingly practical—approach based on the teachings of Jewish mysticism and Kabbalah.

"Lovely, simple introduction to Kabbalah....a singular contribution...."
—*American Library Association's* Booklist

•AWARD WINNER•
6" x 9", 192 pp. Quality PB, ISBN 1-58023-009-1 **$14.95**; HC, ISBN 1-879045-53-2 **$19.95**

THE DEATH OF DEATH
Resurrection and Immortality in Jewish Thought
by *Neil Gillman*

Explores the original and compelling argument that Judaism, a religion often thought to pay little attention to the afterlife, not only offers us rich ideas on the subject—but delivers a deathblow to death itself.

6" x 9", 336 pp., HC, ISBN 1-879045-61-3 **$23.95**

THE EMPTY CHAIR: FINDING HOPE & JOY
Timeless Wisdom from a Hasidic Master,
Rebbe Nachman of Breslov
Adapted by *Moshe Mykoff* and the *Breslov Research Institute*

A "little treasure" of aphorisms and advice for living joyously and spiritually today, written 200 years ago, but startlingly fresh in meaning and use.
Teacher, guide and spiritual master—Rebbe Nachman provides vital words of inspiration and wisdom for life today for people of any faith, or of no faith.

"For anyone of any faith, this is a book of healing and wholeness, of being alive!"
— *Bookviews*
•AWARD WINNER•
4" x 6", 128 pp., 2-color text, Deluxe Paperback, ISBN 1-879045-67-2 **$9.95**

THE GENTLE WEAPON
Prayers for Everyday and Not-So-Everyday Moments
Adapted by *Moshe Mykoff* and *S.C. Mizrahi*,
together with the *Breslov Research Institute*

A small treasury of prayers for people of all faiths, based on the Jewish wisdom tradition. The perfect companion to *The Empty Chair: Finding Hope and Joy,* and to our stressful lives.

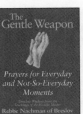

4" x 6", 144 pp., 2-color text, Deluxe Paperback, ISBN 1-58023-022-9 **$9.95**

Spirituality

"WHO IS A JEW?"
Conversations, Not Conclusions
by *Meryl Hyman*

Who is "Jewish enough" to be considered a Jew? And by whom?

Meryl Hyman courageously takes on this timely and controversial question to give readers the perspective necessary to draw their own conclusions. Profound personal questions of identity are explored in conversations with Jews and non-Jews in the U.S., Israel and England.

6" x 9", 272 pp. Quality Paperback, ISBN 1-58023-052-0 **$16.95**
HC, ISBN 1-879045-76-1 **$23.95**

THE JEWISH GARDENING COOKBOOK
Growing Plants and Cooking for Holidays & Festivals
by *Michael Brown*

Wherever you garden—a city apartment windowsill or on an acre—with the fruits and vegetables of your own labors, the traditional repasts of Jewish holidays and celebrations can be understood in many new ways!

Gives easy-to-follow instructions for raising foods that have been harvested since ancient times. Provides carefully selected, tasty and easy-to-prepare recipes using these traditional foodstuffs for holidays, festivals, and life cycle events. Clearly illustrated with more than 30 fine botanical illustrations. For beginner and professional alike.

6" x 9", 224 pp. HC, ISBN 1-58023-004-0 **$21.95**

WANDERING STARS
An Anthology of Jewish Fantasy & Science Fiction
Edited by *Jack Dann;* with an Introduction by *Isaac Asimov*

Jewish science fiction and fantasy? *Yes!* Here are the distinguished contributors: Bernard Malamud, Isaac Bashevis Singer, Isaac Asimov, Robert Silverberg, Harlan Ellison, Pamela Sargent, Avram Davidson, Geo. Alec Effinger, Horace L. Gold, Robert Sheckley, William Tenn and Carol Carr. Pure enjoyment. We laughed out loud reading it. A 25th Anniversary Classic Reprint.

6" x 9", 272 pp. Quality Paperback, ISBN 1-58023-005-9 **$16.95**

THE ENNEAGRAM AND KABBALAH
Reading Your Soul
by *Rabbi Howard A. Addison*

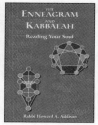

What do the Enneagram and *Kabbalah* have in common? Together, can they provide a powerful tool for self-knowledge, critique, and transformation?

How can we distinguish between acquired personality traits and the essential self hidden underneath?

6" x 9", 176 pp. Quality Paperback Original, ISBN 1-58023-001-6 **$15.95**

Spirituality

PARENTING AS A SPIRITUAL JOURNEY
Deepening Ordinary & Extraordinary Events into Sacred Occasions
by *Rabbi Nancy Fuchs-Kreimer*

A perfect gift for the new parent, and a helpful guidebook for those seeking to re-envision family life. Draws on experiences of the author and over 100 parents of many faiths. Rituals, prayers, and passages from sacred Jewish texts—as well as from other religious traditions—are woven throughout the book.

6" x 9", 224 pp. Quality Paperback, ISBN 1-58023-016-4 **$16.95**

STEPPING STONES TO JEWISH SPIRITUAL LIVING
Walking the Path Morning, Noon, and Night
by *Rabbi James L. Mirel & Karen Bonnell Werth*

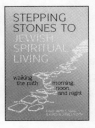

How can we bring the sacred into our busy lives?

Transforms our daily routine into sacred acts of mindfulness. Chapters are arranged according to the cycle of each day—and the cycle of our lives—providing spiritual activities, creative new rituals, meditations, acts of *kavannah* (spiritual intention) and prayers for any lifestyle.

6" x 9", 240 pp. HC, ISBN 1-58023-003-2 **$21.95**

THE YEAR MOM GOT RELIGION
One Woman's Midlife Journey into Judaism
by *Lee Meyerhoff Hendler*

A frank, thoughtful, and humorous "spiritual autobiography" that will speak to anyone in search of deeper meaning in their religious life. The author shares with the reader the hard lessons and realizations she confronted as a result of her awakening to Judaism, including how her transformation deeply affected her lifestyle and relationships. Shows that anyone, at any time, can deeply embrace faith—and face the challenges that occur.

6" x 9", 208 pp. Quality Paperback ISBN 1-58023-070-9 **$15.95**
HC, ISBN -000-8 **$19.95**

MOSES—THE PRINCE, THE PROPHET
His Life, Legend & Message for Our Lives
by *Rabbi Levi Meier, Ph.D.*

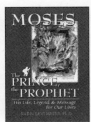

How can the struggles of a great biblical figure teach us to cope with our own lives today? A fascinating portrait of the struggles, failures and triumphs of Moses, a central figure in Jewish, Christian and Islamic tradition. Draws from Exodus, *midrash*, the teachings of Jewish mystics, modern texts and psychotherapy. Offers new ways to create our own path to self-knowledge and self-fulfillment—and face life's difficulties.

6" x 9", 224 pp. Quality Paperback, ISBN 1-58023-069-5 **$16.95**
HC, ISBN -013-X **$23.95**

Spirituality—The Kushner Series

EYES REMADE FOR WONDER
A Lawrence Kushner Reader
Introduction by *Thomas Moore*

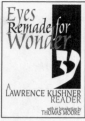

A treasury of insight from one of the most creative spiritual thinkers in America. Whether you are new to Kushner or a devoted fan, you'll find inspiration here. With samplings from each of Kushner's works, and a generous amount of new material, this is a book to be savored, to be read and reread, each time discovering deeper layers of meaning in our lives. Offers something unique to both the spiritual seeker and the committed person of faith.

6" x 9", 240 pp. Quality PB, ISBN 1-58023-042-3 **$16.95**; HC, ISBN -014-8 **$23.95**

INVISIBLE LINES OF CONNECTION
Sacred Stories of the Ordinary
by *Lawrence Kushner*

Through his everyday encounters with family, friends, colleagues and strangers, Kushner takes us deeply into our lives, finding flashes of spiritual insight in the process.

5½" x 8½", 160 pp. Quality Paperback, ISBN 1-879045-98-2 **$15.95**

HC, ISBN -52-4 **$21.95**

•AWARD WINNER•

HONEY FROM THE ROCK
An Easy Introduction to Jewish Mysticism
by *Lawrence Kushner*

"Quite simply the easiest introduction to Jewish mysticism you can read."

An introduction to the ten gates of Jewish mysticism and how it applies to daily life.

6" x 9", 168 pp. Quality Paperback, ISBN 1-879045-02-8 **$14.95**

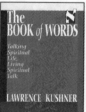

THE BOOK OF WORDS
Talking Spiritual Life, Living Spiritual Talk
by *Lawrence Kushner*

In the incomparable manner of his extraordinary *The Book of Letters*, Kushner now lifts up and shakes the dust off primary religious words we use to describe the spiritual dimension of life. For each word Kushner offers us a startling, moving and insightful explication. He concludes with a short exercise that helps unite the spirit of the word with our actions in the world.

6" x 9", 152 pp. 2-color text, Quality PB ISBN 1-58023-020-2 **$16.95**; HC, ISBN 1-879045-35-4 **$21.95**

THE BOOK OF LETTERS
A Mystical Hebrew Alphabet
by *Rabbi Lawrence Kushner*

In calligraphy by the author. Folktales about and exploration of the mystical meanings of the Hebrew Alphabet. Draws from ancient Judaic sources, weaving Talmudic commentary, Hasidic folktales, and kabbalistic mysteries around the letters.

• **Popular Hardcover Edition** 6" x 9", 80 pp. HC, two colors, inspiring new Foreword. ISBN 1-879045-00-1 **$24.95**

• **Deluxe Gift Edition** 9" x 12", 80 pp. HC, four-color text, ornamentation, in a beautiful slipcase. **$79.95**

•AWARD WINNER•

• **Collector's Limited Edition** 9" x 12", 80 pp. HC, gold-embossed pages, hand-assembled slipcase. With silkscreened print. **Limited to 500 signed and numbered copies.** ISBN 1-879045-04-4 **$349.00**

Spirituality

GOD WAS IN THIS PLACE & I, i DID NOT KNOW
Finding Self, Spirituality & Ultimate Meaning
by *Lawrence Kushner*

Who am I? Who is God? Kushner creates inspiring interpretations of Jacob's dream in Genesis, opening a window into Jewish spirituality for people of all faiths and backgrounds.

6" x 9", 192 pp. Quality Paperback, ISBN 1-879045-33-8 **$16.95**

THE RIVER OF LIGHT
Spirituality, Judaism, Consciousness
by *Lawrence Kushner*

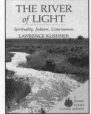

A "manual" for all spiritual travelers who would attempt a spiritual journey in our times. Taking us step by step, Kushner allows us to discover the meaning of our own quest: "to allow the river of light—the deepest currents of consciousness—to rise to the surface and animate our lives."

6" x 9", 180 pp. Quality Paperback, ISBN 1-879045-03-6 **$14.95**

GODWRESTLING—ROUND 2
Ancient Wisdom, Future Paths
by *Arthur Waskow*

This 20th-anniversary sequel to a seminal book of the Jewish renewal movement deals with spirituality in relation to personal growth, marriage, ecology, feminism, politics, and more.

6" x 9", 352 pp. Quality Paperback, ISBN 1-879045-72-9 **$18.95**

HC, ISBN -45-1 **$23.95**

•AWARD WINNER•

ECOLOGY & THE JEWISH SPIRIT
Where Nature & the Sacred Meet
Edited and with Introductions by *Ellen Bernstein*

What is nature's place in our spiritual lives?

A focus on nature is part of the fabric of Jewish thought. Here, experts bring us a richer understanding of the long-neglected themes of nature that are woven through the biblical creation story, ancient texts, traditional law, the holiday cycles, prayer, *mitzvot* (good deeds), and community.

6" x 9", 288 pp. HC, ISBN 1-879045-88-5 **$23.95**

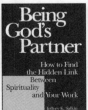

BEING GOD'S PARTNER
How to Find the Hidden Link Between
Spirituality and Your Work
by *Jeffrey K. Salkin*; Introduction by *Norman Lear*

Will challenge people of every denomination to reconcile the cares of work and soul. A groundbreaking book about spirituality and the work world, from a Jewish perspective. Offers practical suggestions for balancing your professional life and spiritual self.

6" x 9", 192 pp. Quality Paperback, ISBN 1-879045-65-6 **$16.95**

HC, ISBN -37-0 **$19.95**

Spirituality

MEDITATION FROM THE HEART OF JUDAISM
Today's Teachers Share Their Practices, Techniques, and Faith
Edited by *Avram Davis*

A "how-to" guide for both beginning and experienced meditators, it will help you start meditating or help you enhance your practice.

Twenty-two masters of meditation explain why and how they meditate. *A detailed compendium of the experts' "Best Practices"* offers practical advice and starting points.

6" x 9", 256 pp. Quality Paperback, ISBN 1-58023-049-0 **$16.95**

HC, ISBN 1-879045-77-X **$21.95**

SELF, STRUGGLE & CHANGE
Family Conflict Stories in Genesis and Their Healing Insights for Our Lives
by *Norman J. Cohen*

How do I find greater wholeness in my life and in my family's life?

The people described by the biblical writers of Genesis were in situations and relationships very much like our own. We identify with them. Their stories still speak to us because they are about the same problems we deal with every day. Here a modern master of biblical interpretation brings us greater understanding of the ancient text and of ourselves in this intriguing re-telling of conflict between husband and wife, father and son, brothers, and sisters.

6" x 9", 224 pp. Quality Paperback, ISBN 1-879045-66-4 **$16.95**; HC, ISBN-19-2 **$21.95**

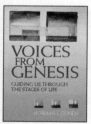

VOICES FROM GENESIS
Guiding Us through the Stages of Life
by *Norman J. Cohen*

A brilliant blending of modern *midrash* and the life stages of Erik Erikson's developmental psychology. Shows how the pathways of our lives are quite similar to those of the leading figures of Genesis who speak directly to us, telling of their spiritual and emotional journeys.

6" x 9", 192 pp. HC, ISBN 1-879045-75-3 **$21.95**

ISRAEL—A SPIRITUAL TRAVEL GUIDE
A Companion for the Modern Jewish Pilgrim
by *Rabbi Lawrence A. Hoffman*

Be spiritually prepared for your journey to Israel.

A Jewish spiritual travel guide to Israel, helping today's pilgrim tap into the deep spiritual meaning of the ancient—and modern—sites of the Holy Land. Combines in quick reference format ancient blessings, medieval prayers, biblical and historical references, and modern poetry. The only guidebook that helps readers to prepare spiritually for the occasion. More than a guide book: It is a spiritual map.

4¾" x 10", 256 pp. Quality Paperback Original, ISBN 1-879045-56-7 **$18.95**

•AWARD WINNER•

Spirituality

HOW TO BE A PERFECT STRANGER, In 2 Volumes
A Guide to Etiquette in Other People's Religious Ceremonies
Edited by *Stuart M. Matlins & Arthur J. Magida*

"A book that belongs in every living room, library and office!"

Explains the rituals and celebrations of America's major religions/denominations, helping an interested guest to feel comfortable, participate to the fullest extent possible, and avoid violating anyone's religious principles.

•AWARD WINNER•

Answers practical questions from the perspective of *any* other faith.

VOL. 1: America's Largest Faiths

VOL. 1 COVERS: Assemblies of God • Baptist • Buddhist • Christian Science • Churches of Christ • Disciples of Christ • Episcopalian • Greek Orthodox • Hindu • Islam • Jehovah's Witnesses • Jewish • Lutheran • Methodist • Mormon • Presbyterian • Quaker • Roman Catholic • Seventh-day Adventist • United Church of Christ

6" x 9", 432 pp. Hardcover, ISBN 1-879045-39-7 **$24.95**

VOL. 2: Other Faiths in America

VOL. 2 COVERS: African American Methodist Churches • Baha'i • Christian and Missionary Alliance • Christian Congregation • Church of the Brethren • Church of the Nazarene • Evangelical Free Church of America • International Church of the Foursquare Gospel • International Pentecostal Holiness Church • Mennonite/Amish • Native American • Orthodox Churches • Pentecostal Church of God • Reformed Church of America • Sikh • Unitarian Universalist • Wesleyan

6" x 9", 416 pp. Hardcover, ISBN 1-879045-63-X **$24.95**

GOD & THE BIG BANG
Discovering Harmony Between Science & Spirituality
by *Daniel C. Matt*

Mysticism and science: What do they have in common? How can one enlighten the other? By drawing on modern cosmology and ancient Kabbalah, Matt shows how science and religion can together enrich our spiritual awareness and help us recover a sense of wonder and find our place in the universe.

"This poetic new book...helps us to understand the human meaning of creation."
—*Joel Primack, leading cosmologist, Professor of Physics, University of California, Santa Cruz*

•AWARD WINNER•

6" x 9", 216 pp. Quality Paperback, ISBN 1-879045-89-3 **$16.95**; HC, ISBN-48-6 **$21.95**

MINDING THE TEMPLE OF THE SOUL
Balancing Body, Mind, & Spirit through Traditional Jewish Prayer, Movement, & Meditation
by *Tamar Frankiel* and *Judy Greenfeld*

This new spiritual approach to physical health introduces readers to a spiritual tradition that affirms the body and enables them to reconceive their bodies in a more positive light. Relying on Kabbalistic teachings and other Jewish traditions, it shows us how to be more responsible for our own psychological and physical health. Focuses on the discipline of prayer, simple Tai Chi–like exercises and body positions, and guides the reader throughout, step-by-step, with diagrams, sketches and meditations.

7" x 10", 184 pp. Quality Paperback Original, illus., ISBN 1-879045-64-8 **$16.95**

Audiotape of the Blessings, Movements & Meditations (60-min. cassette) **$9.95**
Videotape of the Movements & Meditations (46-min. VHS) **$20.00**

Healing/Recovery/Wellness

Experts Praise *Twelve Jewish Steps to Recovery*

"Recommended reading for people of all denominations."
—*Rabbi Abraham J. Twerski, M.D.*

TWELVE JEWISH STEPS TO RECOVERY
A Personal Guide to Turning from Alcoholism & Other Addictions...Drugs, Food, Gambling, Sex...
by *Rabbi Kerry M. Olitzky & Stuart A. Copans, M.D.*
Preface by *Abraham J. Twerski, M.D.*; Intro. by *Rabbi Sheldon Zimmerman*; "Getting Help" by *JACS Foundation*

A Jewish perspective on the Twelve Steps of addiction recovery programs with consolation, inspiration and motivation for recovery. It draws from traditional sources and quotes from what recovering Jewish people say about their experiences with addictions of all kinds. Inspiring illustrations of the twelve gates of the Old City of Jerusalem introduce each step.

6" x 9", 136 pp. Quality Paperback, ISBN 1-879045-09-5 **$13.95**

Recovery from Codependence: A Jewish Twelve Steps Guide to Healing Your Soul
by Rabbi Kerry M. Olitzky

6" x 9", 160 pp. Quality Paperback Original, ISBN 1-879045-32-X **$13.95**; HC, ISBN -27-3 **$21.95**

Renewed Each Day: Daily Twelve Step Recovery Meditations Based on the Bible
by Rabbi Kerry M. Olitzky & Aaron Z.

6" x 9", Quality Paperback Original **V. I**, 224 pp., ISBN 1-879045-12-5 **$14.95**
V. II, 280 pp., ISBN 1-879045-13-3 **$16.95**

One Hundred Blessings Every Day: Daily Twelve Step Recovery Affirmations, Exercises for Personal Growth & Renewal Reflecting Seasons of the Jewish Year
by Rabbi Kerry M. Olitzky

4½" x 6½", 432 pp. Quality Paperback Original, ISBN 1-879045-30-3 **$14.95**

HEALING OF SOUL, HEALING OF BODY
Spiritual Leaders Unfold the Strength and Solace in Psalms
Edited by *Rabbi Simkha Y. Weintraub, CSW, for The Jewish Healing Center*

A source of solace for those who are facing illness, as well as those who care for them. The ten Psalms which form the core of this healing resource were originally selected 200 years ago by Rabbi Nachman of Breslov as a "complete remedy." Today, for anyone coping with illness, they continue to provide a wellspring of strength. Each Psalm is newly translated, making it clear and accessible, and each one is introduced by an eminent rabbi, men and women reflecting different movements and backgrounds. To all who are living with the pain and uncertainty of illness, this spiritual resource offers an anchor of spiritual comfort.

"Will bring comfort to anyone fortunate enough to read it. This gentle book is a luminous gem of wisdom."
—*Larry Dossey, M.D., author of* Healing Words: The Power of Prayer & the Practice of Medicine

6" x 9", 128 pp. Quality Paperback Original, illus., 2-color text, ISBN 1-879045-31-1 **$14.95**

Art of Jewish Living Series for Holiday Observance

THE SHABBAT SEDER
by *Dr. Ron Wolfson*

A concise step-by-step guide designed to teach people the meaning and importance of this weekly celebration, as well as its practices.

Each chapter corresponds to one of ten steps which together comprise the Shabbat dinner ritual, and looks at the *concepts, objects,* and *meanings* behind the specific activity or ritual act. The blessings that accompany the meal are written in both Hebrew and English, and accompanied by English transliteration. Also included are craft projects, recipes, discussion ideas and other creative suggestions for enriching the Shabbat experience.

"A how-to book in the best sense...."
—*Dr. David Lieber, President, University of Judaism, Los Angeles*

7" x 9", 272 pp. Quality Paperback, ISBN 1-879045-90-7 **$16.95**

Also available are these helpful companions to *The Shabbat Seder*:	
•Booklet of the Blessings and Songs	ISBN 1-879045-91-5 $5.00
•Audiocassette of the Blessings	DNO3 $6.00
•Teacher's Guide	ISBN 1-879045-92-3 $4.95

HANUKKAH
by *Dr. Ron Wolfson*
Edited by *Joel Lurie Grishaver*

Designed to help celebrate and enrich the holiday season, *Hanukkah* discusses the holiday's origins, explores the reasons for the Hanukkah candles and customs, and provides everything from recipes to family activities.

There are songs, recipes, useful information on the arts and crafts of Hanukkah, the calendar and its relationship to Christmas time, and games played at Hanukkah. Putting the holiday in a larger, timely context, "December Dilemmas" deals with ways in which a Jewish family can cope with Christmas.

"Helpful for the family that strives to induct its members into the spirituality and joys of Jewishness and Judaism...a significant text in the neglected art of Jewish family education."
—*Rabbi Harold M. Schulweis, Cong. Valley Beth Shalom, Encino, CA*

7" x 9", 192 pp. Quality Paperback, ISBN 1-879045-97-4 **$16.95**

THE PASSOVER SEDER
by *Dr. Ron Wolfson*

Explains the concepts behind Passover ritual and ceremony in clear, easy-to-understand language, and offers step-by-step procedures for Passover observance and preparing the home for the holiday.

Easy-to-Follow Format: Using an innovative photo-documentary technique, real families describe in vivid images their own experiences with the Passover holiday. **Easy-to-Read Hebrew Texts:** The Haggadah texts in Hebrew, English, and transliteration are presented in a three-column format designed to help celebrants learn the meaning of the prayers and how to read them. **An Abundance of Useful Information:** A detailed description of how to perform the rituals is included, along with practical questions and answers, and imaginative ideas for Seder celebration.

"A creative 'how-to' for making the Seder a more meaningful experience."
—*Michael Strassfeld, co-author of* The Jewish Catalog

7" x 9", 336 pp. Quality Paperback, ISBN 1-879045-93-1 **$16.95**

Also available are these helpful companions to *The Passover Seder*:	
•Passover Workbook	ISBN 1-879045-94-X $6.95
•Audiocassette of the Blessings	DNO4 $6.00
•Teacher's Guide	ISBN 1-879045-95-8 $4.95

Children's Spirituality

For ages 8 and up

BUT GOD REMEMBERED
Stories of Women from Creation to the Promised Land
by *Sandy Eisenberg Sasso*, Full-color illus. by *Bethanne Andersen*

NONDENOMINATIONAL, NONSECTARIAN

A fascinating collection of four different stories of women only briefly mentioned in biblical tradition and religious texts, but never before explored. Award-winning author Sasso brings to life the intriguing stories of Lilith, Serach, Bityah, and the Daughters of Z, courageous and strong women from ancient tradition. All teach important values through their faith and actions.

9" x 12", 32 pp. HC, Full-color illus., ISBN 1-879045-43-5 **$16.95**

•Award Winner•

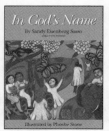

IN GOD'S NAME
by *Sandy Eisenberg Sasso*

For ages 4 and up

Selected as Outstanding by Parent Council, Ltd.™

Full-color illustrations by *Phoebe Stone*

MULTICULTURAL, NONDENOMINATIONAL, NONSECTARIAN

Like an ancient myth in its poetic text and vibrant illustrations, this modern fable about the search for God's name celebrates the diversity and, at the same time, the unity of all the people of the world. Each seeker claims he or she alone knows the answer. Finally, they come together and learn what God's name really is, sharing the ultimate harmony of belief in one God by people of all faiths, all backgrounds.

•Award Winner•

9" x 12", 32 pp. HC, Full color illus., ISBN 1-879045-26-5 **$16.95**

For ages 4 and up

GOD IN BETWEEN
by *Sandy Eisenberg Sasso*
Full-color illustrations by *Sally Sweetland*

NONDENOMINATIONAL, NONSECTARIAN, MULTICULTURAL

If you wanted to find God, where would you look?

A magical, mythical tale that teaches that God can be found where we are: within all of us and the relationships between us.

9" x 12", 32 pp. HC, Full-color illus., ISBN 1-879045-86-9 **$16.95**

IN OUR IMAGE
God's First Creatures

For ages 4 and up

Selected as Outstanding by Parent Council, Ltd.™

by *Nancy Sohn Swartz*
Full-color illustrations by *Melanie Hall*

NONDENOMINATIONAL, NONSECTARIAN

For ages 4 and up

A playful new twist to the Creation story. Celebrates the interconnectedness of nature and the harmony of all living things.

•Award Winner•

9" x 12", 32 pp. HC, Full-color illus., ISBN 1-879045-99-0 **$16.95**

For ages 4 and up

GOD'S PAINTBRUSH
by *Sandy Eisenberg Sasso*
Full-color illustrations by *Annette Compton*

MULTICULTURAL, NONDENOMINATIONAL, NONSECTARIAN

Invites children of all faiths and backgrounds to encounter God openly in their own lives. Wonderfully interactive, provides questions adult and child can explore together at the end of each episode.

11" x 8½", 32 pp. HC, Full-color illus., ISBN 1-879045-22-2 **$16.95**

***Also Available!* Teacher's Guide: A Guide for Jewish & Christian Educators and Parents**

8½" x 11", 32 pp. PB, ISBN 1-879045-57-5 **$6.95**

Children's Spirituality

A PRAYER FOR THE EARTH
The Story of Naamah, Noah's Wife

For ages 4 and up

by *Sandy Eisenberg Sasso*
Full-color illustrations by *Bethanne Andersen*

NONDENOMINATIONAL, NONSECTARIAN

This new story, based on an ancient text, opens readers' religious imaginations to new ideas about the well-known story of the Flood. When God tells Noah to bring the animals of the world onto the ark, God *also* calls on Naamah, Noah's wife, to save each plant on Earth.

"A lovely tale....Children of all ages should be drawn to this parable for our times."
—*Tomie dePaola, artist/author of books for children*

•AWARD WINNER•

9" x 12", 32 pp. HC, Full-color illus., ISBN 1-879045-60-5 **$16.95**

THE 11TH COMMANDMENT
Wisdom from Our Children

For all ages

by The Children of America

MULTICULTURAL, NONDENOMINATIONAL, NONSECTARIAN

"If there were an Eleventh Commandment, what would it be?"

Children of many religious denominations across America answer this question—in their own drawings and words—in *The 11th Commandment*.

"Wonderful....This unusual book provides both food for thought and insight into the hopes and fears of today's young."
—*American Library Association's* Booklist

8" x 10", 48 pp. HC, Full-color illus., ISBN 1-879045-46-X **$16.95**

SHARING BLESSINGS
Children's Stories for Exploring the Spirit of the Jewish Holidays

For ages 6 and up

by *Rahel Musleah* and *Rabbi Michael Klayman*
Full-color illustrations by *Mary O'Keefe Young*

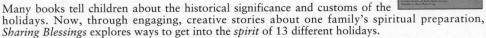

What is the spiritual message of each of the Jewish holidays?
How do we teach it to our children?

Many books tell children about the historical significance and customs of the holidays. Now, through engaging, creative stories about one family's spiritual preparation, *Sharing Blessings* explores ways to get into the *spirit* of 13 different holidays.

"A beguiling introduction to important Jewish values by way of the holidays."
—*Rabbi Harold Kushner, author of* When Bad Things Happen to Good People *and* How Good Do We Have to Be?

7" x 10", 64 pp. HC, Full-color illus., ISBN 1-879045-71-0 **$18.95**

THE BOOK OF MIRACLES
A Young Person's Guide to Jewish Spiritual Awareness

For ages 9–13

by *Lawrence Kushner*

With a Special 10th Anniversary Introduction and all new illustrations by the author.

From the miracle at the Red Sea to the miracle of waking up this morning, this intriguing book introduces kids to a way of everyday spiritual thinking to last a lifetime. Kushner, whose award-winning books have brought spirituality to life for countless adults, now shows young people how to use Judaism as a foundation on which to build their lives.

6" x 9", 96 pp. HC, 2-color illus., ISBN 1-879045-78-8 **$16.95**

Life Cycle

GRIEF IN OUR SEASONS
A Mourner's Kaddish Companion
by *Rabbi Kerry M. Olitzky*

Strength from the Jewish tradition for the first year of mourning.

Provides a wise and inspiring selection of sacred Jewish writings and a simple, powerful ancient ritual for mourners to read each day, to help hold the memory of their loved ones in their hearts. It offers a comforting, step-by-step daily link to saying *Kaddish*.

"A hopeful, compassionate guide along the journey from grief to rebirth from mourning to a new morning."
—*Rabbi Levi Meier, Ph.D., Chaplain, Cedars–Sinai Medical Center, Los Angeles*

4½" x 6½", 448 pp. Quality Paperback Original, ISBN 1-879045-55-9 **$15.95**

MOURNING & MITZVAH
• WITH OVER 60 GUIDED EXERCISES •
A Guided Journal for Walking the Mourner's Path Through Grief to Healing
by *Anne Brener, L.C.S.W.*
Foreword by *Rabbi Jack Riemer;* Introduction by *Rabbi William Cutter*

"Fully engaging in mourning means you will be a different person than before you began." **For those who mourn a death, for those who would help them,** for those who face a loss of any kind, Brener teaches us the power and strength available to us in the fully experienced mourning process. Guided writing exercises help stimulate the processes of both conscious and unconscious healing.

"A stunning book! It offers an exploration in depth of the place where psychology and religious ritual intersect, and the name of that place is Truth."
—*Rabbi Harold Kushner, author of* When Bad Things Happen to Good People

7½" x 9", 288 pp. Quality Paperback Original, ISBN 1-879045-23-0 **$19.95**

A TIME TO MOURN, A TIME TO COMFORT
A Guide to Jewish Bereavement and Comfort
by *Dr. Ron Wolfson*

A guide to meeting the needs of those who mourn and those who seek to provide comfort in times of sadness. While this book is written from a layperson's point of view, it also includes the specifics for funeral preparations and practical guidance for preparing the home and family to sit *shiva*.

"A sensitive and perceptive guide to Jewish tradition. Both those who mourn and those who comfort will find it a map to accompany them through the whirlwind."

—*Deborah E. Lipstadt, Emory University*
7" x 9", 336 pp. Quality Paperback, ISBN 1-879045-96-6 **$16.95**

WHEN A GRANDPARENT DIES
A Kid's Own Remembering Workbook for Dealing with Shiva and the Year Beyond
by *Nechama Liss-Levinson, Ph.D.*

Drawing insights from both psychology and Jewish tradition, this workbook helps children participate in the process of mourning, offering guided exercises, rituals, and places to write, draw, list, create and express their feelings.

"Will bring support, guidance, and understanding for countless children, teachers, and health professionals."
—*Rabbi Earl A. Grollman, D.D., author of* Talking about Death

8" x 10", 48 pp. HC, illus., 2-color text, ISBN 1-879045-44-3 **$15.95**

Life Cycle

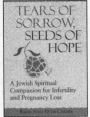

TEARS OF SORROW, SEEDS OF HOPE
A Jewish Spiritual Companion for Infertility and Pregnancy Loss
by *Rabbi Nina Beth Cardin*

Many people who endure the emotional suffering of infertility, pregnancy loss, or stillbirth bear this sorrow alone. Rarely is the experience of loss and infertility discussed with anyone but close friends and family members. Despite the private nature of the pain, many women and men would welcome the opportunity to be comforted by family and a community who would understand the pain and loneliness they feel, and the emptiness caused by the loss that is without a face, a name, or a grave.

Tears of Sorrow, Seeds of Hope is a spiritual companion that enables us to mourn infertility, a lost pregnancy, or a stillbirth within the prayers, rituals, and meditation of Judaism. By drawing deeply on the texts of tradition, it creates readings and rites of mourning, and through them provides a wellspring of compassion, solace—and hope.

6" x 9", 192 pp. HC, ISBN 1-58023-017-2 **$19.95**

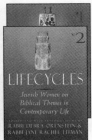

LIFECYCLES
V. 1: Jewish Women on Life Passages & Personal Milestones
Edited and with Introductions by *Rabbi Debra Orenstein*
V. 2: Jewish Women on Biblical Themes in Contemporary Life
Edited and with Introductions by
Rabbi Debra Orenstein and *Rabbi Jane Rachel Litman*

This unique multivolume collaboration brings together over one hundred women writers, rabbis, and scholars to create the first comprehensive work on Jewish life cycle that fully includes women's perspectives.

V. 1: 6" x 9", 480 pp. Quality Paperback, ISBN 1-58023-018-0 **$19.95**
HC, ISBN 1-879045-14-1 **$24.95**

•AWARD WINNER•

V. 2: 6" x 9", 464 pp. Quality Paperback, ISBN 1-58023-019-9 **$19.95**
HC, ISBN 1-879045-15-X **$24.95**

LIFE CYCLE— The Art of Jewish Living Series for Holiday Observance
by Dr. Ron Wolfson

Hanukkah—7" x 9", 192 pp. Quality Paperback, ISBN 1-879045-97-4 **$16.95**

The Shabbat Seder—7" x 9", 272 pp. Quality Paperback, ISBN 1-879045-90-7 **$16.95**;
Booklet of Blessings **$5.00**; Audiocassette of Blessings **$6.00**; Teacher's Guide **$4.95**

The Passover Seder—7" x 9", 336 pp. Quality Paperback, ISBN 1-879045-93-1 **$16.95**;
Passover Workbook, **$6.95**; Audiocassette of Blessings, **$6.00**; Teacher's Guide, **$4.95**

• LIFE CYCLE...Other Books •

A Heart of Wisdom: Making the Jewish Journey from Midlife Through the Elder Years
Ed. by Susan Berrin 6" x 9", 384 pp. Quality Paperback, ISBN 1-58023-051-2, **$18.95**;
HC, ISBN 1-879045-73-7 **$24.95**

Bar/Bat Mitzvah Basics: A Practical Family Guide to Coming of Age Together
Ed. by Cantor Helen Leneman 6" x 9", 240 pp. Quality Paperback, ISBN 1-879045-54-0 **$16.95**

Embracing the Covenant: Converts to Judaism Talk About Why & How
Ed. and with Intros. by Rabbi Allan L. Berkowitz and Patti Moskovitz
6" x 9", 192 pp. Quality Paperback, ISBN 1-879045-50-8 **$15.95**

*For Kids—Putting God on Your Guest List: How to Claim the Spiritual Meaning of Your
Bar or Bat Mitzvah* by Rabbi Jeffrey K. Salkin
6" x 9", 144 pp. Quality Paperback Original, ISBN 1-58023-015-6 **$14.95**

*The New Jewish Baby Book: Names, Ceremonies, Customs—A Guide for Today's
Families* by Anita Diamant 6" x 9", 336 pp. Quality Paperback, ISBN 1-879045-28-1 **$16.95**

*Putting God on the Guest List, 2nd Ed.: How to Reclaim the Spiritual Meaning of
Your Child's Bar or Bat Mitzvah* by Rabbi Jeffrey K. Salkin
6" x 9", 224 pp. Quality Paperback, ISBN 1-897045-59-1 **$16.95**; HC, ISBN 1-879045-58-3 **$24.95**

So That Your Values Live On: Ethical Wills & How to Prepare Them
Ed. by Rabbi Jack Riemer & Professor Nathaniel Stampfer
6" x 9", 272 pp. Quality Paperback, ISBN 1-879045-34-6 **$17.95**

Theology/Philosophy

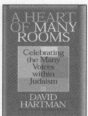

A HEART OF MANY ROOMS
Celebrating the Many Voices within Judaism
by *David Hartman*

With clarity, passion and outstanding scholarship, David Hartman addresses the spiritual and theological questions that face all Jews and all people today. From the perspective of traditional Judaism, he helps us understand the varieties of 20th-century Jewish practice and shows that commitment to both Jewish tradition and to pluralism can create bridges of understanding between people of different religious convictions.

"An extraordinary book, devoid of stereotypic thinking; lucid and pertinent, a modern classic."
—*Michael Walzer, Institute for Advanced Study, Princeton*

6" x 9", 352 pp. HC, ISBN 1-58023-048-2 **$24.95**

WINNER, National Jewish Book Award

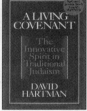

A LIVING COVENANT
The Innovative Spirit in Traditional Judaism
by *David Hartman*

The Judaic tradition is often seen as being more concerned with uncritical obedience to law than with individual freedom and responsibility. Hartman challenges this approach by revealing a Judaism grounded in a covenant—a relational framework—informed by the metaphor of marital love rather than that of parent-child dependency.

"Jews and non-Jews, liberals and traditionalists will see classic Judaism anew in these pages." —*Dr. Eugene B. Borowitz, Hebrew Union College–Jewish Institute of Religion*

6" x 9", 368 pp. Quality Paperback, ISBN 1-58023-011-3 **$18.95**

• THEOLOGY & PHILOSOPHY...Other books •

Aspects of Rabbinic Theology by Solomon Schechter, with a new Introduction by Neil Gillman 6" x 9", 440 pp, Quality Paperback, ISBN 1-879045-24-9 **$19.95**

The Last Trial: On the Legends and Lore of the Command to Abraham to Offer Isaac as a Sacrifice by Shalom Spiegel, with a new Introduction by Judah Goldin 6" x 9", 208 pp, Quality Paperback, ISBN 1-879045-29-X **$17.95**

Judaism and Modern Man: An Interpretation of Jewish Religion by Will Herberg; new Introduction by Neil Gillman 5½" x 8½", 336 pp, Quality Paperback, ISBN 1-879045-87-7 **$18.95**

Seeking the Path to Life: Theological Meditations On God and the Nature of People, Love, Life and Death by Rabbi Ira F. Stone 6" x 9", 132 pp, Quality Paperback, ISBN 1-879045-47-8 **$14.95**; HC, ISBN 1-879045-17-6 **$19.95**

The Spirit of Renewal: Finding Faith After the Holocaust by Edward Feld 6" x 9", 224 pp, Quality Paperback, ISBN 1-879045-40-0 **$16.95**

Tormented Master: The Life and Spiritual Quest of Rabbi Nahman of Bratslav by Arthur Green 6" x 9", 408 pp, Quality Paperback, ISBN 1-879045-11-7 **$18.95**

Your Word Is Fire Ed. and trans. with a new Introduction by Arthur Green and Barry W. Holtz 6" x 9", 152 pp, Quality Paperback, ISBN 1-879045-25-7 **$14.95**

Or phone, fax or mail to: JEWISH LIGHTS Publishing
Sunset Farm Offices, Route 4 • P.O. Box 237 • Woodstock, Vermont 05091
Tel (802) 457-4000 Fax (802) 457-4004 www.jewishlights.com
Credit card orders (800) 962-4544 (9AM–5PM ET Monday–Friday)
Generous discounts on quantity orders. SATISFACTION GUARANTEED. Prices subject to change.

DATE DUE

APR 19 2011			
			Printed in USA

HIGHSMITH #45230

WITHDRAWN